AF896452

Design(s) for Law

Rossana Ducato, Alain Strowel,
and Enguerrand Marique (eds)

Ledizioni

Co-funded by
the European Union

Funded by the European Union. Views and opinions expressed are however those of the author(s) only and do not necessarily reflect those of the European Union or the European Education and Culture Executive Agency (EACEA). Neither the European Union nor EACEA can be held responsible for them.

We published the Open Access PDF version on Zenodo on 18/03/2024. We received a rectification request on 25/04/2024 regarding Chapter 2. We have republished the corrected version on 20/05/2024.

Unless otherwise stated, this work is released under a Attribution 4.0 International (CC BY 4.0 Deed), https://creativecommons.org/licenses/by/4.0/.

Rossana Ducato, Alain Strowel, and Enguerrand Marique (eds), *Design(s) for Law*
First print edition: May 2024

ISBN print: 9791256000845
ISBN ePub: 9791256000852
ISBN PDF Open Access: 9791256000869

Catalogue and reprints information: www.ledipublishing.com, www.ledizioni.it

Printed in Italy in May 2024 by Infolio digital print srl - Sant'Egidio del Monte Albino (Salerno)

TABLE OF CONTENTS

NARRATIVE AND STORYTELLING

Legal Design interventions against misleading design and misinformation online

LIST OF CONTRIBUTORS

Vincent Couronne, PhD, is co-founder and director of Les Surligneurs, fellow researcher at Versailles Institutions Publiques research centre (Paris-Saclay University), and Lecturer in Law at Sciences Po Saint-Germain-en-Laye.

Marie-Sophie de Clippele is Assistant Professor of law at UCLouvain Saint-Louis - Brussels, with a chair in nature law and cultural law at the Centre d'étude en droit de l'environnement (CEDRE). Her research focuses mainly on issues relating to heritage (cultural, natural and common). Besides contributions in research books and papers in peer-reviewed journals on topics related to heritage and environmental law, she has also published two books on the subject, *Protéger le patrimoine culturel, à qui incombe la charge?* published by Presses de l'Université Saint-Louis in 2020, and recently *Restes humains et patrimoine culturel: de quels droits?* published by Anthémis in October 2023.

Santiago de Francisco Vela is a designer and an associate professor in the School of Design at the University of Los Andes in Bogotá, Colombia. He has worked in emotions and positive design, fostering emotional experiences and positive behaviours through product design. His areas of interest involve design for well-being, financial and social innovation, behavioural design, and design for justice. He is co-leader of Labjuticia (Design for Justice Lab) and leads the "emotionally driven design" research group.

Robert de Rooy is a practising commercial attorney, non-executive director on the boards of several companies and the founder of Creative Contracts (Pty) Ltd. In 2016, Robert developed the world's first fully illustrated legally binding contracts for farm workers, known as Comic Contracts. The purpose of Creative Contracts is to affirm the dignity of vulnerable people, by creating legal contracts and other important information that vulnerable people can autonomously and easily understand. Robert more recently developed the Composite Comic Contract application to leverage the power of digital technology to improve and scale the delivery of Comic Contracts. He was born in Cape Town, and studied business (BComm) and law (LLB) at the University of Stellenbosch and the University of Leiden in Holland and an MBA specialising in Executive Management at the University of Cape Town.

In 2016 he was the winner of the Innovation Award for his work on Comic Contracts, awarded by IACCM's Program of Visionary Change, now known as World Commerce and Contracting. In 2019, Comic Contracts was awarded 3rd place in the Hague Institute for Innovation of Law (HiiL) international Social Justice Innovation competition. Robert has authored and co-authored several academic articles and book chapters about Comic Contracts and Dignity and Contracting. He is currently also working on his doctorate in Business Law at the University of Vaasa, Finland.

Together with his wife, two daughters and a son, he lives in Cape Town, South Africa, where he tries to balance his work, studies and family life with some cycling and surfing.

Rossana Ducato is Senior Lecturer in IT Law and Regulation at the School of Law of the University of Aberdeen. She is also affiliated to UCLouvain, where she teaches in the Erasmus+ Jean Monnet course "Clinic on EU Digital Rights, Law, and Design". Her research interests are always pursued in a comparative vein and range from Privacy and Data Protection to Consumer protection, Intellectual Property Law, and Law and Design, with a special focus on the problems related to new technologies and their impact on society. She is the author of several peer-reviewed articles and chapters in scholarly books about issues related to law and technology with a particular attention to the platform economy, artificial intelligence and data regulation.

Laura Guzmán-Abello is an industrial engineer and an assistant professor at the School of Design of Universidad de los Andes. She has experience in research and consulting in organisational design, strategy, and management-oriented decision-making processes with a systemic and participatory approach. Her work has focused on using system dynamics for justice, health, and ICT systems. She is is co-leader of Labjuticia (Design for Justice Lab).

Helena Haapio is Professor of Practice and Docent of Proactive Law and Contract Design at the University of Lapland, Associate Professor of Business Law at the University of Vaasa, and Contract Strategist at Lexpert Ltd in Helsinki, Finland.

She is a lawyer on a mission: a practitioner by day and a researcher, author, and editor by night. She has devoted her life to improving contracts, especially for people who lack legal training: engineers, business and project managers, entrepreneurs who encounter contracts on a daily basis. Her mission is to fundamentally change the way contracts are designed, communicated, perceived and taught. Together with information designers and colleagues she has explored new contract genres and designs. She has authored several book chapters and articles and recently co-edited two books for Edward Elgar, one on Legal Design and the other on Contract Design.

After completing her legal studies at the University of Turku, Finland, and Cambridge University, England, she served for several years as an in-house Legal Counsel in Europe and the US, working with cross-border contracts. She started at the University of Vaasa as a Teacher of Strategic Business Law and defended her doctoral dissertation on Next Generation Contracts: A Paradigm Shift in 2013. She supervises doctoral students whose research interests focus on merging proactive legal thinking with design: helping people and businesses use contracts and law proactively to achieve better business and societal results, balance risk with reward, and stay away from unnecessary problems. Together with Stefania Passera she co-created the WorldCC Contract Design Pattern Library. Her work has been recognized with the European Women of Legal Tech 2020 Award. She is also a co-founder of the Nordic School of Proactive Law, the International Network for Proactive Law and the Legal Design Alliance and a co-author of its Legal Design Manifesto.

Margaret Hagan is the executive director of Stanford Legal Design Lab. She is a lawyer with a JD from Stanford and a PhD from Queen's University Belfast. Margaret works on public interest technology -- teaching classes in partnership with courts and self help centres and leading R&D around new applications, visuals, policies, and artificial intelligence to improve access to justice.

Pablo Hermansen is a Designer and Associate Professor at the School of Design of the Pontificia Universidad Católica de Chile and holds a PhD in Architecture and Urban Studies from the same university. Dr. Hermansen's research and publications focus on the material conditions of interspecies coexistence, prototyping as a more-than-human research device, and performative strategies for the political visibility of counter-hegemonic groups in public space. He works in the fields of digital museography and interactive installation and provides consulting services in the area of critical service design for public institutions. From the question of the material conditions for a more-than-human coexistence, his main research areas are (1) Interspecies prototyping, (2) Performative strategies for political visibility in public space, and (3) Public services as a public space. Professionally, he serves as a creative director and consultant (1) on projects of digital museography and interactive installations, and (2) on service design, organisational processes, and change management, especially in the public sector. In 2022, he served as an advisor to the cabinet of the Minister of Health. In July 2021, he was part of the winning team that designed the Chile Pavilion for the London Design Biennale. The museographic proposal of this pavilion won the highest distinction of the Biennale, the most important event of the discipline worldwide. He recently co-edited the book *Design For More-Than-Human Futures - Towards Post-Anthropocentric Worlding* published in 2023 by Routledge.

Anne Ketola is a senior research fellow at The Faculty of Information Technology and Communication Sciences at Tampere University, Finland. She is a communication researcher who specialises in accessible visual communication. Ketola currently works in the Sarjis research group, which produces and examines comic-style versions of complex, institutional documents.

Anne is intrigued by how information changes when we turn words into images and vice versa. She has published extensively about how people interpret the combination of words and images in illustrated texts. In her PhD, she cognitively modelled how illustrations affect verbal text comprehension when reading illustrated technical texts. She has recently authored a practical guide on cognitively accessible visual communication for the Finnish Centre for Easy Language.

Anne is also passionate about accessibility on a more general level. She has been in charge of developing an interdisciplinary accessibility education curriculum at Tampere University and she regularly consults researchers on how to make academic communication more accessible, for instance, by illustrating participant consent forms aimed at vulnerable readers. Anne is also actively involved with developing audio description practices in Finland, and she actively collaborates with the Finnish Cultural Services for the Visually Impaired in projects related to improving the visual accessibility of culture and online services. Anne Ketola's contribution to the chapter is supported by the *Graphic Justice* research project (2020–2024), funded by the Academy of Finland (decision number 333367).

Apolline Le Gall is Research Director at Où sont les Dragons. She is a teacher and researcher who works in multiple fields. She has completed a thesis in Innovation Management, Sociology, and Design, with a specialisation in Service Design. Her research explores how design contributes to public innovation, organisations, law, and design education. She is currently associated researcher at Ecole Normale Supérieure de Paris-Saclay.

Emily MacLoud is a Senior Design Strategist at Portable, a research and design agency that is dedicated to identifying critical areas of social need and policy failure and driving transformational change through the innovative use of design and technology. While at Portable, Emily has worked with community legal centres, justice departments, and court services across Australia. Through her work, she has developed a deep understanding of the importance of adopting a systems lens when addressing complex problems. Emily's extensive experience in the community legal sector in the UK has also given her a unique perspective on the intersection of design and law, and she is passionate about finding ways to make legal services more accessible and user-friendly. Emily currently serves as a member of the Macquarie University Law School Advisory Board.

Enguerrand Marique is currently a Universitair Docent for digital conflict resolution at the department of European and International law of

Radboud Universiteit, and a guest lecturer in digital and business law at the department of Economic law of the UCLouvain. Between 2016 and 2021, he carried out doctoral research on the regulation of digital platforms in the European Union. He has examined the tools to regulate digital services, and the mechanisms that platforms put in place in order to steer the behaviour of their business and individual users. Enguerrand is the author of several peer-review articles and book chapters on the regulation of digital services in the EU, especially with a particular attention to the e-commerce directive and digital services act. Throughout his work, Enguerrand is also working on the role of algorithms in decision-making processes, both for private actors as well as the public sector (including the use of algorithms in judicial systems).

Barbara Pasa is Full Professor of Comparative Law at the Università IUAV of Venezia. Her research interests focus on Comparative Law and Legal Theory, Law and Design, Contract Law and Consumer protection at the intersection with Intellectual Property Rights, with specific emphasis on Artificial Intelligence issues. She is a member of the International Academy of Comparative Law; a member of the European Law Institute; a member of the executive board of the Italian Society for Research on Comparative Law (SIRD) and a member of the Italian Association of Comparative Law (AIDC).

Hallie Jay Pope is a legal educator and information designer. She is the inaugural Director of Seton Hall Law School's New Jersey Legal Design Lab, a social transformation laboratory that combines law, design, and education to channel power into local movements. Hallie's work focuses on using participatory design processes and visual storytelling to share legal knowledge and advance social justice.

Marie Potel-Saville is the founder of Amurabi, an award-winning legal innovation studio, and www.fairpatterns.com, a platform dedicated to fight against dark patterns and train all stakeholders to avoid them. She is an international keynote speaker in human-centric law and legal innovation by design (IAPP Global Privacy Summit, W@Privacy, Computer Privacy and Data Protection, Legal Design Summit, LegalGeek...) Before founding Amurabi, she worked in private practice for 10 years (Freshfields, Allen & Overy) in Europe, then moved in-house to become GC EMEA of a US listed group. She holds a Master's Degree in Innovation by Design at ENSCI. She is also a member of the Advisory Board of the Serpentine Galleries' Legal Lab and is involved in pro bono access to access initiatives. Marie teaches innovation by design at Singapore Management University, Sciences Po and Assas.

Marika Salo-Lahti is an Assistant Professor (tenure track) of Business Law at the University of Vaasa. Her research interests include legal design, AI, fintech, and other topics combining digitalization and law. Recently, she has also been exploring EU legislative actions related to sustainability. She tries to balance her time between research, teaching, thesis supervision, as well as family life and living in a century-old house and having too many ideas about how to decorate it.

Joaquín Santuber is Assistant Professor of Law and Technology at the Faculty of Law, Universidad de Los Andes, Colombia. He has been a postdoctoral researcher on the topic of designing for posthuman legalities—human-nature-machine relations at the Center for Advanced Design Studies, Palo Alto, USA. He obtained a Ph.D. in Design in IT Systems and Technologies at the Hasso-Plattner-Institute, Germany. His doctoral studies focused on designing for digital justice, studying innovation, law, and technologies in Chilean courts. Taking an interdisciplinary approach, Joaquín's work addresses questions around design and governance of technology in public sector organisations, and the tensions between the regulative power of digital technologies and the traditional sources of regulation by the State. While part of the HPI-Stanford Design Thinking Research Program, Joaquín published on the topic of design theory and methodology focused on new educational approaches. His research also extends to the field of health, as part of the HPI Digital Health Design Lab, Potsdam, Germany and the Neurodesign Research initiative at Stanford University. He has also been guest scholar at the Center for Social Studies (CES), University of Coimbra, Portugal and the Humboldt's Institute for Internet and Society, Berlin, Germany. Joaquín was also co-founder of This is Legal Design, Berlin, and the Center for Advanced Design Studies, Palo Alto, USA. He holds a law degree from the Pontificia Universidad Católica de Chile.

Joachim Savin is Design Director at Où sont les Dragons. He is a service designer who is interested in systems, how they are structured, and how they work together. Initially trained in woodworking, Joachim graduated from ENSCI Les Ateliers, where he shifted from physical objects to spaces, then to services, and finally to strategy. Together with Vincent Couronne, he co-founded Les Surligneurs.

Gianni Sinni is Associate Professor of Communication Design at the Università IUAV of Venezia. His research topics and publications deal with communication design applied to social innovation, complex information and data visualisation with a focus on public utility. He was an identity consultant to the Digital Transformation Team at the Prime Minister's Office for the "Digital Republic" project and a member of the Steering Committee of the Agency for Digital Italy (Agid) for the definition of the "Design Guidelines for the Public Administration Websites".

Alain Strowel is professor at UCLouvain where he teaches intellectual property, IT and media law. He also teaches at the Munich IP Law Center and the University of Alicante. Alain is avocat at the Brussels bar since 1988. Alain graduated in law, economics and philosophy at UCLouvain and the University of Amsterdam. He holds a PhD in Law from UCLouvain. Today his research focuses on data governance, Artificial Intelligence and online platforms. He has been appointed as a trustee of the European Law Academy (ERA, 2012-2019). Since 2019, he chairs the Intellectual Property working group of All European Academies (ALLEA).

Nina Toivonen is a lawyer and doctoral researcher in law at the University of Helsinki, Finland. Her doctoral research studies legal theoretical foundations for systemic design of law, especially for the purposes of legal drafting and policy design. Toivonen has a master's degree in legal design and legal expertise from the Laurea University of Applied Sciences, and she is the co-founder and co-host of Legal Design Podcast. Toivonen has also worked as a Legal Designer at the City of Helsinki Legal Services.

PREFACE

The Editors

Legal design has been with us for over a decade. Its core idea, i.e. to use design methods to make the world of law accessible to all, blossomed at the beginning of the 2010s in what can be considered its two main 'cribs': the Legal Design Lab in Stanford, directed by Margaret Hagan, and the Finnish environment, fuelled by thinkers like Helena Haapio, Stefania Passera, or initiatives like the Legal Design Summit.

Since then, legal design has been embraced by academics, researchers, and professionals almost worldwide. New initiatives, courses, projects, and publications (including a dedicated academic journal)[1] are emerging at a constant pace, showing that such a practice is more than just hype.

The reflection about what we mean by legal design, which design practices are key to the legal field, what we can do with them, whether they work and how to evaluate their outcomes, and what the values of the community of 'legal designers' are, has been going on. The constant questioning about its impact and value is probably the reason for this discipline's healthy and steady growth.

This book can be inserted in the *continuum* of such collective reflection. It starts from the observation that legal design has entered an age of adolescence. One of the predominant approaches has been the 'design thinking' method and its problem-solving orientation. However, the awareness that this framework does not exhaust the *spectrum* of legal design practices has grown over the years, and the palette of tools and applications available to everyone has become more diverse and colourful.

The volume contains twelve contributions presented at the 'Legal Design Roundtable' dedicated to 'Design(s) for Law' and organised in Brussels in 2023 within the Erasmus+ Jean Monnet clinic on 'EU Digital Rights, Law, and Design'. These perspectives from academics and professionals add important nuances to the literature, either presenting new

---

1 The 'Legal Design Journal' <https://legaldesign-journal.com> accessed 31 December 2023.

approaches, applying consolidated practices to new contexts and areas, and showcasing actual and potential applications.

The first part of the book explores the significance of speculative design for law. Speculative design has been popularised by Dunne and Raby as a practice to critically reflect on social, cultural, and ethical issues through future scenarios or artefacts (the 'provotypes', i.e. provocative prototypes). However, it is not a sort of sci-fi exercise: it is an intellectual effort for the present to think about where we are headed as a society and direct our future.

Chapter 1 opens the series with an interdisciplinary work by a comparative lawyer and a designer in one of the most interesting European hubs for architects, visual artists, and designers (the IUAV University of Venice). In their piece, Barbara Pasa and Gianni Sinni outline the potential of speculative design for legal change. Pasa and Sinni present a selection of works created during a series of workshops with their students that will certainly challenge the imagination of the readers and let them think about the implications of those propositions.

Emily MacLoud continues in this direction in Chapter 2. Building on a series of examples, including her direct experience during the workshop 'Experimenting with Design in Legal Education', organised by Amanda Perry-Kessaris and Emily Allbon in 2022, she distils some lessons learned when applying speculative techniques in the legal domain.

The second group of contributions deals with another set of tools that can enrich the legal reflection: narratives and storytelling.

In Chapter 3, Emily MacLoud critically engages with one of the most popular instruments used in design thinking, i.e. the 'persona', the fictional representation of the user serving as a benchmark during the design process. Drawing from Kate Raworth's work as an example, she argues that the power of storytelling can contribute to developing stories and narratives to embrace (legal) complexity and inspire systemic change.

Hallie Jay Pope explores the role of critical play as a means to support collective and organising efforts by 'ordinary people' in Chapter 4. By showing ways – such as video games – in which dominant and elite narratives can be challenged, her vibrant piece speaks to legal designers concerned with inequalities, imbalance of power, and oppressive systems.

The third part of the book hosts works answering the call of imaging legal design beyond the user-centred approach or re-imagining its implementation.

Chapter 5 builds on an important vein that has characterised the evolution of legal design over the years: proactive law. Moving from a preventive and problem-solving dimension of design, Robert de Rooy, Anne Ketola, and Helena Haapio present their work on Composite Comic Contracts, a tool to make the contractual artefact more 'cognitively accessible' through a combination of strategies, including visualisation. They acknowledge the chance that the visual aspect of contracts might generate legal uncertainty, but they argue that this will not be an insurmountable obstacle for the tools of legal hermeneutics.

The proactive approach to law is also at the centre of Chapter 6. Here, Marika Salo-Lahti and Helena Haapio combine it with the framework of possibility-driven design, intended as a method to explore possibilities to improve people's lives even when there is no problem to solve on the horizon. They contextualise their proposition within the case of disclosure duties in sustainability legislation at the EU level, also offering a critical take on how and to what extent some AI instruments, notably OpenAI's ChatGPT, can be used for presenting legal information.

In Chapter 7, Nina Toivonen and Santiago De Francisco Vela open the section on the role of participatory design practices in legal design. The authors note that despite the emphasis on the 'human element' as the main focus of legal design, the idea and baggage of participation struggle to materialise in practice (what they call the 'paradox of participation'). In their contribution, the authors argue for such a participatory turn in legal design and discuss five methods and tools to facilitate it.

Santiago De Francisco Vela and Laura Guzman-Abello ideally continue along this line of argumentation in Chapter 8, where they present the transdisciplinary approach developed during 'Design for Justice Lab', an undergraduate course for students in law, design, and engineering at the Universidad de los Andes in Bogotá. They outline and discuss their teaching case, which combines the principles of legal systems, Legal Design, and systemic design, which can serve as a source of inspiration for other educators.

Joaquin Santuber and Pablo Hermansen close this section in Chapter 9 with a philosophical and methodological piece, reflecting on how a posthuman approach can contribute to the understanding and structural ontology of legal design as a discipline.

The final part of the volume presents some challenging applications of legal design in the field of misleading design and misinformation in the online environment. Such a practical and applicative perspective feeds important takeaways into the theoretical discussion on legal design as a practice.

In Chapter 10, Margaret Hagan presents the origin and evolution of a Stanford Legal Design Lab project focusing on counteracting online misinformation and disinformation about public services in the US context. Acknowledging the pervasive role of BigTech actors, as powerful informational intermediaries between public services and users, their 'Better Legal Internet design initiative' proposes cooperation mechanisms to make reliable information discoverable and easy to retrieve by the public.

Vincent Couronne, Joachim Savin, Marie-Sophie de Clippele, and Apolline Le Gall make up the interdisciplinary group of authors that, in Chapter 11, presents a critical reflection on legal design through the lenses of the project 'Les Surligneurs', a media outlet to fact-check the legal accuracy of statements made in the press, in particular by politicians. The initiative embedded the legal design ethos and principles, and the paper constructively reflects on the limitations of its current understanding in France.

Dulcis in fundo, Marie Potel-Saville presents her ongoing work on one of the key problems that has attracted the intervention of legislators, notably the European one in the recent Digital Services Act: dark patterns. Such deceptive and misleading design practices can harm consumers who are in a situation of ontological vulnerability (as humans are structurally affected by cognitive biases and heuristics). In her piece, the author introduces the concept of 'fair patterns' as a tool to support individuals' decision-making processes.

This journey through various approaches in legal design will, we hope, be inspirational and nourish further reflections and new experimentations in integrating design into the realm of law.

SPECULATIVE DESIGN

1. NEW FRONTIERS OF LEGAL KNOWLEDGE: HOW DESIGN *PROVOTYPES* CAN CONTRIBUTE TO LEGAL CHANGE

Barbara Pasa and Gianni Sinni

Abstract

Legal change is a complex phenomenon. Transplants, imitations, borrowings, assimilations by chance or for prestige, adoptions and rejections, and cross-fertilisation are all dynamic processes, which correspond to the past and the present of world legal systems—and they are not just a matter of the "sovereign will" of a state and its sovereign power. Beyond the state, supranational institutions of various kinds are the global agents responsible for shaping legal order reform. Their actions are the preserve of a multitude of forces, including transnational epistemic communities across the globe. What is less explored is how legal change can be the outcome of individual and collective actions, in an age when, for the first time in human history, social organisations depend on the use of information and communication technologies (ICTs). This fact radically affects the legal sphere. How do these collectives and individuals exercise their rights and how are they reminded of their duties, thus playing a major role in delineating the boundaries of the relationship between themselves, legal institutions, and legal change? What legal change is implied by the empirical analysis of the social acts involved in what they do? While legal transplantation theory explicitly deals with how legal change is produced with reference to national and transnational legal institutions, the recognition of speculative design practice in the legal domain can raise awareness of pressing societal issues and bolster individual and collective civic agency over transformation and legal change, through imagination and critical thinking.

1. Legal Change: Setting the Scene and its Narratives

Legal change can be described through the agents vested with the power to change the law.

The following are the main (simplified) narratives aimed at reconstructing legal change from the modern era to the present day; they constitute a minimum common ground of shared knowledge between jurists and designers, a starting point for contributing to a critical and speculative reflection on future scenarios about legal change.

In Western legal tradition, the agents of legal change are judges and lawmakers, with the former acting through case law, and the latter through government and parliamentary legislation. Legitimised from below, as institutions of the *Rechtsstaat* founded on the archetype of the will of the people, these agents decide whether to adopt or reject legal change, controlling it within state borders, with the aim of arriving at new and more efficient legal solutions for fairer legislative reform. The Western-style sovereign state therefore assumes that changes in legal rules are the result of a complex function that is entirely internal to its organs, in which an independent body of specialist-expert judges, together with good legislative practice by state officials, can be steered towards specific policy objectives, such as the recognition of human rights, democratic values, non-discrimination principles and justice, improved economic performance, greater investments and efficiency (but also towards diametrically opposed political goals, as was the case with the Nazi-fascist regimes in Europe). It later also assumed that good rules can be exported to countries transitioning to democracy and the market, because most legal rules can operate in very different societies from the one for which they were originally created through the almost surgical operation of "legal transplants," to use the fortunate expression coined by Alan Watson (1974).

This first narrative of legal change characterised the modern era until the Second World War. It then came to overlap with a more complex transnational narrative, which ever since the Bretton Woods agreements has been guided by economic liberalism and legal functionalism. Private international financial institutions and corporations regarded the World Bank's activities (granting of loans) as complementary to their interests: public works projects to improve the economic infrastructure could only be good for private foreign investors, too.

The fundamental idea is that policy choices and legal rules have a direct effect on the functioning of markets and economic growth, with spill-over effects on sectors not directly dependent on economic mechanisms. In this transnational dimension,[1] multiple agents steer legal

1 Philip Jessup, *Transnational Law* (Yale Law University 1956) p 2: 'transnational law,

change. On these premises, over the last fifty years, the dynamics of legal change have been based on specific alliances between states, forming more or less cooperative networks that act at different speeds. Such alliances range from the maximalist political and economic integration model of the European Union and its Member States, to the minimalist model of the Commonwealth of Independent States (CIS), created in the wake of the break-up of the Soviet Union to prevent the sudden disappearance of an alliance system that for seventy years had kept the Soviet Socialist Republics together; from purely economic cooperation for the elimination of tariff barriers –operating on a macro or mega-regional scale, where for macro-areas we have, for instance, the United States–Mexico–Canada Agreement (USMCA, formerly NAFTA) in North-Central America, the Canada-European Union Comprehensive Economic and Trade Agreement (CETA), the Gulf Cooperation Council (GCC) in the Persian Gulf, the ASEAN Free Trade Area Agreement in Southeast Asia, or the MERCOSUR in Latin America; and for mega-areas we have, for example, the World Trade Organization (WTO), which deals with the global rules of trade between nations, and the Comprehensive and Progressive Agreement for Trans-Pacific Partnership (CPTPP)– to cooperation that integrates economic aspects into a future framework of political integration, such as the Andean Community, the Union of South American Nations (UNASUR), the African Union, the Arab League, and the Council of Europe, to name but a few. By accommodating these transnational dynamics, legal change is driven by a range of factors, which can be simplified in terms of military force, political influence, and economic power, even once colonialism had ceased. Of these three factors, improving economic performance is perhaps the most visible goal in terms of joint statements and declarations of intent; however, it is also the least relevant for the dynamics of legal change, as what usually matters most in these cases is not the effectiveness of legal reform, but the reputation-based legitimacy acquired by joining a prestigious "club of peers" or group of "reliable states."

in general terms, is the law that regulates actions or events that transcend national borders, including both public and private international law, as well as other rules that fall outside the national source system (post-Westphalian model)'.

Regional or international financial organisations, such as the EBRD in Europe, the IMF, or the World Bank,[2] often fund legal change processes, but they propose a "one size fits all" approach to be implemented as quickly as possible, with funding conditional on the adoption by recipient countries of the rule of law and democratic reforms. By proposing the adoption of economic theories and models that make the effectiveness of legal change dependent on the time needed to evaluate its effects on markets' performances, legal systems become market-dependent variables. In this functionalist paradigm, legal rules become a tool of social engineering, a mere technique of utility in the service of better economic performance.

Endorsing this approach and its neo-liberalist version, other players have joined in the global dissemination of standardised, high-performance rules. They include not only public entities, but also private, or public-private, organizations, foundations, associations, corporations, professional firms, NGOs from all sectors, standardisation organisations–such as, for example, the International Organization for Standardization (ISO), and ICANN, a US-based non-profit corporation with global capital, which manages the domain name system–, and even big law firms, that have an exceptional regulatory role and play an important part in processes of legal change through contractual instruments and property rights adjudication procedures.[3]

---

2 For an empirical study of commercial law making within the United Nations, including the UN itself, the World Bank, the IMF, and UNIDROIT, see Susan Block-Lieb and Terence Halliday, *Global Lawmakers: International Organizations in the Crafting of World Markets* (CUP 2017); Michael Likosky (ed), *Transnational Legal Processes Globalisation and Power Disparities* (Butterworths 2002).

3 The reinvention of the legal space by new agents and the resulting pluralism has long been investigated by Italian scholars, including Maria Rosaria Ferrarese, Mauro Bussani, Gianamaria Ajani, Michele Graziadei, Ugo Mattei, Pier Giuseppe Monateri and other younger scholars belonging to the Turin school of comparative law founded by Rodolfo Sacco, in dialogue with other leading thinkers, from Norberto Bobbio and Sabino Cassese, not only in the field of law— to Duncan Kennedy, David Trubek, Martin Shapiro, Gunther Teubner, Mireille Delmas-Marty, Alvaro Santos, Pierre Legrand, Annelise Riles, Roger Cotterell, William Twining, Zygmunt Bauman, Pierrick Le Golf, Ulrich Beck, Saskia Sassen, Robert Reich, Susan Strange, Boaventura de Sousa Santos, etc.

Non-state regulatory solutions are, *de facto*, extremely pervasive in the post-Westphalian environment. Tech giants, with their technological management of the Internet, show how technology can transform the way regulatory and legal functions are performed nowadays, in the space that Roger Brownsword called "the Law 3.0".[4] Technology is changing both the idea of existing law as a coherent system of legal rules and standards, and the way that lawyers, judges, and legislators think about the law's role, and about the national and international architecture of legal and regulatory institutions, including whether A.I. and algorithms could count as legitimate institutions as well.[5]

Our regulatory mind-set needs then to focus on the disruption of the fundamental assumptions on which traditional legal thinking is built, and to take up the challenge on the monopoly concentrations of the "attention merchants"[6] and their business models in terms of data access/data protection. This is our time, the time we live in, where "code" and "architecture" can be more important than formal laws, where IT programmers, computer scientists and neuroscientist teams have a greater effect on a risk management approach to law than the legislators. It is, indeed, the "architecture" that Lawrence Lessig, in his seminal essay, called "code"[7] that plays the most important role today, in the digital ecosystem in which not only markets, but also our social relations have been moving for some time. The Internet is more subject to non-state forms of control than the offline world.[8] And it could not be otherwise. The Internet is (for now) entirely human-made, and it is online that "code" is the most powerful lever for shaping and regulating our behaviours.

---

4 Roger Brownsword, *Rethinking Law, Regulation, and Technology* (Edward Elgar 2022).

5 Woodrow Barfield and Ugo Pagallo (eds), *Research Handbook on the Law of Artificial Intelligence* (Edward Elgar 2018).

6 Tim Wu, *The Attention Merchants: The Epic Scramble to Get Inside Our Heads* (Alfred A Knopf 2016).

7 Code is 'the software and hardware that constitute(s) cyberspace as it is — the set of protocols, the set of rules, implemented, or codified, in the software of cyberspace itself, that determine how people interact, or exist, in this space' at p 4, *The Laws of Cyberspace*, draft 3, essay presented at the Taiwan Net '98 conference, in Taipei, March, 1998. Available online.

8 Lawrence Lessig, *Code: and other laws of cyberspace*, Version 2.0 online (Basic Books 2006).

These continuous transformations of the normative dimension have led political and economic uncertainty to grow worldwide.

In such a complex framework, agents of legal change also seek to measure the effects of their reforms and understand whether time is still an essential factor for reforms to take root—as it was in the past, when the control and steering of legal change was firmly in the hands of the state, and local epistemic communities[9] could be swayed to construct a consensus for a reform. But the quantitative analyses, and the Law and Finance theory as initiated by La Porta, Lopez-de Silanes, Shleifer, and Vishny[10] appear to be backward-looking reference systems of knowledge, based on "historical evidence"–as they investigated the differences between legal origins and their impact on economic performance–especially when compared to new ways of understanding complex phenomena, as will be discussed in the following pages.

What has been said so far also applies to non-Western legal traditions, although the main drivers for legal change were, and are, other things: mainly the ideology of the group or party in power, tradition, religion, chance, and even personal factors. This can be seen in the legal systems of the Islamic world, the Indian subcontinent, Far East Asia and in sub-Saharan African traditions, where legal change has coincided with the history of colonisation, *coups d'état*, and non-pacific revolutions, and with the international trade routes marked out by the pressures of interest groups and personal contacts.[11] But when looking at non-Western contexts, what matters above all is "the process" of legal change; a process that unfolds shaped by both the supply side of the reforms, which is generally indifferent to or unaware of the framework in which new legal rules will be received, and the demand side, which often does not understand or is indifferent to the specific content of the new legal rules

9 Against the premise that epistemic communities are constituted at the national level and are dependent on privileges granted by the state see Brook Harrington and Leonard Seabrooke, 'Transnational Professionals' (2020) 46 Annual Review of Sociology 399. On 'measuring the effects' of legal rules see Antonio Gambaro, 'Misurare il diritto?' (2012) Annuario di diritto comparato e di studi legislativi 17.

10 For a summary: Mathias Siems, Comparative Law (3rd ed, CUP 2022).

11 Li-Wen Lin, 'Legal Transplants through Private Contracting: Codes of Vendor Conduct in Global Supply Chains as an Example' (2009) 57 The American Journal of Comparative Law 711; John Gillespie, 'Globalisation and legal transplantation: Lessons from the past' (2001) 286 Deakin Law Review 286.

(examples of content include redistributive effects, the degree of compatibility with pre-existing legal rules in the system, the time required for adaptation to the local hermeneutic tradition, etc.). The supply/demand division reflects the tension between the legal change and the framework for its reception—a tension that is more significant where countries are less homogeneous than, for example, EU Member States following their European political and economic integration. Thus, at the root of legal change processes we find a lack of understanding, a network of informational asymmetries, and fallacious simplifications that are of little help in grasping the various facets of legal change, in particular of legal transplants shaped by religious factors, personal interests, chance and prestige.[12]

In the wake of the coronavirus pandemic, and the fears and negative effects associated with the transnational dynamics of Covid-19, Western and Global North institutions are fully aware of how legal changes are complex and non-linear multifactor processes, with no clear boundaries between what is local (nationalism) and what is global (transnationalism/supranationalism).[13] Instead they are mutually constitutive dynamics, in which local and global construct each other, becoming "glocal". Local customs, practices, and traditions are real elements of all legal systems, not a cultural invention in response to the neoliberal international legal order. [14]

What we are therefore experiencing today on a global level is the contradictory coexistence of very different regulatory systems: on the one hand, customary rules, practices, and traditions that are the effective components of all legal systems; and on the other, the architecture of the Internet, and coding techniques, which are equally real elements of

12 Gianmaria Ajani, 'By Chance and Prestige: Legal Transplants in Russia and Eastern Europe' (1995) 43 The American Journal of Comparative Law 93.

13 Michele Graziadei, 'What Does Globalisation Mean for the Comparative Study of Law?' (2021) 16 Journal of Comparative Law 511.

14 Graziadei (n 13) 514; Michele Graziadei, 'Legal Transplants and the Frontiers of Legal Knowledge' (2009) 10 Theoretical Inquiries in Law 723; Michele Graziadei, 'Comparative Law as the Study of Transplants and Receptions' in Mathias Reimann and Reinhard Zimmermann (eds) *The Oxford Handbook of Comparative Law* (OUP 2006) 441-476.

contemporary legal systems. As such, they raise issues of justice, responsibility, sustainability, and solidarity.

2. Legal Change: The Good Practice of Interdisciplinary Research in Comparative Law

Comparative law, like other domains of study, looks at legal knowledge from an interdisciplinary point of view. Legal knowledge has porous boundaries and fault lines. By displaying overarching patterns of difference and similarity, comparative law has, for some time now, opened the "black box" of law, revealing its many dimensions and pushing for an examination of the actual and potential possibilities available when legal change is necessary or desired.

The consolidation of interdisciplinary approaches has led comparative law to tap into a composite and collective knowledge that is methodologically robust and, at the same time, flexible and not self-referential. After all, stateless issues such as global warming, environmental destruction, social injustice, poverty, natural disasters, and pandemics are not inevitable events, or the result of historical determinism, and can only be addressed by bringing together different disciplines, practising interdisciplinarity, and pursuing wide-scale participatory action—without which the well-known goals of the UN 2030 Agenda, "a plan of action for people, planet and prosperity", as it states in its preamble,[15] will remain a dead letter.

Interdisciplinary inquiry, for instance, has brought to light the deep malaise in Western legal and political thought based on the values of civilised nations.[16] The dualistic tendency it shows of identifying bad local rules based on tradition, implying they are synonymous with backwardness, and good global norms of a universal, cosmopolitan, and rational nature, based on the supposed existence of a natural law (for which one is against landmines/for the protection of dolphins, against racism/for equal gender rights, against genocide/for human rights, etc.) has been

15 See <https://sdgs.un.org/2030agenda> accessed 12 January 2023.

16 The charter of the International Court of Justice is also based on these principles: see Marija Dordeska, *General Principles of Law Recognized by Civilized Nations (1922–2018)* (Brill Nijhoff 2020).

widely commented on and criticised as a functionalist approach to legal change based on the so-called "Washington consensus," leading to the "Americanisation" of the world[17]—although the same can be said today about Europe and the so-called "Brussels effect" beyond European borders.[18]

Interdisciplinary inquiry, furthermore, has provided an alternative explanation in response to the observation that many rules that have been imitated or transplanted have remained on paper and have not always produced the legal uniformity hoped for in terms of promoting trade and better market performance. Scholars usually proceed with a historical analysis to explain that it is all the fault of the past which conditions the present, and that legal change is bound to events that happened in the past, as taught by the path dependency theory. Those past events have a solid impact on legal culture, which becomes the catch-all factor that is used to emphasise how and how much the past conditions the present. But this explanation only partially satisfies us.

In countries in transition and in the Global South, the ineffectiveness of legal change is usually associated with the antagonistic relationship that arises between local institutions and role-occupants (generally judges, public officials, and Western consultants) sent to carry out reforms or provide local training, who treat legal data according to the principle of the indifference and technical neutrality of the law,[19] for which societies that are different from each other can be governed by the same rules.[20] That same mechanism, however, is also observed in

---

17 Ex multis, Francis Snyder, 'Economic Globalization and the Law in 21st Century' in Austin Sarat (ed), *The Blackwell Companion to Law and Society* (Blackwell Publishers 2004) 2-17; Ugo Mattei, 'A Theory of Imperial Law: A Study on U.S. Hegemony and the Latin Resistance' (2003) 10 Indiana Journal of Global Legal Studies 383; Mathias Reimann, 'Beyond National Systems: A Comparative Law for the International Age' (2001) 75 Tulane Law Review 1103.

18 Anu Bradford, *The Brussels Effect: How the European Union rules the World* (OUP 2020); Marise Cremona and Joanne Scott (eds*) EU law beyond EU borders: the extraterritorial reach of EU Law* (OUP 2019).

19 On neutrality, see among Italian scholars: Gianmaria Ajani, 'Trapianto di norme informato e globalizzazione alcune considerazioni' in Gianmaria Ajani and others (eds), *Studi in onore di Aldo Frignani Nuovi orizzonti del diritto comparato europeo e transnazionale* (Jovene 2011) 3–15.

20 On the "one size fits all" approach see Section 1.

the legal systems of the Global North, where the failure of legal reforms carried out according to the functionalist approach is associated with the dialectical tension between the autonomy of local constituencies and the central institutions that impose top-down legal reforms. Empirical observation studies suggest that resistance to change is not linked to cultural differences, as an exoticising view of non-Western laws might initially seem to suggest.[21] Reiterated conclusions as to the ineffectiveness of legal change when pursued according to the abstract model of legal transplants and the logic of "one size fits all" have recently prompted legal scholars to explore the deeper relationship between law, considered the main tool of legal change, and "societal forces", "different vested interests," and "political interests".[22] Thus, it turns out that legal change, in both the Global South and the Global North, depends on a number of additional variables, such as the effects of informal processes on the standardised discourse about the rule of law and democracy, political choices and ideology, the role of cryptotypes, and customary practices shaping implementational rules, as well as social practices that shape the law.[23] This implicit dimension of normativity that silently rules the actions of individuals and communities may in fact be unveiled by applying the normative variant of Paul Grice's theory of conversation developed by Marina Sbisa,[24] and Rodolfo Sacco's theory of cryptotypes:[25] the "underlying patterns" can be revealed, or made visible through mi-

21 Franz and Keebet von Benda-Beckmann, 'Why not Legal Culture' (2010) Journal of Comparative Law 104.

22 Graziadei 'What Does Globalisation Mean for the Comparative Study of Law?' (n 13).

23 On law and society see Lester Salomon, *The Tools of Government: A Guide to the New Governance* (OUP 2022); see Antonina Bakardjieva Engelbrekt and Joakim Nergelius (eds), *New Directions in Comparative Law* (Edward Elgar 2010).

24 Herbert-Paul Grice, *Logic and conversation*, in Peter Cole and Jerry Morgan (eds), *Syntax and semantics, vol. 3: Speech acts* (Academic Press 1975) 41–58; Marina Sbisa, *Detto non detto. Le forme della comunicazione implicita* (Laterza 2007); Marina Sbisà, 'Normativita e comunicazione' in Lucia Morra and Barbara Pasa (eds), *Questioni di genere nei testi normativi: crittotipi e impliciti* (Giappichelli 2015) 15–38.

25 In the seminal work by Rodolfo Sacco, *Introduzione al diritto comparato* (Giappichelli 1980). See also Rodolfo Sacco, 'Mute Law' (1995) 43 The American Journal of Comparative Law 455; a fresh reflection, by the same author, is contained in the book *Il diritto muto* (Il Mulino 2015).

cro-comparisons of legal rules among different legal systems. The discovery of a cryptotype is facilitated when, as happens, a legal rule, a concept, or a principle implicit in one legal system is explicit in another one. By logical and non-logical inferences of textual information from an explicit rule, pragmatics tools unveil the connections between what lies outside the text and what is inside it, what can plausibly be considered as part of what a statute, a judgment, or a decree communicated when it was produced, and what can enrich a legal rule without affecting its truth value.[26]

In the background lies the idea that law is a socially valuable practice of regulation in a given time and place, a practice that reflects the variability of socio-legal conditions and contexts.[27] What thus counts in defining what is legal are particular social settings: law is not only what law officials do and say they are doing, it is also a reflection of social values, educational conditioning, ideology and economics.[28]

The law then can appear for what it is: an interpretative socially valuable practice of formal regulations and customary rules in a given time and place, made up of embodied subjectivities that find protection under a wider notion of "citizenship" as part of the legal change itself; a procedural notion of citizenship, understood as the social process of being engaged that facilitates cohesion, rather than a status, or a goal in itself (a reward for being integrated) is then needed.

3. Choice is Good, but Community Engagement is Better: Citizenship

The uglier face of globalisation is shown when the law and legal change processes admit their powerlessness in setting out the moral limits of markets. One remedy that is often proposed is to lower their level of complexity and then essentially solve the problem by reducing it to a matter of self-determination and freedom of choice—because "choice

26 Barbara Pasa and Lucia Morra, '6. Implicit Legal Norms' in Jacqueline Visconti (ed), *Handbook of Communication in the Legal Sphere* (De Gruyter Mouton 2018) 141-168.

27 Roger Cotterrell, 'Why jurisprudence is not legal philosophy' (2014) Jurisprudence 41, 51.

28 William Twining, *Law in context: enlarging a discipline* (OUP 1997); William Twining, 'Social science and diffusion of law' (2005) 32 Journal of Law and Society 203.

is good".[29] Such a solution, however, is not altogether convincing. We believe that the question—or rather, the questions—should be restated: how can states, markets, and other players involved in legal change—both in the Global South and in advanced post-industrial, multicultural countries—come to terms with deeply-rooted social structures that they cannot change? To what extent does public opinion impact public policy? What difference does individual behaviour make? How do networks of higher civil service elites (public administration, public management, judiciary, etc.) shape legal change? In identifying the institutions that organise social, economic, and political interaction, can we also say, drawing from cognitive science and ethnology, that the human mind "is the first institution", one shared by all human societies? Might the unity of the human mind—because all humans share important common cognitive frameworks, both with each other and with other hominids[30]—be a crucial factor in social organisation and legal change?

It is at this point that a broad vision of citizenship comes into play. Based on active community engagement, it is citizenship understood as a social process in which the greatest possible number of people partake;[31] and not only humans,[32] considering that the general principles of

29 The topic of personal self-determination in private law is the subject of extensive debate, for example in the area of surrogate motherhood agreements, contracts promoting sex work, and marriage brokerage contracts, nuptial agreements, but also usurious contracts as well as immoral suretyships, etc. See Aurelia Colombi Ciacchi, Chantal Mak, Zeeshan Mansoor (eds), *Immoral Contracts in Europe* (Intersentia 2020).

30 We have an innate ability for the "mental score-keeping of services," that is, a mechanism for social exchange based on reciprocity, as psychological, anthropological, and ethnological studies appear to show; see Raffaele Caterina, 'Comparative Law and the Cognitive Revolution' (2003-2004) 78 Tul L Rev 1501 inspired by Dan Sperber, *Explaining Culture: A Naturalistic Approach* (Blackwell 1996); see, Dan Sperber and Deirdre Wilson, *Relevance*: *Communication and Cognition* (Blackwell 1986; 2nd ed 1995).

31 The desire to make law "work better for people," and to design legal systems "fit for real humans" weaves through many of the interviews conducted by Henna Tolvanen and Nina Toivonen for their Legal Design Podcast: see the episodes at <https://legaldesignpodcast.com/> accessed 12 January 2023.

32 On post-human, more-than-human agency in legal design see Joaquín Santuber and Lina Krawietz, 'The Sociomateriality of Justice: A Relational Ontology for Legal Design' (2021) Revista Chilena de Diseño 1.

perceptual organisation and the common framework of basic assumptions of the world, built on our genetic system, are something we share with all species, or at least with all vertebrates.

The citizenship debate first originated from concerns about social cohesion and the maintenance of public order in nation-states. It was a censorious citizenship[33] that arose within certain territorial boundaries, based on a legitimisation of sovereignty of an ascending (from the people), and no longer descending (from the divine) kind, referring to the people, the nation, a singular identity.[34] Today, the criteria for becoming a citizen contained in national legislations have in practice become obstacles to achieving citizenship itself, and to integration.[35]

One of the basic principles of liberal states is that all citizens are formally equal to each other and before the law. But as we all know, the equality of citizens is intersected by many inequalities (by ethnicity, gender, physical and mental disability, income, and so on) and compromised by the substantial exclusion to the enjoyment of rights for noncitizens (migrants, asylum seekers, refugees). For if there were no inequalities, there would indeed be no need for anti-discrimination laws and inclusion practices.

Today, moreover, there can be no citizenship without taking the digital dimension into account, just as there can be no "mature citizens" regardless of the digital dimension.[36] The point is not only the recognition of a digital citizenship that has broken through the territorial boundaries of nation-states, expanding to coincide with the concept of "neti-

---

33 Stefano Rodotà, 'Antropologia dell'homo dignus' (2010) Storia e memoria 107.

34 On the process of forming nation-states and "authentic citizens", in particular with regard to the destruction of local crafts in favour of nationally integrated workers, shaped by the technical requirements of their jobs and by their participation in national culture, by their speaking one common national language, by their reading the same newspapers and going to the same coffee-houses and sharing the same dress code etc. see Melissa Aronczyk and Craig Calhoun, 'Nationalism' in Richard A Couto (ed), *Political and Civil Leadership, A Reference Handbook* (Sage 2010) 490–497 [the "violence" of the state, 494]. See also Bryan Roberts, *The Making of Citizens. Cities of Peasants Revisited* (Routledge 1995).

35 Steven Vertovec, 'Super-Diversity and its Implications' (2007) 30 Ethnic and Racial Studies 1024.

36 Alfonso Fuggetta, *Cittadini ai tempi di Internet. Per una cittadinanza consapevole nell'era digitale* (Franco Angeli 2018) 62.

zenship"—from [Inter]net + [cit]izenship.[37] Current research is outlining the figure of the "happy citizen"[38] based on the principle of well-being, as intangible collective capital, which is expressed in the preservation and transmission of cultural heritage, collective memory, political participation, peace, environmentalism, social equity and the inclusion of minorities and vulnerable social groups. The idea of happy citizenship is already at the core of political and regulatory decisions aimed at increasing people's well-being and life satisfaction, as witnessed by the OECD projects.[39]

The relationship between citizenship and the ideals of happiness and well-being, integration, and equality is complex. In particular, the goals of citizenship policies are not well defined, and generally at odds with those of immigration. Among other things, the differentiation between citizens and noncitizens sharpens when migrants travel mainly in South-North and East-West directions.[40] This makes it desirable to have a flexible notion of citizenship, based on solidarity-building mechanisms, traceable to the idea of pan-citizenship, to help further active community engagement[41] and greater tolerance of different lifestyles and values, a notion that embraces social responsibility and aims to reduce the number of people with extremely limited rights. That means a broader definition of citizen to include migrants, refugees, and marginalised people in general, with stronger value placed on active community engagement. Here, public participation goes beyond the turnout of vot-

37 In the pioneering definition given by Michael and Ronda Hauben, *Netizens – On the History and Impact of Usenet and the Internet* (IEEE Operations Center 1997).

38 Galit Wellner, Aharon Aviram, Yael Rozin, Alfredo Ronchi, 'Well-Being in the Digital Age' in Alfredo Ronchi (ed) *e-Citizens: Toward a New Model of (Inter) Active Citizenry* (Springer Nature 2019) 28; Michele Graziadei and Barbara Pasa, 'Happiness Once More' (2019) Journal of Comparative Law 203; Sofia Axelsson and Stefan Dahlberg, 'Measuring Happiness and Life Satisfaction Amongst Swedish Citizens. An inquiry into semantic equivalence in comparative survey research' (2018) *Working Paper Series* 2018:2, University of Bergen.

39 See <https://www.oecdbetterlifeindex.org/topics/life-satisfaction/>; <https://www.oecd.org/wise/measuring-well-being-and-progress.htm> accessed 12 January 2023.

40 Stephen Shulman, 'Challenging the Civic/Ethnic and West/East Dichotomies in the Study of Nationalism' (2002) 35 Comparative Political Studies 554.

41 Russell Dalton, 'Citizenship Norms and the Expansion of Political Participation' (2008) 56 Political Studies 76.

ers at elections,[42] entailing new forms of consultation and governance,[43] where the latter is understood as a process through which institutions, businesses, and community members articulate their interests, exercise their rights, and allocate choices and opportunities, while mediating their differences.[44]

4. The Contestability of Decision-Making Processes and the Micro-Dimension of Persons as Agents of Legal Change

In thinking about legal change, the focus should therefore be shifted onto the dialectic between policy-making and the law. It can be observed how the domestic politics of states and major changes within the national political arena project outwards and reshape the legal structure of the global system.[45] Law cannot act as a substitute for political choices, as witnessed by the adjudication process[46]—a privileged site of interaction between the legal and the political—and by widely documented policy transfers.[47] While it is true that legal change is based on selective ad-

42 Considering the record abstention rate of more than 40% of voters during the last three years of political and administrative elections in many European member states, such as Italy, France, Germany, Spain, Ireland, Latvia, Estonia, Lithuania, Croatia and Bulgaria, but the same phenomenon is also noted in other countries: see Pew Research Center, November 1, 2022 at <https://www.pewresearch.org/fact-tank/2022/11/01/turnout-in-u-s-has-soared-in-recent-elections-but-by-some-measures-still-trails-that-of-many-other-countries/> accessed 12 January 2023.

43 Nico Krisch and Benedict Kingsbury, 'Introduction: Global Governance and Global Administrative Law in the International Legal Order' (2006) 17 European Journal of International Law 1. For connections between design and citizenship see Veronica Dal Buono, Gianni Sinni and Michele Zannoni, 'Design for Citizenship' (2020) 10 MD Journal.

44 This is the definition given by the Second Global Knowledge Conference GKII (2000), see Second Global Knowledge Conference (GKII): building knowledge societies: access-empowerment-governance 7-10 March 2000, Kuala Lumpur: Global Knowledge Partnership (2000).

45 Charles B Roger, *The Origins of Informality: Why the Legal Foundations of Global Governance Are Shifting, and Why It Matters* (OUP 2020).

46 Duncan Kennedy, *A critique of adjudication: fin de siècle* (Harvard University Press 1997).

47 Fabrizio Gilardi and Fabio Wasserfallen, 'The Politics of Policy Diffusion' (2019) 58

aptation under the pressure of specific political-economic interests,[48] it is also true that legal change is centred on the "contestability" of decision-making processes, where contestable means that there are no major barriers to change.[49]

In this changed epistemological horizon, the theory of legal change is called on to explore the subjective micro-dimension, on a dual level: on the one hand, individuals and, on the other, the collective. The key notion advanced to explore this micro-dimension, proposed by Michele Graziadei, inspired by psychological studies of the social formation of the mind,[50] is that of "mediated action". Mediated action denotes action performed by people through the instrumentality of material objects and other kinds of artifacts, such as mnemonic techniques, algebraic symbol systems, works of art, writing, schemes, diagrams, maps, mechanical drawings, all sorts of conventional signs, and so on.[51]

This brings us to the question of languages, laws, and their design. Drawing on the intuition that languages are social tools, the approach we embrace provides the theoretical bases for understanding how legal change processes occur in "places of engagement", where discourse

---

European Journal of Political Research 1245; Diane Stone, 'Between Policy Failure and Policy Success: Bricolage, Experimentalism, and Translation in Policy Transfer' in Claire Dunlop (ed) *Policy Learning and Policy Failure* (Policy Press 2020) 71-92.

48 Tobias Hofmann, 'How Long to Compliance? Escalating Infringement Proceedings and the Diminishing Power of Special Interests' (2018) 40 Journal of European Integration 785.

49 Decision-making process is "contestable" if decision-makers are open to adopting new methods, such as the "seven-generation rule" of indigenous peoples, when making decisions. See Eliezer Yudkowsky, *Inadequate Equilibria. Where and How Civilizations Get Stuck* (Machine Intelligence Research Institute 2017), who uses the term "contendible": "a contendible situation is one in an inadequate equilibrium, which is still an equilibrium (that is why it has not changed), but it is inadequate, so it might be possible to disrupt it with a reasonable effort"; see the Sci-Fi Economics Lab, involved in the Long Termism Deep Demonstration (2020) at <https://www.climate-kic.org/programmes/deep-demonstrations/long-termism/publications/> accessed 12 January 2023.

50 Graziadei 'What Does Globalisation Mean for the Comparative Study of Law?' (n 13) 518.

51 Lev Seme¨novich Vygotsky, 'The Instrumental Method in Psychology' in James Wertsch (ed), *The Concept of Activity in Soviet Psychology* (ME Sharpe Inc 1981) at 134, 137.

turns into action,[52] starting from schools and universities, where emphasis can be placed on the importance of graphic communication design in creating not only visual communication, but also in changing people's attitudes and capabilities.[53]

The reflection on words, terminologies, and "language" in general is a fruitful and common starting point for the dialogue between law and graphic communication design. In both areas, a tacit or mute dimension[54] is admitted and represents much of what lies beneath the surface. There are many silent rules, with people often knowing how to put them into practice, but without being able to formulate them. However, knowing "how to do" something is different from knowing "what to do", just as "knowing that" is distinct from "knowing how"[55]—a fact and an awareness that are ultimately shared by both law and design. Knowing what is the law is not only about the content of detailed legal rules and the structures and concepts used by doctrine and legal actors, but also about implicit sources, foundational principles and values underpinning them; it is just as important as knowing how to go beyond written texts or spoken words in legal communication, including images, rituals, feelings and public performances as modes of human ruling and interpretation, [56] since legal texts imply more than they say.

Continuing along this line of reasoning, it seems worth emphasising that law and graphic communication design studies share the reflection

52 Sigrid Norris and Rodney H Jones (eds), *Discourse in Action: Introducing Mediated Discourse Analysis* (Routledge 2005); see for example Yoram Shachar, who illustrates how mediated action works with respect to legal transplants in the drafting of the Israeli Declaration of Independence: Yoram Shachar, 'Jefferson Goes East: The American Origins of the Israeli Declaration of Independence' (2009) 10 Theoretical Inquiries in Law 589.

53 Jorge Frascara, 'Graphic Design: Fine Art or Social Science?' (1998) Design Issues 18.

54 Above, Section 2.

55 Gilbert Ryle, *The Concept of Mind* (Barnes & Noble 1949).

56 The reflection on law & language covers a vast spectrum, from the absence of written forms to the multiplicity of representations forms: for instance, the performance of an act, or of a duty, acquiescence, or exercise of a right can be implied by silent, normative, rules: see Sacco 1995, 2015 (n 25); pictures and images have a normativity in themselves: see Anne Wagner and Richard Sherwin (eds), *Law, Culture and Visual Studies* (Springer 2014); Volker Boehme-Neßler, *Pictorial Law. Modern law and the power of pictures* (Springer 2011).

on the relationship between alphabetical writing and visual codes in the formulation and communication of complex messages.[57] While recognising the dominance of verbal language in human communication, at least in our cultural context, both law and graphic communication design specifically acknowledge that not all writing is alphabetical (such as in China) and that not all writing is verbally oriented (such as the graphic symbols used to represent numbers).

The fact that all writing is a set of conventional graphic signs used to represent, preserve, and transmit information by organising language in physical and digital space[58] is another relevant aspect for a promising dialogue between law and design.

Furthermore, transformative processes are completed through ideologies, which are tools that legitimise normativity.[59] Ideologies are forms of action aimed at orienting social beliefs, responding to the need to build consensus, or resistance, towards legal change. It is in the nature of ideology, given that its adherents will act in largely the same way in similar situations, to facilitate the carrying out of joint tasks and contribute to group cohesion. In this sense, an ideology is essentially an "interface" between individual practice and collective action,[60] and interface is another key word that can unite jurists and designers in contemporary thinking, on which design studies can project their theoretical and practical knowledge. Ideology has primarily been studied as a tool of

57 Emily Allbon, 'Beyond text: exploiting the visual in law' (2018) Australian Law Librarian 54. On the production of user-friendly legal documents, using for example graphic symbols and icons that are machine-interpretable and able to elicit information effectively, see Arianna Rossi and Monica Palmirani, 'From Words to Images Through Legal Visualization' in Ugo Pagallo, Monica Palmirani, Pompeu Casanovas, Giovanni Sartor and Serena Villata (eds) *AI Approaches to the Complexity of Legal Systems*. AICOL 2015 2016 2017. Revised selected papers, Lecture Notes in Computer Science, vol 10791 (Springer 2018) 72–85. This area studies have been also called "legal information design": Arianna Rossi, Rossana Ducato, Helena Haapio, Stefania Passera and Monica Palmirani, 'Legal Design Patterns: Towards a New Language for Legal Information Design' in *Internet of Things. Proceedings of the 22nd International Legal Informatics Symposium* IRIS (2019) 517-526.

58 Giovanni Lussu, *La grafica è scrittura, una lezione*, A.A.M Architettura Arte Moderna e Istituto Europeo di Design di Roma (Stampa Graffiti Roma 1996).

59 Ajani 'By Chance and Prestige: Legal Transplants in Russia and Eastern Europe' (n 12).

60 Teun A van Dijk (ed), *Discourse as Social Interaction* (Sage 1997) 25.

domination, or as an expression of benevolent paternalism—and both, at certain times and under certain conditions, have been interpreted as the realisation of ideals of justice.[61] However, ideologies are above all ambiguous and contradictory, and they have a finite temporal horizon. They change over time, adapt to the context, and tolerate multiple personal affiliations and subtle variations in personal commitments; they are forced to make continuous adjustments to accommodate what lives on the margins, the singularities that animate the collective. As a circular process, it is the behaviour of the individuals that determines that of the entire system, and obtaining the desired behaviour depends on individual incentives and the individual framing of information.[62] At the same time, the behaviour of the system is deduced from that of the collective. Thus rebound and other second-order effects, which refer to behavioural or other systemic responses after the implementation of new laws, are important as well for legal change.[63] The expected effects are not equivalent to an engineering estimate, because of systemic and behavioural adjustments; habits and lifestyles are also factors that lead to the mitigation or, more frequently, amplification of the rebound effect. If we accept the shortcomings of a positivistic research paradigm, then there is room to understand the indirect and society-wide rebound effects from a qualitative and theoretical perspective.

Our micro-dimension starting point is therefore a stimulus for investigating legal change from the perspective of the well-being of the final recipients of the normative message, of different subjectivities and their positions in respect to the collective. But that is not all. What drives

---

61 See Christopher L Tomlins, 'Transplants and Timing: Passages in the Creation of an Anglo-American Law of Slavery' (2009) 10 Theoretical Inquiries in Law 389 (for the justification of slavery); Jane Dailey, 'Race, Marriage and Sovereignty in the New World Order' (2009) 10 Theoretical Inquiries in Law 511 (for the justification of racial superiority). See also Joseph Berger and others, 'The Legitimation and Delegitimation of Power and Prestige Orders' (1998) 63 American Sociological Review 379.

62 On the nudge theory see Richard H Thaler and Cass R Sunstein, *Nudge: Improving Decisions About Health, Wealth, and Happiness* (Yale University Press 2008).

63 It is worth noting that the literature regarding the rebound effect does not distinguish between policy-driven rebound and "autonomous" rebound. It suggests that rebound effects are plural because a number of mechanisms are involved: see Hans Jakob Walnum, Carlo Aall, and Søren Løkke, 'Can Rebound Effects Explain Why Sustainable Mobility Has Not Been Achieved?' (2014) 12 Sustainability 9510.

us to adopt this analytical and subjective perspective is the recognition that the so-called Fourth Revolution,[64] based on information and communication technologies (ICT), has changed our understanding of the world in the Internet and social media age, highlighting our nature as "permanently interconnected informational organisms".[65] This nature of ours is shared with both other biological organisms and artificial agents (A.I.) within an ecosystem of information and message communication.[66] Breaking free from human exclusivity in law and approaching a post-anthropocentric legality is an ontological turn that we can accomplish with legal design.[67] The more the ICT-dependency of contemporary societies consolidates, the more important it becomes to delve into the issue of regulatory profiles of digital technologies and the more important the role played by post-human-centred design becomes in designing the objects and environments in which we live, interact, and socialise,[68] especially considering the fact that we have all become "infomaniacs" and "phono sapiens".[69]

5. The Transformative Power of Law and Design

With the aim of clarifying what we propose as a different approach to legal change from analyses based on backward-looking reference systems,[70] in the following Sections we will introduce possible scenarios of legal change led by collective practices and individual actions based on speculative design and storytelling as tools for legal and policy change: what we have named forward-looking reference systems.

---

64 Luciano Floridi, *The Fourth Revolution: How the Infosphere is Reshaping Human Reality* (OUP 2014).

65 Ugo Pagallo, *Il diritto nell'età dell'informazione* (Giappichelli 2014).

66 For McLuhan the medium is itself the message: Marshall McLuhan, *Understanding Media: The Extensions of Man* (McGraw-Hill 1964).

67 Arturo Escobar, *Designs for the Pluriverse. Radical Interdependence, Autonomy, and the Making of Worlds* (Duke University Press 2017); Santuber and Krawietz (n 32).

68 Marij Swinkels, 'How ideas matter in public policy: a review of concepts, mechanisms, and methods' (2020) International Review of Public Policy 281.

69 Byung-Chul Han, *Undinge: Umbruche der Lebenswelt* (Ullstein Verlag 2022) at 7 and 46.

70 Those mentioned in Section 1.

Engaging with design is only a recent topic of interest for jurists and lawyers,[71] in which design is generally treated as a skill that can be picked up along the way, while the true experts in the room remain the jurists. This has much to do with the mythical "lawyers' mindset"[72] that would appear to be an insurmountable hurdle to the empathy that is central to design—a mindset in which a jurist's value is determined by their assumed knowledge, made up of words and by the manipulation of words, where failure must be avoided at all costs, the group of experts must contain the least possible cognitive diversity, creating a situation of homophily, and the problem-solver is the leading role they can play.[73] Below, we will capture the opposite dynamic, when designers engage with law, and in which design is applied to a legal context, to achieve that "well-being of law as a practical idea", a duty that we all have, as Roger Cotterrell suggests[74]—what we might call service design, or systemic design (we will not linger here on the issues that certain taxonomies raise). By relating the story of some practices carried out at our university, we would like to stress the naivety of the assumption that a jurist or a lawyer can turn their hand to being a service designer, or a graphic commu-

71 For a summary of the different positions on what legal design is see Rossana Ducato and Alain Strowel (eds), *Legal Design Perspectives* (Ledizioni 2021); see also Dan Jackson, Jules R Sievert, Miso Kim and Sankalp Bhatnagar 'What legal design could be: Towards an expanded practice of inquiry, critique, and action' in Dan Lockton, Sara Lenzi, Paul Hekkert, Arlene Oak, Juan Sádaba, and Peter Lloyd (eds) *DRS2022: Bilbao* (Design Research Society 2022) <https://doi.org/10.21606/drs.2022.281> accessed 12 January 2023. Initiated by Margaret Hagan with her work *Law by Design* (2016), online at <https://lawbydesign.co/>, the discussion is ongoing. LeDA, What is Legal Design? (2018), online at <https://www.legaldesignalliance.org/> and the NuLawLab, the interdisciplinary innovation laboratory at Northeastern University School of Law at <https://www.nulawlab.org/> accessed 12 January 2023.

72 Rae Morgan and Emily Allbon, 'Is Law Really that Special?' in Ducato and Strowel (n 71) 139–158; Anne-Marie Slaughter, 'On Thinking Like a Lawyer' (2002) *Harv L Today* <https://www.princeton.edu/~slaughtr/Commentary/On%20Thinking%20Like%20a%20Lawyer.pdf> accessed 12 January 2023; Stefania Passera, *Beyond the wall of contract text - Visualizing contracts to foster understanding and collaboration within and across organizations* (Aalto University publication series Doctoral Dissertations 134/2017).

73 Lawrence Krieger, *The Hidden Sources of Law School Stress: Avoiding the Mistakes that Create Unhappy and Unprofessional Lawyers* (Kindle 2014) 7–9.

74 Roger Cotterrell, *Sociological Jurisprudence Juristic Thought and Social Inquiry* (Routledge 2018).

nication, or information designer. The training, aptitude, and experience required to be skilled in design practices is relevant. The relationship between jurists and designers ought to be mutually constructive. Design methods draw on humanistic and technical knowledge and their experience can break through the legacy of formal thinking,[75] opening up the legal setting to empathy, fictitious descriptions of users, visualisations, peripheral information, and the experiences of others, while the legal experience that designers require can be provided in co-design processes, through the participation of jurists and the community at large, and in speculative design practices. These practices[76] do not run the risk of distraction or self-indulgence: on the contrary, the vision of multiple possible, or probable futures trains our serendipity, our ability to notice the unexpected and make it constructive for change, our ability to detect, interpret and connect accidental data or random phenomena from the existing. Thus, in planning legal change for the benefit of society as a whole, and for the individuals who interact under the law's protection, we may be able to move from where we are now to where we would like to be.

6. Speculative Design for Legal Change in Public Services

Law and design are not knowledge for themselves, but knowledge for action. They are social practices and poietic disciplines that can build change in the future, starting from the observation of the present. By exploring alternative hypotheses to the question about people's real needs in a post-anthropocentric view that assumes a new relationship with nature and for nature, they enable us to see the future possibilities for what seems inadequate, ineffective, or unjust in the present (enabling capacity of speculative design).

Our hypothesis is that legal change can be successfully experimented within the interdisciplinary space where law and design meet. Our ex-

75 See Amanda Perry-Kessaris, 'Legal design could and should be more sociolegal' in Lockton, Lenzi, Hekkert, Oak, Sádaba, and Lloyd (n 71) [she also traces the history of the idea that design can enhance cross-disciplinary thinking and practice]; Amanda Perry-Kessaris, 'Making sociolegal research more social by design: Anglo-German roots, rewards and risks' (2020) 21 German Law Journal 1427.

76 As we will see in Sections 7-8.

perimental work focuses, in particular, on design strategies that speculate on the future and are implemented through participatory and social interaction practices in the public services sector.[77]

Public services are the sector that has attracted the most social innovation, involving the direct engagement of citizens.[78] An exemplary case is the UK Gov design team,[79] which has had similar experiences in

77 Mauricio Vico, Santiago de Francisco Vela, and Monica Pachón Buitrago, 'Cuando el pensamiento en Diseño y el mundo legal se encuentran: Innovación para mejorar la prestación de servicios públicos' (2021) RChD: creación y pensamiento 1. On public service design and some examples, such as the UNESCO Global Futures Literacy Network, the UK Policy Lab, the OECD Directorate for Public Governance and its Observatory of Public Sector Innovation, the Danish Design Center Future Welfare, the EU Policy Lab The Future of Government 2030+ and others, a summary in Barbara Pasa and Gianni Sinni, 'Democracy in Outer Space. Speculative Design for Future Citizenship' forthcoming (2024).

78 On the relevance, for the designer, of reflecting on civic and political issues, and in particular on public services, see the first debates in Italy with the 1984 First Cattolica Graphics Biennial; among others, Giovanni Anceschi, *Prima Biennale della grafica*: *propaganda e cultura* (Mondadori 1984).

79 Louise Downe, *Good Services: Decoding the Mystery of What Makes a Good Service: How to Design Services that Work* (Bis Publishers 2019).

France,[80] Italy,[81] Spain,[82] Denmark,[83] and Belgium,[84] just to name but a few examples. In these cases, co-design activities focus on including user needs in the actual design process of digital services.[85] The degree of community engagement varies from citizens as "co-implementers" of services and activities formerly carried out by the government, to citizens as "co-designers", involved in designing the content and delivery process of the services, to citizens as "initiators" of the design of specific services.[86] In general terms, some suggest using "co-production" "as an

80 DINSIC (*Direction interministérielle du numérique et du système d'information et de communication de l'État*) – now DINUM (*Direction interministérielle du numérique*), for example, included the *MonAvis* button (I give my opinion) on public websites to test the satisfaction of citizens with administrative processes. See <https://www.plus.transformation.gouv.fr/engagement/7> accessed 12 May 2023.

81 The *Team per la Trasformazione Digitale* has a large developer community (Developers Italia) that creates new software and allows developers on other levels of government to reuse developed tools: developers, suppliers, civil servants, and citizens can collaborate to improve a common code base and customise public services using open-source architecture.

82 The Spanish Central Administration, via its Secretary General for Digital Transformation, since the program "2017 Digital Strategy for an Intelligent Spain", has used co-assessment *ex-ante* and *ex-post* evaluation for digital public services, where stakeholders are essential to measure the economic and social impact. A success case of co-assessment has been in the selection of the non-working days for notifications at the Tax Agency, based on a massive evaluation feedback from all stakeholders.

83 The Danish Business Authority is part of the Ministry of Business and Finance and includes stakeholders in order to define user needs as the basis for any kind of co-creation activities. See <https://www.co-val.eu/case-studies/blog/project/the-danish-business-authority-dba/> accessed 12 May 2023.

84 BOSA's DG Digital Transformation has set up the reporting website managed by the Administrative Simplification Agency, where citizens can report feedback on administrative experiences they have had, and signal issues and what can be improved: <https://www.kafka.be/fr> accessed 12 May 2023.

85 Ines Mergel, 'Digital Service Teams in Government: An International Comparison of New IT Governance Structures' available at https://www.economie.gouv.fr/igpde-editions-publications/comparative-analysis_n6. See also the material gathered by the "25th International Government Design Community Call," where maturing and scaling up design is discussed: <https://www.youtube.com/watch?v=apGPATMrvKg> accessed 12 January 2023.

86 William Voorberg, Victor Bekkers and Lars Tummers, 'A Systematic Review of Co-Creation and Co-Production: Embarking on the social innovation journey' (2015) 17 Public Management Review 1333, 1347; Ezio Manzini, *Design, When Everybody*

umbrella concept that captures a wide variety of activities that can occur in any phase of the public service cycle and in which state actors and lay actors work together to produce benefits".[87] With co-production, the commissioning of services—seen as a "core public sector task [to be] undertaken by politicians and top managers"[88]—is generally done by state institutions and lay actors working together. This practice of "co-commissioning", used by digital government service teams in several European countries, is prospective in nature, in that it is oriented towards the future (a near future) and concerned with activities that may take place at a later (but not too far) date.

While this is the starting point for service design for public sector, involving designers at multiple levels—in user consultation, service design labs, customer journey mapping, neighbourhood and community regeneration forums, ethnographic research, participatory research, and so on to redesign, for example, the websites for health care services, public education, and senior citizens creating opportunities for interdependent living— our experimental practices draw more on speculative design and design fiction as disrupting, visionary, imaginative, and provocative methods[89] that can fuel active participation by multiple actors with different interests and have a strong impact on legal change.

The influence of future studies on design is not new; however, interest has been growing especially late in design schools, and it seems to reemerge in times of crisis, when the need to think about alternative futures becomes pressing. Nevertheless, future-oriented research methods and interdisciplinary studies are currently only included in curricula at the initiative of individual lecturers. Interest in future studies in the field of law instead lags behind. Although in some cases the expression "future studies and law" appears to indicate an interest in exploring critical issues in law, emerging technologies, and society, future studies have yet to be in-

Designs: An Introduction to Design for Social Innovation (MIT Press 2015).

87 Tina Nabatchi, Alessandro Sancino and Mariafrancesca Sicilia, 'Varieties of Participation in Public Services: The Who, When, and What of Coproduction' (2017) Public Administration Review 766, 769.

88 Tony Bovaird and Elke Loeffler (eds), *Public Management and Governance* (Routledge 2015) 6.

89 Hallie Jay Pope, 'Liberatory legal design and radical imagination' in Lockton, Lenzi, Hekkert, Oak, Sádaba, and Lloyd (n 71).

corporated into regulatory processes and legal reforms—processes that continue to be non-speculative and non-participatory, failing to engage people and the community in the creation, planning, and organisation of services, which in some sectors are crucial for their well-being (such as environment, education, infrastructure, energy, and others).

The tertiary education system and public institutions have a responsibility to identify ways of engaging design students in the design of public services, in the knowledge that only the active engagement of designers in new interdisciplinary contexts can ensure the development of the public services sector. At the same time, universities have a similar responsibility towards law students, who are called upon to abandon their traditional isolation, uniqueness, and specialness, and participate in non-lawyer-dominated but rather interdisciplinary design activities. Collaboration as a mode of dialogue between jurists and designers and, indeed, as a wider template for social and political life, is the way forward:[90] legal change is embedded in the collaborative framework.

7. Storytelling and Design Fiction as Tools for Legal Change

The speculative design approach does not begin with product design but "with laws, ethics, political systems, social beliefs, values, fears, and hopes, and how these can be translated into material expressions".[91] That enables designers co-designing with legal experts and end-users, i.e., the people to whom the legal regulations are addressed, to anticipate and imagine the future and concretely represent, through various artifacts, the implications of legal choices made in the present.[92]

Design fiction is the practice of creating artifacts that are not intended to meet market needs, but rather to stimulate public debate and reflection through the construction of a narrative context. These artifacts are effectively "thinking objects"—sometimes provocative in nature, so

90 Annelise Riles, 'From Comparison to Collaboration: Experiments with a New Scholarly and Political Form' (2015) 78 Law and Contemporary Problems 147.

91 Anthony Dunne and Fiona Raby, *Speculative Everything: Design, Fiction, and Social Dreaming* (MIT Press 2013) 70.

92 Gianni Sinni, 'Speculative Design for the Public Sector. Design Fiction as a Tool for Better Understanding Public Services' (2021) *Design Culture(s)*. Cumulus Conference Proceedings Rome 2021.

called provotypes—that encourage critical discourse about changing the status quo.[93] Narrative, on the other hand, is an effective tool for overcoming resistance to legal change by using empathetic language rather than solely informative language. As all research on human cognitive biases has widely shown,[94] an abundance of information can lead to greater resistance, rather than to a better understanding of the context.[95] This is the so-called "backfire effect," an expression coined to denote the apparent impossibility of rationally correcting deeply ingrained beliefs.[96] By raising public awareness of specific themes, narrative media, such as cinema and literature, have demonstrated their ability to exert a direct influence on the orientation of government policy in the United States, for example, in the reorganisation of the psychiatric system, in building consensus on massive investments in space exploration, in the overhaul and modification of the administrative-bureaucratic apparatus, and in the reorganisation of the health care system.[97]

Starting in the designer's educational career, design fiction can combine law and politics, foresight and civic participation, within a conscious and ethical narrative framework.[98] This is not a mere exercise in futur-

---

93 Bruce M Tharp and Stephanie M Tharp, *Discursive Design: Critical, Speculative, and Alternative Things* (MIT Press 2019).

94 Daniel Kahneman, Olivier Sibony and Cass R Sunstein, *Noise: A Flaw in Human Judgment* (Hachette Book Group 2021); Daniel Kahneman, *Thinking, Fast and Slow: Daniel Kahneman* (Penguin Books 2011).

95 Alberto Cairo, *The Truthful Art: Data, Charts, and Maps for Communication* (New Riders Pub 2016) 84-85.

96 Brenda Nyhan and Jason Reifler, 'When Corrections Fail: The Persistence of Political Misperceptions' (2010) 32 Political Behavior 303.

97 Howard McCurdy, 'Fiction and Imagination: How They Affect Public Administration' (1995) 55 Public Administration Review 499; Christian Sauvé, 'The Public Service in Science Fiction. Institutionalized Evil, Perfect Incompetence or Invisible Efficiency', presented at Science-Fiction and Long-Term Projections for the Public Service. Public Service Commission of Canada (1998, June) <https://www.christian-sauve.com/essays/the-public-service-in-science-fiction/>; Lyn Holley and Rebecca Lutte, 'Public Administration at the Movies' (2017) 4-10 available at <https://www.researchgate.net/publication/313034742_Public_Administration_at_the_Movies> accessed 12 January 2023.

98 In support of ethical design see Emily Allbon and Amanda Perry-Kessaris (eds), *Design in Legal Education* (Routledge 2022) [a summary is available at <https://designinlegaleducation.net/book-home.html>] accessed 12 January 2023.

ology. Rather, speculative design in general can help address the shortcomings of our current understanding of how legal change takes place and broaden our understanding of key aspects of the law.[99]

One of the crucial aspects that design fiction can help clarify in the contemporary debate is the relationship between law and power, delving into the question of whether the law is a product of power, as Norberto Bobbio held.[100] This assertion raises questions of justice, as power—being a flexible concept, understood as the authority to act for personal or collective purposes, either through orders or through freedom—offers only to those who hold it "a large space for the self".[101] Conversely, the space for social participation is very limited. Whenever we lack the right to participate on an equal footing, justice is called into question. Including the needs of the individuals and collective through speculation on the future in the actual process of designing public services and in the regulations that govern them is a step towards an effective right to participate. Furthermore, speculative design helps to develop tools that are applicable to public policies and regulations, placing the necessary emphasis on ethical concerns, as it has a counterfactual dimension and provokes us to imagine a different reality from the one we are immersed in, exploring it with awareness using scientific, technological, political, and social knowledge to represent desirable futures.

As argued in the previous Sections, our reflections offer a particularly stimulating opportunity to critically engage in a discourse—in the spirit of speculative design and storytelling—on legal change from a perspective of sustainability and equity.

The complexity of the implications of such speculation can be addressed by drawing on interdisciplinary skills.

---

99 Arianna Rossi, Regis Chatellier, Stefano Leucci, Rossana Ducato, Estelle Hary, 'What If Data Protection Embraced Foresight and Speculative Design?' in Lockton, Lenzi, Hekkert, Oak, Sádaba, and Lloyd (n 71).

100 Norberto Bobbio, *Diritto e Potere: Saggi su Kelsen* (Giappichelli 2014). On the need to develop counterstorytelling to contrast the actual experience of power see Hallie Jay Pope, 'Designing to Dismantle', Chapter 13, in Allbon and Perry-Kessaris (n 98).

101 Byung-Chul Han, *Was ist Macht*? (Reclam Philipp Jun 2005) at 15.

Legal design is one such example,[102] with the potential it has to change and improve the status quo in the legal domain by using critical discursive and fictional tools and exploring alternative regulatory approaches.

Policy design is another example, as the dynamics of legal change make it clear that the law is closely linked to politics. Hence, with the general term policy design, we describe the action of defining the goals of policies and the interdisciplinary design tools necessary to achieve them.[103]

Often the definition of a public policy constitutes a "wicked problem",[104] one of those problems whose cause can derive from bureaucratic, normative, technological, organisational constraints, or from political conditions or a combination of all of these. In such cases, the solution to a single problem, isolated from an overall vision, fatally risks exacerbating the criticalities, rather than contributing to their resolution.

The characteristics of a systemic design, which places relationships and their sustainability at the centre, can therefore be particularly useful in policy and legal design. The goals can be of various types: to modify the policy-making practices, to allow the necessary institutional change,

---

102 Here we do not enter the discussion of whether legal design is or should be seen as a distinct discipline within design and/or law, or a post-disciplinary movement, or a nomadic practice, or a broad array of practices and studies: for a summary Ducato and Strowel (n 71), Allbon and Perry-Kessaris (n 98), Jackson and others (n 71), Santuber and Krawietz (n 32). See also Phoebe Walton, 'James v Birnmann: The potential of critical design for examining legal issues' in Lockton, Lenzi, Hekkert, Oak, Sádaba, and Lloyd (n 71); Marcelo Corrales Compagnucci, Helena Haapio, Margaret Hagan and Michael Doherty (eds), *Legal Design: Integrating Business, Design and Legal Thinking with Technology* (Edward Elgar 2021); Amanda Perry-Kessaris, 'Legal Design for Practice, Activism, Policy and Research' (2019) 46 Journal of Law and Society 185.

103 Michael Howlett and Ishani Mukherjee (eds), *Routledge Handbook of Policy Design* (Routledge 2018).

104 According to the definition by Horts Rittel, a mathematician, designer, and former teacher at the Hochschule fur Gestaltung (HfG) Ulm: "wicked problems are a class of social system problems which are ill-formulated, where the information is confusing, where there are many clients and decision makers with conflicting values, and where the ramifications in the whole system are thoroughly confusing". This approach suggests that there is a fundamental indeterminacy (in the sense that there are no definitive conditions or limits to design problem) in all but the most trivial design problems. See Richard Buchanan, 'Wicked Problems in Design Thinking' (1992) 8 Design Issues 5, 15-16.

or to build the capacity to co-design and implement systemic strategies that can lead to potentially transformative policies and actions; and the methods can be of diverse inspiration too: for example, the Polak Game, where persons are asked to indicate their position with respect to the experience of change (things are getting better/worse) and their own contribution to change (I can do little/I can do a lot),[105] the Futures Wheel, a visual representation in which future repercussions are hypothesised in various categories of thought—social, economic, philosophical, religious, health, legal, ethical, and environmental,[106] the Futures Cone, with the representation of the alternatives of probable, plausible or possible futures among which to identify, by untangling the contingencies represented by the wild cards, the preferable future,[107] and the reverse archaeology of the game The Thing from the Future, where participants create a story from a set of random premises—temporal location, trend, reference context, object type, and state of mind.[108]

Instead of limiting ourselves to thinking about concrete answers and solutions in terms of legal change or transformative policies, what is even more interesting is that speculative design emphasises the implications rather than the applications; this means that it entrusts designers—and their expertise drawing from different disciplines—with the task of asking the right questions and no longer providing only answers as problem-solvers. From this perspective, speculative design can make a significant contribution to the formation of aware, informed, and empowered "citizens" (above Section 3) capable of rising to the challenges of our present (design as world making).[109]

---

105 Peter Hayward and Stuart Candy, 'The Polak Game' in Richard Slaughter and Andy Hines (eds), *The Knowledge Base of Futures Studies* (Association of Professional Futurists, 2020) 326-340.

106 Jerome C Glenn 'The Futures Wheel' in Jerome C Glenn and Theodore J Gordon (eds), *Futures Research Methodology* (Version 3.0 [CD-ROM] (2009).

107 Joseph Voros, 'A Primer on Futures Studies, Foresight and the Use of Scenarios' (2001) *Prospect. The Foresight Bulletin* 6 available at <https://thinkingfutures.net/foresight-primer> accessed 12 January 2023.

108 Stuart Candy and Jeff Watson, *The Thing from the Future* (Situation Lab 1st ed., 2014, Print-and-Play ed., 2015, 2nd ed., 2018). Available at <https://situationlab.org/wp-content/uploads/2015/10/FUTURETHING_Print-and-Play.pdf> accessed 12 May 2023.

109 Gianni Sinni, 'Designing Implications. Design Fiction as a Tool for Social Change'

The use of narrative fiction does not compromise the concreteness of co-designing legal change. This is evident if one considers the extent to which imaginary scenarios are fundamental for the construction of the social system. Narrative is indeed at the core of our ability to organise extended and remote collaborative networks. The search for alternative and ethically sustainable futures cannot, therefore, avoid questioning the dominant narrative. Design fiction thus has the unique potential to tackle the structural problems of our society, creating narratives of possible futures that help us question the reasons for the present. As said, the goal of design fiction is to focus on a plurality of futures—probable, plausible, and possible[110]—so as to steer reality towards those considered preferable, but in the awareness that the future, like any chaotic system, contains all those forms of discontinuity and variability ("wild-cards") that, far from the classical deterministic view, make it unpredictable and not predetermined. Design fiction is also a tool for innovating social practices because it presupposes broad participation in those practices. Ultimately, this relationship between law, politics, and design is the essence of the "design hope" invoked by Tomás Maldonado: "Politically speaking, the revolutionary sense of dissent is really only attainable through design. Dissent that rejects hope in design is nothing but a subtle form of consent."[111]

8. Working with Futures: Some Examples

At a series of design communication workshops organised as of 2016 for masters' students at the University of the Republic of San Marino and at the University Iuav of Venice,[112] we experimented with the potential of storytelling and design fiction to bring students to reflect on the implications of public service design and legal change—topics generally not present in traditional design (nor in legal) curricula. The experience led to the development of design communication workshops at the Univer-

---

in Alessandra Bosco and Silvia Gasparotto (eds), *Updating Values. Perspectives on Design Education* (Quodlibet 2020); Sinni (n 92); Pasa and Sinni (n 77).

110 Voros (n 107).

111 Tomás Maldonado, *La Speranza Progettuale* (Einaudi 1970) at 60.

112 Laura Badalucco and Luca Casarotto (eds), *Design e formazione. Continuità e mutamenti nella didattica per il design* (Il Poligrafo 2018) 80-89.

sity Iuav of Venice in collaboration with different institutions and, for the last two years, with the Italian Government Department for Digital Transformation.[113] In the workshops, students were encouraged to map the ecosystems, archetypes, and touchpoints of the main public administration services such as land management, mobility, health, education, and culture, with the aim of tackling complex projects on the future of the public services sector, playing with heterogeneous and hybrid visual languages. [114]

The results of the projects, some of which are illustrated below through the synopses developed by the students themselves, can help highlight the dual function inherent to this learning approach: on the one hand, building a common ground between future designers and public decision-makers; and, on the other hand, transporting the project into a critical and sometimes antagonistic dimension. Speculative design frees the mind from the constraints of dominant thinking and allows us to question even those socio-economic assumptions that, like cognitive biases, prevent us from fully grasping the real opportunities for change. Here, in the speculative narrative's immersive space, it seems entirely reasonable to propose radical legal change, such as, to cite just some of the projects developed in the workshops: the end of the consumer system and private property through a widespread goods sharing service; demanding the disposal of one's biometric data upon reaching legal age; using a highly connected IoT network to do away with the prison system through social control (utopia or dystopia? The choice is yours); or even the design of a direct democracy system for guiding human communities living in the hostile Martian environment.

---

113 Gianni Sinni, 'Un atlante per la collaborazione tra design e PA' in Luca Casarotto, Raffaella Fagnoni and Gianni Sinni (eds), *Dialoghi oltre il visibile. Il design dei servizi per il territorio e i cittadini* (Ediz illustrata Ronzani 2021).

114 The visual restitution of the investigations makes up the pages of an atlas for collaboration between design and public administration. The Projects are also available at <https://sites.google.com/iuav.it/design/design-open-lab/202122-primo-semestre/212-i-lm-design-comunicazione-1?authuser=0> accessed 12 May 2023.

8.1. Delete-me

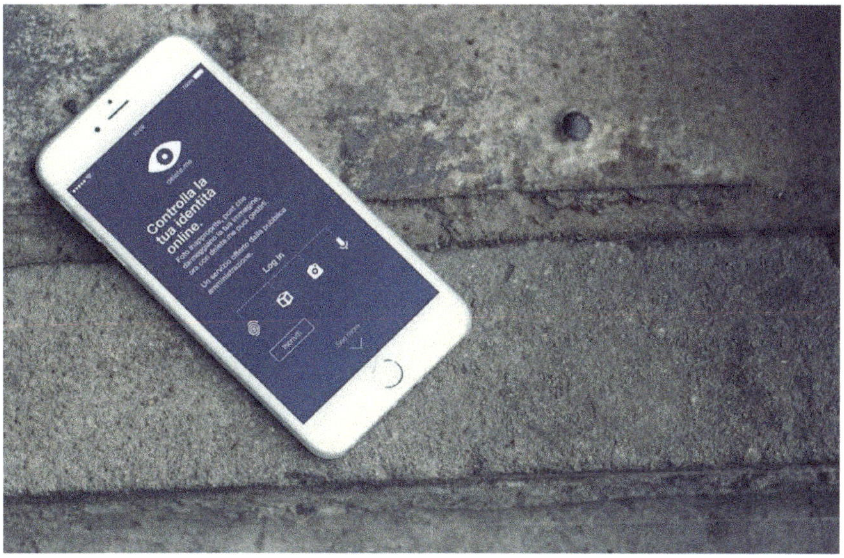

Fig. 1. Delete-me. © Luca Barbieri, Elena Cavallin and Irene Trotta. Hybrid design workshop, led by Gianni Sinni with Tommaso Bovo. Master's degree program in design, University of the Republic of San Marino, 2016/2017. Licensed under CC-BY-SA 4.0

Synopsis: By 2030, web platforms will all be connected to each other, becoming the place where people constantly share information and personal data. The increasingly detailed info-trail they leave of themselves online, however, will also be increasingly difficult to erase. Simply deleting one's profile will not be enough, as the information entered over time remains recorded and available to everyone. As such, the government will provide a service that helps citizens understand the weight of their shared information, offering the possibility to reset the data as they feel is appropriate. That solution will be *delete.me*, an application that communicates with social networks. People will be able to manage their online image by deciding which content to obscure and, if necessary, restore later, or delete permanently. In addition, they will have the possibility, through 3D scanning, facial recognition, and voice and text recognition to track down content, uploaded by others, that depicts them. Such content will automatically come under a person's control when they reach the age of eighteen, as they contain their image and data. Finally, the app will provide a documentation section that explains the steps to take to eliminate one's online presence.

8.2. OP!

Fig. 2. OP!. © Giorgia Perich, Violeta Tufonic and Simone Zorzetto. Communication design lab 3, led by Gianni Sinni with Irene Sgarro. Bachelor's degree program in design, University Iuav of Venice, 2020/2021. Licensed under CC-BY-SA 4.0

Synopsis: Year 2040. After decades of crisis, the country is finally recovering. The digitisation of services and public administration, initiated at the beginning of the 21st century, will now be a reality. *OP!* is an institutional monitoring and public participatory planning application. By accessing the service with their digital identity, people will be able to monitor public activities and view active projects in their residential area, as well as national projects of interest. They will be able to actively contribute to projects with appraisals, advice, and criticism. They will also be able to propose original projects and see them implemented with community support. This service will involve citizens in collective interest projects and optimise public spending.

8.3. Independent Theater

Fig. 3. Independent Theater. © Anna Bigaran, Rosa Corazza, Febe Corba and Martina Valente. Communication design workshop 3, led by Gianni Sinni with Irene Sgarro. Bachelor's degree program in design, University Iuav of Venice, 2020/2021. Licensed under CC-BY-SA 4.0

Synopsis: In 2050, the world is in crisis. The environment, the economy, and the demographic crisis are pressing problems. Complexity, unpredictability, risk, and technologies have taken over, creating a digitalised society at the expense of analog-human society. The situation has corroded society to the point of its disintegration. As a result, individuals have adopted more and more anti-social and introverted behaviour, neglecting the need to establish human relationships. In response to the need to focus on human beings and protect the environment in which they live, a participatory system will be developed, which allows people to express their thoughts within an *Independent Theater*. The idea of a social theatre service is based on the ideal of classical Greek theatre, which socialised citizens, and is therefore educational in its purpose, while seeking to gather people's opinions to pursue concrete actions based on shared ideas. The social theatre service will be based on three values considered fundamental: concertation, as there can be no dialogue without others; inclusiveness, as respect and personal opinions all deserve equal importance; and physical experience, as it is important to meet in person to fully understand what one does.

8.4. Smart jail

Fig. 4. Smart Jail. © Matteo Boem, Miriam David, Giovanni Maraga and Erica Penazzo. Communication design lab 3, led by Gianni Sinni with Irene Sgarro. Bachelor's degree program in design, University Iuav of Venice, 2020/2021. Licensed under CC-BY-SA 4.0

Synopsis: In 2050, the world is made up of smart cities, real jungles of IoT systems where there is a constant exchange of information. In this ultra-technological environment, *Smart Jail* will be a new type of prison, developed using IoT systems to monitor all the movements of people who have committed crimes. In 2050, the term "inmate" will no longer be used, because *Smart Jail* will be designed to do away with prisons as physical places and the concept of detention, for which people tracked through *Smart Jail* will simply be known as "offenders". The idea is to replace prisons with a correctional environment that becomes a rehabilitation experience. Alongside the use of IoT systems, offenders will be monitored through a localising wristband, equipped with hologram technology enabling them to interact and self-organise their daily tasks within a programme designed to stimulate socialisation and reeducation, aimed at their reintegration into society.

8.5. Oright

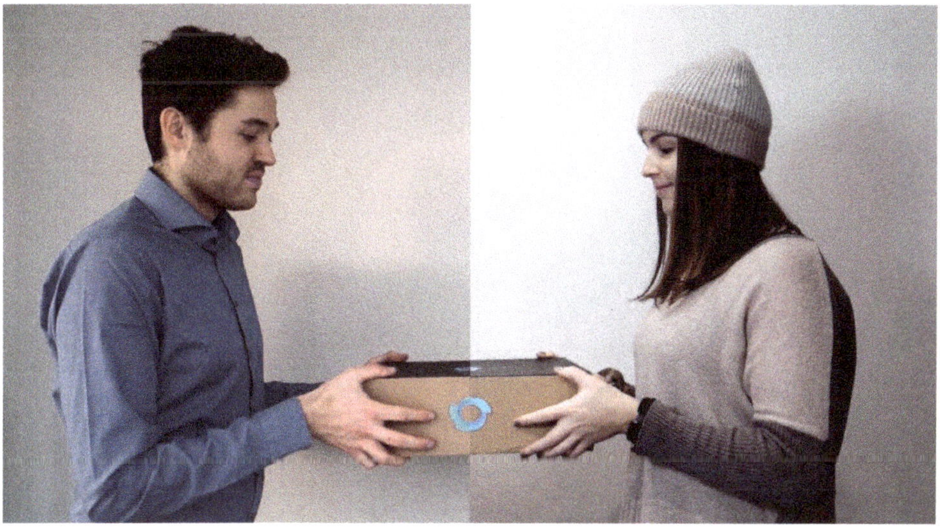

Fig. 5. Oright. © Lisa Bachmann, Sarah Maglio, Valentina Phung and Elettra Pignatti. Communication design lab 3, led by Gianni Sinni with Irene Sgarro. Bachelor's degree program in design, University Iuav of Venice, 2020/2021. Licensed under CC-BY-SA 4.0

Synopsis: Year 2060. Climate troubles and the scarcity of raw materials have led to a new awareness, enabling the sharing economy to take hold much more than in the past, to the point that private property no longer matters. Due to the unsustainability of the capitalist consumption model, people in 2060 will seek durable, high-quality products and services for all their needs and lifestyle choices like never before. Artificial intelligence will help people to be more aware of what is unnecessary, to know their needs and manage their lives more wisely. Since people will no longer have to perform and devote time to certain tasks, the time saved can be spent on leisure or educational activities, as well as on personal interests and hobbies. *Oright* will therefore operate in a post-capitalist scenario, where the quality and circularity of products and services prevails. Sharing high-quality products and services at affordable prices will help break down the social barriers raised by ownership, in favour of a different logic of collective utility. *Oright* will be designed for sharing any material or digital good and service. Not having to own what one needs can only be advantageous: guaranteed assistance and maintenance, savings on objects of little use, technological updates without supplements, and flexible loans, etc.

8.6. Harmonia

Fig. 6. Harmonia. © Robert Cosmin Oanca, Anna Laura Pascon, Emiliano Rainis and Caterina Sartorello. Communication design lab 3, led by Gianni Sinni with Irene Sgarro. Bachelor's degree program in design, University Iuav of Venice, 2020/2021. Licensed under CC-BY-SA 4.0

Synopsis: Year 2100, planet Mars. *Harmonia* is a human settlement of one million inhabitants on Martian territory. The planet is not yet terraformed, but daily life is possible thanks to a system of pressurised buildings and the local, self-sufficient production of resources. The governance of *Harmonia* is ethical, welcoming, and human-scale. Its inhabitants come from various countries on Earth, but on Mars they all become citizens of *Harmonia* (and use only English as the common language). Their motivations for joining the settlement vary—for scientific research, humanitarian reasons, artistic inspiration, or simply adventure, but as volunteers they are selected for their ability to contribute to the sustainability and development of human society on Mars. *Harmonia* is a direct democracy, in which all propose and vote on decisions collectively. *Harmonia* is also a welfare state, in which everyone is a public employee, essential goods are guaranteed for free and luxury goods can be enjoyed through credits earned by performing activities useful to the community. Public services in *Harmonia* are provided through a digital platform that people can access via the numerous public terminals available and via the personal devices they are each assigned. All political, economic, and administrative life is managed through the *Harmonia* portal.

9. Conclusions

The future scenarios depicted by our students in their "objects of the future" and provotypes projects can serve as inspiration for policy-makers and legal change. The common themes addressed include socialisation, engagement, co-participation, training, education, and direct democracy. This shows that legal change can be supported by design fiction and speculative design, starting with the reform of public services co-designed with people, as individuals and as a collective, to enhance confidence and cooperation, and potentially reduce public spending. Incorporating the experiences, practices, and speculative imagination of individuals and communities into the design, planning, and implementation of public services through an outside-in approach allows the agents of legal change to better understand how public services can be designed to be of greatest use and benefit for individuals and communities.

Our complex ecosystem—populated by states and markets, but also individuals who perform social acts and by collective actions that are conceived and actuated through verbal and nonverbal behaviours—is constitutive of the ethical dimension of the law. The projects we have presented, based on speculative design, storytelling, and design fiction, focus on the ethical dimension of the law and regulatory processes.

As said, many pressing issues of justice in the contemporary world intertwine with legal change and its complex institutional and legal dimensions, which include multiple perspectives that often emerge through comparative law. The public space of the future and the common interests of citizens and society need to be filled with inclusive and accessible services that aim to reduce social barriers through a logic of collective utility and well-being. We believe in the power of mistakes, provocation, speculation, and fiction in designing alternative legal changes, relying on inclusive, participatory forms of law-making and policy-making from the bottom up, driven by a collective civic agency that steers transformation. To further this goal, a pedagogical turn is necessary, which involves building different educational tools for legal scholars and designers, including teaching legal basics in design schools and incorporating provotypes, design fiction and co-design processes into legal training. This pedagogical shift requires a radical change in the legal process as well, incorporating co-design and speculative practices into the creation of legal rules, and ultimately leading to a quest for justice.

Bibliography

Ajani G, 'Trapianto di norme informato e globalizzazione alcune considerazioni' in Gianmaria Ajani and others (eds), *Studi in onore di Aldo Frignani. Nuovi orizzonti del diritto comparato europeo e transnazionale* (Jovene 2011)

—, 'Legal Change and Institutional Reforms' in Torstein Frantzen, Helge Johan Thue, Giuditta Cordero Moss, Johan Giertsen (eds), *Rett og toleranse. Festkrift til Helge Johan* Thue: 70 år (Glydendal Norsk Forlag 2007)

—, 'By Chance and Prestige: Legal Transplants in Russia and Eastern Europe' (1995) 43 The American Journal of Comparative Law 93

Allbon E, 'Beyond text: exploiting the visual in law' (2018) 26 Australian Law Librarian 54

— and Perry-Kessaris A, *Design in legal education* (Routledge 2022)

Anceschi G, *Prima Biennale della grafica: propaganda e cultura* (Mondadori Milano 1984)

Aronczyk M and C Calhoun, 'Nationalism' in Richard A Couto (ed*), Political and Civil Leadership, A Reference Handbook* (Sage 2010)

Axelsson S and Dahlberg S, 'Measuring Happiness and Life Satisfaction Amongst Swedish Citizens. An inquiry into semantic equivalence in comparative survey research' (2018) *Working Paper Series* 2, University of Bergen

Badalucco L and Casarotto L (eds), *Design e formazione. Continuità e mutamenti nella didattica per il desig*n (Il Poligrafo 2018)

Bakardjieva Engelbrekt A and Nergelius J (eds), *New Directions in Comparative Law* (Edward Elgar 2010)

Barfield W and Pagallo U (eds), *Research Handbook on the Law of Artificial Intelligence* (Edward Elgar 2018)

Berger J and others, 'The Legitimation and Delegitimation of Power and Prestige Orders' (1998) 63 American Sociological Review 379

Block-Lieb S and Halliday T, *Global Lawmakers: International Organizations in the Crafting of World Markets* (CUP 2017)

Bobbio N, *Diritto e Potere: Saggi su Kelsen* (Giappichelli 2014)

Boehme-Neßler V, *Pictorial Law. Modern law and the power of pictures* (Springer 2011)

Bovaird T and E Loeffler (eds), *Public Management and Governance* (Routledge 2015)

Bradford A, *The Brussels Effect: How the European Union rules the World* (OUP 2020)

Brownsword R, *Rethinking Law, Regulation, and Technology* (Edward Elgar 2022)

Buchanan R, 'Wicked Problems in Design Thinking' (1992) 8 *Design Issues* 5

Byung-Chul Han, *Undinge: Umbruche der Lebenswelt* (Ullstein Verlag 2022)

—, *Was ist Macht*? (Reclam Philipp Jun 2005)

Cairo A, *The Truthful Art: Data, Charts, and Maps for Communication* (New Riders Pub 2016)

Candy S and Watson F, *The Thing from the Future* (Situation Lab 1st ed, 2014, Print-and-Play ed, 2015, 2nd ed, 2018)

Caterina R, 'Comparative Law and the Cognitive Revolution' (2003-2004) 78 Tul L Rev 1501

Colombi Ciacchi A, C Mak, Z. Mansoor (eds), *Immoral Contracts in Europe* (Intersentia 2020)

Compagnucci M C, Haapio H, Hagan M, Doherty M (eds) *Legal Design: Integrating Business, Design and Legal Thinking with Technology* (Edward Elgar 2021)

Cotterrell R, 'Why jurisprudence is not legal philosophy' (2014) Jurisprudence 41

Cremona M and Scott J (eds*) EU law beyond EU borders: the extraterritorial reach of EU Law* (OUP 2019)

Dailey J, 'Race, Marriage and Sovereignty in the New World Order' (2009) 10 Theoretical Inquiries in Law 511

Dal Buono V, Sinni G and Zannoni M, 'Design for Citizenship' (2020) 10 MD Journal

Dordeska M, *General Principles of Law Recognized by Civilized Nations (1922–2018)* (Brill Nijhoff 2020)

Downe L, *Good Services: Decoding the Mystery of What Makes a Good Service: How to Design Services that Work* (Bis Publishers 2019)

Ducato R and A Strowel (eds), *Legal Design Perspectives* (Ledizioni 2021)

Dunne A and Raby F, *Speculative Everything: Design, Fiction, and Social Dreaming* (MIT Press 2013)

Escobar A, *Designs for the Pluriverse. Radical Interdependence, Autonomy, and the Making of Worlds* (Duke University Press 2017)

Floridi L, *The Fourth Revolution: How the Infosphere is Reshaping Human Reality* (OUP 2014)

Frascara J, 'Graphic Design: Fine Art or Social Science?' (1988) Design Issues 18

Fuggetta A, *Cittadini ai tempi di Internet. Per una cittadinanza consapevole nell'era digitale* (Franco Angeli 2018)

Gambaro A, 'Misurare il diritto?' (2012) Annuario di diritto comparato e di studi legislativi 17

Gilardi F and F Wasserfallen, 'The Politics of Policy Diffusion' (2019) 58 European Journal of Political Research 1245

Gillespie J, 'Globalisation and legal transplantation: Lessons from the past' (2001) 286 Deakin Law Review 286

Glenn J C, 'Futures Wheel' in Jerome C Glenn and Theodore J Gordon (eds), *Futures Research Methodology* (Version 3.0 [CD-ROM] 2009)

Graziadei M, 'Comparative Law, Transplants, and Receptions' in Mathias Reimann and Reinhard Zimmermann (eds), *The Oxford Handbook of Comparative Law* (1st edn, OUP 2006; 2nd edn, OUP 2019)

—, 'Legal Transplants and the Frontiers of Legal Knowledge' (2009) Theoretical Inquiries in Law 723

—, 'What Does Globalisation Mean for the Comparative Study of Law?' (2021) Journal of Comparative Law 511

— and Pasa B, 'Happiness Once *More'* (2019) Journal of Comparative Law 203

Grice H-P, 'Logic and conversation' in Peter Cole and Jerry Morgan (eds), *Syntax and semantics, vol. 3: Speech acts* (Academic Press 1975)

Hagan MD, *Law by Design* (2016) <https://lawbydesign.co/> accessed 12 January 2023

Harrington B, Seabrooke L, 'Transnational Professionals' (2020) 46 Annual Review of Sociology 399

Hauben M and R, *Netizens – On the History and Impact of Usenet and the Internet* (IEEE Operations Center 1997)

Hayward P and Candy S, 'The Polak Game' in Richard Slaughter and Andy Hines (eds), *The Knowledge Base of Futures Studies* (Association of Professional Futurists 2020)

Hofmann T, 'How Long to Compliance? Escalating Infringement Proceedings and the Diminishing Power of Special Interests' (2018) 40 Journal of European Integration 785

Holley L and Lutte R, 'Public Administration at the Movies' (2017) 4 *Public Voices* <https://www.researchgate.net/publication/313034742_Public_Administration_at_the_Movies> accessed 12 January 2023

Howlett M and Mukherjee I (eds), *Routledge Handbook of Policy Design* (Routledge 2018)

Jackson D, Sievert JR, Kim M, and Bhatnagar S, 'What legal design could be: Towards an expanded practice of inquiry, critique, and action' in Dan Lockton, Sara Lenzi, Paul Hekkert, Arlene Oak, Juan Sádaba, Peter Lloyd (eds), *DRS2022: Bilbao* (Design Research Society 2022)

Jessup P, *Transnational Law* (Yale Law University 1956)

Kahneman D, *Thinking, fast and slow* (Penguin Books 2011)

— and Sibony O, Sunstein CR, *Noise: A Flaw in Human Judgment* (Hachette Book Group USA 2021)

Kennedy D, *A critique of adjudication: fin de* siècle (Harvard University Press 1997)

Krieger L, *The Hidden Sources of Law School Stress: Avoiding the Mistakes that Create Unhappy and Unprofessional Lawyers* (Kindle 2014)

Krisch L and B Kingsbury, 'Introduction: Global Governance and Global Administrative Law in the International Legal Order' (2006) 17 European Journal of International Law 1

LeDA, *What is Legal Design?* (2018) <https://www.legaldesignalliance.org/> accessed 12 January 2023

Lessig L, *Code: and other laws of cyberspace*, Version 2.0 online (Basic Books 2006)

Li-Wen Lin, 'Legal Transplants through Private Contracting: Codes of Vendor Conduct in Global Supply Chains as an Example' (2009) 57 The American Journal of Comparative Law 711

Likosky M (ed), *Transnational Legal Processes Globalisation and Power Disparities* (Butterworths 2002)

Lussu G, *La grafica è scrittura, una lezione*, A.A.M Architettura Arte Moderna e Istituto Europeo di Design di Roma (Stampa Graffiti Roma 1996)

Maldonado T, *La Speranza Progettuale* (Einaudi 1970)

Manzini E, *Design, When Everybody Designs: An Introduction to Design for Social Innovation* (MIT Press 2015)

Mattei U, 'A Theory of Imperial Law: A Study on U.S. Hegemony and the Latin Resistance' (2003) Indiana Journal of Global Legal Studies 383

McCurdy H E, 'Fiction and Imagination: How They Affect Public Administration' (1995) 55 Public Administration Review 499

McLuhan M, *Understanding Media: The Extensions of Man* (McGraw-Hill 1964)

Mergel I, 'Digital Service Teams in Government: An International Comparison of New IT Governance Structures' <https://www.economie.gouv.fr/igpde-editions-publications/comparative-analysis_n6> accessed 12 January 2023

Nabatchi T, A Sancino, M Sicilia, 'Varieties of Participation in Public Services: The Who, When, and What of Coproduction' (2017) Public Administration Review 766

Nyhan B and Reifler J, 'When Corrections Fail: The Persistence of Political Misperceptions' (2010) 32 Polit Behav 303

Norris S and Jones R H (eds), *Discourse in Action: Introducing Mediated Discourse Analysis* (Routledge 2005)

Pagallo U, *Il diritto nell'età dell'informazione* (Giappichelli 2014)

Pasa B and Sinni G, 'Democracy in Outer Space. Speculative Design for Future Citizenship' forthcoming

Pasa B and Morra L, 'Implicit legal norms' in Jacqueline Visconti (eds) *Handbook of Communication in the Legal Sphere* (De Gruyter Mouton 2018)

Passera S, 'Beyond the wall of contract text - Visualizing contracts to foster understanding and collaboration within and across organizations' (Aalto University publication series Doctoral Dissertations 134/2017)

Perry-Kessaris A, 'Legal design could and should be more sociolegal' in Lockton D, Lenzi S, Hekkert P, Oak A, Sádaba J, Lloyd P (eds), *DRS2022*: *Bilbao* (Design Research Society 2022)

—, 'Making sociolegal research more social by design: Anglo-German roots, rewards and risks' (2020) 21 German Law Journal 1427

—, 'Legal Design for Practice, Activism, Policy and Research' (2019) 46 Journal of Law and Society 185

Pope HJ, 'Liberatory legal design and radical imagination' in Lockton D, Lenzi S, Hekkert P, Oak A, Sádaba J, Lloyd P (eds), *DRS2022*: *Bilbao* (Design Research Society 2022)

Reimann M, 'Beyond National Systems: A Comparative Law for the International Age' (2001) 75 Tulane Law Review 1103

Riles A, 'From Comparison to Collaboration: Experiments with a New Scholarly and Political Form' (2015) 78 Law and Contemporary Problems 147

Roberts B, *The Making of Citizens. Cities of Peasants Revisited* (Routledge 1995)

Rodotà S, 'Antropologia dell'homo dignus' (2010) Storia e memoria 107

Roger CB, *The Origins of Informality: Why the Legal Foundations of Global Governance Are Shifting, and Why It Matters* (OUP 2020)

Rossi A, Chatellier R, Leucci S, Ducato R, and Hary E, 'What if data protection embraced foresight and speculative design?' in Lockton D, Lenzi S, Hekkert P, Oak A, Sádaba J, Lloyd P (eds), *DRS2022*: *Bilbao* (Design Research Society 2022)

Ryle G, *The Concept of Mind* (Barnes & Noble 1949)

Sacco R, *Il diritto muto. Neuroscienze, conoscenza tacita, valori condivisi* (Il Mulino 2015)

—, *Antropologia giuridica. Contributo ad una macrostoria del diritto* (Il Mulino 2007)

—, 'Mute Law' (1995) 43 The American Journal of Comparative Law 455

—, *Introduzione al diritto comparato* (Giappichelli 1980)

Salomon L, *The Tools of Government: A Guide to the New Governance* (OUP 2022)

Santuber J and Krawietz L, 'The Sociomateriality of Justice: A Relational Ontology for Legal Design' (2021) Revista Chilena de Diseño 1

Sauvé C, 'The Public Service in Science Fiction. Institutionalized Evil, Perfect Incompetence or Invisible Efficiency' (Science-Fiction and Long Term Projections for the Public Service. Public Service Commission of Canada, 26 June 1998) <https://www.christian-sauve.com/essays/the-public-service-in-science-fiction/> accessed 12 January 2023

Sbisa M, *Detto non detto. Le forme della comunicazione implicita* (Laterza 2007)

—, 'Normativita e comunicazione' in Lucia Morra and Barbara Pasa (eds), *Questioni di genere nei testi normativi: crittotipi e impliciti* (Giappichelli 2015)

Shachar Y, 'Jefferson Goes East: The American Origins of the Israeli Declaration of Independence' (2009) 10 Theoretical Inquiries in Law 589

Shulman S, 'Challenging the Civic/Ethnic and West/East Dichotomies in the Study of Nationalism' (2002) 35 Comparative Political Studies 554

Siems M, *Comparative Law* (3rd edn, CUP 2022)

Sinni G, 'Designing Implications. Design Fiction as a Tool for Social Change' in Bosco A and Gasparotto S (eds), *Updating Values. Perspectives on Design Education* (Quodlibet 2020)

—, 'Speculative Design for the Public Sector. Design Fiction as a Tool for Better Understanding Public Services' in *Design Culture(s).* Cumulus Conference Proceedings Roma 2021 (Cumulus 2021)

—, 'Un atlante per la collaborazione tra design e PA' in Luca Casarotto, Raffaella Fagnoni and Gianni Sinni (eds), *Dialoghi oltre il visibile. Il design dei servizi per il territorio e i cittadini* (Ediz illustrata Ronzani 2021)

Slaughter A-M, 'On Thinking Like a Lawyer' (2002) Harv L Today <https://www.princeton.edu/~slaughtr/Commentary/On%20Thinking%20Like%20a%20Lawyer.pdf> accessed 12 January 2023

Snyder F, 'Economic Globalization and the Law in 21st Century' in Austin Sarat (ed), *The Blackwell Companion to Law and Society* (Blackwell Publishers 2004)

Sperber D, *Explaining Culture: A Naturalistic Approach* (Blackwell 1996)

— and D Wilson, *Relevance*: *Communication and Cognition* (Blackwell 1986; 2nd ed 1995)

Stone D, 'Between Policy Failure and Policy Success: Bricolage, Experimentalism, and Translation in Policy Transfer' in Claire Dunlop (ed), *Policy Learning and Policy Failure* (Policy Press 2020)

Swinkels M, 'How ideas matter in public policy: a review of concepts, mechanisms, and methods' (2020) International Review of Public Policy 281

Thaler RH and Sunstein CR, *Nudge: Improving Decisions About Health, Wealth, and Happiness* (Yale University Press 2008)

Tharp BM and Tharp SM, *Discursive Design: Critical, Speculative, and Alternative Things* (MIT Press 2019)

Tomlins CL, 'Transplants and Timing: Passages in the Creation of an Anglo-American Law of Slavery' (2009) 10 Theoretical Inquiries in Law 389

Twining W, *Law in context: enlarging a discipline* (OUP 1997)

—, 'Social science and diffusion of law' (2005) 32 Journal of Law and Society 203

van Dijk TA (ed), *Discourse as Social Interaction. Discourse Studies: A Multidisciplinary Introduction* (Sage 1997)

Vertovec S, 'Super-Diversity and its Implications' (2007) 30 Ethnic and Racial Studies 1024

Vico M, de Francisco Vela S and Pachón M, 'Cuando el pensamiento en Diseño y el mundo legal se encuentran: Innovación para mejorar la prestación de servicios públicos' (2021) RChD: creación y pensamiento 1

Voorberg W, Bekkers V and Tummers L, 'A Systematic Review of Co-Creation and Co-Production: Embarking on the social innovation journey' (2015) 17 Public Management Review 1333

von Benda-Beckmann F and K, 'Why not Legal Culture' (2010) 5 Journal of Comparative Law 104

Voros J, 'A Primer on Futures Studies, Foresight, and the Use of Scenarios' (2001) *Prospect. The Foresight Bulletin* 6 <https://thinkingfutures.net/foresight-primer> accessed 12 January 2023

Vygotsky L, 'The Instrumental Method in Psychology' in James Wertsch (ed), *The Concept of Activity in Soviet Psychology* (M E Sharpe Inc 1981)

Wagner A and Sherwin R (eds), *Law, Culture and Visual Studies* (Springer 2014)

Walnum H J, All C, and Løkke S, 'Can Rebound Effects Explain Why Sustainable Mobility Has Not Been Achieved?' (2014) 12 Sustainability 9510

Walton P, 'James v Birnmann: The potential of critical design for examining legal issues' in Lockton D, Lenzi S, Hekkert P, Oak A, Sádaba J, Lloyd P (eds), *DRS2022: Bilbao* (Design Research Society 2022)

Watson A, *Legal Transplants: An Approach to Comparative Law* (Charlottesville 1974)

Weimann J, Knabe A, Schoeb R (eds) *Measuring Happiness: The Economics of Well-being* (Gildan Media Corporation 2015)

Wellner G, Aviram A, Rozin Y, Ronchi A, 'Well-Being in the Digital Age' in Alfredo Ronchi (ed) *e-Citizens: Toward a New Model of (Inter) Active Citizenry* (Springer Nature 2019)

Wu T, *The Attention Merchants: The Epic Scramble to Get Inside Our Heads* (Alfred A Knopf 2016)

Yudkowsky E, *Inadequate Equilibria. Where and How Civilizations Get Stuck* (Machine Intelligence Research Institute 2017)

2. AN EXERCISE IN SPECULATIVE LEGAL DESIGN

Emily MacLoud

Abstract
Speculative design addresses concerns about the status quo by supporting critical and creative thinking. As a methodology, it has been relatively under-utilised in the domain of law. This article will explore what speculative design is, why it should be employed in law and considerations to keep in mind when applying it in the legal landscape. Speculative legal design presents a promising way to reflect on the implications of emerging technologies and bring to light the various issues that plague justice systems around the world. By reflecting on several examples including an experience that was facilitated by the author hosting an interactive stall at the book launch of Design in Legal Education edited by Emily Allbon and Amanda Perry-Kessaris, the intention of this article is to provide legal design practitioners with practical and complementary tools that they can apply in their own work. This article contributes to the growing body of literature that explores how design can be used to make the world of law better, pushing the boundaries of the conversation beyond the confines of design thinking.

1. Introduction

Design thinking is a problem-solving method that applies the creative design process to traditional business problems.[1] It has gained significant traction as a way of solving the many problems that exist within the legal field. Yet, another type of design may be better suited at identifying problems that don't yet exist and imagining the radically new socio-economic and political paradigms that are needed for us to realise truly sustainable and equitable futures. Design thinking is not enough. It doesn't enable people to step out of their current paradigm. It maintains the status quo. Speculative design falls within the umbrella concept of critical design, which offers a way to confront and challenge existing power im-

1 Sarah Gibbons, 'Design Thinking 101' (*NNG Nielsen Norman Group*, 31 July 2016) <https://www.nngroup.com/articles/design-thinking/> accessed 9 May 2023.

balances. By speculating on the future, this largely under-utilised design method promises a way for those working in the legal field to explore a wide range of possibilities outside the current realm. When conducted respectfully and thoughtfully it can also allow for a greater diversity of perspectives to be heard.

This paper will begin with an introduction of what speculative design is and present existing examples of how it is already being used within the domain of law (Section 2). It will then describe the preparation, design and delivery of a speculative design experience and explore the elements of the experience that had the most impact on participants (Section 3), It will then conclude with a discussion about considerations to keep in mind if legal designers want to start experimenting with this methodology in their own practice (Section 4). The intention of this paper is that it provides practitioners with the know-how to use this methodology in their own work and inspires even more practitioners to start speculating.

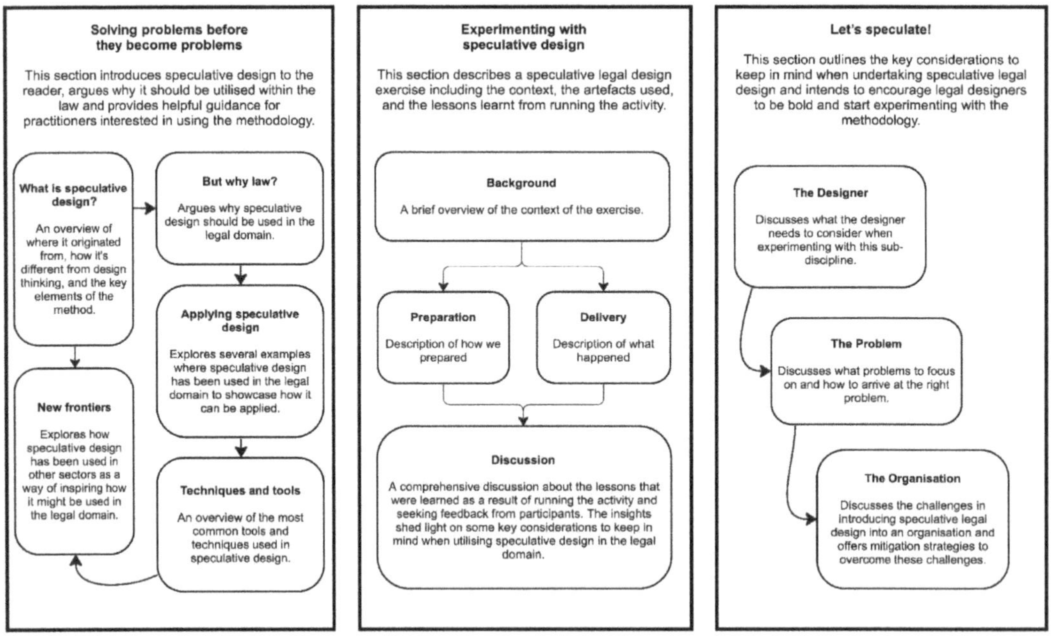

Fig. 1. A visual summary of the article

2. Solving Problems before They Become Problems

2.1. What Is Speculative Design?

The term speculative design was first coined by Anthony Dunne and Fiona Raby, two British design theorists, in 2001. The two popularised the concept in their book, *Speculative Everything: Design, Dreaming, and Social Dreaming.*[2] The term was used to describe their work, which was focused on exploring relationships between humans, technology, and culture. The term has since been adopted by the broader design community and has been used to describe a wide variety of projects and approaches.

Many are familiar with design thinking, where problems are identified at the beginning and after ideating on a series of novel solutions and pathways, an approach is selected and tested.[3] Speculative design differs in a number of ways. Firstly, instead of identifying problems, speculative designers identify hopes and fears, weak signals and insights generated from extrapolating data and projections.[4] Once this intel is collated, prototyping can then commence. The second way speculative design differs from design thinking is in the way it handles artefacts at the prototyping stage.[5] They are designed not to *fix* things, but rather to *unfix* them. The outputs of speculative design are created to make future possibilities tangible and to call into question aspects of the here and now. When these outputs are done well, they have the potential to make the impact of the future possibilities compelling in a way that no amount of data can. Finally, speculative design is concerned with facilitating dialogue and decision-making more so than it is about creating things. By "showing not telling",[6] people are empowered to become active participants

---

2 Anthony Dunne and Fiona Raby, *Speculative Everything: Design, Fiction, and Social Dreaming* (MIT Press 2013) 2.

3 Gibbons (n 1).

4 See Superflux, 'The Future Energy Lab' (*Superflux*, 2017) <https://superflux.in/index.php/work/futureenergylab/#> accessed 18 January 2023.

5 See Nick Foster, 'Designing for the unknown' (*X, the moonshot factory*, 16 June 2021) <https://blog.x.company/designing-for-the-unknown-5156fde8ffb3> accessed 30 January 2023.

6 Interview with Jason Tashea, Georgetown Law (Virtual, 3 February 2023).

in carving out the future they want to see. It is a multi-faceted design method that can complement design thinking. The main elements of the method are set out below.

2.2. Speculative Design Broadens The Scope of Problems that Design Can Solve

Speculative design is part of a wider movement of design known as critical design. More of a mindset than a methodology, through this lens designers seek to critique the status quo. Described as the opposite of affirmative design, which focuses on improving systems that currently exist, critical design challenges "narrow assumptions, preconceptions, and givens."[7] It challenges designers to see their role as provocateurs of paradigms and to think laterally.

Given the wide remit of critical design, those who practise speculative design have the opportunity to solve problems that may not yet be problematic. For instance, for Jason Tashea, producing the speculative podcast series *40 Futures*,[8] provided him an outlet to share what he had heard from academics and scientists during his days as a journalist: "A lot of those interviews... would usually end with them saying, 'So we're talking about the thing that's happening now, but just wait five years when X is going to occur.'"[9] Tashea recounts that this material was also often more interesting than what he was tasked to write about. In this way, speculative design provides the means to focus on problems that are not yet problems, thereby broadening the scope of problems that design can usually solve for.

Crucially though, designers who dabble in speculative design may propose concepts that lie beyond the boundaries of reality or dominant paradigms and venture into the imagination,[10] but they do so with an eye on critiquing aspects about the present state. For example, at first glance the project *James v Birnmann*, produced by speculative designer Phoebe

7 Dunne and Raby (n 2).

8 40 Futures is a speculative fiction series about the criminal justice system. See Jason Tashea, '40 Futures' (*40 Futures,* n.d.) <https://podcasts.apple.com/us/podcast/40-futures/id1607895300> accessed 28 January 2023.

9 Tashea (n 6).

10 Amanda Perry-Kessaris, *Doing sociolegal research in design mode* (Routledge 2021) 80.

Walton, could be mistaken for simply an imaginative version of a future courtroom.[11] However, it is much more than that. It is an intentional, critical examination of the problems within western legal systems that exposes deep-rooted injustices and inequalities by exacerbating the ethical, social and cultural implications of technology gone wrong and social and cultural biases unchallenged. This project makes fears and concerns tangible and broadens the remit of what design can fix beyond existing service experiences.

2.3. Speculative Design Provides a Way to Collectively Imagine

Speculative design not only feeds the imagination of the design professional who takes on the task of creating new worlds, it also feeds the imaginations of those who engage with the designs. Given what we understand about history and the oppressors' fondness for "policing the imagination",[12] this is crucial. Human beings are not very good at thinking long term or outside the box,[13] and often need help to think about the future or about alternate realities. Speculative design enables a collective to gather together and delve into imaginary possibilities, so that they can make the right decisions in the present. It not only makes the future tangible, it also offers the opportunity for more diverse voices to be heard.

Speculative design can also unleash people from their current realities and stimulate their imaginations by offering a bridge between the current reality and future possibilities. Speculative design proposals can be thought of as devices that can "snap [participants] into the future,"[14] and can prove very effective at helping people to collectively travel at speed to imagined future-states. For example, a vignette about a possible future could act as a device that helps participants to discuss the implications of future problems that might not exist yet. This can help

11 Phoebe Walton, 'James v Birnmann: The potential of critical design for examining legal issues' (DRS2022, Bilbao, July 2022).

12 Saidiya Hartman, 'Under the Blacklight: Storytelling While Black and Female: Conjuring Beautiful Experiments' (*African American Policy Forum*, 5 August 2020) <https://youtu.be/xGS5aP5Vi7g> accessed 28 January 2023.

13 Interview with Sarah McArthur, Director, CityLab (Virtual, 18 January 2023).

14 Interview with Sarah Kaur, Principle Business Designer, Portable (Virtual, 7 November 2022).

participants collectively engage in discourse and think deeply together about the ethical, political, social and cultural ramifications of current behaviours, decisions and technologies.

By enabling collective imagination, the designer can foster sustainable and equitable change. As social imagination agency Canopy puts it, "without new and shared imaginations our society will stay stuck in its current destructive and unequal patterns."[15] Finding ways to imagine together is vital so that "the future is not built based on imaginations that are incomplete, one-sided and disconnected".[16] Speculative design creates the conditions for shared imagining, thereby bringing forward the opportunity to align on preferable futures that are inclusive, fair and just.

2.4. Speculative Design Forges New Perspectives through Discussion and Debate

Speculative design is not only focused on producing future visions, it also facilitates dialogue between people. The design artefacts which are produced to catapult people into alternate realities are often just the starting point. Fostering discussion between participants who engage in speculative design is crucial if the experience is to be impactful. As directed by Damien Lutz, the Founder of Future Scouting,[17] which is a database of simple and effective speculative design resources, "whoever your audience is – stakeholders, fellow designers, social media followers, or the general public – make it easy for them to offer their interpretation of your product".[18] This step is essential for it is often in the discussion that ensues after a speculative design experience, where new perspectives can be reached. Lutz encourages designers to provide questions to participants to support them to articulate "why they do or don't like your future concept, how it might affect them personally, and what they

15 Canopy, 'Canopy in a nutshell' (*Canopy,* 2021) <http://www.canopy.si/> accessed 27 January 2023.

16 ibid.

17 Future Scouting, 'The Future Scouting approach' (*Future Scouting*, n.d.) <https://futurescouting.com.au/> accessed 28 January 2023.

18 Damien Lutz, 'Future Thieving #2—Speculative design methods and tools' (*UX Collective*, 4 August 2020) <https://uxdesign.cc/future-thieving-2-speculative-design-methods-tools-45b655096d95> accessed 28 January 2023.

might prefer".[19] In doing so, people who are engaged can reflect on why it matters to them and form their own opinions. Crucially, this paves the way for people to respond to the speculative design experience and empowers them to take concrete steps towards the future they want to see.

2.5. Speculative Design Fosters Alignment towards Preferable Futures

As alluded to above, beyond imagining what futures may be possible and relating it to oneself, speculative design also seeks to discern what futures are *preferable* and encourages stakeholders to commit to action. The Futures Cone first conceptualised by Trevor Hancock and Clement Bezold in 1994,[20] based on the taxonomy proposed by futurist Norman Henchey in 1978,[21] is often utilised to frame how to think about the different types of futures that are possible, plausible, probable and preferable:[22]

- The possible cone includes futures that *may* happen;
- The plausible cone includes futures that *could* happen;
- The probable cone includes futures that are *likely* to happen; and
- The preferable cone includes futures that we *want* to happen.

Most design efforts are orientated around what is probable. Speculative design is most interested in identifying futures that sit within the preferable zone.

This framing can be useful for mapping speculative futures. For example, scenarios, which are described as "compilations of trends into differing images of the future",[23] can be mapped onto the futures cone and provide a clear way to compare a range of options. This mapping provides the opportunity to examine these futures in depth, which can be at once liberating and sobering. In making a choice between different futures, designers also enable values, held both individually and collectively, to be

---

19 ibid.

20 Trevor Hancock and Clement Bezold, 'Possible futures, preferable futures' (1994) 37 The Healthcare Forum Journal 23.

21 Norman Henchey, 'Making Sense of Future Studies' (1978) 7(2) Alternatives 24 <http://www.jstor.org/stable/45030200> accessed 28 January 2023.

22 Hancock and Bezold (n 20).

23 ibid 24.

made visible.[24] Alignment is fostered by realising where various futures are and having discussions about how to get to the preferred future.

2.6. Speculative Design Catalyses Action

Once the speculative designer has identified what they want to critique, provided a way for participants to collectively imagine a new world, forged new perspectives through discussion and debate and aligned participants around the preferred future, the final step is to elicit a "commitment to action".[25] Without this final step, a lack of control may start to set in and along with it, the preferable futures may become just another workshop relic, that's too distant, too fleeting and too hard to attain. Depending on the size of the project, this step could either involve back-casting a future strategy and optimising and adapting it in order to stay on track toward the preferred future, or it could be as simple as creating a website that shows what the future could be and tracking and recording feedback and reactions.[26] As designers, there is a need to create things that have an impact and are useful. This last element gives speculative design its edge.

2.7. But Why Employ Speculative Design in Law?

Using speculative design in the legal domain makes sense for many reasons. Primarily, speculative design can be most useful when it critiques the status quo.[27] As described succinctly by Paul Magrath, Head of Product Development and Online Content at Incorporated Council of Law Reporting for England and Wales, "whether you get the future right or wrong – it doesn't matter – it makes you question the present".[28] Similarly, as Walton highlights in her reflective piece about her student project

24 ibid.
25 ibid 23.
26 Lutz (n 18).
27 Karma Dabaghi, 'Beyond design thinking and into speculative futures in legal design' (DRS2022, Bilbao, July 2022) 2.
28 Interview with Paul Magrath, Head of Product Development and Online Content, ICLR (Virtual, 5 January 2023).

James v Birnmann, it is only by stepping into the impossible, and offering speculations that are far-fetched that it is possible to crystallise concerns with the status quo.[29] To demonstrate this, it is useful to look at one of the concepts she focuses on, which is that "law is a continual performance" and that "courtrooms are the epicentre of this charade".[30] By including seating for an audience in front of the typical courtroom and featuring "ON AIR" signs on top of the doors (see Figure 2), she makes tangible the illusory nature of the law as objective and calls into question the role of rituals and symbols used in the law. This example demonstrates how design artefacts can challenge our preconceptions about the law and reveal areas that need critical attention.

Fig. 2. Screenshots of James v Birnmann*, a design fiction that depicts a never ending legal drama, situated in a future where law is controlled by AI.*[31]
© Phoebe Walton, 2021. Reproduced with permission.

Using speculative design in the legal domain also addresses what Dabaghi describes as "the most potent drawback of design thinking",[32] which is the fact that it is "focused on solving problems that already exist".[33] Speculative design can explore the unintended consequences of introducing new technologies into the courtroom,[34] or the implica-

29 Walton (n 11).

30 Phoebe Walton, 'James v Birnmann' (*James v Birnmann*, n.d.) <https://phoebewalton.com/James-v-Birnmann> accessed 28 January 2023.

31 ibid.

32 Dabaghi (n 27) 3.

33 ibid.

34 Eeda Da Gyung Lee, 'Virtual Justice: Courts of the Future' (*Architectural Association School of Architecture*, 2021) <https://pr2021.aaschool.ac.uk/students/da-

tions of possible future criminal justice processes,[35] before they happen. It acts as a way to forward-plan and start thinking about the possible issues to come.[36] As Daniel Hoadley, Head of Data Science & Analytics at Mishcon de Reya LLP highlights, the biggest challenge facing his team isn't the obvious technical hurdles of introducing data science into legal processes, but rather it's trying to understand both the positive and negative implications of introducing new technologies.[37] He notes that this methodology would be relevant for his team as it could usefully act as another form of data governance. By reimagining what the law *might* be, speculative design can spark critical debate about what the law *should* be.

When done well, speculative design can also be a useful way to elicit an empathetic response and make the law "palpable."[38] *The Touching Contract* is a live performance and an example of an especially emotive design fiction that makes the law relatable (and at times physical), chilling and uncomfortable. It was an immersive evocative performance that explored "law's relationship to violence, suffering and vulnerability" by using the female body as a "repository for legal histories."[39] Indeed, Karma Dabaghi contends that speculative design intends to create a "strange or unsettling atmosphere" that "generates a feeling of menace or fear of what might come as a result of current practices".[40] Speculation isn't just about exercising the brain, crucially it is also about engaging the heart. In so doing, it can capture audiences in new ways and make people *feel* differently about the law.

Using speculative design in the legal domain can also act as another way to get wider audiences interested and engaged. Justice is known to suffer from a publicity problem, often not getting the same recognition or public support as other fields like health and medicine. Even Shake-

---

gyung-lee> accessed 28 January 2023.

35 Tashea (n 6).

36 Dabaghi (n 28) 3.

37 Interview with Daniel Hoadley, Head of Data Science & Analytics, Mishcon de Reya LLP (Virtual, 26 January 2023).

38 Máiréad Enright and Tina Kinsella, 'Legal Aesthetics in The Touching Contract: Memory, Exposure and Transformation' (2021) Law, Culture and the Humanities <https://doi.org/10.1177/1743872120987113> accessed 28 January 2023.

39 ibid 5.

40 Dabaghi (n 27) 4.

speare pokes fun at this: "The first thing we do, let's kill all the lawyers."[41] By being approachable and relatable, these designs can entice people into the domain of law and enable them to engage in important subject matter that they may not think about often. As one commentator described the successful speculative fiction series *40 Futures*: "[it's] kind of like sitting with your very smart, engaging friend at a bar and talking about what they think the world will look like in 2060."[42] For Jason Tashea, the creator of the series, this was his exact intention: "I was hoping that people that are not in our world would use it as an on-ramp to be interested in our world."[43] By opening up the world of law to new and larger audiences, speculative design has the potential to engage even more people in critical debate and ensure the justice system not only remains accountable to the people but also retains its relevance as a cornerstone of our society.

2.8. Applying Speculative Design

Although applying speculative design in the domain of law is quite novel, a number of topics are emerging as popular focal points for these types of projects. The courtroom tends to be a favoured subject for speculative designers. Described as the "epicentre" of legal structures,[44] its rituals and symbols have been examined, critiqued and modified by these designers in a number of ways. Some projects have used the courtroom as a platform to consider fundamental aspects of the law, while others have speculated about humanity's place within a wider ecosystem of justice that also involves animals and our shared environment.[45] Regardless of the setting, speculative design projects tend to be densely packed with meaning and cover multiple topics. Helpfully, explanations are often provided alongside the design artefacts as supportive commentary.

---

41 William Shakespeare, *Henry VI* (1591) Part 2, Act IV, Scene 2.

42 Mimi.9, 'Thought-provoking, entertaining, and informative' (*Apple Podcasts*, 4 July 2022) <https://podcasts.apple.com/us/podcast/40-futures/id1607895300> accessed 28 January 2023.

43 Tashea (n 6).

44 Walton (n 30).

45 Jack Tan, 'Four Legs Good' (*Jack Tan*, n.d.) <https://jacktan.wordpress.com/artwork/four-legs-good/> accessed 22 January 2023.

The projects below have been selected because they each share similar focal points (the principle of open justice), but their approaches and interpretations are drastically different. The comparison intends to highlight the variety of speculative design techniques. It also seeks to show how the same subject matter can be portrayed and the result is a better understanding of the nuances of the challenges that we face.

In the already mentioned *James v Birnmann*, Phoebe Walton presents a future where the legal system is maintained by AI.[46] This project has several layers, one being the contention that "law is a continual performance".[47] She amplifies this in a number of ways, including presenting the courtroom as a stage complete with props and costumes, lighting booms, spectator seats and artificial crowd noise. By presenting the courtroom theatrically, Walton is calling attention to not only the impact of the media framing the public's perception of law through fictional legal dramas and televising real cases,[48] but laterally she is also highlighting the implications of the principle that law must be seen to be done, commonly referred to as the open justice principle. It showcases the risk of reducing the principle to its performative quality. In her words, the project "invites the audience to question their current relationship to the legal system and perception of the law."[49] As the next two examples demonstrate, this is just one way to examine and elicit responses about this fundamental principle of the legal system.

The Policy Lab team that brings its "multidisciplinary expertise to help teams understand the present, imagine the future and design ways to achieve the policy impact they intend,"[50] also explored the principle that justice must be done in the open so that it can be subjected to public and professional scrutiny, but took a drastically different approach. In 2019, the team was tasked with the challenge: *How do we maintain open justice in a digital world?* and to address this, the team prepared and ran four 2-hour sessions with members of the public.[51] The sessions were

46 Walton (n 30).
47 ibid.
48 ibid.
49 ibid.
50 Policy Lab, 'About Policy Lab' (*Policy Lab*, n.d.) <https://openpolicy.blog.gov.uk/about/> accessed 9 May 2023.
51 Policy Lab, 'Exploring the Future of Open Justice' (*HM Courts and Tribunals Ser-

split into two parts, where the first part focused on what people already knew and thought about open justice and the second part (the bulk of the session) was focused on using provocations to understand what the participants thought and felt about open justice. The provocations were hypothetical future scenarios that were loosely based on options being considered by HM Courts and Tribunals Service (HMCTS). The team at the Policy Lab used the provocations to ignite discussions about the future between participants. After a process of synthesis, common principles were distilled and packaged up for HMCTS so they could be used as helpful guides when designing future open justice delivery mechanisms. On reflection, HMCTS noted that speculative design revealed "interesting findings in a more emotive way".[52] The HMCTS team also spoke about wanting to use provocations again and highlighted that the methodology could be used to explore "the more emotive and organic reactions to the topic".[53] This example showcases how speculative design can be used to influence strategic policy decisions within mainstream government services.

The third example that tangentially explores the principle of open justice is from Eeda Da Gyung Lee, who produced *Virtual Justice: Courts of the Future* which, put simply, presents a VR court platform that manages criminal activities committed in virtual space.[54] The project stems from her own experience as a juror in criminal trials, in which she had "difficulty in understanding the legal processes" and had felt "really frustrated with the adversarial environment that [she was] not familiar with".[55] Like Walton's project, this project also has many layers. With relevance to the open justice principle, this project may be perceived as critiquing the adversarial built environment and brings into question the need to be physically present in the courtroom in order to access court proceedings. In this fictional courthouse there exists a separate space,

---

vice, 1 November 2019) <https://assets.publishing.service.gov.uk/government/uploads/system/uploads/attachment_data/file/844189/20190820_Open_Justice_-_Write-Up_V3.pdf> accessed 22 January 2023.

52 ibid.

53 ibid.

54 Da Gyung Lee (n 34).

55 Interview with Eeda Da Gyung Lee, Architect, Architectural Association School of Architecture (Virtual, 27 January 2023).

called the Archive Portal, in which the public can easily navigate through all the previous cases that are stored in cubes (see Figure 3). Virtual reality (VR) technologies enable the public to immerse themselves in the evidence and testimonies, which is bringing attention to the emerging trend of using VR in criminal cases today.[56] The public are provided with comprehensive access "so that [they] can understand and participate in a more engaging way".[57] Da Gyung Lee also represents those participating in the trial as avatars because of her own experience of feeling "insecure" when the accused looked at her when she was a juror. In order to access the trial, these participants are required to pass through an identification system. In contrast, she felt that the public who were simply perusing cases in the Archive Portal need not identify themselves. By bringing to light her own concerns with the justice system, she has tangentially also critiqued the principle of open justice by pondering how it might materialise in the future.

Fig. 3. Screenshot of Virtual Justice: Courts of the Future*, a design fiction that allows the public access to all of the collected cases and their verdicts, through an Archive Portal. © Eeda Da Gyung Lee, 2021. Reproduced with permission.*

56 For example, VR technology has been used in a homicide trial at the Beijing First Intermediate People's Court, where the witness in the case wore VR glasses and returned to the scene of the simulated crime describing the process of the case from his perspective. Zhang Ruiyu Du Jiang, 'The visualisation system is first applied to the court trial where the witness wears VR glasses and returns to the scene of the crime' (*China Youth Network*, 1 March 2018) <http://news.youth.cn/gn/201803/t20180301_11458901.htm> accessed 29 January 2023.

57 Da Gyung Lee (n 34).

These three projects present different perspectives and value judgments about the future. They each focus on the idea of open justice, but portray very different worlds where this principle remains intact. In so doing, they reveal the nuances of the principle and how it can operate now and into the future.

2.9. The Techniques and Tools of The Trade

Borrowing from Futures work and art forms like cinema and literature, speculative design uses a variety of techniques and tools to critique, engage, elicit empathy and foster debate. Designers who practise speculative design may use techniques and tools that are familiar but they use these to critically reflect on the current paradigm and the corresponding interplay between social, economic and technological developments. The key difference is that these techniques and tools aim to destabilise the status quo, rather than just improve it.

2.9.1. Scenarios

Speculation on the future can lead to the generation of a range of scenarios. These snippets of the future-state can take the form of short stories and describe new possibilities or new challenges related to a critical issue. The scenarios produced by the Policy Lab (described as "provocations") are good examples because they are plausible, logically coherent and internally consistent.[58] Scenarios can either act as prompts where the speculative designer develops the scenario themselves and presents it as a way of fostering discussion,[59] or they can be developed by participants in a workshop so that participants consider elements of critical issues that are relevant to them.[60] Regardless of how they are utilised, most practitioners note that scenarios should avoid straying into the zone of fantasy,[61] nor should they present a world where everyone gets

58 European Foresight Platform, 'Scenario Method' (*European Foresight Platform*, n.d.) <http://foresight-platform.eu/community/forlearn/how-to-do-foresight/methods/scenario/> accessed 29 January 2023.

59 Dunne and Raby (n 2).

60 European Foresight Platform (n 58).

61 Dunne and Raby (n 2) 4.

along or where technological silver bullets have saved the day.[62] Futures that are spelt out in scenarios are "not a destination or something to strive for" but rather they are "a medium to aid imaginative thought".[63] Scenarios form the basis of many other speculative techniques and tools.

2.9.2. Design Fictions

Design fictions make these scenarios tangible. They stretch beyond mere stories and envision the worlds in which those stories take place.[64] Described by Nick Foster as "expertly designed artefacts" that can "communicate complex information in ways that are generative and provocative, but also systematic and precise", design fictions are the output of careful and critical design.[65] For example, a design fiction may be a cereal box that takes the elements of a normal cereal box (the contents, where things are made, where they were sold, how they were sold and the technology used) and re-imagines this in the future while simultaneously critiquing the social, economic and technological dynamics of the status quo.[66] The best design fictions are meticulous and believable.

2.9.3. What if... *Prompts*

Questions beginning with "what if" can be used as a tool to help build scenarios and design fictions. Unfinished, these prompts open space for discussing and considering alternative possibilities and options. The power of this simple technique is that it can cover paradigm shifts (for example *What if we abandoned the dominant common law model?*), systemic shifts (for example *What if we redesigned legal systems for the*

62 Jim Dator, 'Some hints on writing scenarios of preferred futures' (*Hawaii Research Center for Futures Studies,* n.d.) <https://manoa.hawaii.edu/futures-center/publications/futures-theories-methods/WritingScenarios1994.pdf> accessed 22 April 2022.

63 Dunne and Raby (n 2).

64 Elvia Vasconcelos, 'Part 3 – What is Speculative / Critical / Fiction / Design?' (*Elivia's Blog of Everything*, 23 July 2017) <https://elviavasconcelosblog.wordpress.com/2017/07/23/part-3-what-is-speculative-critical-fiction-design/> accessed 29 January 2023.

65 Nick Foster, 'What is Design Fiction?' (*Futurist*, 23 June 2022) <https://futurist.com/2022/06/23/what-is-design-fiction/> accessed 22 January 2023.

66 ibid.

end user?[67] or *What If Psychology Redesigned the Criminal Justice System?*[68]) or product and service shifts (for example *What if we no longer needed to consider regulation?*[69]). They are a flexible and effective tool but require structure. Participants who complete what if prompts should be given the space to engage in discourse with others after they frame this new world, in order to think them through and consider any relevant implications.

2.9.4. Social Dreaming

Social dreaming techniques recognise that imagination is both a "resource and a battleground"[70] and acknowledges that "most people are forced to live inside someone else's imagination".[71] This technique has been described as a "way of working with dreams where the focus is on the dream and not the dreamer, where dreams are shared amongst people who come together solely for this purpose."[72] Key to social dreaming is the ability to build dreams through association, which requires participants to share and also engage with each other's contributions. The difference between scenarios and social dreams is that scenarios are often developed independently, whereas social dreams are developed collectively. Social dreaming allows groups of people to build worlds together, which can then act as effective platforms for developing design fictions

67 Margaret Hagan, 'What if we redesigned legal systems for the end user?' (*Justice Innovation Stanford Legal Design Lab*, December 2014) <https://justiceinnovation.law.stanford.edu/redesigned-legal-systems-end-user/> accessed 29 January 2023.

68 Joel Dvoskin and others, 'What If Psychology Redesigned the Criminal Justice System?' in Joel Dvoskin and others (eds), *Using Social Science to Reduce Violent Offending* (Oxford Academic 2011).

69 LexisNexis, 'Lawyers and Robots? Conversations Around the Future of the Legal Industry' (*LexisNexis*, n.d.) <https://www.lexisnexis.com.au/__data/assets/pdf_file/0003/187644/Lawyers_and_Robots_Whitepaper.pdf> accessed 29 January 2023.

70 Professor Ruha Benjamin, 'Race to the Future: Rethinking Innovation, Inequity, and Imagination in Everyday Life' (*Emerson College,* 19 October 2019) <https://emerson.hosted.panopto.com/Panopto/Pages/Viewer.aspx?id=9e233ca9-c5ca-49fb-85c0-abd60131e64a> accessed 29 January 2023.

71 ibid.

72 The Centre For Social Dreaming, 'Social Dreaming' (*The Centre For Social Dreaming*, n.d.) <http://socialdreaming.squarespace.com/socialdreaming> accessed 29 January 2023.

that are provocative and tangible.

2.9.5. Backcasting Activity

Backcasting reverses the process of forecasting. It is often used to identify the actions, policies and programs needed to arrive at a desired future-state.[73] The use of backcasting techniques, also makes the process of achieving the vision more manageable by breaking it into components (actions, policies and programs) bringing greater focus and clarity in the short-term. This activity is a useful way to catalyse action given it sets people up to assign responsibility and keep one another accountable.

2.9.6. Worst Case Scenario Planning

Worst case scenario planning is another form of analysis that, similarly to backcasting, can be used to determine the steps involved to bring about a particular future. The key difference is that the particular future that is focused on in worst case scenario planning is one that is *not* desirable. It is a powerful technique to identify the multiple steps that would need to be taken in order for society to reach the worst case scenario, as it is often a combination of technical, social, economic, political, and legal changes that occur incrementally and combine that bring about the futures we don't want.[74] The technique also presents ample opportunity to reflect on the "story arc" of new technologies,[75] and identify what interventions could look like and when they should occur.

There are several other useful techniques and tools. Databases such as *The SpeculativeEdu Online Repository,*[76] are useful as they contain further documentation about various methods, approaches and tools speculative designers use in their practice. Depending on the speculative

---

73 Roxi Nicolussi, 'Backcasting: Creating a Strategic Roadmap from the Future' (*Medium*, 29 November 2020) <https://bigpictureroxi.medium.com/backcasting-creating-a-strategic-roadmap-from-the-future-dcc06f118592> accessed 29 January 2023.

74 Tashea (n 6).

75 ibid.

76 SpeculativeEdu, 'Speculative Edu – the online repository' (*GitHub*, 10 July 2021) <https://github.com/speculativeedu/The-SpeculativeEdu-Online-Repository> accessed 29 January 2023.

design approach undertaken, these techniques and tools can be tailored for the desired effect.

2.10. New Frontiers

These examples are helpful in establishing how to apply speculative design in the law. But they are limited. In considering how else speculative design can be applied in the domain of law, it is useful to look at how it has been used in other sectors that have been using the methodology for much longer.

In the architecture and urban planning field, speculative design has been used to win work and create projects that explore alternative futures and the potential impact of new technologies on social and economic life, to great effect. A prime example is the work of speculative design agency Superflux, which was invited by the United Arab Emirates government to develop a way for their senior decision-makers to experience numerous possible futures around energy and stress test their implications.[77] They created several models of future metropolises to make the data (that they extrapolated from the Ministry' of Energy's econometric data and projections) experientially evocative. These models helped the participants to understand the dynamics between financial investments and social, economic and technological developments and the impact this would have on the environment and society. Participants were taken through five different future worlds that contained various design artefacts to make these futures more real. The most compelling artefacts were the series of air samples from the years 2020, 2028, and 2034. Samples contained a combination of chemicals such as carbon monoxide, sulphur dioxide, and nitrogen dioxide based on climate and fossil fuel emission projections. Described by Superflux as "noxious stuff" and "impossible to inhale",[78] this crystalised the disastrous impacts of current behaviour in a way that predictions and data simply cannot. The experience had an almost immediate effect on the participants and is said to have informed the UAE's National Energy

77 Superflux, 'The Future Energy Lab' (*Superflux*, 2017) <https://superflux.in/index.php/work/futureenergylab/#> accessed 18 January 2023.

78 ibid.

Strategy 2050, which will invest $163 billion in renewables.[79] This example highlights the importance of engaging the right stakeholders in the experience and the role of design artefacts to make the future *feel* real. It also presents several provocations for legal design practitioners, like *how might we use smell to engage people in policy change* or *how might we make the dynamics between social, economic and technological developments tangible so that we can evaluate the impact this will have on the justice space?*

Major companies are also spinning up teams focused on the future. For example, Google X, which is the so-called "moonshot factory at Alphabet" is a lab that is trying to resurrect dreaming big and inventing things.[80] They conceive prototyping "in its broadest possible terms" and make the future tangible by creating things like imaginary corporate websites or receipts for future dinners.[81] They also employ different kinds of specialists, who each bring a certain perspective to the table. Explained simply by Derek Thompson, the method they follow is threefold: "First, [they] must address a huge problem; second, [they] must propose a radical solution; third, [they] must employ a relatively feasible technology."[82] This set up poses a challenge to those working in the legal domain: *What if we created a Speculative Legal Design Lab? What if we invited a cross section of specialists to solve some of the biggest problems facing the justice sector? What if we followed the three part formula to identify problems before they become problems?* These frontiers are yet unexplored and present an exciting space to experiment in.

79 ibid.

80 Derek Thompson, 'Google X and the Science of Radical Creativity' (*The Atlantic*, November 2017) <https://www.theatlantic.com/magazine/archive/2017/11/x-google-moonshot-factory/540648/> accessed 30 January 2023.

81 Nick Foster, 'Designing for the unknown' (*X, the moonshot factory*, 16 June 2021) <https://blog.x.company/designing-for-the-unknown-5156fde8ffb3> accessed 30 January 2023.

82 Thompson (n 80).

3. Experimenting with Speculative Design

3.1. Background

The editors of *Design in Legal Education*,[83] Emily Allbon and Amanda Perry-Kessaris, wanted the launch for their book outlining what design can do for legal education, to give attendees an immersive experience into legal design.

- Making ideas visible and tangible: Participants were invited to use Lego to imagine different ways of teaching/learning and other real-world legal scenarios.
- Get user-centred: Participants were invited to use personas and journey maps to consider different types of legal environments and appropriate responses.
- Thinking outside your box: Participants were invited to use the *5 Whys* technique to understand the root cause of problems.
- Simplify legalese: Participants were invited to re-write legalese using simple and straightforward language.
- Speculative Design: Participants were invited to imagine future legal environments, prompted through sound, imagery and scenarios.
- Comic Strips: Participants were invited to create a comic strip explaining something legal.

Each attendee was given a legal design passport (see Figure 4) and could engage with the activity as much or as little as they liked, and in whatever order suited them (whilst collecting a 'stamp' at each stall). They were also given a "Spot the case" card;[84] an illustration of an attic where pictorial clues for various landmark UK cases lay amidst the clutter. There were prizes for the most successful clue unravellers.

83 Emily Allbon and Amanda Perry-Kessaris, *Design in Legal Education* (Routledge 2022). The book website offers summaries of all chapters and a conversation between the editors, see https://designinlegaleducation.net/book-home.html

84 Stephen Eccles and Emily Allbon, 'Spot the Case' (tl;dr, n.d.) <https://tldr.legal/resource/spot-the-case-at-our-book-launch.html> accessed 13 April 2024.

Fig. 4. Each participant was given a Legal Design Passport and invited to participate in different design activities. Legal Design Passport ©, *Emily Allbon and Amanda Perry-Kessaris, 2022. Photograph by Emily MacLoud, 2022.*

The following sections describe the preparation and delivery of the speculative design stall, which sought to pose critical questions about the future of legal environments (and other related topics) and facilitate discussion between participants. This section ends with a discussion about what we learnt about using speculative design in the legal domain through the experience.

3.2. Preparation: What We Did

Prior to the event, three learning goals were developed in connection with the speculative design stall. These learning goals sought to clarify the purpose of the experience and helped guide not only the preparatory steps and the delivery of the experience, but also the reflection that is set out below.

Desktop research was undertaken about the various types of speculative design techniques and tools that could be used, taking into account constraints such as the time, space and budget available and the expected number of participants. As a source of inspiration, other examples of speculative design experiences were also explored. In particular, previous work undertaken by Portable in the death and ageing space,[85] and the economic and taxation space were examined and elements identified that were going to be crucial for success (such as having a way to catapult participants into a future-thinking state). An approach was subsequently developed, which clarified:

- Why we were using speculative design as a methodology (the why);
- What we would be speculating about (the what);
- How we would engage participants (including the invitations we would offer participants, what artefacts would act as inputs, what artefacts would be created as outputs, and constraints to consider) (the how); and
- How we would make sense of the data after the experience and what we would do with it (the next steps).

This approach worked well as it narrowed the focus of the exercise and provided the scaffolding to start developing the design artefacts that would be utilised.

Artefacts were then created, which were made available on the day of the event (Figure 5).

85 See Portable, 'Lymbo' (*Portable*, n.d.) <https://www.designyourdeath.com.au/> accessed 8 November 2022; Portable, 'The World's Most Deathable City' (*Portable*, n.d.) <https://www.deathable.city/> accessed 8 November 2022.

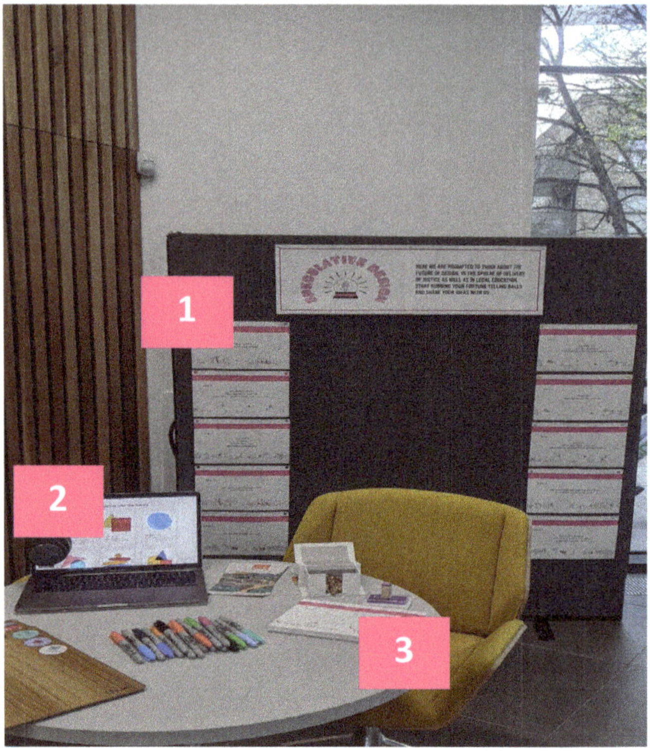

Fig. 5. The Speculative Design stall at the launch of Design in Legal Education, *prepared by Emily Allbon and Amanda Perry-Kessaris, 2022. Photograph by Emily MacLoud, 2022.*

1 A series of simple, fictional provocations that began with *What if*… These questions were intended to provide prompts for discussion and also to exemplify the types of contributions participants could make on their own. Examples included:

- What if we replaced “access to justice” with “access to equity and wellbeing”?
- What if you could choose to have your case decided by an algorithm?
- What if you lost your senses as retribution for your crimes?
- What if students redesigned our law schools?

2 A laptop, with headphones, was made available for participants to engage in the website: https://speculativejustice.softr.app/ The website was created for the event. The website contains:

- A series of short videos about speculative scenarios set in the future,
- A series of informal speculations about the future of justice and legal education (since updated with the participants contributions),
- Resources about speculative design, and
- A form to submit feedback.

Participants were invited to write their own hypothetical scenarios about the future. The prompt cards contained the words "What if" followed by three blank lines, inviting participants to write down their framings of the future. They were guided by a facilitator to use the existing provocations as examples.

The space was also arranged so that participants felt comfortable while watching the videos or writing down their own hypothetical scenarios (seats were provided) and also felt that they had enough room to add their contributions to the board, read other contributions and engage in dialogue relating to the contributions.

3.3. Delivery: What Happened

Approximately 30 attendees participated in the speculative design experience (see Figure 5). Several participants engaged in discussion after reading the provocations, watching the videos or writing their own hypothetical scenarios about the future. This led to several insightful conversations.

Fig. 6. Participants engaging in activities at the Speculative Design stall of the Design in Legal Education *launch, prepared by Emily Allbon and Amanda Perry-Kessaris, 2022. Photograph by Emily MacLoud, 2022.*

3.4. Discussion: What We Learnt about Speculative Design

During the event, through observation and engagement with participants, a number of patterns started to emerge. Following the event, we also spoke with a couple of attendees to gather their reflections about the elements that were most impactful. The insights below provide an outline about what we learnt and shed light on some key considerations to keep in mind when utilising speculative design in the legal domain.

3.4.1. Be Intentional about the Space

Given this particular exercise was conducted in person, we were fortunate to be able to also consider the experiential component of the exercise. As pictured in Figure 6, the space was arranged so that it felt inviting. It also sought to encourage participants to make their own connections between ideas. As one of the participants commented in relation to the arrangement of the table and chairs, "it was very conversational" and in relation to the board arrangement, "the way the boards were arranged meant that after you made your contribution and you put it up... the way the ideas were put together meant that they weren't in isolation... they were intersecting with one another.[86] Working in the physical space was a great opportunity, as it afforded a range of ways for participants to engage not only with the prompts but also with each other's ideas.

86 Interview with Vic Duarte, Student, City University (Virtual, 28 January 2023).

3.4.2. Enable Participants to Engage in Dialogue and Associate Ideas with One Another

Although several participants engaged in debate and discussion with the facilitator and/or other fellow participants after submitting their own What if scenario or watching the videos, there were many that did not. This presented a missed opportunity. If we were to run a similar exercise, we would provide a way for participants to associate their ideas with others and offer this through simple dialogue with others or, for those participants that may be a bit uneasy with this step, offering them a chance to associate ideas using string or some other more passive medium.

Regardless, one participant noted that they appreciated being able to pin their contribution to the board because it felt like they were "adding to a conversation."[87] This participant also liked being able to read other people's work, which encouraged her to "push [her] brain to think about it differently."[88] However, other commentators have noted that this may potentially limit the thinking of the participant since they'll immediately (perhaps subconsciously) work within the same style and constraints as the examples they see and that it may in fact be more effective to let people see other contributions only after making their own.

3.4.3. Have a Device that Can Snap Participants into the Future

Providing the prompts (in the form of provocations and the series of short videos about speculative scenarios set in the future) provided structure for open responses from participants and enabled people to have reflective, relevant and meaningful conversations. As one participant put it: "It's a good exercise for us lawyers because we're so used to rules. It's hard for us to be creative."[89] The devices painted the scene and positioned participants in the future which enabled them to unpack these worlds and start creating their own. Indeed, one of the participants later reflected that it was helpful having so many aides that did not steer people in a certain direction but instead sought to "push them forward".[90] Providing these devices meant the exercise felt approachable

87 ibid.

88 ibid.

89 Interview with anonymous, Lawyer (London, 18 November 2022).

90 Duarte (n 86).

and intentional, which the participants appreciated.

Participants are also more likely to engage in second-order thinking, if they are provided with a prompt to start from. During the exercise, participants who read through the provocations, then participated in the exercise by creating their own hypothetical scenarios, felt challenged and subsequently channelled this thinking and applied this thinking to their current reality. One participant who was challenged by the provocation *What if you could choose to have your case decided by algorithm?* subsequently wrote as his hypothetical scenario *What if a legal AI machine designed to solve cases hides a bug?* This example demonstrates how speculative thinking can kick-start a series of questions, expand thinking and reframe possibilities.

3.4.4. Provide Neutral Provocations; Participants Are Likely to Apply Them to Their Own Context and Make Them Personally Relevant

Many participants engaged in conversation after reading the provocations that were provided. Discussions were initiated by the provocations, but traversed into areas that were personally of importance to participants. For example, a participant who was a shipping lawyer focused on the provocation *What if you could choose to have your case decided by algorithm?* Rather than focusing on this particular topic, he discussed that he wasn't taught about algorithms at law schools or their ethical implications, but regardless of his line of work, he was facing legal decisions about ships being controlled by AI-powered navigation systems.[91] This highlighted for him that legal education is less about the factual nature of right now, and more about equipping the lawyers of tomorrow with the ethical logic needed to make decisions about technology that doesn't even exist yet. This is contrasted with another participant, a lecturer, who told me that after reading the provocation *What if the environment could appear in court as defendants, complainants and witnesses?* She was prompted to think about what she would need to teach her law students about complainants and witnesses in order for them to make those decisions in the future.[92] Interestingly, these two participants arrived at the same conclusion (i.e. that legal education should fo-

91 Interview with anonymous, Lawyer (London, 18 November 2022).

92 Interview with anonymous, Professor (London, 18 November 2022).

cus on principles and build foundational knowledge) but through different routes, highlighting the power of speculative design to bring about alignment between people.

3.4.5. Enable Anonymity so People can Contribute Freely
The prompts were effectively blank cards, with three lines that invited participants to frame a speculative future of their choice. No names were attached to the cards. One participant highlighted the positive effect this had on her and her willingness to be vulnerable: "It's hard to be vulnerable like that and put the first thing that comes to mind out there, especially when it's in front of people. I think there was something about each of the cards being slightly anonymous to write and an extension of the stall."[93] This reflection highlighted the importance of providing different ways to contribute, from the passive to the active.

3.4.6. Provide a Psychologically Safe Space
Speculating about the future can provide an opportunity to critique the status quo in an emotive way. For example some participants described the emotional impact of the experience, noting that it felt and presented a good opportunity to vent.[94] This highlights how speculative design can not only highlight weaknesses within the status quo, but it can also be an emotional outlet for people providing a space for them to engage in the subject matter with their heart, not just their head.

Speculating about the future can also highlight redundancies, which can be uncomfortable. Some participants used the opportunity in their hypothetical scenarios to imagine a world without their profession or organisation in it. For example, one participant who was himself a lecturer wrote *What if there were no lectures only problems, solutions, teams and mentors?* and highlighted that he did not think lectures were an effective learning tool.[95] Another participant, when speculating about a world where his professional role may become redundant, highlighted that "speculative thinking could be scary for people".[96] Speculative de-

93 Duarte (n 86).
94 Interview with anonymous, Professor (London, 18 November 2022).
95 Interview with anonymous, Professor (London, 18 November 2022).
96 Interview with Paul Magrath, Head of Product Development and Online Content, ICLR (Virtual, 5 January 2023).

sign can make us face our darkest fears and areas that need attention by bringing into the spotlight that which we often wish to brush away.

4. Let's Speculate!

Experimenting with speculative design can feel daunting. It not only requires the designer to be critical and creative, but also boldness and bravery. The following discussion breaks down the key considerations to keep in mind when starting to experiment with this methodology. It begins with a discussion about what the designer needs to consider before they can get going (the designer). It then speaks about the challenges associated with choosing the right focal point for the speculation (the problem), before considering how it might be introduced at an organisation (the organisation). Given the present challenges facing the legal domain, it's time to be bold and start speculating. Below we discuss how.

4.1. The Designer

Fundamentally, the designer has to consider themselves as creative. For many legally trained professionals, this can be challenging. As Vic Duarte, a student who participated in the speculative legal design exercise reflected about her own legal education, she described feeling "the need and pressure to shut down creativity... because [she] felt like that's the way that it's interpreted and how [she] had preconceived what it meant to be someone who is part of the law, studying the law contributing to the law."[97] Regardless, there is a strong movement of lawyers embracing new mindsets and embracing creativity.[98] Unleashing the creativity within oneself is the first step to becoming a speculative designer.

For every designer, recognising one's own values and drivers is key if one wants to create an authentic practice.[99] For designers who undertake this work, they are often motivated by long-term thinking and wanting to bring about more equitable futures. Indeed, Sarah McArthur who de-

---

97 Duarte (n 86).

98 Margaret Hagan, *Law by Design* (n.d.) <https://lawbydesign.co/design-mindsets/> accessed 31 January 2023.

99 Melis Senova, *Design Character* (BIS Publishing 2022).

scribes herself as a "tinkerer in emergent technology, speculative design and experiential futures" talks about wanting to be "a good ancestor".[100] She speaks about employing "cathedral thinking", which is a concept that recognises that success of a strategy lies not in its implementation, but in its outcome.[101] Like many who worked on the great cathedrals during mediaeval times who would never see their completion, speculative designers are implored to not lose sight of the preferable future they are aiming for even if that vision isn't realised within their lifetime. Despite being challenging, this perspective is key when speculating.

Designers experimenting with speculative design should also adopt a bias towards action. Starting somewhere is always better than never starting. Given the increasing interest in speculative design methods, there are several databases that are full of useful resources such as *Speculative Edu* and *Future Scouting,*[102] which provide practical and accessible guides and templates that can be followed when starting out. The increase in numbers of people doing this work also means there are more conversations taking place and more case studies being produced, leading to more reflection about how to tackle complicated problems.

Involving those who are experiencing the problem as designers is also key, as this enables new perspectives to be included in the discourse relating to some of the most challenging issues facing society. As one participant noted on reflection of the speculative legal design experience, "I think having adults, children, people who feel limitations to equitable access... write, draw, anything that allows them to visualise what a just world looks like for them specifically" would be useful as it could "reveal barriers that we never [have] seen before".[103] By offering people the chance to develop the designs themselves, speculative design has the potential for unleashing a new wave of insights about what futures are preferable.

100 McArthur (n 13).

101 Meredith James, 'Advancing Design Thinking Towards a Better Understanding of Self and Others' (2017) 10(2) FormAcademic 1.

102 SpeculativeEdu (n 76); Future Scouting, 'The Future Scouting approach' (*Future Scouting*, n.d.) <https://futurescouting.com.au/> accessed 28 January 2023.

103 Duarte (n 86).

Being mindful of the readiness of those participating is also necessary. Speculative design is a potentially unsafe medium for people who may have experienced trauma.[104] Asking a person to imagine may be dangerous as it may mean inviting them to step into a realm where they have little control. Using language that takes this into account is wise.

Giving oneself constraints is also helpful. As Jason Tashea recounts when he was producing the vignettes for the speculative series *40 Futures*: "I only had two rules for writing the pieces. One was that the technology had to be likely based on what we know today, regardless of how far down the road it was going to be. And it had to fit in the moral universe that we currently embody in the United States when it comes to how we treat people in the criminal justice system."[105] These constraints ensured the process of generating the fictions was free-flowing and unhampered by the hurdles that are commonplace in journalistic and academic writing.

4.2. The Problem

Choosing the right problem space is also challenging. As Da Gyung Lee reflects, the first major hurdle she faced was choosing what she would critique.[106] Moreover, because the problems that speculative design calls into question are often so nebulous and systemic, they can be hard to define. These problems are often ingrained in the fabric of our society and understanding their complexities without a clear definition can be a rather daunting task. But even though the problems that speculative design focuses on are big, it doesn't mean the projects have to be big too. By using simple prompts like "What if…", imaginations can be ignited, a plethora of different futures can be conjured up and discussions can ensue.

Like other design methods, identifying problems is best achieved by beginning with thorough research. To demonstrate this inherent complexity, it is useful to consider the lengths Superflux employed when working with the United Nation Development Program (UNDP) team

104 Interview Aishling Costello, Senior Strategic Designer, Portable (31 January 2023).
105 Tashea (n 6).
106 Da Gyung Lee (n 55).

to develop Mantis Systems, which is a speculative design that proactively identifies and prevents global systems risks.[107] For the project, they carried out extensive ethnographic research, facilitated workshops with various practitioners across the development sector, sourced data, spoke with experts and extrapolated trends, weak signals and uncertainties. This was brought together to inform the world building stage, which was then used as a launch pad for developing design fictions. This example highlights the rigour involved and the types of research that can be carried out to ensure the speculative designs focus on problems that are relevant and of concern to the audience of interest.

4.3. The Organisation

Introducing speculative design into a workplace can be challenging for a number of reasons. Firstly, it's not typical for design to work in this way. As noted earlier, design is often thought of as fixing problems that exist in the present. It follows that creating artefacts in speculative design projects without context can cause widespread confusion as people may believe that the designs represent what the organisation is *actually* producing or intending to produce. For example, Nick Foster recounts a project he worked on in which he developed a speculative product, which was prematurely released and was subsequently interpreted as a typical 'product vision'.[108] He talks about the anxiety and distress this caused and highlights the crucial role of commentary alongside these artefacts to avoid these designs being misinterpreted.

Secondly, when introducing speculative design into an organisation a certain level of literacy is required in order for stakeholders to buy-in to the design process. Yet this can be especially challenging when working in a highly publicised setting, like government. Within these settings, it's not only about getting buy-in from stakeholders within the organisation, it's also about "getting across to the community the value of speculative work".[109] This is best done through small structured workshops, as

107 Superflux, 'Mantis Systems' (*Superflux*, 2018) <https://superflux.in/index.php/work/mantissystems/#> accessed 18 January 2023.
108 Foster (n 65).
109 McArthur (n 13).

demonstrated by the work of the Policy Lab, who expertly facilitated several sessions to better understand public perceptions about the principle of open justice.[110] Speculative design holds a lot of potential as a design method, but it often requires significant upfront investment in justifying why it should be used. It also requires a lot of planning, which can present an obstacle in time-poor organisations.

Thirdly, unique to the legal context, is the consideration of the regulatory landscape in which legal entities operate. When considering how to introduce speculative design into law firms, there is a risk that any speculative designs may be shut down by the regulators.[111] It begs the question whether there may be a need to set up regulatory sandboxes that are not just focused on considering the implications of technologies in the present, but can also extend these so that they can consider the implications of technologies that don't yet exist.

5. Conclusion

Employing speculative design in law makes sense for many reasons. It can be used to critique the status quo; by reimagining what the law *might* be, speculative design can spark critical debate about what the law *should* be. It can also capture audiences in new ways and make people *feel* differently about the law. By opening up the world of law to new and larger audiences, speculative design also has the potential to engage even more people in critical debate. Given the opportunities that this methodology affords, many pioneers have started experimenting with speculative design in the legal domain.

When utilising this approach, it's important to consider the space, enable dialogue and idea association, provide future scenarios or a device that can snap participants into the future, offer neutral provocations, enable anonymity so people can contribute freely, and provide a psychologically safe space. Speculative design can make us face our darkest fears and areas that need attention. It is important to wield this methodology respectfully and thoughtfully.

110 Policy Lab (n 51).
111 Hoadley (n 37).

Speculative design offers a novel way to confront and challenge existing power structures and systems in the legal domain, allowing for the exploration of a wide range of possible futures and alignment towards what is preferable. By engaging with this approach, we can create artefacts that help to bridge the gap between our current state and possible future states and evolve the legal ecosystem into something that works for everyone.

Bibliography

Allbon E and A Perry-Kessaris, *Design in Legal Education* (Routledge 2022)

Benjamin R, 'Race to the Future: Rethinking Innovation, Inequity, and Imagination in Everyday Life' (Emerson College, 19 October 2019) <https://emerson.hosted.panopto.com/Panopto/Pages/Viewer.aspx?id=9e233ca9-c5ca-49fb-85c0-abd60131e64a> accessed 29 January 2023

Canopy, 'Canopy in a nutshell' (Canopy, 2021) <http://www.canopy.si/> accessed 27 January 2023

Da Gyung Lee E, 'Virtual Justice: Courts of the Future' (Architectural Association School of Architecture, 2021) <https://pr2021.aaschool.ac.uk/students/da-gyung-lee> accessed 28 January 2023

—, Architect, Architectural Association School of Architecture (Virtual, 27 January 2023)

Dabaghi K, 'Beyond design thinking and into speculative futures in legal design' (DRS2022, Bilbao, July 2022)

Dator J, 'Some hints on writing scenarios of preferred futures' (Hawaii Research Center for Futures Studies, n.d.) <https://manoa.hawaii.edu/futures-center/publications/futures-theories-methods/WritingScenarios1994.pdf> accessed 22 April 2022

Dvoskin J and others, 'What If Psychology Redesigned the Criminal Justice System?' in Joel Dvoskin and others (eds), *Using Social Science to Reduce Violent Offending* (Oxford Academic 2011)

Duarte V, Student, City University (Virtual, 28 January 2023)

Dunne A and Raby F, *Speculative Everything: Design, Fiction, and Social Dreaming* (MIT Press 2013)

Enright M and T Kinsella, 'Legal Aesthetics in The Touching Contract: Memory, Exposure and Transformation' (2021) Law, Culture and the Humanities <https://doi.org/10.1177/1743872120987113> accessed 28 January 2023

European Foresight Platform, 'Scenario Method' (European Foresight Platform, n.d.) <http://foresight-platform.eu/community/forlearn/how-to-do-foresight/methods/scenario/> accessed 29 January 2023

Foster N, 'Designing for the unknown' (X, the moonshot factory, 16 June 2021) <https://blog.x.company/designing-for-the-unknown-5156fde8ffb3> accessed 30 January 2023

—, 'What is Design Fiction?' (Futurist, 23 June 2022) <https://futurist.com/2022/06/23/what-is-design-fiction/> accessed 22 January 2023

Future Scouting, 'The Future Scouting approach' (Future Scouting, n.d.) <https://futurescouting.com.au/> accessed 28 January 2023

Gibbons S, 'Design Thinking 101' (NNG Nielsen Norman Group, 31 July 2016)

<https://www.nngroup.com/articles/design-thinking/> accessed 9 May 2023

Hagan M, Law by Design (n.d.) <https://lawbydesign.co/design-mindsets/> accessed 31 January 2023

—, 'What if we redesigned legal systems for the end user?' (Justice Innovation Stanford Legal Design Lab, December 2014) <https://justiceinnovation.law.stanford.edu/redesigned-legal-systems-end-user/> accessed 29 January 2023

Hancock T, and C Bezold, 'Possible futures, preferable futures' (1994) 37 The Healthcare Forum Journal 23

Hartman S, 'Under the Blacklight: Storytelling While Black and Female: Conjuring Beautiful Experiments' (African American Policy Forum, 5 August 2020) <https://youtu.be/xGS5aP5Vi7g> accessed 28 January 2023

Henchey N, 'Making Sense of Future Studies' (1978) 7(2) Alternatives 24

Hoadley D, Head of Data Science & Analytics, Mishcon de Reya LLP (Virtual, 26 January 2023)

James M, 'Advancing Design Thinking Towards a Better Understanding of Self and Others' (2017) 10(2) FormAcademic 1

Kaur S, Principle Business Designer, Portable (Virtual, 7 November 2022)

LexisNexis, 'Lawyers and Robots? Conversations Around the Future of the Legal Industry' (LexisNexis, n.d.) <https://www.lexisnexis.com.au/__data/assets/pdf_file/0003/187644/Lawyers_and_Robots_Whitepaper.pdf> accessed 29 January 2023

Lutz D, 'Future Thieving #2—Speculative design methods and tools' (UX Collective, 4 August 2020) <https://uxdesign.cc/future-thieving-2-speculative-design-methods-tools-45b655096d95> accessed 28 January 2023

Magrath P, Head of Product Development and Online Content, ICLR (Virtual, 5 January 2023)

McArthur S, Director, CityLab (Virtual, 18 January 2023)

Mimi.9, 'Thought-provoking, entertaining, and informative' (Apple Podcasts, 4 July 2022) <https://podcasts.apple.com/us/podcast/40-futures/id1607895300> accessed 28 January 2023

Nicolussi R, 'Backcasting: Creating a Strategic Roadmap from the Future' (Medium, 29 November 2020) <https://bigpictureroxi.medium.com/backcasting-creating-a-strategic-roadmap-from-the-future-dcc06f118592> accessed 29 January 2023

Perry-Kessaris A, *Doing sociolegal research in design mode* (Routledge 2021)

Phoebe Walton, 'James v Birnmann' (James v Birnmann, n.d.) <https://phoebewalton.com/James-v-Birnmann> accessed 28 January 2023

Policy Lab, 'About Policy Lab' (Policy Lab, n.d.) <https://openpolicy.blog.gov.uk/about/> accessed 9 May 2023

Policy Lab, 'Exploring the Future of Open Justice' (HM Courts and Tribunals Service, 1 November 2019) <https://assets.publishing.service.gov.uk/government/uploads/system/uploads/attachment_data/file/844189/20190820_Open_Justice_-_Write-Up_V3.pdf> accessed 22 January 2023

Portable, 'Lymbo' (Portable, n.d.) <https://www.designyourdeath.com.au/> accessed 8 November 2022

Portable, 'The World's Most Deathable City' (Portable, n.d.) <https://www.deathable.city/> accessed 8 November 2022

Ruiyu Du Jiang Z, 'The visualisation system is first applied to the court trial where the witness wears VR glasses and returns to the scene of the crime' (China Youth Network, 1 March 2018) <http://news.youth.cn/gn/201803/t20180301_11458901.htm> accessed 29 January 2023

Senova M, *Design Character* (BIS Publishing 2022)

Shakespeare W, *Henry VI* (1591) Part 2, Act IV, Scene 2

SpeculativeEdu, 'Speculative Edu – the online repository' (GitHub, 10 July 2021) <https://github.com/speculativeedu/The-SpeculativeEdu-Online-Repository> accessed 29 January 2023

Superflux, 'Mantis Systems' (Superflux, 2018) <https://superflux.in/index.php/work/mantissystems/#> accessed 18 January 2023

Superflux, 'The Future Energy Lab' (Superflux, 2017) <https://superflux.in/index.php/work/futureenergylab/#> accessed 18 January 2023

Tan J, 'Four Legs Good' (Jack Tan, n.d.) <https://jacktan.wordpress.com/art-work/four-legs-good/> accessed 22 January 2023

Tashea J, Georgetown Law (Virtual, 3 February 2023)

—, '40 Futures' (40 Futures, n.d.) <https://podcasts.apple.com/us/podcast/40-futures/id1607895300> accessed 28 January 2023

The Centre For Social Dreaming, 'Social Dreaming' (The Centre For Social Dreaming, n.d.) <http://socialdreaming.squarespace.com/socialdreaming> accessed 29 January 2023

Thompson D, 'Google X and the Science of Radical Creativity' (The Atlantic, November 2017) <https://www.theatlantic.com/magazine/archive/2017/11/x-google-moonshot-factory/540648/> accessed 30 January 2023

Vasconcelos E, 'Part 3 – What is Speculative / Critical / Fiction / Design?' (Elivia's Blog of Everything, 23 July 2017) <https://elviavasconcelosblog.wordpress.com/2017/07/23/part-3-what-is-speculative-critical-fiction-design/> accessed 29 January 2023

Voros J, 'Big History and anticipation: Using Big History as a framework for global foresight' in R Poli (ed), *Handbook of anticipation: Theoretical and applied aspects of the use of future in decision making* (Springer International 2017)

Walton P, 'James v Birnmann: The potential of critical design for examining legal issues' (DRS2022, Bilbao, July 2022)

NARRATIVE AND STORYTELLING

3. THE POWER OF STORIES TO UNITE, INSPIRE, AND COLLECTIVELY IMAGINE NEW FUTURES

Emily MacLoud

Abstract

Within the field of law, stories can be a powerful tool. They can help to articulate how individuals experience the justice system and compel people to take action by evoking empathy. However, when stories are used reductively in the context of legal design, such as part of a case study or persona, they can lose their nuance and the context that surrounds them and may even reinforce harmful stereotypes or biases. This article will explore the relationship between stories and narratives and how stories have been used in other sectors to bring people together, inspire systemic change, and help envision a better future. It will also seek to promote a systemic sensibility in legal design practitioners, so they can develop stories and narratives that appreciate the interconnectedness of the systems within which they operate. The intention of this article is to enable legal practitioners to better manage complex systems change and to be able to tell stories about it.

1. Introduction

In a recent legal design project, Liz contemplated how to best present the observations she had witnessed and the opinions she had heard in interviews with end-users back to her client. She knew that the data she had collected was reliable enough to draw meaningful conclusions. However, she wanted to make sure that this was communicated in a way that enabled her audience, the client, to fully comprehend the complexities and nuances of the insights she had gained. She wanted to express the potential benefits users would gain as well as the risks involved in proceeding ahead. She also wanted to warn the client about the implications if her findings were incorrectly interpreted. She needed a way to communicate this complexity and make her insights engaging.

Liz created four behavioural personas that showcased the needs, motivations and challenges of the target user group. However, she was concerned that these outputs could be forgotten or misused because they were reductionistic and only revealed a small piece of the puzzle. As she continued to ponder, she realised how the stories she collected from people she engaged could be misconstrued as a result of transforming them into personas. As a designer who acted as the conduit between the target user group and her client, she felt the weight of responsibility to ensure the stories she told were authentic and truly representative of the people she had engaged. She felt that it was essential to consider the implications of storytelling carefully.

Stories are commonly used in the legal domain to articulate the lived experiences of people involved in the justice ecosystem. They can often engage the target audience in a way that evidence and reports cannot. In the story above, Liz is contemplating the implications of using stories as a tool to communicate the findings from her research. She highlights her anxiety about the outputs of her work being forgotten, misused or misconstrued – a concern many designers often grapple with. She ponders the far-reaching impacts of her work and posits that one must carefully consider the implications of using specific techniques, such as storytelling, when embarking on design projects. This paper seeks to do just that.

Recognising that the synergy between law and literature is not new,[1] this paper will explore how stories can be powerful devices for communicating needs, inspiring change, and compelling stakeholders to consider the broader implications of their decisions in the legal context. It will also expose the shadow side of stories. That is, it will scrutinise what can go wrong when stories are used reductively by design practitioners, like in a case study or presented as static personas. When this happens the subtle complexities of stories and their contexts can be overlooked. This paper shows how developing a *systemic sensibility* can be a useful way to ensure stories fully capture the complexity of the legal domain. Stories have already been utilised in other industries to tackle issues from a systemic perspective. It's time we started using them more often in the legal domain.

The article will begin with an overview of systems thinking to enhance the reader's systemic sensibility (Section 2). By highlighting examples where stories have been used reductively, the article will then explore

1 Richard Posner, *Law and Literature* (Harvard University Press 2009).

the complexity of wielding stories in legal settings (Section 3). It will conclude with a discussion about how stories can be used for systems change in law (Section 4).

2. Systems Thinking in the Law

2.1. Enhancing Legal Design with Systems Thinking

Applying a systems thinking lens to better understand and make sense of the legal domain is not new.[2] Previous scholars have explored systems analysis as a methodology and explored different examples of systems projects,[3] why it's important and how to introduce systems thinking to law schools through a pedagogical lens,[4] and even how to reconfigure the criminal justice response to human trafficking through a complex-systems perspective.[5] Systems thinking confirms the "tacit understanding" that the law is both a system and is an element of much broader social systems.[6] The legal domain is an especially pertinent subject for systems thinking.

For legal designers, who use design to make the world of law better, systems thinking can be thought of one of the many designerly mindsets that they already adopt.[7] Once systems thinking is revealed, it is similar to "taking the blinders off" as one is able to perceive connections and relationships between different forces in a refreshed way.[8] Systemic sensibility provides the know-how to be able to "see the water"; that

2 Petra Hietanen-Kunwald, Helena Haapio, and Nina Toivonen, 'Systems Theory as a Research Framework for Dispute Prevention and Resolution by Design' in Rossana Ducato and Alain Strowel (eds), *Legal Design Perspectives: Theoretical and Practical Insights from the Field* (Ledizioni 2021) 71.

3 Lynn M LoPucki, 'Systems Approach to Law' (1997) 82 Cornell Law Review 479.

4 Tomar Pierson-Brown, '(Systems) Thinking Like a Lawyer' (2020) 26 Clinical Law Review 515.

5 Marcel van der Watt and Amanda van der Westhuizen, '(Re)configuring the criminal justice response to human trafficking: a complex-systems perspective' (2017) 18(3) Police Practice and Research 218.

6 Pierson-Brown (n 4) 532.

7 Margaret Hagan, Law by Design (n.d.) <https://lawbydesign.co/design-mindsets/> accessed 31 January 2023.

8 Pierson-Brown (n 4) 532.

is, to be able to recognise and describe the often "translucent context" that gives rise to problems.[9] Many legal designers already do this without knowing it. Systemic sensibility gives awareness to this untapped resource, and systems literacy provides legal designers with enhanced skills and competencies to address the ever-more complex challenges that they are being tasked to undertake. With this, legal designers are then empowered to apply systems thinking in their own work.

2.2. Systemic Sensibility: Introducing Systems Thinking Into a Designers' Toolkit

The term system can be applied in any context (be it a situation or a project) where "items" regularly interact with one another.[10] In the legal context, a good example is the criminal justice system. The "items" within this system include not only the victims, offenders, police, lawyers, and judges, but also the tangible institutions such as the courts and prisons.[11] Systems thinking involves seeing these interdependent groups of items as relational, rather than linear, that function together in a way that gives rise to emergent properties.[12] Emergent properties can be thought of as "unexpected behaviours" that materialise as a result of interaction between the various elements of a system.[13] Regardless of the intended purpose of the system (for example, the purpose of the criminal justice system is to protect society and its members from criminal activity), emergent properties can appear unintentionally (for example, arguably an emergent property of the criminal justice system is that it marginalises vulnerable groups). These emergent properties are often not caused by individual players in the system, but because of the way the system oper-

---

9 Pierson-Brown (n 4) 533.

10 Merriam-Webster, 'System' <https://www.merriam-webster.com/dictionary/system> accessed 11 February 2023.

11 LoPucki (n 3) 482.

12 Jim Woodhill and Juliet Millican, 'Systems Thinking and Practice: A guide to concepts, principles and tools for FCDO and partners' (Brighton: Institute of Development Studies, February 2023).

13 Christopher W. Johnson, 'What are Emergent Properties and How Do They Affect the Engineering of Complex Systems?' (*University of Glasgow*, n.d.) <https://www.dcs.gla.ac.uk/~johnson/papers/RESS/Complexity_Emergence_Editorial.pdf> accessed 13 February 2023.

ates. Awareness of this has been described as systemic sensibility, and it is the first step to developing a systems lens (see Figure 1).

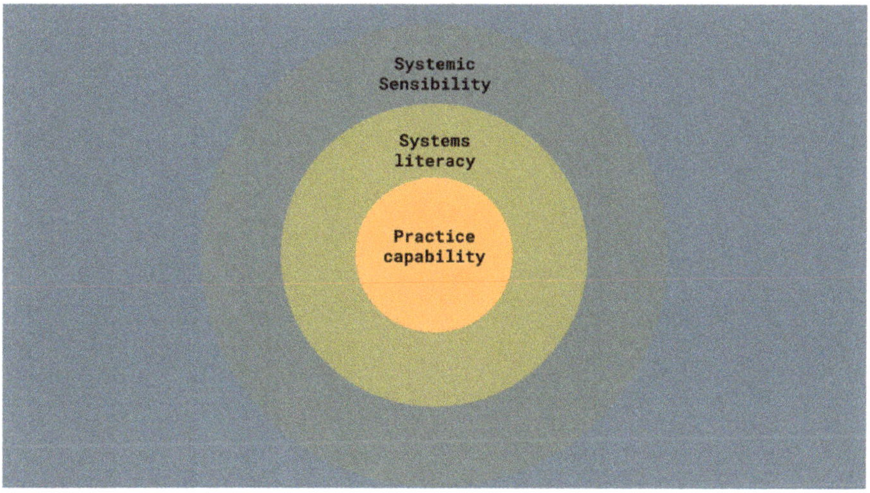

Fig. 1. There are three different layers of systems thinking capability - systemic sensibility, systems literacy and systems thinking in practice capability. © Edson, Tuddenham and Buckle-Henning, 2016. Reproduced with permission.[14]

It follows that a system's behaviour cannot be understood by focusing on the experience of just one person or one entity within the system. The system as a whole must be comprehended.[15] For legal designers, this means that they cannot truly grasp the experiences of a group of people (for example victims or police), without examining the entire system. They need to appreciate the wider context in which those people are situated in order to establish the ways that the system influences and is influenced by them.

2.3. Systems Literacy: Recognising Different Types of Systems

For legal designers, sharing a language around systems means that com-

---

14 Mary Edson, Peter D Tuddenham and Pamela Buckle-Henning, 'Systems Research: A Foundation for Systems Literacy' (2016) Proceedings of the 2016 IFSR Conversation Team 3: Systems Research Team.

15 Pierson-Brown (n 4) 528.

monly encountered behaviours and relationships found in systems can be expressed easily. Recognising that different types of systems exist and behave in different ways is often the first step to developing this literacy. Dave Snowden's Cynefin Framework is particularly helpful for this task (see Figure 2).[16] It is a decision framework that helps to identify the differences between system types and how to respond appropriately. Disorder occurs when there is no clarity about the type of situation one is facing.

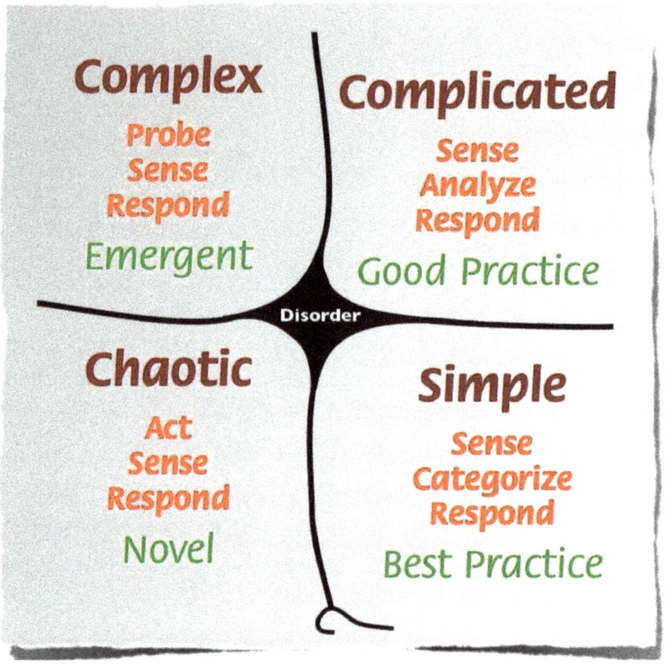

Fig. 2. "Cynefin Framework" © 2011 by Dave Snowden is licensed under Creative Commons Attribution 3.0 Unported license.[17]

In the legal domain, some situations may seem ordered, requiring a "systematic" response that involves following a step-by-step plan and engaging in linear thinking. These situations can be described as "sim-

16 David J Snowden and Mary E Boone, 'A Leader's Framework for Decision Making' (Harvard Business Review, November 2007) <https://hbr.org/2007/11/a-leaders-framework-for-decision-making> accessed 13 February 2023.

17 Dave Snowden, 'The Cynefin Framework' (CognitiveEdge, 12 July 2010) <https://youtu.be/N7oz366X0-8> accessed 10 February 2023.

ple" or "complicated" and the recommended approach to tackling these sorts of problems is to follow "best practice" or "good practice" respectively. An example may be how to approach the situation of charging clients. Many legal professionals approach this fairly "simple" situation by adopting "best practice" which dictates that one should track the hours they work and keep their time entries consistent. This task is often an assumed part of a lawyer's everyday practice and for years, many law firms followed this model. However, as Dave Snowden highlights, there is a danger in becoming complacent about processes and their success.[18] The once "simple" situation can drift towards the "complacency cliff", represented in the Cynefin Framework as a ridge between the "simple" and "chaotic" parts of the diagram. If one is not careful, a simple situation can easily turn into a crisis that can be very expensive to recover from.[19] As with our example above, many law firms are re-considering the billable hour and switching to other models like retainers, fixed and capped fees and event costed litigation, as they recognise that these pricing models are more practicable for their clients, and prevent their clients from experiencing nasty surprises that can result in mistrust.[20] As the example above demonstrates, in most situations it is often better, in the long run, to perceive most situations as complex to prevent the feeling of complacency.

Complex systems are "unordered" systems where causality is circular. The appropriate approach in these situations is to conduct safe experiments to probe the system, make sense of the results of that intervention and amplify it if the experiment succeeds or dampen it if not. This practice is often called "emergent practice" and involves a constant iterative process of learning and responding to what is learnt.[21] The Stanford Legal Design Lab is carrying out emergent practice as it "researches, designs, and develops new interventions to ensure equal access to justice for all."[22] In attempting to address the complex access to justice problem,

18 ibid.

19 ibid.

20 For example, see Marque Lawyers 'How We Charge' (Marque Lawyers, n.d.) <https://www.marquelawyers.com.au/litigation> accessed 10 February 2023.

21 Snowden and Boone (n 16).

22 Stanford Law School, 'The Legal Design Lab' (*Stanford Law School*, n.d.) <https://law.stanford.edu/organizations/pages/legal-design-lab/#slsnav-gallery> accessed

the Lab is working in the "realm of unknown unknowns" and "unpredictability and flux."[23] They are letting patterns emerge and then helpfully highlighting these in the form of taxonomies,[24] case studies,[25] and pattern libraries.[26] Being able to recognise complex systems allows us to re-frame situations. What might feel like a complicated situation where a problem-solving framework, like design thinking, can be applied by experts, may in fact be a complex situation, where we need to employ emergent practice. For legal designers working in the complex legal system, this can be both a liberating and a sobering realisation.

In contrast, chaotic systems require rapid responses and can be particularly challenging because these situations often lack any sort of recognisable patterns that could be used to better understand the relationships and connections between different parts of the system.[27] For example, the situation that many community legal centres had to contend with in the early days of the COVID-19 pandemic could be described as chaotic. These situations required decisive action to be taken that could enable these organisations to remain open. For example, Speakeasy Law Centre, a community legal centre operating in Cardiff (Wales), responded to the chaotic situation by changing its practices overnight and installing a postbox so that legal papers could be dropped off by members of the public in a hygienic manner.[28] These examples demonstrate how an enhanced systemic sensibility can enable the legal designer to approach situations appropriately and how vastly different the approaches need to be. This further underscores the importance of being able to identify when a one-size-fits-all approach is insufficient and when a more tailored approach is necessary.

---

12 February 2023.

23 Snowden and Boone (n 16).

24 LIST, 'LIST=Legal Issues Taxonomy' (*Stanford Legal Design Lab*, n.d.) <https://taxonomy.legal/> accessed 13 February 2023.

25 Stanford Legal Design Lab, 'Legal Design and Innovation' (*Stanford Legal Design Lab*, n.d.) <'https://medium.com/legal-design-and-innovation> accessed 12 February 2023.

26 A better legal internet, 'A better legal internet' (*Stanford Legal Design Lab*, n.d.) <https://betterinternet.law.stanford.edu/> accessed 13 February 2023.

27 Snowden and Boone (n 16).

28 Speakeasy Law Centre, 'Speakeasy Law Centre' (Speakeasy Law Centre, n.d.) <https://www.speakeasy.cymru/eng> accessed 12 February 2023.

In addition to recognising different system types, a shared language regarding the different components of systems is particularly useful for legal designers for they can be a way to describe concepts that are sometimes difficult to explain or non-obvious. It is outside the scope of this article, but a good understanding of the concepts of self-organisation, emergent behaviour, context and information flow is useful for it can enhance a legal designer's ability to recognise what system they are embedded within and how to make sense of what might be happening within the system. This also enables the legal designer to tell stories about systems that can encapsulate complexity easily and simply.

3. Storytelling in the Law

3.1. How Legal Designers Use Stories

If systems thinking is how a legal designer can *think* about the situations that they come across, storytelling is how a legal designer can *describe* what is happening. Storytelling is an integral part of a legal designer's toolkit. As a method, stories can be used by legal designers to elicit contextual information,[29] or when utilised as a part of "Anecdote Circles", which involves supporting a group of people to engage in a discussion relating to a set of themes, they can be used in a group setting to "reveal insights one could never predict from the outset."[30] Stories can also be a way to share insights from user research activities, and when done well can make the problems relatable and inspire action.[31] But when used poorly, they can be at best unmemorable and at worst lead to misrep-

---

29 Kim Gausepohl, Woodrow Winchester, Tonya Smith-Jackson, Brian Kleiner and James Arthur, 'A conceptual model for the role of storytelling in design: leveraging narrative inquiry in user-centered design (UCD)' (2016) 6(2) Health and Technology 125, 125.

30 Shawn Callahan, Andrew Rixon and Mark Schenk, 'The Ultimate Guide to Anecdote Circles' (*anecdote*, 2006) <https://www.anecdote.com/pdfs/papers/Ultimate_Guide_to_ACs_v1.0.pdf> accessed 13 February 2023.

31 Raya Raycheva, 'Communicating user research learnings is a storytelling exercise' (*UX Collective*, 13 March 2019) <https://uxdesign.cc/communicating-user-research-learnings-is-a-storytelling-exercise-2c163e21058e> accessed 13 February 2023.

resentation about the subject of the story. In this section, we will focus on the way stories are used to share insights from research activities, and explore the way legal designers typically use stories for this purpose and the pitfalls to which they are often susceptible.

Personas are a great tool for communicating the needs, motivations and challenges of research subjects. They provide a useful framework for organising and visualising user research data in a meaningful way, helping to identify patterns, similarities, and differences in the behaviour and attitudes of the people being studied. Personas provide a way to bring user research data to life, helping to create an image of the user with specific traits, needs, and motivations. Often represented as cards, with a profile of a fictional character and relevant demographic and behavioural information alongside it, personas seek to encapsulate the research data and present it in a way that's memorable.[32]

However, as Kim Salazer points out "these are just the representations of personas... What you really want is to get personas off the paper and into the minds of your colleagues. You want personas to be naturally and organically referenced in every discussion and decision that is made."[33] If not utilised well, personas run the risk of remaining static artefacts. Personas also run the risk of being reductive to the point that they focus on only the aspects that are relevant to the product, service or system rather than encapsulating the whole person and their context. This can lead to a single-dimensional view of a user and result in a lack of understanding of the complexities and nuances of the user's experience.

Case studies are also used by legal designers to share knowledge and experiences from successful projects, and to celebrate success with colleagues and peers. Through this form of collaboration, legal designers can learn from each other and improve their practice. However, the lack of them may also misrepresent what is happening in reality. As one LegalTech commentator raised in a recent post on social media, she was unsure whether the definition of legal design had narrowed due to a recent trend she had observed where proponents were mainly focused

32 Christin Roman, 'The Problem with Personas' (*Type/Code*, 27 February 2019) <https://medium.com/typecode/the-problem-with-personas-b6734a08d37a> accessed 6 February 2023.

33 Kim Salazar, 'Why Personas Fail' (*Nielsen Norman Group*, 28 January 2018) <https://www.nngroup.com/articles/why-personas-fail/> accessed 6 February 2023.

on the design of contracts.[34] She made this assumption based on the number of case studies that had been published that showcased the success of these projects. Moreover, how the success is shared is often questionable. Many of these case studies, developed by private companies, are not genuinely shared or data about their evaluation is not made available.[35] Yet, this is simply a misrepresentation of the work that is happening in this space. Arguably, one of the reasons why we may hear about contract design projects is that it's often easier to write about these projects as they can be neatly packaged up and produce tangible results. Another possible reason is that contract design is one of the first "cribs" of legal design. Information design projects in this field were the first ones to be developed and not just within the confines of "legal design" rhetoric. Why are case studies about systemic change so few and far between? How might we write stories that encapsulate these hard-to-define inputs and outputs?

3.2. Using Stories for Systems Change

Stories are especially powerful devices for presenting the complexity found within systems. For the rest of this article, we will explore the way that stories can be used as a device to not only drive systems change but also help to shine a light on the way systems change.[36] Inspired by the work of Thea Snow and others,[37] the focus of this article will be looking at how legal designers can use stories for systems change to engage both hearts and minds.

---

34 Nicola Shaver, CEO and Co-Founder, Legaltech Hub, (*LinkedIn*, 10 February 2023) <https://www.linkedin.com/posts/nicola-shaver-21b436b_legal-legaldesign-legal-services-activity-7029531338076487680-g5_n?utm_source=share&utm_medium=member_desktop> accessed 12 February 2023.

35 See, for instance: Rae Morgan and Emily Allbon, 'Is law really that special?' n Rossana Ducato and Alain Strowel (eds), *Legal Design Perspectives: Theoretical and Practical Insights from the Field* (Ledizioni 2021).

36 Thea Snow, David Murikumthara, Teya Dusseldorp, Rachel Fyfe, Lila Wolff and Jane McCracken, 'Storytelling for Systems Change: insights from the field' (Centre for Public Impact, n.d.) <https://www.centreforpublicimpact.org/assets/documents/storytelling-for-systems-change-report.pdf> accessed 10 February 2023.

37 ibid.

The definition of systems change that we will use is that offered by the UK think tank and consultancy for the social sector, New Philanthropy Capital (NPC): “Systems change aims to bring about lasting change by altering underlying structures and supporting mechanisms which make the system operate in a particular way. These can include policies, routines, relationships, resources, power structures and values.”[38] This definition is useful as it captures both the intent behind systems change (the what) as well as possible ways to bring about systems change (the how).

It is well known that changes in how systems function are unlikely until “a critical mass of people hold a particular view and the system reaches a tipping point”.[39] Stories and messages are often viewed as the most effective way at engaging a critical mass of people to alter these underlying structures and supporting mechanisms. This has been recognised by many community organisations, like the First Nations collective *Passing the message stick*, which is on a mission to change the mainstream narrative about Aboriginal and Torres Strait Islander peoples.[40] They speak about the importance of repetition: “when we all use the same effective messages we can shift public support and win a transformative policy agenda.”[41] Groups like *Passing the message stick* are creating change in their communities by disrupting the predominant narrative. It is through narrative change that systems can change. We explore the interplay between narrative and stories and worldviews below.

Stories have the potential to contribute significantly to systemic change. They can inspire and move people to action, and can be a powerful tool for social and political transformation. However, there are also several intrinsic and extrinsic limits to the impact of storytelling. One of the intrinsic limits is the fact that stories are often subjective and can be interpreted in different ways by different people. This can sometimes lead to misunderstandings and confusion, which can limit the ability of stories to bring about change. Additionally, many stories are limited

38 NPC, ‘Systems change: A guide to what it is and how to do it’ (NPC, 23 June 2015) <https://www.thinknpc.org/resource-hub/systems-change-a-guide-to-what-it-is-and-how-to-do-it/> accessed 13 February 2023.

39 Passing the message stick, ‘About’ (Passing the message stick, n.d.) <https://passingthemessagestick.org/about> accessed 13 February 2023.

40 ibid.

41 ibid.

by their form or medium. Certain types of stories, such as those found within case studies, may not have the time or space to fully explore complex issues or ideas. Extrinsic limits to the impact of storytelling include factors such as access and distribution. Stories that are not widely available or that are not promoted effectively may not reach their intended audience, and may therefore have limited impact. Additionally, the cultural and political context in which stories are presented can also limit their impact. Stories that challenge the status quo or that promote marginalised perspectives may face resistance or backlash from those in power.

3.3. The Interplay Between Stories and Narratives

One of the key aspects of stories that are about systems change is that they can often be presented as disconnected or random, but when sewn together, an underlying narrative can form. The *Narrative Initiative* has crystallised this concept in their *Waves* model that eloquently explains the components of deep narrative change.[42] The framework clearly sets out the dynamics between messages, stories, narratives, worldviews and values (see Figure 3). It uses a very simple metaphor of a wave driven by a current to explain the interplay between values and worldviews and how they drive a narrative. It expands this metaphor to also consider how stories and messages, which can feel independent and disorderly, are often driven by narratives, just as the ocean's surface, which can feel disorientating and unpredictable, is largely driven by what is happening underneath.

---

42 Narrative Initiative, 'Waves: A model for deep narrative change' (*Narrative Initiative* 8 July 2020) <https://narrativeinitiative.org/blog/waves-a-model-for-deep-narrative-change/> accessed 5 February 2023.

Fig. 3. Waves is a simple model to explain the components of deep narrative change.[43]
© Narrative Initiative, 2020. Reproduced with permission.

3.3.1. Messages and Stories

Just like the ocean surface that is subject to the whim of the environment, like a gusty wind, stories and messages are often reactive to the environment. Being surface-level, it is usually what we see when we look out at the ocean and we can be mistaken to believe that that is all there is to the ocean. The ocean's surface, much like stories and messages, is accessible. We can see stories and messages floating on the surface, and if we are not careful, we may not appreciate what lies beneath.

As Fleurie Forbes-Martin, Story & Growth Director at Stronger Stories, describes, "the three principles that we always share are the strongest stories are the ones people already tell themselves; the only thing that can replace that story is a stronger one; and it takes 1,000 stronger stories to change the narrative."[44] The Lean Story Canvas is an effective tool

43 ibid.

44 Interview with Fleurie Forbes-Martin, Story & Growth Director, Stronger Stories (Virtual, 24 January 2023).

for building an effective story.[45] The Canvas contains nine building blocks that aims to help the user refine the target group or individual, the environment, the behaviour that stands in the way of change, the trigger for change, what the first step will look like and so on. It is crucial to think carefully about what story is going to be appropriate for the message one is trying to convey and the environment in which it will be received. When crafting stories, it is important to consider whether the environment is conducive to smooth sailing or whether it will be treacherous high seas.

3.3.2. Narratives

Narratives infuse stories with deeper meaning. Identifying the predominant narratives is one of the key steps that *Stronger Stories* takes when first working with a client.[46] Like waves, they influence what happens on the surface level, but they are often unnoticeable on the water's surface. Narratives are a constellation of stories related to one another, held together by a common thread. By analysing these narratives we can start to identify the values and worldviews that underpin them.

3.3.3. Values and Worldviews

Values and worldviews are deeply embedded in our cultures. They are the currents that drive the waves that influence what we see on the surface of the ocean. They are the beliefs that we each hold, unknowingly or not. These beliefs shape how we interpret what we see and what we hear. Often described as a lens, they inform how we see ourselves, our communities and others. Forbes-Martin from *Stronger Stories* highlights that for their team, they've learned that making stories relatable isn't through demographics, it's by... speaking directly to the values that drive people.[47]

The Waves model can be used as a tool to assist legal designers think about what stories they want to tell and what may be influencing these stories and describe how narratives are influenced by deeply held beliefs. It can also provide legal designers with a way to work with their

45 Stronger Stories, 'The Lean Story Canvas' (Stronger Stories, n.d) <https://strongerstories.org/canvas/> accessed 12 February 2023.

46 Forbes-Martin (n 44).

47 ibid.

clients to articulate and identify dominant narratives and replace these with their desired ones. It's a useful framework for legal designers seeking to engage in more storytelling in their practice.

4. Application to Real Life

Now that we've better understood how systems thinking and storytelling can be applied in the law, it's time to get practical. *How might we use stories for systems change?* Underlying this next section is the understanding that stories bring about change because they operate at two levels simultaneously. At the individual level, they help people to build empathy, shift their mindsets and see new possibilities through discussion and debate.[48] Systems can only change when people change. Stories can act as a powerful catalyst for people to reframe how they see themselves and how they relate to others.[49] At the system level, stories can play a role in "reshaping the rules of the systems" and articulating how systems are changing.[50] Stories can help to make sense of the current landscape and how it has been shaped by the forces that have acted upon it. They can also provide insights into how the system is evolving and how it may look in the future, helping to create a shared understanding of the changes that are taking place.

An analysis of good stories highlights several common features: good stories are known for being "resonant, clear and relatable", and "guided and bound by agreed protocols".[51] Good stories resonate emotionally with the listener, conveying a sense of relatability. They are persuasive and engaging because they connect on a deeper level than mere data points can provide. They avoid academic language and instead offer authentic, inclusive and gentle language. They can also provide more context than numbers alone because they can tap into past experiences and emotions through literary tools like analogies and metaphors.

48 Snow and others (n 36).
49 ibid.
50 ibid.
51 ibid.

4.1. Learning From Other Sectors

Systemic narratives have already been utilised in other industries to tackle issues from a systemic perspective. These unique stories provide a platform for people to come together, to find common ground, to be inspired and motivated, and to create a shared vision for the future. Systemic narratives can be used to draw attention to the complexity of a particular issue, to help to make sense of it, and to provide a framework for collective action. They can help to shift perspectives, to open up possibilities, and to create an environment where new solutions can be imagined and explored. Ultimately, these stories have the power to bring people together, to unify them, and to help them to develop a shared vision of what the future could look like.

A good example of a systemic narrative is the Doughnut. Kate Raworth developed the Doughnut of social and planetary boundaries in 2017, as a "playfully serious approach to framing the challenge of balancing life's essentials (like clean water and food) to overshooting our pressure on Earth's life-supporting systems" (Figure 4).[52] This simple concept has captured the essence of the Sustainable Development Goals and transformed it into a story that has awakened the imaginations of communities across the world. For example, in Melbourne, Australia, Regen Melbourne has co-created the local Melbourne Doughnut (Figure 5), which has been augmented to accommodate Melbourne's unique character, problems and opportunities.[53] Crucially, the Melbourne Doughnut is "organic and alive" and will be shaped as the Regen Melbourne community uses it and contributes to it. As Forbes-Martin from *Stronger Stories* warns, "stories are living and messy things that constantly evolve and change".[54] By remaining "open", this can foster the conditions for people to inject new thoughts and ideas into stories, apply them in different contexts and keep them sustainable.

---

52 Kate Raworth, 'What on Earth is the Doughnut?...' (*Kate Raworth*, n.d.) <https://www.kateraworth.com/doughnut/> accessed 10 February 2023.

53 Regen Melbourne, 'Regen Melbourne: an evolving journey' (Doughnut Economics Action Lab, 16 May 2023) <https://doughnuteconomics.org/stories/252> accessed 28 June 2023.

54 Forbes-Martin (n 44).

Legal designers can learn a thing or two from the humble Doughnut. First, it has enabled the transformation of the Sustainable Development Goals (SDGs) from largely disparate goals into a simplified concise form. What if we took the principles and goals of the General Data Protection Regulation (GDPR) and made sense of them in an easy to remember diagram? It's likely this may make the principles more memorable and therefore, applied more readily. Second, the Doughnut has transitioned the SDGs focus away from growth, to balance.[55] The Doughnut does this by placing an ecological ceiling on each of the SDGs and highlighting when ecosystems are at risk of being unable to sustain our resource consumption. For legal designers, what if we were able to place some visual boundaries on the criminal justice system? What if we could visualise how the system must strike a balance between retributive justice and restorative justice. Third, the Doughnut has made sense of this complex space in a way that is easy to absorb and talk about. The simple use of red and green to signal whether a particular jurisdiction is either overshooting or underperforming with respect to the SDGs makes it clear where effort should be put and what problems should be tackled as a priority. Legal designers can wield their visual design skills in a similar way to pinpoint what is important and what can be deprioritised.

4.2. How Might We Use Stories for Systems Change in the Law?

The focus of this article is to inspire the use of more stories that can be used within the justice space. A good example of using systemic narrative in the legal space is the work of The Chancery Lane Project (TCLP). TCLP is an ambitious collaborative initiative, which brings together close to 3000 legal and industry professionals across the globe in order to address climate change.[56]

---

55 Edwina Landale, Introducing Melbourne To Doughnut Economics (*City of Melbourne,* n.d.) <https://mkw.melbourne.vic.gov.au/insight/introducing-melbourne-to-doughnut-economics/> accessed 25 May 2023.

56 The Chancery Lane Project, 'About The Chancery Lane Project' (*The Chancery Lane Project*, n.d.) <https://chancerylaneproject.org/about/> accessed 13 February 2023.

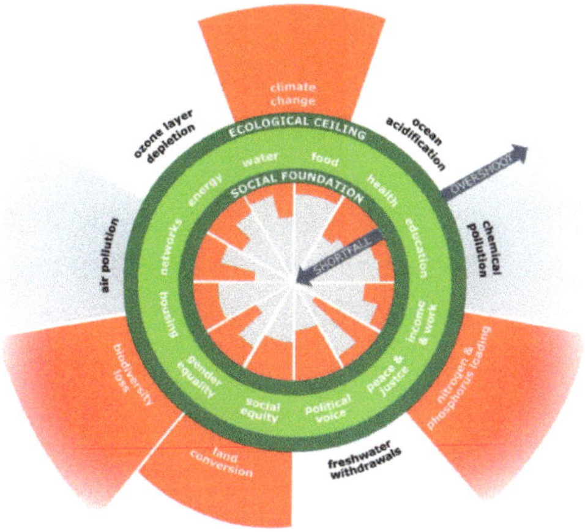

Fig. 4. "The Doughnut of social and planetary boundaries" © Kate Raworth and Christian Guthier, 2017. Creative Commons Attribution-ShareAlike 4.0 International Licence.

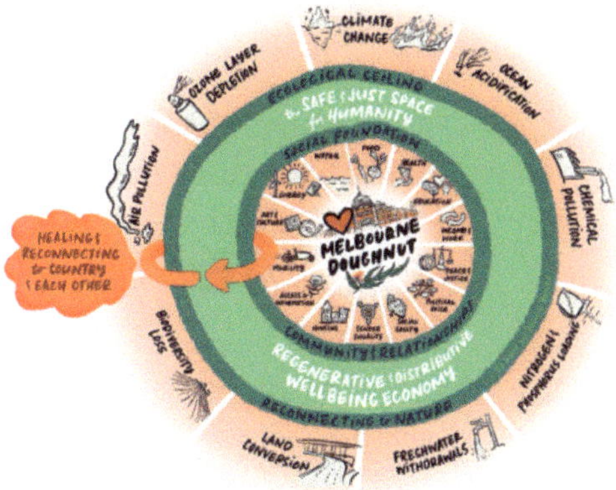

Fig. 5. "The Melbourne Doughnut" © Regen Melbourne, 2021. Creative Commons Attribution-ShareAlike 4.0 International Licence.

Working in close partnership, these professionals use their expertise to create new and practical contractual clauses which can be easily incorporated into law firm precedents and commercial agreements to provide long-term climate solutions.[57] Through this initiative, they are utilising their deep understanding of the complexities of legal systems, contracts and markets, and harnessing these to achieve meaningful and sustainable systemic environmental change. Stories play a key role in inspiring professionals to join in. Ben Metz, Executive Director, talks about the "aha moment" him and his team had at the beginning of TCLP where it dawned on them that they should start using stories: "we had this idea of riffing off superheroes because lawyers are mild-mannered Clark Kents... and underneath great responsibility comes a great power but just nobody's tapping into it."[58] This storyline runs through all of their work. As a next step, Metz also shares that an ambition he has is to cre-

57 ibid.

58 Interview with Ben Metz, Executive Director, The Chancery Lane Project (Virtual, 27 January 2023).

ate an origin story template that would act as the source material for the drafting of a clause that could be used by a lawyer, and then the relevant elements could be adapted to be used by a congressperson to create the wraparound narrative and story. This initiative is yet to commence, but it sounds promising. By using stories, TCLP has tapped into the rich resource of lawyers operating in very different capacities across the world and is incrementally bringing about the change needed to address the very large complex wicked problem: climate change.

4.3. What's Next?

As alluded to above, legal designers are already using stories in multiple ways. By augmenting client-generated stories with observation and empathy, client stories are no longer at the centre of the legal design process.[59] Instead, their needs are. Arguably this enhances the client narratives as they can be more fully realised through the expansive process of legal design. Yet, there is also an inherent risk in making sense of the stories we hear and transforming these into representative artefacts, as legal designers each hold a set of biases that are sometimes hard to discern. Whenever possible, stories should be told in the language and voice of the community being represented.[60] Power should be placed in the hands of story-holders. They must be able to decide which stories should be told and how they should be narrated.

With the advance of ChatGPT, AI presents a new frontier for telling stories. Stronger Stories are exploring how AI compares to what they can produce from "a place of intuition and experience and, you know, heart."[61] Forbes-Martin suspects that AI will struggle to identify what it is about story building blocks that resonate. While AI can parse through data and produce helpful insights, it cannot yet capture the complexity of what really drives people to engage with a story in a meaningful way. That's where legal designers come in.

59 Martha F Davis, 'What Is Essential: Legal Design And Client Stories' (2021) 13 The Elon Law Journal 39, 74.

60 Snow and others (n 36).

61 Forbes-Martin (n 44).

ChatGPT may also be biassed and can produce fake results.[62] In instances where accuracy and impartiality are crucial, this can be particularly concerning. For example, if legal designers were to start building a conversational chatbot based on data that exists about decisions made in the courts, there are several reasons why this might pose issues. The large datasets that are required to develop chatbots like this may be trained on biassed data that may lead to biassed outputs that can perpetuate systemic inequalities. Moreover, it may not be possible to account for the nuances and complexities of legal decision-making, which could lead to inaccurate or incomplete information being provided to users. When developing and implementing ChatGPT in legal contexts, it is crucial to carefully consider the potential risks and drawbacks of this technology.

5. Conclusion

After Liz had researched how stories from other sectors had been used to bring about change, she decided to apply the same techniques to the law. She realised that good stories needed to be guided and bound by protocols, and that stories about systems change needed to embrace nonlinear, dynamic and more fluid forms. She also learned the importance of making sure the stories were resonant, warm and relatable, and that they should not be used to promote any agenda or to claim any kind of dominance.

The legal designer was determined to ensure that the stories she told would be honest, authentic, and inclusive. She wanted to make sure that it was story-holders who had the power to decide which stories should be told, and how they should be told. With a newfound understanding of the power of stories, she was ready to start telling stories that would enable systemic change in the legal domain.

---

62 Tiffany Hsu and Stuart A. Thompson 'Disinformation Researchers Raise Alarms About A.I. Chatbots' (*The New York Times*, 8 February 2023) < https://www.nytimes.com/2023/02/08/technology/ai-chatbots-disinformation.html> accessed 9 May 2023.

She began by creating stories about the lived experiences of individuals within the justice system to communicate their needs and push for change. She used empathy to understand their motivations and feelings, allowing her to create a more holistic narrative that captured the nuances of the situation. She also applied a systems thinking lens to ensure that the nuance and complexity of the system in which the individuals operated within was captured.

Through her stories, she brought people together and helped them envision a better future. People began to understand the implications of their actions and make decisions that would create more equitable and accessible legal systems. Using the Doughnut as inspiration, she created a visualisation of the complex legal landscape and provided her client with a way to talk about the problems they were encountering. Her stories had a ripple effect, inspiring systemic change and transforming the landscape incrementally.

We often hear the cry "We need systems change" to refer to the need to address the many complex and interconnected problems we face in today's society. From climate change to systemic bias held against marginalised groups, the need to address these systemic problems is urgent now more than ever. As society is fragmenting down societal, economic, and political boundaries, finding ways to identify and align around how to shift these complex systems forward is crucial. In the passage above, Liz's reflections are a reminder that stories can be powerful tools to bring about change, and that by wielding stories well, we can create a better future.

Systems thinking offers not only enhanced awareness about these often nonobvious forces but also provides the tools to map these forces, bring them to light and help people to identify where to intervene for the greatest impact. By developing an awareness of the larger social, economic and political systems in which people and entities are embedded, legal designers can gain a deeper insight into the broader implications of their work.

Combining systems thinking with storytelling enables legal designers to be equipped to express the complex situations that they are designing within. By looking at the problem from a holistic perspective, legal designers can gain a better understanding of the interconnections that exist between the various elements of the situation, providing a comprehensive overview and enabling them to bring about the desired outcome.

Bibliography

A better legal internet, 'A better legal internet' (Stanford Legal Design Lab, n.d.) <https://betterinternet.law.stanford.edu/> accessed 13 February 2023

Callahan S, A Rixon and M Schenk, 'The Ultimate Guide to Anecdote Circles' (anecdote, 2006) <https://www.anecdote.com/pdfs/papers/Ultimate_Guide_to_ACs_v1.0.pdf> accessed 13 February 2023

Davis M, 'What Is Essential: Legal Design And Client Stories' (2021) 13 The Elon Law Journal 39

Edson M, P D Tuddenham and P Buckle-Henning, 'Systems Research: A Foundation for Systems Literacy' (2016) Proceedings of the 2016 IFSR Conversation Team 3: Systems Research Team

Forbes-Martin F, Story & Growth Director, Stronger Stories (Virtual, 24 January 2023)

Gausepohl K, W Winchester, T Smith-Jackson, B Kleiner and J Arthur, 'A conceptual model for the role of storytelling in design: leveraging narrative inquiry in user-centered design (UCD)' (2016) 6(2) Health and Technology 125

Hagan M, Law by Design (n.d.) <https://lawbydesign.co/design-mindsets/> accessed 31 January 2023

Hietanen-Kunwald P, H Haapio, and N Toivonen, 'Systems Theory as a Research Framework for Dispute Prevention and Resolution by Design' in R Ducato and A Strowel (eds), *Legal Design Perspectives: Theoretical and Practical Insights from the Field* (Ledizioni 2021)

Hsu T and S Thompson 'Disinformation Researchers Raise Alarms About A.I. Chatbots' (The New York Times, 8 February 2023) < https://www.nytimes.com/2023/02/08/technology/ai-chatbots-disinformation.html> accessed 9 May 2023

Johnson C, 'What are Emergent Properties and How Do They Affect the Engineering of Complex Systems?' (University of Glasgow, n.d.) <https://www.dcs.gla.ac.uk/~johnson/papers/RESS/Complexity_Emergence_Editorial.pdf> accessed 13 February 2023

Landale E, 'Introducing Melbourne To Doughnut Economics' (City of Melbourne, n.d.) <https://mkw.melbourne.vic.gov.au/insight/introducing-melbourne-to-doughnut-economics/> accessed 25 May 2023

LIST, 'LIST=Legal Issues Taxonomy' (Stanford Legal Design Lab, n.d.) <https://taxonomy.legal/> accessed 13 February 2023

LoPucki L, 'Systems Approach to Law' (1997) 82 Cornell Law Review 479

Marque Lawyers 'How We Charge' (Marque Lawyers, n.d.) <https://www.marquelawyers.com.au/litigation> accessed 10 February 2023

Merriam-Webster, 'System' <https://www.merriam-webster.com/dictionary/system> accessed 11 February 2023

Metz B, Executive Director, The Chancery Lane Project (Virtual, 27 January 2023)

Morgan R and Allbon E, 'Is law really that special?' in R Ducato and A Strowel (eds), *Legal Design Perspectives: Theoretical and Practical Insights from the Field* (Ledizioni 2021)

Narrative Initiative, 'Waves: A model for deep narrative change' (Narrative Initiative 8 July 2020) <https://narrativeinitiative.org/blog/waves-a-model-for-deep-narrative-change/> accessed 5 February 2023

NPC, 'Systems change: A guide to what it is and how to do it' (NPC, 23 June 2015) <https://www.thinknpc.org/resource-hub/systems-change-a-guide-to-what-it-is-and-how-to-do-it/> accessed 13 February 2023

Passing the message stick, 'About' (Passing the message stick, n.d.) <https://passingthemessagestick.org/about> accessed 13 February 2023

Posner R, *Law and Literature* (Harvard University Press 2009)

Pierson-Brown T, '(Systems) Thinking Like a Lawyer' (2020) 26 Clinical Law Review 515

Raworth K, 'What on Earth is the Doughnut?...' (Kate Raworth, n.d.) <https://www.kateraworth.com/doughnut/> accessed 10 February 2023

Raycheva R, 'Communicating user research learnings is a storytelling exercise' (UX Collective, 13 March 2019) <https://uxdesign.cc/communicating-user-research-learnings-is-a-storytelling-exercise-2c163e21058e> accessed 13 February 2023

Regen Melbourne, 'The Melbourne Doughnut' (Regen Melbourne, n.d.) <https://www.regen.melbourne/research-content/melbdoughnut> accessed 10 February 2023

Roman C, 'The Problem with Personas' (Type/Code, 27 February 2019) <https://medium.com/typecode/the-problem-with-personas-b6734a08d37a> accessed 6 February 2023

Salazar K, 'Why Personas Fail' (Nielsen Norman Group, 28 January 2018) <https://www.nngroup.com/articles/why-personas-fail/> accessed 6 February 2023

Shaver N, CEO and Co-Founder, Legaltech Hub, (LinkedIn, 10 February 2023) <https://www.linkedin.com/posts/nicola-shaver-21b436b_legal-legaldesign-legalservices-activity-7029531338076487680-g5_n?utm_source=share&utm_medium=member_desktop> accessed 12 February 2023

Snow T, D Murikumthara, T Dusseldorp, R Fyfe, L Wolff and J McCracken, 'Storytelling for Systems Change: insights from the field' (Centre for Public Impact, n.d.) <https://www.centreforpublicimpact.org/assets/documents/storytelling-for-systems-change-report.pdf> accessed 10 February 2023

Snowden D, 'The Cynefin Framework' (CognitiveEdge, 12 July 2010) <https://youtu.be/N7oz366X0-8> accessed 10 February 2023

Snowden D and M Boone, 'A Leader's Framework for Decision Making' (Harvard Business Review, November 2007) <https://hbr.org/2007/11/a-leaders-framework-for-decision-making> accessed 13 February 2023

Speakeasy Law Centre, 'Speakeasy Law Centre' (Speakeasy Law Centre, n.d.) <https://www.speakeasy.cymru/eng> accessed 12 February 2023

Stanford Law School, 'The Legal Design Lab' (Stanford Law School, n.d.) <https://law.stanford.edu/organizations/pages/legal-design-lab/#slsnav-gallery> accessed 12 February 2023

Stanford Legal Design Lab, 'Legal Design and Innovation' (Stanford Legal Design Lab, n.d.) <'https://medium.com/legal-design-and-innovation> accessed 12 February 2023

Stronger Stories, 'The Lean Story Canvas' (Stronger Stories, n.d) <https://strongerstories.org/canvas/> accessed 12 February 2023

The Chancery Lane Project, 'About The Chancery Lane Project' (The Chancery Lane Project, n.d.) <https://chancerylaneproject.org/about/> accessed 13 February 2023

van der Watt M, and A van der Westhuizen, '(Re)configuring the criminal justice response to human trafficking: a complex-systems perspective' (2017) 18(3) Police Practice and Research 218

Woodhill J and J Millican, 'Systems Thinking and Practice: A guide to concepts, principles and tools for FCDO and partners' (Institute of Development Studies, February 2023)

4. SOLIDARITY BY DESIGN: GENERATING COUNTERNARRATIVES ABOUT PEOPLE POWER

Hallie Jay Pope

Abstract
When ordinary people exercise their collective power, they can disrupt and even dismantle systems of elite rule. But in recent decades, the American Left has moved away from organising strategies that regard ordinary people as the authors of their own liberation, instead favouring shallower mobilisation tactics that accept elite rule as incontestable. This shift has coincided with the rollback of many of the progressive victories won by the labour and civil rights movements. How might design methods support a resurgence of deep, transformative organising efforts? This paper will explore critical play as a method for fostering faith in ordinary-people power.

1. Introduction

Legal designers concerned with dismantling oppressive systems must reckon with today's political reality. Over the past few decades, the corporate class in the United States has systematically dismantled many of the gains of the labour and civil rights movements. Economic inequality is deepening, reactionary politics are resurging, and substantial progressive victories are few and far between. Union organiser and scholar Jane McAlevey attributes this trajectory to the Left's shift in strategy "away from deep *organizing* and toward shallow *mobilizing*."[1]

Mobilising and organising are rooted in two very different theories about the power of "ordinary people" (a term McAlevey borrows from sociologist and activist Frances Fox Piven). Mobilising depends on large numbers of ordinary people to participate in campaigns for change, but in a shallow way, reserving meaningful control for professional staffers. This approach rests on the assumption that elite rule is inevitable, that

1 Jane F McAlevey, *No Shortcuts: Organizing for Power in the New Gilded Age* (OUP 2016) 2.

the best we can hope for is to replace bad elites with friendlier elites.[2] Organising, on the other hand, "places the agency for success with a continually expanding base of ordinary people," and seeks "to transfer power from the elite to the majority."[3] This approach "assumes that the very idea of who holds power is itself contestable,"[4] and reflects an understanding that ordinary-people power is essential for meaningful transformation.

Successful organising requires getting ordinary people to recognize and believe in their own power, to reject the notion that the status quo is inevitable; only then will they put their jobs and bodies on the line to fight the corporate elite. It also requires professional activists, lawyers, and other allied "elites" to understand that ordinary people can and should hold power; only then will they wield their own power in solidarity and relinquish it to ordinary people whenever possible. How might we change the way we conceive of our own power and the power of others? We use narratives to make sense of our experiences and ourselves.[5] Fostering a belief in ordinary-people power necessitates the creation of counterstories that challenge the dominant narrative of elite power.

This paper will investigate critical play as a tool for reimagining power, with the aim of contributing to a fruitful mindset for movement organising. Part I examines the transformative role of ordinary-people power—and *belief* in this power—in the context of two pivotal moments in American history: the labour movement in the 1930s, and the civil rights movement in the 1960s. Part II argues that efforts to cultivate belief in ordinary-people power will benefit from the generation of counternarratives, stories that challenge our shared latent understandings of elite power. Finally, Part III explores critical play as one potential method for generating and engaging with counternarratives about ordinary-people power. This paper builds on my previous exploration of convoking radical imagination in the context of liberatory legal design projects.[6] Can play-

2 McAlevey (n 1) 4.

3 ibid 10.

4 ibid.

5 See George Lakoff, *The Political Mind: A Cognitive Scientist's Guide to Your Brain and Its Politics* (Penguin Books 2009) 33.

6 See Hallie Jay Pope, 'Liberatory legal design and radical imagination' in D Lockton, S Lenzi, P Hekkert, A Oak, J Sádaba, P Lloyd (eds), *DRS2022: Bilbao* (2022) <https://

ful immersion in counternarratives contest the inevitability of elite rule and inspire faith in the power of ordinary people?

2. Why Ordinary-people Power Matters

McAlevey begins *No Shortcuts* with an observation that is sobering for anyone striving for collective liberation in the United States: "Many of the biggest victories of the past 100 years, those won in the heyday of the labour and civil rights movements, have been all but rolled back."[7] To be fair, many wins from this era remain embedded in American structures and cultures—so much so that we take them for granted and forget that they were born of mass struggles.[8] But through a decades-long multifront campaign, corporate interests have ushered in a new gilded age, one marked by privatisation, deregulation, mass incarceration, voter suppression, and immense income and wealth inequality.[9]

How did we get here? "Why were the achievements won during the heyday of the pre-McCarthy labour movement and the civil rights movement so substantial compared with the progressive achievements of the past forty years?"[10] McAlevey argues that truly significant and durable movement victories have historically resulted—and indeed, can only result—from the agency and power of ordinary people.[11] Specifically, these gains stem from the threat or exercise of large-scale disruptive power, like strikes, when ordinary people leverage their ability "to disrupt a pattern of ongoing and institutionalized cooperation that depends on their continuing contributions."[12]

---

doi.org/10.21606/drs.2022.689>.

7 McAlevey (n 1) 7.

8 ibid.

9 ibid 7–8. See also Bernie Sanders, 'The US has a ruling class—and Americans must stand up to it' *The Guardian* (2 Sep 2022) <https://www.theguardiancom/commentisfree/2022/sep/02/the-us-has-a-ruling-class-and-americans-must-stand-up-to-it> accessed 27 Jan 2023.

10 McAlevey (n 1) 8.

11 ibid 8, 206.

12 Frances Fox Piven, *Challenging Authority: How Ordinary People Change America* (Rowman & Littlefield Publishers Inc 2006) 20–21. See also McAlevey (n 1) 206.

McAlevey attributes the Left's diminished capacity and willingness to exercise disruptive power to a shift in strategy from *organising* to *mobilising*. Organising relies on the "involvement of specific, large numbers of people whose power is derived from their ability to withdraw labour or other cooperation from those who rely on them."[13] Organising ordinary people who possess disruptive power creates the capacity to engage in mass tactics like strikes and sustained nonviolent direct action, tactics that led to the significant victories of the 1930s labour movement and 1960s civil rights movement. Mobilising, by contrast,[14] focuses on corporate campaigns led by professional staff or volunteer activists and aimed at generating media attention, influencing policy makers, and ultimately pressuring employers to make reforms. While such campaigns do require large numbers of people to participate, "it matters little who shows up, or, why, as long as a sufficient number of bodies appear—enough for a photo good enough to tweet and maybe generate earned media."[15] Under this strategy, staffers are the key agents, and ordinary people with disruptive power, like workers, are simply useful "messengers" for the staffers' vision of change.[16]

According to McAlevey, these two different strategies stem from two competing progressive theories of power.[17] The dominant mobilising model assumes that elite power is unchallengeable.[18] Subscribers to this theory seek to effect change by replacing "a very naughty elite with a 'better' elite, one they 'can work with'" to improve conditions for ordinary people.[19] The ruling class—or what McAlevey dubs the "priestly-kingly-corporate class"[20]—will always be the ruling class, and the best change-makers can strive for is to make their rule more palatable. This

13 McAlevey (n 1) 11.
14 McAlevey notes that organisers sometimes use mobilising as a tactic, but only in support of their overarching strategy of building and exercising mass disruptive power.
15 McAlevey (n 1) 10.
16 ibid 10, 53.
17 McAlevey notes that most liberals also share the belief that elite rule is inevitable. For liberals, this theory supports an advocacy model. For progressives, it underpins a mobilising model.
18 McAlevey (n 1) 4.
19 ibid.
20 ibid 3.

theory of power relegates ordinary people to the peripheral; in a mobilisation strategy, workers are merely one point of leverage among many against the inexorable power-holders. In other words, "[w]orkers are no longer essential to their own liberation."[21]

The organising model, on the other hand, rests on a belief that "the very idea of who holds power is itself contestable."[22] As Piven puts it, "the widely held thesis that power is based on control of wealth and force explains a good deal of our experience. But it does not explain all of our experience."[23] Rule by elites might feel inevitable, but an examination of our own history proves that their power is not absolute. Ordinary people hold a "vast potential power," the power to disrupt society and create change.[24] Adherents to this theory view ordinary people as "the primary agents of their own liberation."[25] This is why ordinary people are central to the organising strategy; the ultimate goal is "to transfer power from the elite to the majority,"[26] a majority "anchored in deep...solidarities and cooperative engagement in class struggle."[27]

2.1. Ordinary-people Power in Action

Movement scholar Charles M. Payne provides a detailed illustration of how ordinary-people power shaped civil rights activism in 1960s Mississippi. The civil rights movement held "two distinct traditions," traditions that parallel McAlevey's mobilising-organising dichotomy.[28] The "community-mobilizing tradition" epitomised by Martin Luther King "focused on large-scale, relatively short-term public events" like the March on Washington.[29] The Student Nonviolent Coordinating Committee (SNCC)'s voter registration efforts in Mississippi, on the other hand, "reflect[ed]

21 ibid 19.
22 ibid 4–5.
23 Piven (n 12) 19.
24 McAlevey (n 1) 5.
25 ibid 30.
26 ibid 10.
27 ibid 30.
28 Charles M Payne, *I've Got the Light of Freedom* (2nd edn, University of California Press 2007) 3.
29 ibid 3.

another tradition of Black activism, one of community organising, a tradition with a different sense of what freedom means and therefore a greater emphasis on the long-term development of leadership in ordinary men and women."[30] In Payne's estimation, SNCC's organising efforts during the early 1960s were "sufficiently transformative—empowering, if you will—that local people who had become active in that period were able to create and sustain several movement-related institutions, even in the face of decreasing help from...outside organizers."[31]

The community organising tradition in Mississippi stemmed largely from the philosophies and practices of Septima Clark, Myles Horton, and Ella Baker. These activists and educators shared a belief that ordinary people can and must be the authors of their own liberation. All three distrusted top-down organisations and leaders who had separate interests from the communities they claimed to serve.[32] As Baker put it, "strong people don't need strong leaders": an effective leader would be more of a teacher than a decision-maker, developing the leadership capacities of others through participatory politics.[33]

SNCC drew deeply from this organising framework when it set about registering Black voters in Mississippi. In 1962, SNCC organisers drafted a plan that "Ella Baker or Septima Clark could have written," stressing the importance of developing local leadership and using registration as "a means to the more important end of getting people politically involved."[34] Organisers facilitated opportunities for community members to take on tasks "they didn't think themselves 'qualified' to handle"—convincing others to vote, speaking at community meetings, engaging in demonstrations, and making decisions about the movement's direction and strategy—and "creat[ed] an atmosphere in which people fe[lt] free to make mistakes and try again."[35] SNCC began using voter registration as an opportunity to build Black Mississippians' capacity and self-determination in the early sixties. By the mid-sixties, "defiance of white

30 ibid 3.
31 ibid 4.
32 ibid 83, 93, 101.
33 ibid 93, 101.
34 ibid 129–30.
35 ibid 331.

supremacy had been institutionalized."[36] And by the late sixties, towns like Greenwood, Mississippi were home to numerous political initiatives developed and run by local folks who "carried on the struggle even as direct influence of SNCC was waning."[37]

Reliance on ordinary-people power also underpinned the Congress of Industrial Organization (CIO)'s successful workplace organising efforts in the early twentieth century. Founded in 1935, the CIO rejected the dominant organising philosophy of the time and built power "across the many 'isms'" by organizing workers of all skill-levels, races, genders, and ethnicities.[38] The CIO's president, John Lewis, was anti-communist and anti-socialist, but he was forced to rely on leftist organizers because they were the best at what they did. According to McAlevey, unions "led by leftist factions were not only the most effective but also the most democratic."[39] Their members fought for control over production, not just for material gains, and successful organizing efforts "resulted in high-quality contracts that cemented a high level of participation, active membership, and a strong relationship between the rank and file and union leaders."[40] In these early days of the CIO, "[s]trikes...were routine, and were evidence that workers *themselves* were the primary agents of their own liberation."[41]

Today, organisers who still follow the CIO model continue to emphasise identifying, recruiting, and developing "organic leaders" who already hold the respect of their fellow workers. Early in an organising effort, these organic leaders must persuade others to join them in high-risk displays of union support—like signing a petition or wearing a union sticker to work with each successive demonstration not only proving the leader's capability, but also facilitating mass involvement and building the workers' confidence in their collective power.[42] Workers who

36 ibid 316.

37 ibid 318.

38 McAlevey (n 1) 30–31.

39 McAlevey (n 1) 32, citing Judith Stephan-Norris and Maurice Zeitlin, *Left Out: Reds and America's Industrial Unions* (CUP 2002).

40 McAlevey (n 1) 32–33, citing Howard Kimeldorf, *Reds or Rackets?* (University of California Press 1992).

41 ibid 30.

42 ibid 34–35.

come to understand their own agency in this way are empowered not only to challenge elite power themselves, but to "unite their workplace and community relationships into a single struggle for decency and respect."[43] This kind of worker-centred organising is rare in our era of mobilisation, but nursing home workers in New England, teachers in Chicago, and factory workers in North Carolina have all successfully employed "whole worker"[44] organising tactics to strike and win, building and exercising ordinary-people power within and beyond the workplace.[45]

While mobilising might achieve limited victories, it cannot deliver us from this new gilded age. Only organising—placing "the primary agency for success on an ever-expanding base of ordinary people"[46]—can generate the disruptive power necessary to challenge elite rule.

2.2. Believing in Ordinary-people Power

When it comes to social change, "the actual limits of what is achievable depend in part on the beliefs people hold about what sorts of alternatives are viable."[47] We see this understanding reflected in both Payne's and McAlevey's accounts, which emphasise that a key part of successful mass organising is cultivating a *belief* in ordinary-people power. The legacy of organisers like Clark and Baker was "a faith that ordinary people who learn to believe in themselves are capable of extraordinary acts."[48] For SNCC activists in Mississippi, "whether a community achieved this or that tactical objective was likely to matter less than whether the people in it came to see themselves as having the right and the capacity to have some say-so in their own lives."[49] They measured success not by voter registration numbers, but by the cultivation of a sense of self-determination in the communities they organised.[50] "SNCC preached a gospel of individual efficacy. What you do matters. In order to move politically,

---

43 ibid 25.
44 ibid 58–59.
45 ibid 25.
46 ibid 206.
47 Erik Olin Wright, *Envisioning Real Utopias* (Verso 2010) 23.
48 Payne (n 28) 5.
49 ibid 68.
50 ibid 318.

people had to believe that."[51]

Similarly, in the labour context, McAlevey observes that "[l]arge numbers of people transition from unthinking 'masses' or 'the grassroots' or 'the workers' to serious and highly invested actors exercising agency when they come to see, to understand, and to value" their own power.[52] In workplace organising, believing in ordinary-people power is often a precursor to exercising it collectively. By deciding to participate in a disruptive action like a strike, a worker puts her livelihood at risk; such a risk is worthwhile only if she believes that she and her fellow workers have the power to prevail.[53] This sentiment is echoed in a list of advice circulated among union organisers: "Workers united can beat the boss. You have to believe that and so do they."[54]

That phrasing—"You have to believe that and so do they"—reveals that faith in ordinary-people power should extend beyond the people most directly affected by a problem of subordination, beyond the people directly participating in disruptive action. The ultimate purpose of organising is to take power from the 1%, the priestly-kingly-corporate elites, and transfer it to the 99%, the majority.[55] But the 99% includes people with a wide range of proximity to subordination and to elite privilege. People who are ideologically aligned with movement goals but who hold institutional or class-based power—professional activists, policymakers, and lawyers, for instance—can hamper organising efforts by consolidating their own power, or they can help facilitate the conditions for a bottom-up swell towards liberation. McAlevey notes that the labour movement's strategic shift from organising to mobilising can be blamed, at least in part, on "the people controlling the movement's resources—the individuals who are decision makers in national unions and in philanthropy."[56] What if these decision makers' imaginations were not limited to the search for "friendly elites"? What if they believed in the power and right of those they "serve" to lead their own efforts to dismantle the status quo?

51 ibid 235.
52 McAlevey (n 1) 6.
53 ibid 36–37.
54 '1199's Advice to Rookie Organizers' in McAlevey (n1) x.
55 ibid 10.
56 ibid 7.

Part of the Mississippi organisers' task was getting wealthier community members to identify with their poor neighbours, and to understand that poor people had the capability and the right to lead themselves rather than being "led by their betters."[57] Activists like Baker, Clark, and Horton believed that "[e]veryone has a contribution to make":

> "The organizer has to be aware of class exploitation, sensitive to class snobbery, without losing sight of the potential contribution to be made by those who do succumb to it. Just as one has to be able to look at a sharecropper and see a potential teacher, one must be able to look at a conservative lawyer and see a potential crusader for justice."[58]

Solidarity rooted in recognition of ordinary people's agency can not only encourage the democratic redistribution of power within the movement, but also channel broader community support into organising efforts. If more of us come to believe in the power of ordinary people, we may set the stage for a self-fulfilling prophecy of grassroots liberation.

3. Why We Need Counternarratives about Ordinary-people Power

How do we cultivate belief in ordinary-people power? In particular, how do we inspire this faith among people whose existing beliefs and previous experiences contradict it?

We form our beliefs about ourselves and the world through our experiences.[59] It makes sense, then, that ordinary people can come to believe in their own power by experiencing their collective agency for them-

---

57 Payne (n 28) 68.

58 ibid 89.

59 I went down a bit of a rabbit hole trying to understand how this process actually happens in our brains. When we have an experience our neurons fire, and the synapses between neurons release chemicals that activate other neurons. Under certain conditions—which I'll get to in Part III—this neural firing can actually strengthen the synaptic connections between neurons, which is how we learn from experience. Although we're more open to learning from experience when our brains are young and still developing, our brains retain the ability to change—known as neuroplasticity—throughout our lives. Daniel J Siegel, *Mindsight: The New Science of Personal Transformation* (Bantam Books 2011) 40–42.

selves. This understanding lay at the heart of the organising strategy in Mississippi. People experienced their individual and collective self-determination through "participatory political and educational activities, in which the people themselves ha[d] a part in defining the problems... and solving them."[60] Leaders like Septima Clark and others who ran the Highlander Folk School developed their faith in ordinary-people power "[t]hrough long experience working with impoverished communities," during which they witnessed first-hand "the ability of communities of the poor to provide much of the leadership for their own struggle."[61] Legal scholar Stephen Wexler makes a similar connection between experiencing and believing in ordinary-people power:

> "If the lawyer negotiates the settlement of a dispute, the people will see, if anything, only that one lawyer can beat another. If the people confront those who oppose them and win, they see that they can beat those whom they will inevitably oppose again. That lesson is more valuable than anything the lawyer can win, or any ease in his style of victory."[62]

But power is an abstract and complex concept. How do we make sense of our experiences with power, and why do we draw certain lessons and beliefs from them rather than others? Cognitive linguist George Lakoff argues that we understand ourselves and each other through narrative frames.[63] In other words, when we are learning from experience, we are encoding a story in our brains about how various events, ideas, and emotions connect.[64] We combine simple narratives into more complex ones, and we share our narratives with each other through storytelling and other cultural exchange.[65] We apply culturally shared "deep narratives"—roles like the Hero, the Villain, the Victim, and the Helper—to our experiences, giving meaning to our lives and the lives of those around

60 Payne (n 28) 68.
61 ibid 77.
62 Stephen Wexler, 'Practicing Law for Poor People' (1970) 79 Yale LJ 1049, 1058.
63 Lakoff (n 5) 24, 33–34.
64 ibid 26–27.
65 ibid 23–27.

us.[66] To an extent, we even experience others' narratives as our own.[67] When we see or experience something, there is rarely one true understanding of it. We must impose meaning with storytelling. "We participate in creating what we see in the very act of describing it."[68]

This means that narratives are central to how we understand power, our own and others. And the cultural "deep narrative" about power in America, the dominant story, is that elite rule is inevitable. Sure, we have shared stories about "ordinary" people transcending overwhelming odds, but these stories hinge on the idea that the "ordinary" person is actually extraordinary in some way: hardworking, virtuous, talented. The hero of the Rags-to-Riches narrative doesn't band together with other poor people to overthrow the rich; she does something exceptional to become one of them.[69] Even our shared narratives about bottom-up movements for social transformation tend to lionise—and sanitise—exceptional individuals, like Martin Luther King. As Payne puts it, the achievements of ordinary people during the civil rights movement "seem extraordinary to us precisely because we have such an impoverished sense of the capabilities of ordinary people."[70]

These dominant narratives that conflate power with extraordinariness reinforce our understanding that elite rule is inevitable, and at the same time they limit our moral imaginations of a better world to a world with friendlier elites. Legal scholar Richard Delgado explores this connection between the descriptive and normative elements of narrative:

> "We decide what is, and, almost simultaneously, what ought to be. Narrative habits, patterns of seeing, shape what we see and that to which we aspire. These patterns of perception become habitual, tempting us to believe that the way things are is inevitable, or the best that can be in an imperfect world."[71]

---

66 ibid 33.

67 ibid 39–40.

68 Richard Delgado, 'Storytelling for Oppositionists: A Plea for Narrative' (1989) 87 Mich L Rev 2411, 2416.

69 See Lakoff (n 5) 29.

70 Payne (n 28) 5.

71 Delgado (n 68) 2416–17.

Even if we recognize the status quo as harmful, our belief in its inevitability leads us to conclude that "there are no other real possibilities that would make things significantly better, and that thus there is little point in struggling to change things."[72] We accept our existing power structures as the limit of what is and what ought to be. And once we accept the dominant narrative about power, we are more likely to dismiss or explain away contradictory experiences of ordinary people successfully challenging elite rule.[73] So developing faith in ordinary-people power may not be as simple as experiencing it. We need counternarratives: stories that "destroy" our conventional understanding of power and "open new windows into reality."[74]

Payne notes that many of the key participants in SNCC's organising in Greenwood, Mississippi came from families that told similarly defiant stories about their place in the world. "The common thread [of these familial narratives was] a refusal to see oneself as merely acted upon, as merely victim. These are families in which children were encouraged to believe that even within an oppressive social structure one retains some control over one's life."[75] By casting themselves as agency-holders in the face of intense subordination, these Black families occupied counternarratives that challenged the absolute nature of white supremacist power in the Deep South. And the folks who grew up with these counternarratives went on to form "much of the core of the movement" in Greenwood, upholding an organising tradition rooted deeply in the agency and power of ordinary people.

The counternarratives of these Mississippi families played out in the reality they challenged: their tellers lived them daily in their acts of defiance. But *fictional* counternarratives can shape our understanding of the world as well. According to Lakoff, "some of the same neural structure in the brain that is used when we live out a narrative is also used when we see someone else living out that narrative, in real life or on TV, or if we imagine it as when we are reading a novel."[76] Action and imagination

72 Wright (n 47) 286.

73 See Lakoff (n 5) 37 ("When you accept a particular narrative, you ignore or hide realities that contradict it.").

74 Delgado (n 68) 2413–14.

75 Payne (n 28) 234–35.

76 Lakoff (n 5) 40.

are bound together in the very fabric of our brains. Just as our understandings of what *is* can limit our imagination of what *could be*, can't our imagination transform our understandings of what is? Fictional counternarratives "can be a catalyst for this: [they] can inspire imagination and a feeling that, if not exactly anything, more is definitely possible."[77]

Counterstorytelling cannot serve as a replacement for the actual experience of power fostered through participation in democratic organising efforts. But maybe it can set the stage for learning from such experiences by priming participants to reframe their understandings of power. Maybe it can encourage participation in the first place by presenting a tangible, "juicy"[78] vision of the kinds of liberatory victories only ordinary-people power can win. And maybe it can promote solidarity within the 99% by serving as a collaborative activity in which the teller and listener "build a world richer than either could make alone."[79]

4. Can We Unplay Elite Power?

How might we use design to generate counternarratives that inspire belief in ordinary-people power? One promising method is designing critical play scenarios. Game scholar and designer Mary Flanagan defines critical play as "creat[ing] or occupy[ing] play environments and activities that represent one or more questions about aspects of human life."[80] Critical play scenarios present a compelling avenue for immersing

---

77 Anthony Dunne and Fiona Raby, *Speculative Everything* (MIT Press 2013) 161. Ironically, despite their critiques of consumerism and their promotion of radical dreaming through design, Dunne and Raby seem resigned to a world in which the only disruptive power ordinary people hold is as consumers, not as workers: "Once workers could exert power by withholding their labor, by striking; today, as we see again and again, this is less so. In today's economy it is as consumers that we have power. The most threatening act of protest for a capitalist system would be for its citizens to refuse to consume." Dunne and Raby 37. Collective worker action can upend the labour-capital power structure by seizing control of the means of production. Can collective consumer action do the same?

78 See Pope (n 6) 3–4, quoting Demita Frazier in Keeanga-Yamahtta Taylor (ed), *How We Get Free: Black Feminism and the Combahee River Collective* (Haymarket Books 2017).

79 Delgado (n 68) 2439.

80 Mary Flanagan, *Critical Play: Radical Game Design* (MIT Press 2009) 6.

players in counterstories about power because they promote (un)learning, delineate subversive separation from the status quo, create non-coercive safety spaces, and facilitate nonlinear narrative through player agency.

4.1. Learning and Unlearning

Play is conducive to learning. Indeed, "[p]lay is an integral and vital part of mental development and learning, and playful activities are essential aspects of learning and creative acts."[81] The conditions under which we strengthen our brain's synaptic connections—allowing us to learn from our experiences and tell ourselves new stories— "include repetition, emotional arousal, novelty, and the careful focus of attention."[82] When I first read that list, I immediately thought of video games. I've been an avid player since I was a kid, dabbling in virtually every genre from classic platformers to ambient interactive narratives. Every video game I've ever enjoyed has used repetition as a tool to teach rules and skills, inspired strong emotional reactions, introduced novelty through elements like worldbuilding, art, music, and play mechanisms, and required focus to overcome challenges. Unsurprisingly, research proves that games can be a highly effective learning tool.[83] Legal designers are already using video games to teach people about legal processes and rights, like the NuLawLab's RePresent games that simulate legal proceedings.[84]

---

81 ibid 4.

82 Siegel (n 59) 40.

83 See, e.g., Douglas B Clark, Emily E Tanner-Smith, and Stephen S Killingsworth, 'Digital Games, Design, and Learning: A Systematic Review and Meta-Analysis' (2016) 86(1) *Review of Educational Research* 79 (finding that "digital games significantly enhanced student learning relative to nongame conditions."); Sara de Freitas, 'Are Games Effective Learning Tools? A Review of Educational Games' (2018) 21(2) *Journal of Educational Technology and Society* 74 ("To the question: are games effective learning tools, the answer from the research is overwhelmingly positive.").

84 NuLawLab, 'RePresent Games' <https://www.nulawlab.org/projects/represent-games>.

With a critical approach, video games and other play scenarios might help us not only to learn, but to *un*learn, question, or "unplay" dominant understandings of abstract concepts like power.

4.2. Subversion of the Status Quo

By definition, play takes place "outside 'ordinary' life" in what historian Johan Huizinga dubbed "the magic circle."[85] While play is not inherently critical of dominant narratives and modes of being,[86] its distance from the status quo lends itself to subversion.[87]

Like any medium, games are embedded with ideologies "whether game designers intend these ideologies or not."[88] Mainstream games tend to reflect the context in which they are designed: "primarily white, primarily male, and primarily profit driven."[89] But if we approach these default assumptions with critical reflection and intent, we can make the magic circle a space for challenging dominant narratives rather than reinforcing them. Play is a natural outlet for revealing "'hidden transcripts' that often lie among the 'official transcripts' of power relations."[90]

4.3. Safety Space

Delagdo points out that "counterstories, to be effective, must be or must appear to be noncoercive."[91] Counternarratives challenge our deep and often unexamined assumptions about the world. Their destructive pow-

85 Johan Huizinga, *Homo Ludens: A Study of the Play Element in Culture* (Beacon Press 1955) 38–39.

86 See, e.g., Flanagan (n 80) 8 (noting that "the invention of organized doll play and 'playing house' during the U.S. industrial revolution [came about] when gender roles needed to be reasserted due to changing labor conditions").

87 Paul Coulton, Dan Burnett, and Adrian Gradinar, 'Games as Speculative Design: Allowing Players to Consider Alternate Presents and Plausible Features' in P Lloyd and E Bohemia (eds), *Future Focused Thinking - DRS International Conference* (2016) 1610 <https://doi.org/10.21606/ drs.2016.15>.

88 Flanagan (n 80) 223.

89 ibid 224.

90 ibid 260 (quoting James C. Scott).

91 Delgado (n 68) 2415.

er can be frightening, triggering our instincts to protect ourselves instead of engaging with an open mind. This makes games an ideal context for generating and exploring counterstories. As Flanagan notes, "play occurs only when players feel comfortable. Play is, by definition, a safety space."[92] Play's natural allergy to coercion and "overly didactic communication"[93] makes games fertile ground for speculating about worlds and ways of being that contradict our conventional understandings.[94]

4.4. Player Agency

In order to believe in ordinary-people power, we must believe in individual efficacy: "What you do matters."[95] Play provides a space to experience this directly in a safe, low-stakes context. *Playing* a counternarrative is different from merely *listening to* or *reading* one in part because of the player's agency. While stories tend to be linear, unfolding the same way each time they are told, games are non-linear: their outcomes will vary based on the decisions the player makes.[96] Rather than using design covertly to "nudge" people into changing their beliefs about power, play is a chance to design opportunities to exercise agency, to present multiple meaningful options.[97] We can ask the player: What happens if you place your faith in the power of ordinary people? What happens if you don't? By replaying or reposing the question in different branches of the game's narrative, players can explore multiple possible worlds with varying proximity from our dominant understanding of reality.

92 Flanagan (n 80) 261.
93 ibid.
94 See Dunne and Raby (n 77) 3 ("We rarely develop scenarios that suggest how things should be because it becomes too didactic and even moralistic. For us futures are not a destination or something to be strived for but a medium to aid imaginative thought—to speculate with").
95 Payne (n 28) 235.
96 Flanagan (n 80) 7, citing Greg Costikyan, 'I Have No Words & I Must Design: Toward a Critical Vocabulary for Games' *Interactive Fantasy 2* (1994).
97 See Dunne and Raby (n 77) 161.

4.5. Ideas for Moving Forward

Flanagan concludes her examination of critical play with a call to action:

> "The challenge, then, is to find ways to make interesting, complex play environments using the intricacies of critical thinking and to encourage designers to offer many possibilities in games, for a wide range of players, with a wide range of interests and social roles. We can manifest a different future."[98]

In imagining the various ways we might inspire faith in ordinary-people power through critical play, I find myself drawn to video games (unsurprising, given how often I play them!). Video games are just one of many categories of "constructed play scenarios,"[99] but at this moment in time, they are "especially prominent aspects of our playculture."[100] For the contemporary player, "digital technology has been inherently bound with interactivity and diversion, and artists who engage in computer-based creation and critique represent the majority of contemporary examples of critical play."[101] With computers becoming increasingly available to most Americans,[102] video games can be made accessible to a wide range of people. And digital technology can facilitate a high level of narrative complexity, interactivity, and collaboration, making video games a promising space for meaningful player agency and rich counterstorytelling.

What are some ways a video game could explore counternarratives about ordinary-people power? One method might be to immerse the player in the role of a ruling elite trying to preserve its kingly-priestly status against challenges by ordinary people. The very fact that maintaining power is a goal of play and not a given would serve to question the dominant narrative of inevitable elite rule. For example, the player could assume the role of a union-busting employer attempting

---

98 Flanagan (n 80) 261.

99 ibid 6.

100 ibid 226.

101 ibid.

102 U.S. Census Bureau, 'Computer and Internet Use in the United States: 2018' (21 April 2021) <https://www.census.gov/newsroom/press-releases/2021/computer-internet-use.html>.

to exploit its workers as efficiently as possible and thwart collective action—or perhaps less literally, a human being training ants to do her bidding in her apartment. Confronted with the ants' growing defiance and unyielding solidarity, the player will have the option to resort to increasingly depraved acts of suppression and violence in an effort to quell their uprising. But the player's task is impossible, an idealistic twist on the "you-can't-win" scenarios that activist games typically employ to highlight the immensity of social problems:[103] the ants always prevail, whether by seizing control of the human's apartment or by driving the human to an existential crisis that renders "winning" undesirable.

Alternatively, a game could play out more sincerely from the perspective of ordinary people building and exercising their power. To defy the dominant narrative of the "exceptional" individual, the player could take on the role of a collective. Perhaps the game could be played primarily from the perspective of a "soup," a melding of individual characters' skills that grows more and more powerful as the game progresses and defeats (or absorbs) a series of increasingly powerful opponents. The game could be a riff on the parable of stone soup,[104] with a mysterious stone acting as the catalyst for the creation of the soup. Is the stone an extraordinary power source the soup needs to succeed? Or is it simply a shared experience that brings the ingredient-characters together to collectively exercise their (delicious) pre-existing power?

Whatever the concept, when it comes to critical play, methods matter. Flanagan proposes a framework for engaging in critical game design, one that embeds values into the iterative design process and carves out space for inclusivity: 1) Set design goals and value goals; 2) develop rules and constraints that support values; 3) design for many different play styles; 4) develop a playable prototype; 5) play test with diverse audiences; 6) verify values and revise goals; and 7) repeat.[105] I have just barely begun the first stage of this process, reflecting on the values and

103 See Flanagan (n 80) 244.

104 Stone soup is a European folk story with many variations. The basic idea is this: a hungry visitor to a town convinces the townspeople that he possesses a magic stone, which produces soup when boiled in water. The curious townspeople end up contributing all kinds of ingredients, resulting in a tasty soup that everyone shares.

105 Flanagan (n 80) 257–58.

design goals for a game that questions the inevitability of elite rule. I made these visual notes before I began working on this paper:

Fig. 1. "I want to create a game that brings delight! What inspires it? The unexpected! Silliness. Hope. A sense of connection. Accomplishment! Rhythm. Genuineness." © 2023 by Hallie J Pope is licensed under CC BY-NC 4.0

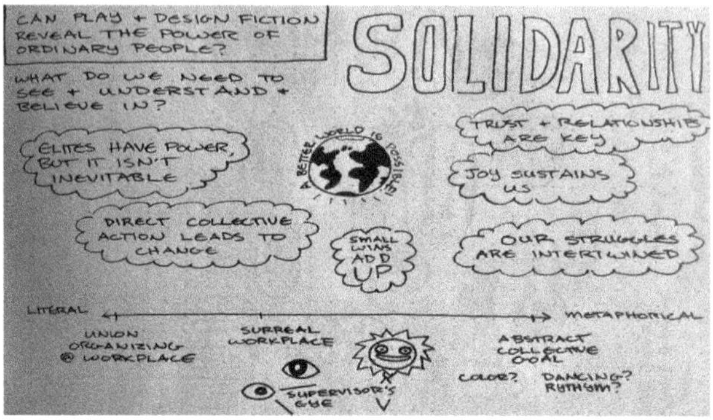

Fig. 2. "Can play and design fiction reveal the power of ordinary people? What do we need to see and understand and believe in? Solidarity. Elites have power, but it isn't inevitable. Trust and relationships are key. Joy sustains us. Direct collective action leads to change. Small wins add up. Our struggles are intertwined." © 2023 by Hallie J Pope is licensed under CC BY-NC 4.0

It will be exciting to revisit these ideas after participating in this roundtable, armed with a fuller understanding of how designing critical play scenarios might support liberatory endeavours. One helpful takeaway is that I should engage in a broader study of historical and fictional narratives about power. My research for this paper did not stretch beyond the U.S. labour and civil rights movements in the early twentieth century. Other contexts, places, moments, and voices will provide a richer perspective on the stories we live and tell about power—both those that affirm elite rule and those that dare to assert the power of ordinary people. It will also be useful to survey existing video games and analyse the extent to which they entrench or challenge dominant power narratives, in order to better understand the possibilities (and pitfalls) of employing the medium for critical ends.

McAlevey makes a compelling argument that meaningful and lasting liberation can be won only when ordinary people organise collectively to exercise their disruptive power. Both hers and Payne's accounts of radical movements in the twentieth century demonstrate that *belief* in ordinary-people power is crucial to its successful exercise. Our conventional narratives may tell us that the kingly-priestly-corporate class will always reign supreme, but by engaging with counternarratives, we can change the stories we tell ourselves about power. Critical play may prove one fruitful method for examining the dominant narrative of elite rule and generating faith in ordinary-people power. All that remains is to give it a try.

5. Conclusion

McAlevey's words inspired the title of this paper: "Solidarity among human beings can happen spontaneously, as in a flood or fire, or by design, through organizing."[106] I am similarly drawn to Payne's description of the civil rights movement as "its own work of art,"[107] a collective crafting of liberatory power and joy. I doubt the authors meant to evoke the practices of art and design on any level other than metaphor, but I can't resist reading these phrases as an invitation.

After all, we have good reason to blur the boundaries between artist, designer, and activist. Flanagan remarks that "if we look to the fundamental reasons for *why we play*, the connection between artistic methods, activism, and game design becomes clear."[108] Those of us engaged in these endeavours must devote "attention to possibility."[109] Acts of creation—artistic or otherwise—are teeming with possibility: What will come to be? What *could* be? Of all the beliefs that bear on our efforts to challenge power structures, "perhaps the most important are beliefs about *what is possible*."[110] We can take our cue from civil rights organisers like Ella Baker, Myles Horton, and Septima Clark, who shared "an

106 McAlevey (n 1) 29.
107 Payne (n 28) 256.
108 Flanagan (n 80) 252.
109 ibid.
110 Wright (n 47) 286.

expansive sense of the possibilities of democracy—an unrealistic sense of the possibilities, their critics would say."[111] If we design, create, and agitate with the goal of dismantling (and not merely reforming) elite rule, our attention to possibility must stretch to include that which most deem impossible.

Bibliography

Clark D, Tanner-Smith E, and Killingsworth S, 'Digital Games, Design, and Learning: A Systematic Review and Meta-Analysis' (2016) 86(1) Review of Educational Research 79

Coulton P, Burnett D, and Gradinar A, 'Games as Speculative Design: Allowing Players to Consider Alternate Presents and Plausible Features' in P Lloyd and E Bohemia (eds), *Future Focused Thinking - DRS International Conference* (2016) 1610 <https://doi.org/10.21606/ drs.2016.15>

Costikyan G, 'I Have No Words & I Must Design: Toward a Critical Vocabulary for Games' *Interactive Fantasy 2* (1994)

De Freitas S, 'Are Games Effective Learning Tools? A Review of Educational Games' (2018) 21(2) Journal of Educational Technology and Society 74

Delgado R, 'Storytelling for Oppositionists: A Plea for Narrative' (1989) 87 Mich L Rev 2411

Dunne A and Raby F, *Speculative Everything* (MIT Press 2013)

Flanagan M, *Critical Play: Radical Game Design* (MIT Press 2009)

Huizinga J, *Homo Ludens: A Study of the Play Element in Culture* (Beacon Press 1955)

Kimeldorf H, *Reds or Rackets?* (University of California Press 1992)

Lakoff G, *The Political Mind: A Cognitive Scientist's Guide to Your Brain and Its Politics* (Penguin Books 2009)

McAlevey J, *No Shortcuts: Organizing for Power in the New Gilded Age* (OUP 2016)

NuLawLab, 'RePresent Games' <https://www.nulawlab.org/projects/ represent-games>

Payne C, *I've Got the Light of Freedom* (2nd edn, University of California Press 2007)

111 Payne (n 28) 68.

Piven F, *Challenging Authority: How Ordinary People Change America* (Rowman & Littlefield Publishers, Inc. 2006)

Pope HJ, 'Liberatory legal design and radical imagination' in D Lockton, S Lenzi, P Hekkert, A Oak, J Sádaba, P Lloyd (eds), *DRS2022: Bilbao* (2022) <https://doi.org/10.21606/drs.2022.689>

Sanders B, 'The US has a ruling class—and Americans must stand up to it' *The Guardian* (2 Sep 2022) <https://www.theguardiancom/commentisfree/2022/sep/02/the-us-has-a-ruling-class-and-americans-must-stand-up-to-it> accessed 27 Jan 2023

Siegel D, *Mindsight: The New Science of Personal Transformation* (Bantam Books 2011)

Stephan-Norris J and Zeitlin M, *Left Out: Reds and America's Industrial Unions* (CUP 2002)

Taylor K (ed.), *How We Get Free: Black Feminism and the Combahee River Collective* (Haymarket Books 2017)

U.S. Census Bureau, 'Computer and Internet Use in the United States: 2018' (21 April 2021) <https://www.census.gov/newsroom/press-releases/2021/computer-internet-use.html>

Wexler S, 'Practicing Law for Poor People' (1970) 79 Yale LJ 1049

Wright E, *Envisioning Real Utopias* (Verso 2010)

THE ‘4PS’: PROACTIVE, POSSIBILITY-DRIVEN, PARTICIPATORY, AND POSTHUMAN APPROACHES FOR LEGAL DESIGN

5. COMIC CONTRACTS 2.0 – CONTRACTS THAT HAVE (AND GIVE) A VOICE

Anne Ketola, Robert de Rooy and Helena Haapio

Abstract

Composite Comic Contracts are the next iteration of contract design, building on the development of legally binding visual contracts, known as Comic Contracts. Making contracts and contractual rights digitally accessible and understandable affords agency and access to justice for the cognitively vulnerable. We describe the creative and contracting processes and discuss the benefits and challenges from a cognitive-linguistic perspective and from a Proactive Contracting legal and interpretive perspective. By enhancing engagement, comprehension and retention of information, Composite Comic Contracts provide the essential preconditions for cognitive accessibility and the success of any contractual relationship with cognitively vulnerable people. We argue that elusive legal certainty on potential legal interpretive issues should not be a barrier to legal innovation and legal design. Composite Comic Contracts are not only contracts that *have* a voice, but also ones that *give* a voice.

1. Introduction

Comic Contracts are designed to be legally binding contracts where the parties to the contract are represented as visual characters and where the contract terms are communicated mainly visually.[1] Comic contracts present the terms of a contract through engaging visuals, an easy-to-follow structure and simplified language. They are designed to make contracts easy to engage with and easy to understand for low-literate and vulnerable people.

---

1 Helena Haapio, Daniela Alina Plewe and Robert de Rooy, 'Next Generation Deal Design: Comics and Visual Platforms for Contracting' in Erich Schweighofer, Franz Kummer, Walter Hötzendorfer and Georg Borges (eds), *Networks. Proceedings of the 19th International Legal Informatics Symposium IRIS 2016* (Österreichische Computer Gesellschaft OCG 2016).

Composite Comic Contracts[2] are the next iteration of contract design towards affording vulnerable people[3] the agency and the dignity to autonomously understand contracts. This new contracting format digitally combines the Comic Contract with an audio narrative of the contract, mediated by synchronising the narrative with pre-set zooming and panning of the relevant images.

Our chapter presents examples of a composite version of a Comic Contract created for seasonal farmworkers on a ClemenGold citrus farm in Letsitele, South Africa.[4] The digital Comic Contract contracting platform[5] consists of two parts: the authoring tool and the contracting tool. The audio-visual experience of the contract is compiled and crafted with the authoring tool and the digital contract signing process is executed by the contracting tool.[6] In this chapter, the samples of the visual and audio elements of the contract are presented in English. In practice, to further aid easy comprehension, we envisage that both the textual and audio elements of the Composite Comic Contract will be presented in the user's mother tongue.

---

2 This contract type can be associated with multisensory legal phenomena, a concept introduced by Colette Brunschwig. See e.g. Colette R Brunschwig, 'Contract Comics and the Visualization, Audio-Visualization, and Multisensorization of Law' (2019) 46(2) The University of Western Australia Law Review 191. See also Colette R Brunschwig, 'Visual Law and Legal Design: Questions and Tentative Answers' (2021) 27 Jusletter-IT.

3 For the purposes of this chapter, 'vulnerable people' refers to people who need help to understand a contract, such as people not fluent in the contracting language or people who struggle to read and understand contracts or legal language. It typically includes ethnic minorities and migrants, and generally people who have poor reading skills.

4 The original Comic Contract created for ClemenGold is discussed, for instance, in Robert de Rooy, 'Nurturing the Dignity of Vulnerable and Marginalized People, One Contract at a Time' (2022) 84 The Clarity Journal 39.

5 The platform is called ShowSmart. Like the original Comic Contracts, it was developed by Creative Contracts (Pty) Ltd, a social enterprise founded by chapter co-author Robert de Rooy.

6 A link to a video demonstrating excerpts from this Composite Comic Contract can be found here: <https://www.youtube.com/watch?v=I4l-fR_V97U>. Process screenshots of this video, along with a sample page showing the visual information that the reader sees at a particular moment, with the corresponding text that the reader hears, are presented in Appendix 1.

Our chapter begins with viewing Composite Comic Contracts in the context of access to justice, as a means to make contracts and contractual rights accessible and understandable to vulnerable people. We describe how Composite Comic Contracts are created and how the contracting process works. We then discuss the benefits and challenges of Composite Comic Contracts from two disciplinary perspectives. We first evaluate Composite Comic Contracts from a cognitive-linguistic perspective. We discuss why images are superior to words when it comes to comprehension and recall of complex content, why having an audio narration of the contract content reduces the reader's cognitive load and why, from a cognitive perspective, the Composite Comic Contract is a combination of information presented in various modes.

We then evaluate Composite Comic Contracts from a legal perspective. We introduce the Composite Comic Contract as an expression of the principles of Proactive Contracting, where the focus is on successful implementation rather than interpretation in dispute resolution. We then discuss some preliminary legal and interpretive implications that emerge from this new contracting format and offer some preliminary views on these based on general principles of contract formation and interpretation common to the jurisdictions with which the authors are familiar. Our chapter does not attempt to draw any legal conclusions, other than to map the territory and discuss some of the key factors that influence the assessment of Composite Comic Contracts by different audiences, including legal audiences.

2. Access to Justice and Comic Contracts

The need to make contracts easy to understand forms part of the broader challenge of providing people with *access to justice*, which is not just about access to a court of law or to easier, quicker or cheaper dispute resolution.[7] Access to justice is also part of the UN's Sustainable Development Goal 16, which aims to promote peaceful and inclusive societies for sustainable development, provide access to justice for all and build

---

7 According to Richard Susskind, there are four elements of access to justice: dispute resolution, dispute containment, dispute avoidance and legal health promotion, Richard Susskind, *Online Courts and the Future of Justice* (OUP 2019).

effective, accountable and inclusive institutions at all levels.[8] Access to justice is a basic principle of the rule of law. In the absence of access to justice 'people are unable to have their voice heard, exercise their rights, challenge discrimination, or hold decision-makers accountable'.[9]

Contracts contain rights and impose obligations, and either party (in theory) can call on the state to enforce these rights and obligations. So, how fit for purpose is a contract when vulnerable people cannot read what they sign, and, more importantly, are not able to access it when they need to rely on the contract? Put differently: *'You can't fight for your rights if you don't know what they are.'*[10]

In addition to making contracts accessible and understandable for vulnerable people, the Composite Comic Contract seeks to address some shortcomings of conventional paper contracts. First, paper contracts get easily damaged and lost. There is a strong correlation between illiteracy and poverty, and people living in poverty are vulnerable to impermanence, displacement and weather. They often do not have the facilities or access to facilities to safely store important documents. Second, paper contracts require printing, completing, copying, and storing. Third, the size of the population of people that are vulnerable and sign contracts that they cannot read or understand requires a more efficient, scalable, and easy-to-manage solution than paper-based contracts. Finally, what about the needs of those vulnerable people who do not have good eyesight or who prefer to, or must, rely on their hearing?

These learnings provoked a journey to develop a solution that continues to build towards the purpose of helping vulnerable people easily access their contractual rights and other important information, and thereby access to justice. While it was obvious that the solution must be a digital contracting platform, for the same reasons that public and private organisations are embracing digital contract management systems, designing and developing a solution for vulnerable users introduces con-

8 'Sustainable Development Goal 16' (*United Nations and the Rule of Law*) <https://www.un.org/ruleoflaw/sdg-16/> accessed 3 March 2023.

9 'Access to Justice' (*United Nations and the Rule of Law*) <https://www.un.org/ruleoflaw/thematic-areas/access-to-justice-and-rule-of-law-institutions/access-to-justice> accessed 3 March 2023.

10 'John G. Roberts, Supreme Court Chief Justice' (ThoughtCo). <https://www.thoughtco.com/john-g-roberts-biography-3322403> accessed 23 October 2022.

straints, for example: lack of access to computers or smartphones, high turnover of phones and phone numbers, high data costs for users, and the challenge of making it engaging and practical to view the pages of a contract on a small screen.

3. Composite Comic Contracts

Most people are familiar with the forbidding format of conventional contracts, which for many present a *wall of text.*[11] Contracts are typically documents written by lawyers who assume that the only reader of the contract will be another lawyer or a judge.[12] When governments and lawyers try to address the difficulties of low-literate people in reading and understanding their contracts, the outcome of that effort often looks something like this:

NOTICE

In terms of Section 49 of the Consumer Protection Act No. 68 of 2008

This agreement contains terms and conditions that resemble the style of words in this notice. These conditions may: - limit the risk or liability of the Service Provider or any third party, - might impose risk or liability on the consumer, - might compel the consumer to indemnify the Service Provider or third party, and/or validate an acknowledgement by the consumer, of a fact.

The Consumer's attention is specifically required to take note of these conditions and clauses as they are important and must be carefully read and understood. By signature of this lease, the Consumer acknowledges that the consumer has carefully perused and understood the content of this agreement.

If the Consumer has not been able to read and understand this agreement, the Consumer confirms that they requested an explanation, and were provided with an explanation and that the Consumer understand the particulars of this agreement, including all clauses that might in any manner limit the risk or accountability of the Service Provider or compel the Consumer to compensate the Service Provider for any reason, and including, but not limited to: clauses 1,2,3,11,14,25,43 of this agreement.

Fig. 1. A typical notice required by Section 58 (1) of the South African Consumer Protection Act, 68 of 2008, elaborated for illustration purposes by Robert de Rooy.

11 Stefania Passera, 'Beyond the Wall of Contract Text: Visualizing Contracts to Foster Understanding and Collaboration Within and Across Organizations' (PhD Thesis, Aalto University 2017).

12 Gerlinde Berger-Walliser, Robert C Bird and Helena Haapio, 'Promoting Business Success Through Contract Visualization' (2011) 17 Journal of Law, Business & Ethics 55.

3.1. The Design of a Composite Comic Contract Template

While it is beyond the scope of this chapter to trace the history of the legal design movement away from such a unidimensional assumption of what a contract must look like, it is safe to say that the growing awareness of Proactive Contracting, legal design and legal tech has removed contracts (and contracting) from the exclusive custody of lawyers, and opened up the design of contracts (*the glue of business*[13] that holds together our modern economies[14]) to professionals from various disciplines. People without a law degree are now invited to collaborate on designing better contracts and contracting processes. It was in this transdisciplinary space that the Composite Comic Contract emerged from a collaboration between a lawyer, a writer, illustrators, designers and software developers.

Composite Comic Contract templates are designed using the authoring tool of the software platform[15]. We take the image files[16] of the pages of a Comic Contract, which are presented mainly in images, together with any important or necessary text. We then write a script that describes the content of the page, and we record a native speaker of the contract's language reading of the script. The image file and the audio file are then uploaded to the authoring tool where zoom points and zoom depths are set to synchronise the narrative with the relevant panels of the visual file to guide the reader's attention to the relevant images and information as it is being discussed in the narrative. This process is facilitated by an instant preview display of the template under construction, allowing the author to fine tune the zoom points and narrative synchronicity for optimal display and readability on any mobile device.

The authoring tool allows for the system to add certain text information to the digital contract as part of the preparation and execution of the contract. Two types of additional text information are accommodated,

---

13 Passera (n 11), 19.

14 'The Sveriges Riksbank Prize in Economic Sciences in Memory of Alfred Nobel 2016' (*NobelPrize.Org*) <https://www.nobelprize.org/prizes/economic-sciences/2016/press-release/> accessed 9 October 2022.

15 The ShowSmart platform referred to in footnote 5 above.

16 The system is configured to be able to use any of the typical image files, for example JPG or PNG.

offer information and acceptor information. Offer information markers allow the party presenting the contract template (for example, a farmer that wants to employ seasonal farm workers) to add information that may vary from contract to contract to blank fields provided for on the image file, based on the same template. This would typically include pay rates, place of work, task lists or working hours. Acceptor information markers provide for the system to add the details of each person who executes the contract (in this case a farm worker) to the relevant blank fields provided for on the relevant contract template. Once the Composite Comic Contract template has been authored, it is published and ready for presentation and execution.

3.2. The Presentation and Execution of a Composite Comic Contract

The platform can present the contract templates for execution in two ways, depending on the employment scenario and the phone available to the intended user: the *remote* (online) mode and the *local* (in-person) mode.

The 'remote mode' is suitable where the employer knows to whom they want to send an employment contract and the prospective worker has a smartphone, or easy access to someone with a smartphone or a computer. Continuing with our farming scenario, this would normally be the case with returning workers or workers who have pre-registered for employment. In the remote mode, an SMS is sent with a link to a personal website that contains a link to the contract. On clicking the link the composite contract is displayed. After the contact has been viewed, the worker is presented with the option to accept or reject the contract offer. The remote mode allows the prospective employee to review and consider the contract offer at their own leisure and in their own time. When the worker has digitally signed the contract, the platform is updated and the farmer is able to monitor which contract offers have been signed, which are outstanding, and which have been refused.

The 'in-person' mode is suitable where the employer is looking to recruit large groups of new workers, or where the prospective workers generally do not have smartphones, or easy access to someone with a smartphone or a computer. The only requirement is that all the workers need to bring a mobile phone that can receive and send an SMS. Mobile phones have become very cheap and are generally available to most people. With the in-person mode each worker's details are captured and their phone number is authenticated before the contract template, completed with all the relevant offer information markers, is presented to all the workers on a screen. At the end of the display of the full contract, the workers are invited to digitally sign the contract by replying to an SMS with the unique code displayed as part of the contract presentation, and thus only available to the workers who are present for the presentation and who have been registered.

In both the remote and the in-person modes, once the contracts have been signed, the system sends an SMS with a link to their phone, which opens up their personal webpage, from where they can open a link to their signed contract in two formats, a PDF format for downloading and printing, and the audio-visual Composite Contract format, for easy access to review the contract whenever needed.

Technically, the integrity of the component parts of the contract is ensured and preserved through the generation of a digital key for each signed contract, by hashing the metadata of all the files that make up the audio-visual experience, including the time and date stamps of the digital signature of the Composite Comic Contract. The system digitally signs all the underlying data that make up the Composite Comic Contract so that it can be independently verified that the underlying data has not been changed since it was signed. To put it differently, the system provides an immutable digital guarantee of the full content of the Composite Comic Contract, when it was seen and heard, and when and by whom it was signed.

Finally, as the cost of data is still a very real barrier to digital inclusivity of the most underserved members of society, the Composite Comic Contract offers a low data solution, as the image and audio files are orders of magnitude smaller than, for example, a typical movie file, which could, in theory and to some extent, offer a similar experience to the user.

3.3. The Business Rationale for the Composite Comic Contract

Businesses routinely contract low-literate and vulnerable people, whether as suppliers of their labour, as consumers of products or services, or as stakeholders in value chains or as communities affected by projects. In an ideal world, any legal product or process designed to make contracts easier for low-literate and vulnerable people to engage with, and easier to understand and remember the content, should suffice as a rationale for the implementation of such solutions. But we don't live in an ideal world, and while there are happily some exceptions, most businesses are ignorant of (or they have more pressing priorities than) the challenges faced by low-literate and vulnerable people when they contract with them. This means that if we want to reach more low-literate and vulnerable people with empowering innovative legal products or processes, these products and services must also have compelling value propositions for a business to implement such solutions.

Applying this lens to Composite Comic Contracts, and staying with our farming scenario, some of the value propositions that this solution offers include: 1) the presentation and execution of the employment contract are much easier and save a lot of time and resources that would otherwise have to be allocated to each contracting session; 2) the contract is always 'explained' and understood consistently, reducing the risk of misunderstanding, Chinese Whispers[17] and potential disputes; 3) the employer has real time reporting of the contracts that were signed, and proof that the contract was properly explained to the workers, which is important, as farmers are often accountable to ethical or due diligence audits by customers or buyers; and 4) the system is paperless, obviating all the challenges of completing, data capture and storing of paper contracts.

4. Composite Comic Contracts from a Cognitive Accessibility Perspective

The term *cognitive accessibility* refers to practices that remove barriers for people who have difficulties in processing information.[18] Readers may be cognitively vulnerable for a variety of reasons: some have poor or non-existing reading skills, some have cognitive challenges that affect

17 'Chinese whispers' refers to a sequence of repetitions of a story, each one differing slightly from the original, so that the final telling bears only a scant resemblance to the original.

18 'What Is Cognitive Accessibility?' (*Bureau of Internet Accessibility*) <https://www.boia.org/blog/what-is-cognitive-accessibility> accessed 10 February 2023.

perception, memory, or attention, and some are non-fluent in a particular language. It is important to bear in mind that all of us can be cognitively vulnerable when, for instance, we visit, or are forced to migrate to, foreign countries and are not familiar with the local language.

When designing information with the goal of removing cognitive accessibility barriers as effectively as possible, the design needs to be in line with how the human mind processes information. A contract does not fulfil its purpose unless the user is able to process, comprehend and remember the information that is presented. The cognitive interpretation is therefore the ultimate threshold in access to justice.

In this section of our chapter, we review research from different areas of psychology and cognitive linguistics to describe how the different information modes of Composite Comic Contracts – images, written text, auditive text, and movement through zooming and panning – are cognitively processed, and how the Composite Comic Contract design cognitively supports information processing. We first discuss comic illustrations on their own (What are the cognitive benefits of images?), then presenting the illustrations with words (How can images support text comprehension?), and finally, presenting the images and text with audio and movement (What are the cognitive benefits of the audio-visual presentation?). We conclude with an assessment of Composite Comic Contracts as a whole (How do the components of the audio-visual product support each other?).

4.1. Comic Illustrations from a Cognitive Perspective

Images are generally recognized with ease and remembered well. Studies in Experimental Psychology have repeatedly demonstrated that the human brain can store a massive number of images with a significant amount of detail.[19] In an oft-quoted visual long-term memory experiment, people were shown 10,000 images, and, in a subsequent recognition memory task, they remembered 83% of them.[20] An extensive body

19 For a comprehensive review of such studies, see e.g. Talia Konkle and others, 'Conceptual Distinctiveness Supports Detailed Visual Long-Term Memory for Real-World Objects' (2010) 139(3) Journal of Experimental Psychology 558.

20 Lionel Standing, 'Learning 10000 Pictures' (1973) 25(2) Quarterly Journal of Exper-

of literature over the past five decades has shown that images are remembered better than words: If a person is shown a series of images and words and then tested for recall, the images are remembered better.[21] This mnemonic advantage of images over words is referred to as *the picture superiority effect.*[22]

Image interpretation is affected by reader characteristics and situational factors. For instance, eye-tracking research has demonstrated that readers with different cultural backgrounds can look, and hence interpret, images in differing ways. One such study compared how American and Chinese participants looked at a set of images of various focal objects (people, objects) against complex backgrounds. The study found that the American participants mainly looked at the focal objects in the images and that the Chinese participants focused more on what could be seen in the background. When subsequently interviewed about the images, what the participants remembered about the images reflected what they had visually focused on.[23] In other words, the same images carried different meanings for viewers with different cultural backgrounds.

Furthermore, we also have individual differences as interpreters of images within cultural communities. Psychological studies have demonstrated that our expectations, attitudes and beliefs influence how we interpret the materials we read, and that we interpret images – and texts – differently in different emotional states.[24] The interpretation we construct of an image when we are frustrated is likely to be different to an interpretation made whilst happy and calm. In addition to affecting our interpretations of images, our feelings also physically affect our vision, in other words, our feelings affect how our eyesight works at a particular

imental Psychology 207.

21 For a comprehensive review of such studies, see e.g. Tyler M Ensor and others, 'Increasing Word Distinctiveness Eliminates the Picture Superiority Effect in Recognition: Evidence for the Physical-Distinctiveness Account' (2019) 47 Memory & Cognition 182.

22 Allan Paivio and Kalman Csapo, 'Picture Superiority in Free Recall: Imagery or Dual Coding?' (1973) 5 Cognitive Psychology 176.

23 Hannah Faye Chua and others, 'Cultural Variation in Eye Movements During Scene Perception' (2005) 102(35) Proceedings of the National Academy of Sciences of the United States of America 12629.

24 Paula M Niedenthal and Adrienne Wood, 'Does Emotion Influence Visual Perception? Depends on How You Look At It' (2019) 33(1) Cognition and Emotion 77.

moment (for instance, when we feel fear, our contrast vision gets better: we are able to distinguish contrast between different areas of an image better than we would if we were comfortable and relaxed).[25]

To sum up, images are a powerful information medium. They are engaging and easily remembered, but their interpretation can be affected by factors such as reader characteristics. Image interpretation can be guided with anchoring the image's meaning with words, either written or spoken.

4.2. Word–Image Combinations from a Cognitive Perspective

Studies in cognitive science have theoretically modelled how the combination of words and images is cognitively processed. This research has concluded that, as a general rule, people understand content better from the combination of words and images than from words alone.[26] These studies propose that when examining a combination of words and images (e.g. reading a comic contract), the reader constructs connections between the word and the images, resulting in conceptual processing that is deeper than for verbal information alone, and the deeper processing results in comprehending and remembering the content better.[27] We may hence argue that, theoretically, images have *the potential* to make words easier to digest. However, as discussed below, the benefits of adding images to complex texts depend on various factors.

Empirical cognitive studies on how adding images to a contract may help or hinder readers in understanding the contract are yet to be conducted. Yet, examining the effects of adding images to verbal content has been the topic of a large body of research in the field of educational psychology and pedagogy. These studies have analysed both individual images used as support for understanding new words or concepts (e.g. individual words matched with images) as well as comics that aim to

25 Elizabeth A Phelps and others, 'Emotion Facilitates Perception and Potentiates the Perceptual Benefits of Attention' (2006) 17(4) Psychological Science 292.

26 Richard E Mayer, 'Cognitive Theory of Multimedia Learning' in Richard E Mayer (ed), *The Cambridge Handbook of Multimedia Learning* (CUP 2013).

27 Stephen D Sorden, 'The Cognitive Theory of Multimedia Learning' in Beverly J Irby and others (eds), *The Handbook of Educational Theories* (Information Age Publishing Inc 2013).

inform the reader about serious content, typically referred to as instructional comics.[28]

The insights gained from these studies have a lot to offer for evaluating the benefits of comic contracts. In this line of research, *learning* refers to being able to retrieve, from one's long-term memory, information one has previously been exposed to. For the non-expert party of an employment contract, the workers, the efficacy of the contract depends on whether they have *learned* at least a part of it, in other words, whether they can recall its content later on. They may not remember all of the details of what was agreed, but as long as they remember the topics that were included in the contract (e.g. 'The contract mentioned something about my sick leave.'), they can be prompted to recover and re-read the contract.

In the following sections, we review educational psychology and pedagogy research that has examined if and how images support the comprehension of complex verbal content and reflect on its implications for comic contract design and use. Our focus is on two central arguments. First, the benefits of adding images to complex text materials are different for different types of content, and second, the benefits of adding images are different for different types of readers.

4.2.1. Adding Images to Text is More Beneficial for Abstract Content than Concrete Content

Within educational psychology, several studies have examined how images can be used as support for learning new concepts and words. Among these studies, one interesting line of research has compared the effect images can have on the reader's ability to learn concrete words (such as *table* and *thirsty*) versus abstract words (such as *regulation*

---

28 In addition to *instructional comics*, this line of research has referred to these comics as *data comics*, *educational comics* or *science comics* when their subject matter is directly related to scientific content; see e.g. Ertugrul Ozdemir, 'Comics in Modern Physics: Learning Blackbody Radiation Through Quasi-History of Physics' (2017) 1(1) Studies in Educational Research and Development 41; Zezhong Wang and others, 'Comparing Effectiveness and Engagement of Data Comics and Infographics' (2019) CHI Conference on Human Factors in Computing Systems Proceedings <https://doi.org/10.1145/3290605.3300483> accessed 1 January 2023; Camillia Matuk and others, 'How Do Teachers Use Comics to Promote Engagement, Equity, and Diversity in Science Classrooms?' (2021) 51 Research in Science Education 685.

and *secure*) in a foreign language they are still learning.[29] The process of learning new words in a foreign language can have parallels with reading a contract: for a vulnerable employee with poor or non-existent reading skills, an employment contract is likely to include words that are new to them, even if the contract is presented in their native language.

This line of research has shown that both types of words, concrete ones as well as abstract ones, are remembered better if presented with corresponding images. However, the improvement effect is small for concrete words, and significant for abstract words.[30] In other words, the more abstract the content, the more readers benefit from image support. The image is remembered well, which strengthens the reader's ability to access the learned item (in other words, the word–image combination that represents the abstract word) in their long-term memory.

Traditional contracts are an archetype of abstract language, full of concepts that a vulnerable reader may struggle to ground in their everyday experience. Research on the development of comic contracts has pointed out that illustrating abstract concepts in comic contracts can be particularly challenging, and that such illustration solutions are often 'visual examples' of abstract ideas, such as an image of a judge's gavel as a symbol for a *court order* or *law*.[31] Yet, these visual examples may have the potential to significantly support readers' comprehension of abstract content. Even if we can't literally draw concepts such as *law*, we can offer a visual hint of what the concept refers to, and hence ground its meaning.

For example, the Composite Comic Contract examined in this chapter explains that the worker will have to pick a minimum number of bags of clementines per day; if they fail to do so, they may receive a *warning*. A

29 Andrew Farley and others, 'The Concreteness Effect and the Bilingual Lexicon: The Impact of Visual Stimuli Attachment on Meaning Recall of Abstract L2 Words' (2012) 16(4) Language Teaching Research 443; Andrew Farley and others, 'Is a Picture Worth a Thousand Words? Using Images to Create a Concreteness Effect for Abstract Words: Evidence from Beginning L2 Learners of Spanish' (2014) 97(4) Hispania 634; Helen H Shen, 'Imagery and Verbal Coding Approaches in Chinese Vocabulary Instruction' (2010) 14(4) Language Teaching Research 485.

30 Farley and others (n 29); Shen (n 29).

31 Eliisa Pitkäsalo and others, 'Image Analysis as a Visualization Tool – Translating Contracts into Comics' in Marcelo Corrales and others (eds) *Research Handbook on Contract Design* (Edward Elgar 2022).

warning is a somewhat abstract concept and is therefore challenging to illustrate precisely. The illustration used in the contract (Figure 2) depicts a visual example of what receiving a warning might look like: it is a serious conversation between a worker and a representative of the employer. The image explains the meaning of the word and the word anchors the meaning of the image.

The word 'warning' is superimposed at the bottom right of the image. This corresponds to one of the cognitively-grounded design principles created within Educational Psychology: the so-called *spatial continuity principle* states that multimodal messages containing words and images are better understood if the words and images are presented near to, rather than far from, each other on a page or a screen[32] (more of these principles are discussed in section 4.3).

Fig. 2. An example image of the Composite Comic Contract illustrating what receiving a warning may look like. © 2016 Creative Contracts (Pty) Ltd. Licensed under CC BY-NC 4.0.

Images also assist in the assimilation of difficult content by making the content more *engaging*. Comprehending complex content requires active cognitive engagement, and the visual appearance of the material

32 Richard E Mayer, *Multimedia Learning* (CUP 2009).

is one of the motivational factors that can either increase or decrease this engagement.[33] Images increase the reader's motivation to engage with the materials – this is, in fact, the premise and starting point for the audio-visual media research reviewed in section 4.3. Research has even been conducted on whether adding purely decorative, topic-irrelevant images to texts increases readers' engagement, the outcome being that they do, in fact, make the reader read the material in more detail, but, unsurprisingly, do not contribute to text comprehension when measured in comprehension post-tests.[34]

4.2.2. Adding Images to Text Benefits Different Readers in Different Ways

Research on instructional comics has compared how factors in the readers' cognitive backgrounds, such as language level or academic abilities, may affect how beneficial image support is. These studies have involved a presentation of complex subject matter either as text-only or as an instructional comic for large groups of readers.

These studies have concluded that the more cognitively vulnerable a reader is, the more their reading comprehension benefits from reading complex content in a comic-format as opposed to text-only. Interestingly, the opposite applies for readers who are not cognitively vulnerable: the comic format can actually hinder their reading comprehension. Examples of these studies include comparing the reading comprehension of nanotechnology-related science text by low- and high-achieving students (i.e. students who have learning difficulties and students who do not)[35] and comparing the reading comprehension of English learning material by readers of low and high proficiency in the English language.[36]

These studies offer similar explanations as to why a skilled reader does not necessarily benefit from the comic-style format: a reader who

33 Roxana Moreno and Richard E Mayer, 'Interactive Multimodal Learning Environments' (2007) 19 Educational Psychology Review 309.

34 Ulrike IE Magner and others, 'Triggering Situational Interest by Decorative Illustrations Both Fosters and Hinders Learning in Computer-Based Learning Environments' (2014) 29 Learning and Instruction 141.

35 Shu-Fen Lin and Huann-shyang Lin, 'Learning Nanotechnology with Texts and Comics: the Impacts on Students of Different Achievement Levels' (2016) 38(8) International Journal of Science Education 1373.

36 Jun Liu, 'Effects of Comic Strips on L2 Learners' Reading Comprehension' (2004) 38(2) TESOL Quarterly 225.

does not need extra support in comprehending a complex text is likely to have *experience* in reading similar complex texts. The comic, in turn, is a very different type of information offering; it differs from how that reader is accustomed to constructing meaning, and it can hence actually make reading more difficult. The value of these findings for comic contract development may lie in acknowledging these reader differences and their possible connection with attitudes towards comic contract use: A high-proficiency reader who is experienced in reading traditional contracts may not always see the value of comic contracts, since for them personally, the traditional text-only format can be easier to cognitively process. The intended users of comic contracts, namely low- or illiterate readers, however, can significantly benefit from the comic-format – the more cognitively vulnerable they are, the more the comic helps.

4.3. Audio-Visual Contracts Format From a Cognitive Perspective

A Composite Comic Contract includes images, movement that guides the reader through the image page, an audio narrative, and a few written keywords and key phrases. In this section of the chapter, we review research on how humans process audio-visual instructive media (i.e. combinations of still images, moving images, written words, spoken words and sound). We discuss how the combination of these elements is cognitively processed and how audio-visual products such as Composite Comic Contracts should best be designed based on these insights.

4.3.1. Composite Comic Contracts and Information Selection

In the sections above, we concluded that, as a general rule, combining words and images has benefits for information processes: the combination leads to cognitive processing that is deeper than for reading words alone. Words can be presented either as written or spoken information, i.e. either as visual information (perceived with eyes) or auditive information (perceived with ears). This presentation modality affects how the words are cognitively processed.

Presenting words as auditive information has obvious benefits for someone who has poor or non-existing reading skills, but it also benefits more skilled readers by reducing their cognitive load. In terms of cognitive load theory, adding auditive information reduces the so-called *split-attention effect*.[37] Split-attention occurs when readers have to split their attention between separate sources of information, such as images and written words in a comic contract. The reader looks at the words, then images, then words again. This switching of visual focus creates extraneous cognitive load: it requires information to be maintained in the working memory while searching for the next information source, which diverts working memory resources away from doing what they are supposed to be doing, namely forming a schema, or an understanding, of the material. If the words are presented as audio narration, the reader does not have to split their attention.

Research in Educational Psychology has similarly argued that presenting identic verbal information as written words and as audio narration is counterproductive in audio-visual instructive media since readers have limited capacity to process visually presented material. This so-called *capacity limitation hypothesis* has been formulated into an audio-visual design technique known as the *redundancy principle*, which states that an audio-visual design with audio narration should only include the most essential words (headings, keywords, key phrases) as written text; the rest is redundant. Repeating the most essential words in writing guides readers' attention by emphasising this content.[38]

The example presented above in Section 4.2, regarding the minimum number of bags of clementines the worker has to pick per day, demonstrates this technique (see Figure 2). The audio narration in this part of the Composite Comic Contract states: ('For example, if you pick only 39 bags in a day,) you will receive a warning, your first warning' (see Process screenshots in Appendix 1). The only word displayed as written text in the Composite Comic Contract is 'Warning'. For those users who are able to read, this visual repetition supports following the contract narrative by offering a reference point. A part of the target readership is illiterate and not able to access written text at all, so from their perspective, all of the written text is redundant. From their perspective, keeping the written text to a minimum also serves to keep the design as clear as possible.

---

37 John Sweller and others, *Cognitive Load Theory. Explorations in the Learning Sciences, Instructional Systems and Performance Technologies* (Springer 2011).

38 Mayer (n 32).

4.3.2. Composite Comic Contracts and Information Interpretation

Cognitively-grounded design principles for audio-visual instructive media emphasise that when presenting images with audio narration, the images and corresponding narration should be presented simultaneously rather than successively (so-called *temporal contiguity principle*).[39] Composite Comic Contracts implement this principle by zooming and panning the image page: the relevant zoom points predetermine where the reader will look when hearing a particular part of the contract.

This temporal integration of words and images is particularly important for page designs with several distinct elements such as comic panels, because we cannot predict the order in which a reader will scan a page. Designers may assume that the scan path starts from the top left and proceeds according to the typical Western reading direction, but eye-tracking research has demonstrated that the reader often first looks at visually salient items in a page design, such as items that are relatively large or bright-coloured.[40] The zooming and panning of the comic contract page is needed to make sure that the reader's visual focus corresponds to the part of the contract page that is being discussed in the audio narration.

The zooming and panning in the Composite Comic Contract are more than mere camera movement: they segment the visual information for the reader and transform the image from something static to an information offering that evolves and progresses in time. For instance, with the clementine bag picking example discussed above, the panning takes the reader from the left panel (a man with a bag of clementines) to the panel on the right (receiving a warning), as the narration states: 'For example, if you pick only 39 bags in a day, you will receive a warning, your first warning' (see Figure 3). The vertical movement from one panel to the next happens within the duration of narrating this sentence, which emphasises cause and effect and the outcome of events.

39 Mayer (n 32).

40 Jana Holsanova, 'In the Eye of the Beholder: Visual Communication From a Recipient Perspective' in David Machin (ed), *Visual Communication* (De Gruyter Mouton 2014).

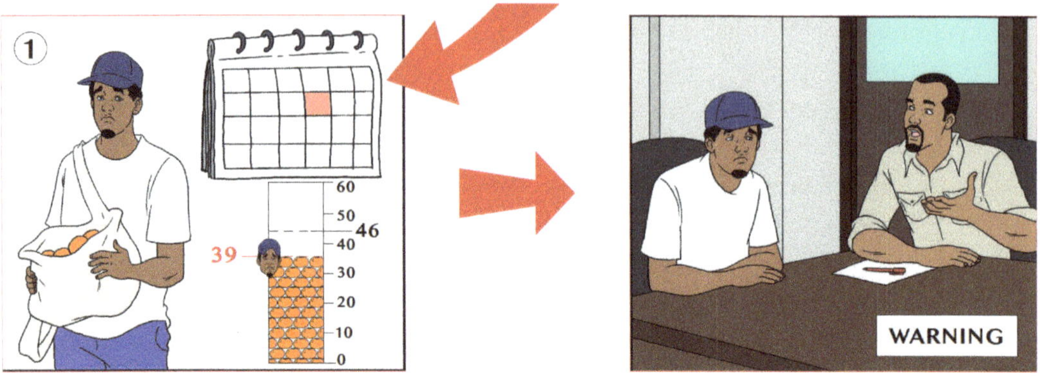

Fig. 3. An example image of the Composite Comic Contract illustrating that the worker will receive a warning if they pick less than 46 bags of clementines per day. In the audio-visual Composite Comic Contract, panning takes the reader from the first panel to the next in a vertical movement. © 2016 Creative Contracts (Pty) Ltd. Licensed under CC BY-NC 4.0.

As the image merges with the movement of zooming and panning, it essentially becomes a different information offer than the image alone. The meanings carried by the other modes of the Composite Comic Contract also merge. The meanings presented through words and images become intrinsically intertwined: the images explain the words and the words anchor the meanings of the images. The keywords that are displayed as written text place a special emphasis on these words as they are uttered in the audio narrative. Hence, from a cognitive perspective, the content of the Composite Comic Contract cannot be reduced down to any of its constituent elements alone: the contract genuinely is a combination of information presented in various modes.

5. Composite Comic Contracts as an Expression of Proactive Contracting

In recent years, researchers and practitioners have started to discover and develop new ways of making and representing contracts, with the focus shifting from winning a legal argument to making it easier for the parties to achieve their business goals and show respect for their counterparties.[41] New contract genres and designs have been introduced, and contract tech has opened up access to new tools, templates and patterns that challenge old beliefs, and even industries.[42] Since the 2010s, visual contracts – contracts with embedded images or infographics to supplement text – and Proactive Contract Design have started to gain recognition in business and academia.[43] The pioneers of *contract visualisation* proposed a visual turn in contract communication: the use of visual representation as a way to enhance contract clarity and ease of use, embedding images such as timelines, flowcharts and icons in actual contracts, contract briefs and guidance, and as planning and thinking tools during negotiations.[44]

Composite Comic Contracts are an expression of the principles of Proactive Contracting, a form of contracting that is deliberately designed to achieve contracting success. The approach builds on proactive legal thinking, where the focus is on preventing unnecessary problems from arising and promoting positive outcomes, such as legal empowerment,

---

41 Examples can be found in publications by Stefania Passera and the chapter authors on SSRN and also at Lexpert Contract Visualization, <https://www.lexpert.com/our-approach/visualization/>, Stefania Passera Contract design / Legal design, <https://stefaniapassera.com/portfolio/legal-design/> and the examples in the WorldCC Contract Design Pattern Library, <https://contract-design.worldcc.com/>.

42 Marcelo Corrales Compagnucci, Helena Haapio and Mark Fenwick, 'The Many Layers and Dimensions of Contract Design' in Marcelo Corrales Compagnucci, Helena Haapio and Mark Fenwick (eds), *Research Handbook on Contract Design* (Edward Elgar 2022); Helena Haapio, Robert de Rooy and Thomas D Barton, 'New Contract Genres' in Erich Schweighofer, Franz Kummer, Ahti Saarenpää and Burkhard Schafer (eds), *Data Protection / LegalTech. Proceedings of the 21st International Legal Informatics Symposium IRIS 2018* (Editions Weblaw 2018).

43 For an overview, see Marcelo Corrales Compagnucci, Helena Haapio and Mark Fenwick (eds), *Research Handbook on Contract Design* (Edward Elgar 2022) and Helena Haapio, 'Visualisation in Contract Education and Practice. The First 25 Years in Emily Allbon and Amanda Perry-Kessaris (eds), *Design in Legal Education* (Routledge 2022). – Strictly speaking, the use of pictures preceded the use of text to capture contracts: Sumerians used pictures to capture the terms of contracts in the 27th century BC. See, for example, the photo of a bill of sale of a male slave and a building in Shuruppak, Sumerian tablet, circa 2600, Musée du Louvre, available at <https://en.wikipedia.org/wiki/Contract#/media/File:Bill_of_sale_Louvre_AO3765.jpg> accessed 7 February 2023.

44 See, e.g. Haapio, Plewe and de Rooy (n 1).

optimal functioning and enhanced access to justice.[45] Proactive legal strategies have been used in many contexts, varying from achieving the business goals of contract parties to promoting societal goals and helping businesses become more sustainable.[46]

To this end, Proactive Contracting promotes the use of visualisation in contracts to achieve the intended success of the transaction or relationship.[47] Visualisation of legal or legally relevant information is not limited to the domain of contracts, of course, as proven in the work on Visual Law.[48] Apart from lawyers and legal scholars, the Proactive Contracting and Proactive Law movement also includes designers and scholars of design, who, through the theories and practice of information design, have actualized and systematised the use of visualisation in contracts.[49] Within this movement, the use of visualisation in the context of contracts has developed to include: 1) visualisation *in* contracts, 2) visualisation *about* contracts, 3) visualisation *for* contracts and 4) visualisation *as* contracts.[50]

---

45 Helena Haapio, Thomas D Barton and Marcelo Corrales Compagnucci, 'Legal Design for the Common Good: Proactive Legal Care by Design' in Marcelo Corrales Compagnucci and others (eds), *Legal Design: Integrating Business, Design and Legal Thinking with Technology* (Edward Elgar 2021).

46 See, e.g. Gerlinde Berger-Walliser, Paul Shrivastava and Adam Sulkowski, 'Using Proactive Legal Strategies for Corporate Environmental Sustainability' (2016) 6 Michigan Journal of Environmental and Administrative Law 1; and Adam Sulkowski and Ruth Jebe, 'Evolving ESG Reporting Governance, Regime Theory, and Proactive Law: Predictions and Strategies' (2022) 59 American Business Law Journal 449. See also Marika Salo-Lahti and Helena Haapio, 'Proactive Legal Design and AI for Better Business and Better Society' (Legal Design Roundtable 2023, Brussels, 17 February 2023).

47 Berger-Walliser, Bird and Haapio (n 12); Thomas Barton, Gerlinde Berger-Walliser and Helena Haapio, 'Visualization: Seeing Contracts for What They Are, and What They Could Become' (2013) 19 Journal of Law, Business and Ethics 47.

48 Colette Brunschwig, 'Visualisierung von Rechtsnormen: Legal Design' (PhD Thesis, University of Zurich, 2001).

49 See, e.g. Robert Waller, 'Designing Contracts for Human Readers' in Marcelo Corrales Compagnucci, Helena Haapio and Mark Fenwick (eds), *Research Handbook on Contract Design* (Edward Elgar 2022) and Waller R, 'Contract Design for Humans: Preventing Cognitive Accidents' (Simplification Centre 2020) <https://www.simplificationcentre.org.uk/reports2/contract-design-for-humans> accessed 29 January 2024. Passera (n 11).

50 Helena Haapio, Daniela Alina Plewe and Robert de Rooy, 'Contract Continuum:

It was these pioneering ideas that inspired the development of the first Comic Contracts, and their ideas and rationale continue to inspire the exploration and design of solutions to achieve contracting success. We argue that the Composite Comic Contracts extend the use of visualisation and harness the other tools of communication, including audio, movement and digital technology to achieve contracting success.

6. Composite Comic Contracts from a Legal Perspective

6.1. Are Composite Comic Contracts Legally Binding?

When presenting the idea of Comic Contracts, we are often asked: 'Are they legally binding?'. While there is no case law on the question, there have been a few remarks and articles on the subject.[51] The former High Court Chief Justice Robert French, speaking at the 'Comic and Creative Contracts Conference' hosted by the University of Western Australia in 2017, stated that there was 'no reason in principle why pictorial contracts explained orally or supplemented textually or contextually could not be enforceable in the same way as any other contract'. Mark Giancaspro concludes: 'There is ample authority supporting the notion that a comic contract can satisfy the legal test of contractual certainty'[52].

We anticipate the same question in respect of Composite Comic Contracts. First, we can state that Composite Comic Contracts are designed to be legally binding and enforceable. They are designed to be an accurate memorandum of the terms of the contract, and for the authenticity of the contract and the electronic signature of the contract to be non-repudiable. Second, from a legal point of view, while Composite Comic Contracts may sound unusual at first, there is no law prohibiting such contracts. The principle of freedom of contract is a universal and essen-

From Text to Images, Comics and Code' in Erich Schweighofer, Franz Kummer, Walter Hötzendorfer and Christoph Sorge (eds), *Trends and Communities of Legal Informatics. Proceedings of the 20th International Legal Informatics Symposium IRIS 2017* (Österreichische Computer Gesellschaft 2017).

51 See, e.g. Mark Giancaspro, 'Picture-Perfect or Potentially Perilous? Assessing the Validity of "Comic Contracts"' (2020) 10(1) The Comics Grid: Journal of Comics Scholarship 7 and the resources mentioned in Section 5.4.

52 Giancaspro (n 51).

tial starting point for contract law. It allows the parties to choose the content and form of their contracts, and the components they consider appropriate for their purposes. Both civil law and common law countries have rules that require certain contracts or contract content to be in writing to be enforceable. But 'in writing' does not necessarily mean just words, nor does it exclude the addition of something to words. Images or spoken words can reflect the intentions of the parties in addition to any required written text. Freedom of contract is not unlimited, of course, and there are other intervening factors. These, however, are beyond the scope of this chapter.

We recognize that we are, to some extent, entering uncharted legal territory, as there are no precedents in terms of rules of interpretation that have been applied to this new contracting format. So, for the purposes of our work, it is important to examine the first principles of contracting based on the requirements and expectations of different contract audiences and how these can be better aligned during the contract design stage, to guide the easy and consistent interpretation of Composite Comic Contracts by all stakeholders: the intended audience of low-literate and vulnerable people, the business users and finally legal users. The goal is to ensure easy comprehension and predictability and to prevent unnecessary disputes. Our work is ongoing, and in this section we present some preliminary legal and interpretive implications for legal users that emerge from this new contracting format. In the following, we also cite some case law as illustrative, not authoritative, examples of jurisprudence in which aspects of the issues raised by this innovation in contracting have been discussed.

6.2. Contracts Come in Many Shapes and Forms

For centuries, the legal enforcement and interpretation of contracts has been about verbal and written contracts. As a result, there is a rich and deep body of contract law literature and case law about the interpretation of such contracts. No treatises currently cover the legal interpretation of Composite Comic Contracts, and few, if any, statutes, cases or other resources address the interpretation of contracts' visual and other non-textual expressions. While different jurisdictions have different requirements for contracts to be valid and enforceable in court, with very few exceptions (such as wills and surety agreements), contracts do not need to be in writing to constitute valid and binding legal agreements. Where there are such legal requirements, the minimum content to comply with such prescribed exceptions can be easily included within a Composite Comic Contract without undermining their purpose of being autonomously accessible to low-literate and vulnerable contracting parties.

Unless specifically regulated – or, if regulated, provided that the regulatory requirements are met – the parties are free to choose the form of their contract, which can be verbal or written, and made on paper or electronically. There should then be no reason why a combination of contracting modes cannot constitute a valid, binding and enforceable legal agreement.

6.3. Which Part of the Composite Comic Contract is 'Legally Binding'?

Conventional drafters of contracts are accustomed to seeking to transfer the risk of contradictions between the text and its explanation to their counterparty, by including statements to the effect that only the writing is legally binding and that any explanations – and even headings – are provided 'for convenience only', or by including text to neutralise rules of interpretation that allow for any ambiguity to be interpreted against the party responsible for drafting the contract. If we were to add to the record of text the record of images, the record of audio narrative, and the record of the digitally predetermined and synchronised zooming and panning mediating these modes of communication, the urge to identify one of the modes as the only legally binding one would easily arise.

Comic Contracts have shown us that visualisation *as* contracts is possible. It extends the idea of what a contract could be and could look like, in other words, that a contract does not need to be a document filled with text. The Composite Comic Contract similarly challenges the assumption of what can constitute a contract. We have shown that from a cognitive assessment perspective, the Composite Comic Contract cannot be reduced to any of its constituent elements alone: the contract genuinely is a combination of information presented in various modes.

From a legal design perspective, the Composite Comic Contract privileges the user's experience and interests. From the user's perspective, especially from the perspective of a low-literate or vulnerable person, any attempt to try and introduce a condition that makes one mode legally binding over another would be artificial and introduce unnecessary complexity. If we cannot predict which of the modes, visual, text or audio, the user understands most easily, in which of the modes do we communicate the fact that one of the modes would be the only legally binding mode?

Finally, from a legal perspective, why is it necessary to 'unscramble the egg' and insist that one mode is more binding than another? In the typical scenarios faced by conventional contract drafters described above, there is normally a text record of an agreement and evidence of a spontaneous or contemporaneous verbal explanation of the agreement. Then it may be prudent to ensure that the weight of the 'more reliable' evidence of the text must prevail over the possibility of 'less reliable' evidence of a verbal explanation. Even if the verbal explanation was recorded, the explanation itself could be spontaneous, dynamic, and less coherent. However, where the modes are prepared and recorded equally and simultaneously as part of a single artefact of the proposed agreement, there is no evidentiary reason for any one mode to prevail over another.

We argue that for these reasons, the Composite Comic Contract cannot and should not be reduced to only the visual Comic Contract, or only the narrative, ignoring the combination of these formats as mediated by the digitally predetermined and synchronised zooming and panning. We argue that what constitutes the legally binding contract is the user's whole experience of the presentation of the contract made up of all its constituent parts.

6.4. How Would Lawyers Interpret a Composite Comic Contract?

With the increased attention to human-friendly contracts such as visual and layered contracts,[53] the possible legal challenges related to their in-

53 See e.g. Waller, 'Designing Contracts for Human Readers' (n 49); Rob Waller, Stefania Passera and Helena Haapio, 'Layered Contracts: Both Legally Functional and Human-friendly' in Kai Jacob, Dierk Schindler, Roger Strathausen and Bernhard Waltl (eds), *Liquid Legal – Humanization and the Law* (Springer 2022).

terpretation and enforcement have started to gain scholarly attention.[54] As regards case law, at the time of writing, we are not aware of any case law directly related to the topic of this chapter.

Two English High Court rulings, Altera Voyageur Production Limited v Premier Oil E&P UK Ltd [2020] EWHC 1891 (Comm) and Starbev GP Ltd v Interbrew Central European Holdings BV [2014] EWHC 1311 (Comm), have dealt with 'illustrations' and 'worked examples', recognizing that these can be integral parts of a commercial contract and may be where the parties' true bargain can be found. In these two cases, the 'illustrations' and 'worked examples' were expressed in words rather than images. In the Altera Voyageur case, the Judge approved of comments in Starbev GP Ltd v Interbrew Central European Holdings BV [2014] EWHC 1311 (Comm) [284] that '[t]here is (...) no reason why illustrations or examples should be construed differently than any other term in a contract' and that 'in the context of lengthy contracts in financial transactions with much boiler plate (...) illustrations or examples deserve particular attention as something to which the parties particularly turned their minds'.

Even though these cases dealt with verbal rather than visual illustrations and examples, the analogy is striking: we argue that there is no reason why visual or voice components of a contract – as long as the parties have made them part of their contract – should be construed or interpreted differently than any other part of a contract. After all, the key goal of the interpretation exercise is to determine what the parties intended should happen.

While Composite Comic Contracts are a novel concept, the legal challenges related to them are not entirely new. Business people and lawyers experienced in contract practice frequently encounter contracts that are partly oral and partly written as well as contracts that are made

54 Jay Mitchell, 'Whiteboard and Black-Letter: Visual Communication in Commercial Contracts' (2018) 20 University of Pennsylvania Journal of Business Law 815; Michael D Murray, 'Cartoon Contracts and the Proactive Visualization of Law' (2021) 16 University of Massachusetts Law Review 98; Michael Murray, 'Toward a Universal Visual Language of Law' (13 March 2021) <https://ssrn.com/abstract=3502568> accessed 7 February 2023; Vesa Annola, Helena Haapio and Merja Koskela, 'Interpreting Images in Contracts' in Marcelo Corrales Compagnucci, Helena Haapio and Mark Fenwick (eds), *Research Handbook on Contract Design* (Edward Elgar 2022).

in many languages. When a contract is written in different languages (including also picture language and multimodality), a number of potential issues can arise due to the challenges of accurate intra- or inter-semiotic translation, which can be hard, especially due to the different concepts, styles and language used in different contexts and legal systems. Courts and arbitrators have dealt with such problems, to which the parties may or may not have provided guidance for example through a prevailing language provision[55] or an integration clause.[56]

As indicated above, it is possible for images to sometimes be subject to differing interpretations. Should an image or a combination of images alone or with text be relevant to a legal dispute, the contract would have to be interpreted and a decision would have to be taken on which interpretation prevails. But does this possibility disqualify the use of visuals in contracting? We argue that it does not, just as the fact that there are legal libraries filled with case law about differing interpretations of text-based agreements does not disqualify the use of text in contracting.

The first point to make is that unlike conventional text-based agreements, it is much more likely that the transparent and easy to understand content of a Composite Comic Contract will surface any ambiguity or contradictions *before* a contract is signed. But we nevertheless need to consider the question of how the courts may deal with differing interpretations of a Composite Comic Contract.

The rules of contract interpretation have developed mainly in the context of text-based agreements. Currently, there is no established legal doctrine for interpreting the combination of written text, images and audio in contracts. However, the idea of visuals as contract components is not entirely new for judges and arbitrators. For certain types of conventional contracts, such as construction and engineering contracts, visuals have been used for quite some time: maps and explanatory drawings

55 A prevailing language provision typically states that in the event of a dispute about interpreting the contract arising from the fact that it exists in multiple languages, the contract in a named, 'official' language will govern the interpretation.

56 Some (but not all) countries' laws require a court to focus on the written contract alone, and the parties can include in their contract a provision, an integration clause (aka a merger clause or an entire agreement clause) to the same effect. See, e.g. Annola, Haapio and Koskela (n 54) and Kim Lewison, *The Interpretation of Contracts* (Sweet & Maxwell 2007) 99.

have traditionally been relied on to provide technical clarity, for example, by showing location, boundaries, shape and size, tolerances, or other aspects of the desired outcome of the performance.[57] Courts and arbitral tribunals have dealt with disputes involving such visuals and have interpreted contracts in relation to them. Again, the parties (or the contract forms they use) may or may not have provided guidance in this respect.[58]

There is the view that not knowing how courts or litigators would view – or challenge – Composite Comic Contracts could create a barrier to their adoption and slow down the development of the field. In the context of visuals, according to Jay Mitchell, '[w]idespread use of visuals by lawyers is unlikely (and unwise) absent the demonstration of a solid legal foundation for such use.'[59]

But as our courts generally do not engage in determining matters of academic interest only, how do we develop this 'solid legal foundation'? The enormous legal foundation built up over centuries of jurisprudence on the interpretation of text agreement has done little to reduce disputes regarding contract interpretation. A decision by a court on any contract, image or text interpretation would only be valid for that image or text in the context of that contract. Conversely, a decision on any defect or issue in a visual or textual agreement would not disqualify or invalidate all visual or textual agreements.

As contracts are made for people to use, and not for lawyers to litigate, we believe that the absence of a solid legal foundation for the use and possible interpretative issues posed by Composite Comic Contracts should not dissuade contract designers from adopting innovative

---

57 Annola, Haapio and Koskela (n 54).

58 The NEC contract flowcharts, for example, expressly state that the flow charts are not contract documents, they are not part of the contract, and they should not be used for legal interpretation of the meaning of the contract. See, e.g., NEC, *Guidance Notes and Flowcharts for the Professional Services Contract – NEC3* (Thomas Telford 2005) 1. – For the purposes, and in the context, of our work, such a solution would be counter-productive and we do not recommend it for Composite Comic Contracts.

59 Mitchell (n 54) 852. For a more general discussion of the potential dangers of visualisation in the legal domain, see Elizabeth Porter, 'Taking Images Seriously' (2014) 114 Columbia Law Review 1687, 1752–53. Porter mentions the lack of legal rules or traditions to mitigate the interpretive risks associated with images among 'three primary dangers of welcoming images into the legal-writing toolbox'.

formats to empower people to easily understand their contracts. We are not aware of writers cautioning the developers and users of smart contracts to wait until there is a solid body of jurisprudence of smart contracts.

7. Conclusion

Composite Comic Contracts are an expression of the principles of Proactive Contracting, a form of contracting that aims to achieve *contracting success* in the best possible way. In the design of the content, we privilege the content that expresses the parties' mutual expectations. The design of the format, in turn, aims to achieve *cognitive success* in the best possible way. We employ the formats that are best at engaging the users' attention and that remove cognitive accessibility barriers: visual information and audio information. We also make the effort of presenting the information in the user's mother tongue. All these facets contribute to enhancing engagement with, and the comprehension and retention of the information, essential preconditions for the success of any contractual relationship.

In this chapter, we have argued that what constitutes the Composite Comic Contract is the whole, and not any of its constituent parts. From the point-of-view of cognitive processing, Composite Comic Contracts are complex combinations of images, movement that guides the reader through the images, written text and audio narration. Each of these elements is a separate information offer, but when presented together they become a single source of information. In other words, the contract is not only the visual comic contract or the narrative, it is the combination of these formats as mediated by the digitally predetermined and synchronised zooming and panning.

Composite Comic Contracts take advantage of the full capacity that humans have for information processing. The images make difficult content easier to engage with, and they assist in explaining and structuring the information. Verbal information is easier to absorb when we hear it as opposed to when we read it, since our visual focus does not have to keep switching between the words and the images on the page.

The Composite Comic Contract challenges the assumption of what can constitute a contract and raises new questions, including whether it can constitute a binding agreement and whether one mode should or could prevail over others. In this chapter we have offered some preliminary views on some of the interpretive issues that may arise. We argue for an approach to innovative contracting formats that privileges the interests of users. Waiting for elusive legal certainty on potential legal issues should not be a barrier to legal innovation and legal design. Composite Comic Contracts afford agency and access to justice for the cognitively vulnerable. Therefore, they are not only contracts that *have* a voice, but also ones that *give* a voice.

Bibliography

Annola V, Haapio H and Koskela M, 'Interpreting Images in Contracts' in Marcelo Corrales Compagnucci, Helena Haapio and Mark Fenwick (eds), *Research Handbook on Contract Design* (Edward Elgar 2022)

Barton T, Berger-Walliser G and Haapio H, 'Visualization: Seeing Contracts for What They Are, and What They Could Become' (2013) 19 Journal of Law, Business and Ethics 47

Berger-Walliser G, Bird RC and Haapio H, 'Promoting Business Success Through Contract Visualization' (2011) 17 Journal of Law, Business & Ethics 55

—, Shrivastava P and Sulkowski A, 'Using Proactive Legal Strategies for Corporate Environmental Sustainability' (2016) 6 Michigan Journal of Environmental and Administrative Law 1

Brunschwig C, 'Visualisierung von Rechtsnormen: Legal Design' (PhD Thesis, University of Zurich, 2001)

—, 'Contract Comics and the Visualization, Audio-Visualization, and Multisensorization of Law' (2019) 46(2) The University of Western Australia Law Review 191

—, 'Visual Law and Legal Design: Questions and Tentative Answers' (2021) 27 Jusletter-IT

Chua HF, Boland JE and Nisbett RE, 'Cultural Variation in Eye Movements During Scene Perception' (2005) 102(35) Proceedings of the National Academy of Sciences of the United States of America 12629

Corrales Compagnucci M, Haapio H and Fenwick M (eds), *Research Handbook on Contract Design* (Edward Elgar 2022)

Corrales Compagnucci M, Haapio H and Fenwick M, 'The Many Layers and Dimensions of Contract Design' in Marcelo Corrales Compagnucci, Helena

Haapio and Mark Fenwick (eds), *Research Handbook on Contract Design* (Edward Elgar 2022)

de Rooy R, 'Nurturing the Dignity of Vulnerable and Marginalized People, One Contract at a Time' (2022) 84 The Clarity Journal 39

Ensor TM, Surprenant AM and Neath I, 'Increasing Word Distinctiveness Eliminates the Picture Superiority Effect in Recognition: Evidence for the Physical-Distinctiveness Account' (2019) 47 Memory & Cognition 182

Farley A, Pahom O and Ramonda K, 'Is a Picture Worth a Thousand Words? Using Images to Create a Concreteness Effect for Abstract Words: Evidence from Beginning L2 Learners of Spanish' (2014) 97(4) Hispania 634

Farley A, Ramonda K and Liu X, 'The Concreteness Effect and the Bilingual Lexicon: The Impact of Visual Stimuli Attachment on Meaning Recall of Abstract L2 Words' (2012) 16(4) Language Teaching Research 443

Giancaspro M, 'Picture-Perfect or Potentially Perilous? Assessing the Validity of "Comic Contracts"' (2020) 10(1) The Comics Grid: Journal of Comics Scholarship 7

Haapio H, 'Visualisation in Contract Education and Practice. The First 25 Years' in Emily Allbon and Amanda Perry-Kessaris (eds), *Design in Legal Education* (Routledge 2022)

—, Barton TD and Corrales Compagnucci M, 'Legal Design for the Common Good: Proactive Legal Care by Design' in Marcelo Corrales Compagnucci and others (eds), *Legal Design: Integrating Business, Design and Legal Thinking with Technology* (Edward Elgar 2021)

—, de Rooy R and Barton TD, 'New Contract Genres' in Erich Schweighofer, Franz Kummer, Ahti Saarenpää and Burkhard Schafer (eds), *Data Protection / LegalTech. Proceedings of the 21st International Legal Informatics Symposium IRIS 2018* (Editions Weblaw 2018)

—, Plewe DA and de Rooy R, 'Next Generation Deal Design: Comics and Visual Platforms for Contracting' in Erich Schweighofer, Franz Kummer, Walter Hötzendorfer and Georg Borges (eds), *Networks. Proceedings of the 19th International Legal Informatics Symposium IRIS 2016* (Österreichische Computer Gesellschaft OCG 2016)

—, Plewe DA and de Rooy R, 'Contract Continuum: From Text to Images, Comics and Code' in Erich Schweighofer, Franz Kummer, Walter Hötzendorfer and Christoph Sorge (eds), *Trends and Communities of Legal Informatics. Proceedings of the 20th International Legal Informatics Symposium IRIS 2017* (Österreichische Computer Gesellschaft 2017)

Holsanova J, 'In the Eye of the Beholder: Visual Communication from a Recipient Perspective' in David Machin (ed), *Visual Communication* (De Gruyter Mouton 2014)

Konkle T, Brady TF, Alvarez GA and Oliva A, 'Conceptual Distinctiveness Supports Detailed Visual Long-Term Memory for Real-World Objects' (2010) 139(3) Journal of Experimental Psychology 558

Lewison K, *The Interpretation of Contracts* (Sweet & Maxwell 2007)

Lin, SF and Lin HS, 'Learning Nanotechnology with Texts and Comics: The Impacts on Students of Different Achievement Levels' (2016) 38(8) International Journal of Science Education 1373

Liu J, 'Effects of Comic Strips on L2 Learners' Reading Comprehension' (2004) 38(2) TESOL Quarterly 225

Magner UIE, Schwonke R, Aleven V, Popescu O and Renkl A, 'Triggering Situational Interest by Decorative Illustrations both Fosters and Hinders Learning in Computer-Based Learning Environments' (2014) 29 Learning and Instruction 141

Matuk C, Hurwich T, Spiegel A and Diamond J, 'How Do Teachers Use Comics to Promote Engagement, Equity, and Diversity in Science Classrooms?' (2021) 51 Research in Science Education 685

Mayer RE, *Multimedia Learning* (CUP 2009)

—, 'Cognitive Theory of Multimedia Learning' in Richard E Mayer (ed), *The Cambridge Handbook of Multimedia Learning* (CUP 2013)

Mitchell J, 'Whiteboard and Black-Letter: Visual Communication in Commercial Contracts' (2018) 20 University of Pennsylvania Journal of Business Law 815.

Moreno R and Mayer RE, 'Interactive Multimodal Learning Environments' (2007) 19 Educational Psychology Review, 309

Murray MD, 'Cartoon Contracts and the Proactive Visualization of Law' (2021) 16 University of Massachusetts Law Review 98

—, 'Toward a Universal Visual Language of Law' (13 March 2021) <https://ssrn.com/abstract=3502568> accessed 7 February 2023

Niedenthal PM and Wood A, 'Does Emotion Influence Visual Perception? Depends on How You Look at it' (2019) 33(1) Cognition and Emotion 77

Ozdemir E, 'Comics in Modern Physics: Learning Blackbody Radiation Through Quasi-History of Physics' (2017) 1(1) Studies in Educational Research and Development 41

Paivio A and Csapo K, 'Picture Superiority in Free Recall: Imagery or Dual Coding?' (1973) 5 Cognitive Psychology 176

Passera S, 'Beyond the Wall of Contract Text: Visualizing Contracts to Foster Understanding and Collaboration Within and Across Organizations' (PhD Thesis, Aalto University 2017)

Phelps EA, Ling S and Carrasco M, 'Emotion Facilitates Perception and Potentiates the Perceptual Benefits of Attention' (2006) 17(4) Psychological Science 292

Pitkäsalo E, Ketola A, Haavisto L and Kalliomaa-Puha L, 'Image Analysis as a Visualization Tool – Translating Contracts into Comics' in Marcelo Corrales and others (eds) *Research Handbook on Contract Design* (Edward Elgar 2022)

Porter E, 'Taking Images Seriously' (2014) 114 Columbia Law Review 1687

Salo-Lahti M and Haapio H, 'Proactive Legal Design and AI for Better Business and Better Society' (Legal Design Roundtable 2023, Brussels, 17 February 2023)

Shen HH, 'Imagery and Verbal Coding Approaches in Chinese Vocabulary Instruction' (2010) 14(4) Language Teaching Research 485

Sorden SD, 'The Cognitive Theory of Multimedia Learning' in Beverly J Irby and others (eds), *The Handbook of Educational Theories* (Information Age Publishing Inc. 2013)

Standing L, 'Learning 10000 Pictures' (1973) 25(2) Quarterly Journal of Experimental Psychology 207

Sulkowski A and Jebe R, 'Evolving ESG Reporting Governance, Regime Theory, and Proactive Law: Predictions and Strategies' (2022) 59 American Business Law Journal 449

Susskind R, *Online Courts and the Future of Justice* (OUP 2019)

Sweller J, Ayres P and Kalyuga S, *Cognitive Load Theory. Explorations in the Learning Sciences, Instructional Systems and Performance Technologies* (Springer 2011)

Waller R, 'Contract Design for Humans: Preventing Cognitive Accidents' (Simplification Centre 2020) <https://www.simplificationcentre.org.uk/reports2/contract-design-for-humans> accessed 29 January 2024

—, 'Designing Contracts for Human Readers' in Marcelo Corrales Compagnucci, Helena Haapio and Mark Fenwick (eds), *Research Handbook on Contract Design* (Edward Elgar 2022)

—, Passera S and Haapio H, 'Layered Contracts: Both Legally Functional and Human-friendly' in Kai Jacob, Dierk Schindler, Roger Strathausen and Bernhard Waltl (eds), *Liquid Legal – Humanization and the Law* (Springer 2022)

Wang Z, Wang S, Farinella M, Murray-Rust D, Henry-Riche N and Bach B, 'Comparing Effectiveness and Engagement of Data Comics and Infographics' (2019) CHI Conference on Human Factors in Computing Systems Proceedings <https://doi.org/10.1145/3290605.3300483> accessed 1 January 2023

Appendix 1. ***Process screenshots of the ClemenGold Composite Comic Contract.***

© 2022 by Creative Contracts (Pty) Ltd is licensed under CC BY-NC 4.0.

	This new contracting format combines our visual comic contract with an audio narrative of the contract, mediated by zooming and panning to the relevant panels in sync with the narrative. We call this new contracting format Composite Comic Contracts.
	While our system also supports a process where the users don't have smartphones, here we present the typical contracting process which assumes the user has a smartphone. The contracting process starts when the user receives an SMS with a link to view a presentation of their contract offer.
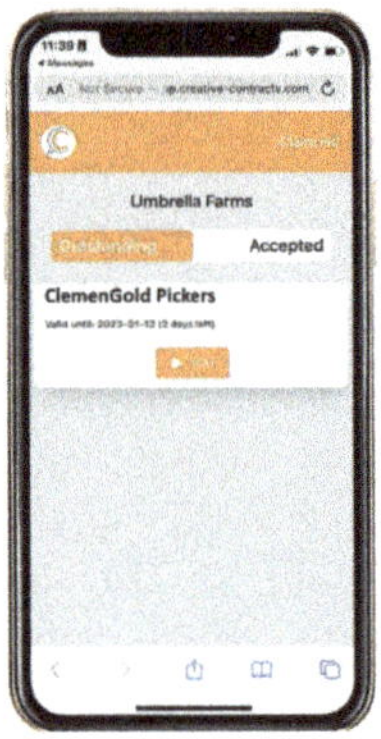	When the new employee clicks on the link, it takes them to their own personal website where they can see an outstanding contract offer. When they click on the PLAY button, their digital comic contract is presented.

<table>
<tr>
<td>
</td>
<td>For purposes of this annexure, we only show one sample page of how the user will experience the composite contract offer.

The textual and audio elements of the Composite Comic Contract are presented in the user's mother tongue to further aid comprehension.</td>
</tr>
<tr>
<td>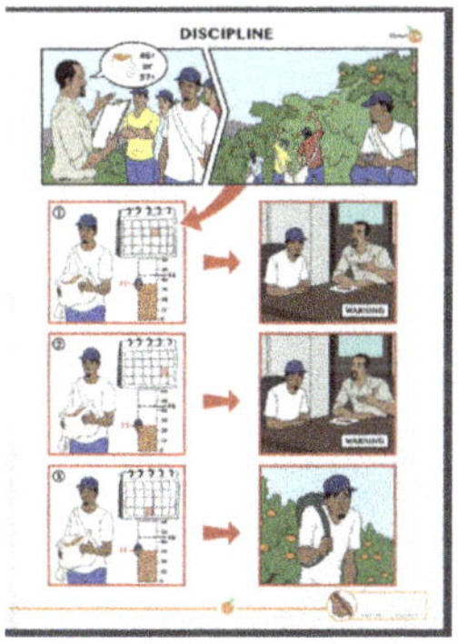
</td>
<td>This is a script of the narration of the adjacent image file that is part of a typical Comic Contract

'Discipline

You need to pick a minimum of 46 bags of clementines per day.

You may take a break every now and then, but if you end up picking less than 46 bags, you may receive a warning.

For example, if you pick only 39 bags in a day, you will receive a warning, your first warning.

If you later again fail to pick the required 46 bags of clementines per day, for example, if you only pick 25 bags instead of 46 bags, you will again receive a warning, your second warning.

If you later then again fail to pick the required 46 bags of clementines, your employment contract will be terminated and you will have to leave the farm.'</td>
</tr>
<tr>
<td colspan="2">But the display of a whole page on a phone is too cluttered and small, so we have also developed the zooming and panning function, so that the contract is easy to follow on a small screen.</td>
</tr>
</table>

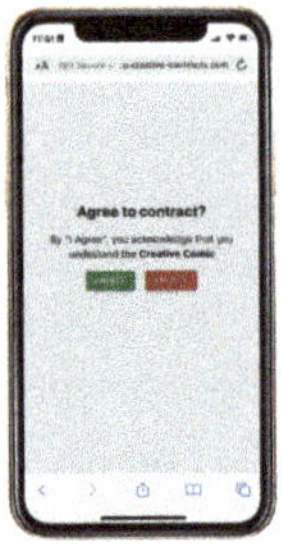	At the end of the presentation of the Composite Comic Contract, the users will be invited to accept the contract by clicking 'I Agree', or they may decline the offer of the contract.
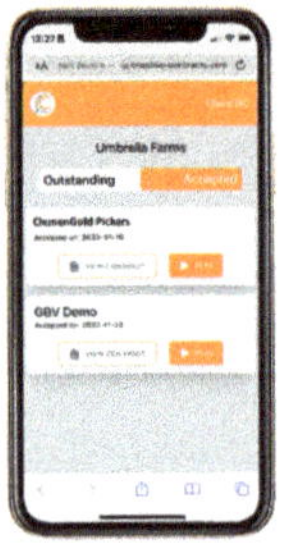	After accepting the contract, the users' signed contract will be displayed under the 'accepted' screen. When users click on the PLAY CONTRACT button, they can review the audio visual version of the contract to check their rights, obligations and procedures as many times as they like whenever they like.
	When users click on the VIEW CONTRACT button, they can view, download and print the PDF version of the signed contract, together with the date and time and other metadata of the presentation and signature of their contract.
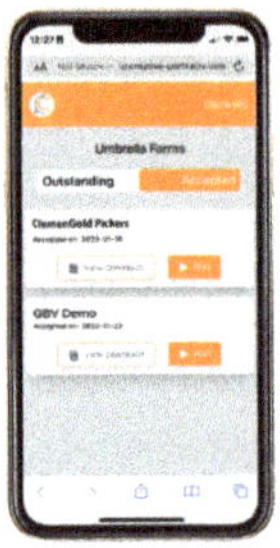	The same composite format and contracting process may be used to communicate and confirm all other important information to the user, for example, various workplace policies, health and safety advice or notices.

6. POSSIBILITY-DRIVEN DESIGN AND RESPONSIBLE USE OF AI FOR SUSTAINABILITY

Marika Salo-Lahti and Helena Haapio

Abstract

Much of the legal scholarship has focused on past or present problems and issues rather than future possibilities. Practitioners involved in legal drafting have focused primarily on conflicts and legal enforcement, rather than on goals and successful implementation. For scholars and practitioners with a proactive legal and design mindset, goals and possibilities drive the work. In addition to mindset and thinking, doing – implementation – is critical. In this paper, we merge proactive legal thinking with possibility-driven design and move from thinking to doing, using templates, design patterns and AI tools. Our examples illustrate how the responsible use of AI tools can help navigate the new legal landscape of sustainability, and how possibility-driven legal design can be used as a framework for balancing the needs and expectations of people, businesses and society at large. By working in this way, we argue, it is possible to achieve better investment decisions and more sustainable and responsible contracting – ultimately better business and a better society.

1. Proactive Legal Thinking and Doing for Legal Design

1.1. Combining Possibility-Driven Design with a Proactive Approach to Law

Design affects all aspects of our society: homes, workplaces, transportation and communication. The challenging years of the pandemic forced a new approach to their design. All designed products, services, environments and systems can influence our wellness and health to a greater or lesser extent.[1] *Positive design* refers to the forms of design that consider the impact of design on the well-being of individuals and societies.[2]

---

1 Mariluz Soto, Haian Xue and Emmanuel Tsekleves, 'Design for Balance: Wellness and Health' (2022) 7(6) Base, Diseño E Innovación 4.

2 Delft Institute of Positive Design, 'Our Mission' <https://diopd.org/about-us/mission/> accessed 12 February 2023. According to the Positive Design Manifest, 'positive design is an umbrella term for all forms of design, design research, and design intention that pay explicit attention to the impact of design on the subjective

For a long-time, however, neither doctors nor lawyers focused on well-being. Instead, they mostly provided *ex post* services: curing the sick and solving legal problems.[3] With a new mindset and legal design, law can be used *ex ante,* proactively, to promote what is desirable and prevent what is not. A proactive, possibility-driven approach to law makes it possible to design the legal well-being of people and organisations, rather than focusing on curing their illnesses, such as disputes and litigation. By integrating legal considerations into the design process, it is possible to create solutions that are legally sound, user-friendly, and effective: an excellent example of the promotive dimension of proactive law[4]. In this paper, we merge our proactive law perspective with a positive, possibility-driven design approach. These approaches, we argue, can enrich the understanding and use of legal design.

While the traditional design approach is typically used in situations where a specific problem or set of problems has been identified, the possibility-driven design process can be initiated and guided by the exploration of possibilities even when there are no problems in sight. Rather than focusing on identifying, analysing and addressing problems or challenges, possibility-driven design envisions *what could be,* rather than *what is.* To continue the health analogy, even healthy people can feel better, and it is important to take care of oneself even when one is not sick. While the problem-driven approach focuses on removing and resolving existing problems and preventing future ones, the possibili-

---

well-being of individuals and communities'. Positive design is noted to create possibilities: it 'envisions and realizes optimistic futures. Rather than merely reducing people's problems, it offers them opportunities to improve their well-being'.

3 It should be noted that in medicine, since the development of genetic studies, there has been a greater emphasis on personalised care and health management. In these respects, legal design could do for law what personalised medicine has done for medicine. For the latter, see, e.g., Laura H Goetz and Nicholas J Schork, 'Personalized Medicine: Motivation, Challenges, and Progress' (2018) 109(6) Fertility and Sterility 952.

4 The proactive law approach differentiates two aspects of proactivity, one being the promotive dimension (promoting what is desirable; encouraging good behaviour) and the other being the preventive dimension (preventing what is not desirable, keeping legal risks from materialising). See, e.g., Opinion of the European Economic and Social Committee on 'The proactive law approach: a further step towards better regulation at EU level' [2009] Official Journal of the European Union C175/26, para 5.3.

ty-driven design goes beyond this, seeking to design artefacts that ultimately improve people's lives.[5]

Both approaches are important and necessary dimensions of legal design. They are not mutually exclusive and can often be used in combination or in sequence during the design process. We argue for a greater focus on possibilities and ways to use the law and design to achieve new and more ambitious goals, not just to remove barriers and resolve or prevent problems. To turn this vision into action, we need to set goals, navigate the legal landscape, move *from thinking to doing* and improve individuals' self-care by promoting their *financial* and *legal literacy*. This will lead to positive outcomes, such as legal empowerment, optimal functioning, and improved access to justice.[6]

As with all human-centred design, our proposed approach seeks positive solutions that take into account people's different characteristics.[7] This is necessary if we want to empower people and promote their legal self-care. Rather than the passive transfer of information – which is often the case with conventional legal drafting and documents – this requires knowledge of user needs, technological possibilities and the context in which the user will make sense of the information provided.[8] As with design in general, user needs are put at the core, and, where appropriate, technology is used to respond to the needs of different audiences. The Nobel laureate Richard H. Thaler uses the term 'choice architecture' to refer to the practical fact that how the environment in which people make decisions is designed affects the decisions they make.[9] In other

---

5 For possibility-driven design, see, e.g., Pia Tamminen, *Possibility-Driven Design in Design-Oriented Communities* (Aalto University publication series Doctoral dissertations 235/2016, 2016) 22.

6 Helena Haapio, Thomas D Barton and Marcelo Corrales Compagnucci, 'Legal Design for the Common Good: Proactive Legal Care by Design' in Marcelo Corrales Compagnucci, Helena Haapio, Margaret Hagan and Michael Doherty (eds), *Legal Design: Integrating Business, Design and Legal Thinking with Technology* (Edward Elgar 2021).

7 For possibility-driven design, see, e.g., Tamminen (n 5) 22.

8 James Utterback, Bengt-Arne Vedin, Eduardo Alvarez, Sten Ekman, Susan Walsh Sanderson, Bruce Tether and Roberto Verganti, *Design-Inspired Innovation* (World Scientific Publishing Co. 2006) 163–164.

9 See, e.g., Richard H Thaler, 'From Cashews to Nudges: The Evolution of Behavioral Economics' (2018) 108(6) American Economic Review 1265, 1283. See also Richard

words, design is not about decorating, it has a huge impact on people's decisions and their outcomes.

A search on SSRN or Google Scholar for topics such as proactive law, proactive legal design, legal health or legal well-being will reveal resources related to research, particularly in the Nordic countries, that shows how design can help bring future-oriented legal thinking into practice. Scholars of proactive/preventive law and proactive legal design have for some time seen lawyers not only as fighters or problem-solvers, but also as planners and designers. Moving beyond problem-solving thinking, they have applied foresight and design in their search for desirable futures, legal well-being and the common good. In this paper we build on the work of these scholars and expand our radar to cover two specific areas of application, namely, 1) sustainability disclosure and reporting, and 2) sustainable and responsible business-to-business (B2B) contracting, both of which are highlighted in the new EU sustainability legislation.

1.2. Towards Action: Merging Possibility-Driven Legal Design with AI

According to the Legal Design Alliance (LeDA), legal design is about using human-centred design in the legal domain to facilitate positive results and proactively address issues before they escalate into conflicts and disputes.[10] Based on this definition, legal design aligns with the essence of possibility-driven thinking. Legal design encourages interdisciplinary cooperation and places emphasis on the perspectives of *all* users, not just lawyers, judges, and regulators.[11] In order to 'make the legal system work better for people',[12] legal design has very practical goals. It seeks

---

H Thaler and Cass Sunstein, *Nudge: Improving Decisions about Health, Wealth, and Happiness* (Yale University Press 2008).

10 See The Legal Design Alliance, 'What is legal design?' <www.legaldesignalliance.org/> accessed 31 August 2023. LeDA, according to the website, is 'a network of lawyers, designers, technologists, academics, and other professionals who are committed to making the legal system more human-centered and effective, through the use of design'.

11 ibid.

12 Michael Doherty, Marcelo Corrales Compagnucci, Helena Haapio and Margaret Hagan, 'A New Attitude to Law's Empire: the Potentialities of Legal Design'

to make the best of law and legal information. In the context of legal information, the core topic of this paper, this includes using information design tools and methods such as visualisation and simplification.[13] Here the perspective is closely linked to the goals of proactive law: enabling and empowering people to make better choices and have clarity about their rights and responsibilities.

This paper highlights the opportunities of legal design by linking it to the promotive dimension of the proactive approach. Moreover, if the aim is to make legal information work better, the focus must be on action. Rather than simply aiming for human-readable information, we should be more ambitious and aim for human-actionable information – something that is actually likely to be used and implemented by the target audience.[14] AI, together with more traditional legal design tools, can help achieve this goal.

The potential of new technologies is well recognised in the field of legal design.[15] In the context of information design, AI tools can assist both readers and writers of legal information. For example, language models such as *GPT-4* and *ChatGPT* can generate simplified summaries of long texts and translate legalese into human language (and vice versa). Our examples here and elsewhere[16] show that AI-powered writing assistants

---

in Marcelo Corrales Compagnucci, Helena Haapio, Margaret Hagan and Michael Doherty (eds), *Legal Design: Integrating Business, Design and Legal Thinking with Technology* (Edward Elgar 2021) 1.

13 See, e.g., Marcelo Corrales, Mark Fenwick, Helena Haapio and Erik PM Vermeulen, 'Tomorrow's Lawyer Today? Platform-Driven Legal Tech, Smart Contracts & the New World of Legal Design' (2019) 22(10) Journal of Internet Law 3, 9.

14 We are not the first to discuss the need for actionable information in the context of contract-related research. This need has also been discussed and solutions proposed in other contexts, such as privacy and disclosure documents, where complex legal information is involved. See, e.g., Arianna Rossi, Rossana Ducato, Helena Haapio and Stefania Passera, 'When Design Met Law: Design Patterns for Information Transparency' (2019) (122–3) Droit de la Consommation – Consumenterecht 79; for contracts, see also Helena Haapio, Robert de Rooy and Thomas D Barton, 'New Contract Genres' in Erich Schweighofer, Franz Kummer, Ahti Saarenpää and Burkhard Schafer (eds), *Data Protection / LegalTech. Proceedings of the 21st International Legal Informatics Symposium IRIS 2018* (Editions Weblaw 2018).

15 Doherty and others (n 12) 1–2.

16 See, e.g., Marika Salo-Lahti, Mikko Ranta and Helena Haapio, 'AI Tools for Sustainability – Actionable Information for Both Humans and Machines' in Erich Schweig-

can also generate helpful first drafts of contract and clause summaries, explanations and reports. As AI tools have certain limitations, which are described later in Section 3.4, we argue that the role of human experts as responsible users of AI is crucial. In this way, AI tools can make a significant contribution to making information more actionable.

1.3. Possibility-Driven Design for Better Contracts, Better Business and a Better Society

Contracts play an important role in business, not only as a legal tool but also as a management tool. Contract negotiation can help to identify and align expectations and clarify objectives, roles and responsibilities. When used in this way, contracts can help reduce the risk of unnecessary misunderstandings and disputes. They can be used proactively to promote what is desirable and prevent what is not.

The proactive approach to law in fact originated in the context of contracting. The first publication in the field was 'Quality Improvement through Proactive Contracting' in 1998, written by one of the authors of this paper.[17] In the beginning, the approach was about using contracts to merge quality and risk management with preventive legal thinking in order for the parties to reach their business objectives and prevent problems and negative surprises. The goal, according to *Pohjonen*, was to ensure that the contracting parties achieve their desired results in accordance with their intentions; this requires a thorough examination of their goals and intentions and the ability to create a clear and legally sound framework for their implementation.[18]

---

hofer, Jakob Zanol and Stefan Eder (eds), *Legal Informatics as Science of Legal Methods. Proceedings of the 26th International Legal Informatics Symposium IRIS 2023* (Editions Weblaw 2023).

17 Helena Haapio, 'Quality Improvement through Proactive Contracting: Contracts Are Too Important to Be Left to Lawyers!' in *Proceedings of Annual Quality Congress (AQC), American Society for Quality (ASQ)*, vol 52 (American Society for Quality 1998).

18 Soile Pohjonen, 'Johdanto' ['Introduction'] in Soile Pohjonen (ed), *Ennakoiva sopiminen – liiketoimien suunnittelu, toteuttaminen ja riskien hallinta [Proactive Contracting – Planning, Implementing and Managing Risk in Business Transactions]* (WSOY Lakitieto 2002) v.

The early adopters of proactive contracting wanted to shift the view of contracts from merely legal tools to operational tools, with a focus on their users, especially people in charge of contract implementation.[19] When searching for ways to create contracts that are both legally and operationally functional and user-friendly, the pioneers of the approach were informed by insights from information design about matters such as people's literacy proficiencies, reading habits, information processing and overload, understanding and memory. Merging these learnings with proactive legal thinking and putting users at the centre became the mission, and proactive legal thinkers and information designers became natural allies. Proactive contract design was born. It was applied not only in the context of the design of contract documents – their content, structure, language, and presentation – but also in the design of contracting processes and their integration into business processes.[20]

The thinking, tools and methods were tested in a number of projects and contexts, which provided proof of concept beyond the domain of contracts. The first Legal Design Jam events[21] conducted in 2013 showed

19 A proactive contract has been described as one 'crafted for the parties, especially for the people in charge of its implementation in the field, not for a judge who is supposed to decide about the parties' failures' in Gerlinde Berger-Walliser, Robert C Bird and Helena Haapio, 'Promoting Business Success through Contract Visualization' (2011) 17 Journal of Law, Business & Ethics 55, 61. The authors note that most contracts are not crafted in this way. Instead, they 'contain concepts and language that non-lawyers often find overly complicated, obscure, and unappealing. This is because most contracts seem to be written by lawyers for lawyers' (ibid 56). Chris Simkins calls such contracts 'lawyer-to-lawyer' or 'L2L contracts' – contracts where 'it's lawyers that lead the process of writing, reading, negotiating and finalising the contract documents on both sides' (Chris Simkins, 'L2L Contracts: Thinking beyond B2C and B2B' (*Improving Contracts. Blog*) <https://improvingcontracts.com/l2l-contracts-thinking-beyond-b2c-and-b2b/> accessed 5 September 2023).

20 Helena Haapio, *Next Generation Contracts: A Paradigm Shift* (Lexpert Ltd 2013); Stefania Passera, *Beyond the Wall of Contract Text: Visualizing Contracts to Foster Understanding and Collaboration within and across Organizations* (Aalto University 2017); Milva Finnegan, *User-Centered Design: A Key to Contract Simplification* (University of Vaasa 2021). For reported business benefits achieved, see, e.g., Paula Doyle and Stefania Passera, 'Contract Design and Simplification – Is This Now a Must-do?' (2021) 14(56) International In-house Counsel Journal 7243.

21 See <http://legaldesignjam.com/jams/past-jams/>. Stefania Passera developed the idea and coined the concept of Legal Design Jam as a by-product of her doctoral research. The first Legal Design Jam events were organised in 2013, first on the

that contracts, conventions, policies, licences and legal information need not be boring, complex and inaccessible, and that designing engaging legal communication is possible even with a limited, or no budget.

Contracts have a significant impact on better business and a better society, too. Better contracts can help businesses and supply chains operate more effectively and sustainably, and contribute to a better society by promoting responsible business and procurement practices. For example, contracts can be used for setting ESG (Environmental, Social, and Governance) goals and improving transparency and accountability in transactions and relationships. In recent years, the proactive contracting approach has broadened to also include the promotion of societal goals, aiming at achieving and maintaining environmental, social and economic well-being for present and future generations. Responsible and sustainable contracting has emerged as a topic of growing interest in research and practice.[22]

Recently, the EU has proposed a plethora of new legislation related to sustainability. These proposals are well-intentioned and aim to make the EU's ambitious sustainability goals a reality. At the same time, they will impose a heavy burden of new and increased reporting requirements on companies. They will also force companies to review their procurement and contracting practices throughout their value chains. We will explore how possibility-driven design and AI can work together to help investors make better investment decisions, help companies meet their new sustainability reporting requirements, and drive sustainable and responsi-

---

CISG, the Convention on Contracts for the International Sale of Goods, as part of the Information Design Summer School on Syros, Greece, and then on the Wikimedia Trademark Policy at the d.school at Stanford University in Stanford, CA, and in San Francisco, CA, USA.

22 See, e.g., Gerlinde Berger-Walliser, Paul Shrivastava and Adam Sulkowski, 'Using Proactive Legal Strategies for Corporate Environmental Sustainability' (2016) 6 Michigan Journal of Environmental and Administrative Law 1; Adam Sulkowski and Ruth Jebe, 'Evolving ESG Reporting Governance, Regime Theory, and Proactive Law: Predictions and Strategies' (2022) 59 American Business Law Journal 449; Nevena Jevremovic, 'Enforcing Sustainability Clauses in Global Supply Chains with a Focus on Proactive and Relational Contract Theory: Case of SDG 12' (2022) 25 ZEuS Zeitschrift für Europarechtliche Studien 393; and Juho Saloranta and Anna Hurmerinta-Haanpää, 'Proactive Contract Theory in the Context of Corporate Sustainability Due Diligence' (2022) 6 Journal of Strategic Contracting and Negotiation 221.

ble contracting practices – all ultimately contributing to better business and a better society.

2. Sustainability and the Need for Tools to Help Navigate the Legal Landscape

2.1. Managing the Flood of New Legislation on Sustainability

Sustainability is at the heart of the European Union. In particular, it is guided by the European Green Deal, which is a comprehensive and ambitious set of sustainability objectives for the Union. The most important goal is to become the world's first climate-neutral continent by 2050. Climate Law (EU) 2021/1119[23] makes this target legally binding on EU Institutions and Member States. In addition, there are a number of subgoals, such as clean water, energy efficiency, and healthy food.[24] The Green Deal also implements the United Nations' 2030 Agenda and the UN Sustainable Development Goals.[25] These global goals include, among others, ending poverty and hunger, achieving gender equality, and taking urgent action to combat climate change.[26]

To translate sustainability goals into action, investors, citizens and other stakeholders need *information* on the sustainability efforts of companies and other actors. However, the Corporate Sustainability Reporting Directive (CSRD) EU 2022/2464[27] identifies a gap between users' information needs and the sustainability information provided by com-

23 Regulation (EU) 2021/1119 of the European Parliament and of the Council of 30 June 2021 establishing the framework for achieving climate neutrality and amending Regulations (EC) No 401/2009 and (EU) 2018/1999 ('European Climate Law') [2021] OJ L243/1.

24 European Commission, 'The European Green Deal' (Communication) COM(2019) 640 final, 4, 6–15.

25 ibid 3.

26 United Nations, 'Transforming Our World: the 2030 Agenda for Sustainable Development' (Resolution adopted by the General Assembly on 25 September 2015, A/RES/70/1, 21 October 2015) 14.

27 Directive (EU) 2022/2464 of the European Parliament and of the Council of 14 December 2022 amending Regulation (EU) No 537/2014, Directive 2004/109/EC, Directive 2006/43/EC and Directive 2013/34/EU, as regards corporate sustainability reporting (CSRD) [2022] OJ L322/15.

panies. This gap is expected to widen if no action is taken. This would have significant negative consequences, such as the inability of investors to take sustainability into account when making investment decisions, and potential systemic risks that could even threaten financial stability. Without adequate information and a common understanding of what is 'sustainable', it is difficult to hold companies and other actors accountable for their impacts on the environment, people and society. The lack of common measures and definitions will also make it difficult for companies to assess, manage and respond to their sustainability efforts.[28]

Legislation is an important tool for achieving sustainability goals. As a result, the EU has recently issued a wealth of new regulations, directives and legislative proposals related to sustainability. To name just a few, the EU Taxonomy Regulation (EU) 2020/852[29] provides a classification framework for sustainable activities. It provides a definition of 'environmentally sustainable' economic activities and new disclosure requirements. Standardised definitions and measures are intended to prevent 'greenwashing', the marketing of products as environmentally friendly, when they are not.[30] The CSRD also introduces new and much broader reporting requirements for companies. In addition, the Sustainable Finance Disclosure Regulation (SFDR)[31] imposes new disclosure requirements for financial market participants and financial advisors at both the company and product level.

The proposal for a Directive on Corporate Sustainability Due Diligence (CSDDD) recognises the role of companies' day-to-day activities in achieving sustainability goals. The proposed Directive covers large companies as well as listed companies.[32] It aims to ensure that companies

28 ibid recital 14.

29 Regulation (EU) 2020/852 of the European Parliament and of the Council of 18 June 2020 on the establishment of a framework to facilitate sustainable investment, and amending Regulation (EU) 2019/2088 [2020] OJ L198/13.

30 ibid recitals 11–12, 19, arts 1, 3, 5–8.

31 Regulation (EU) 2019/2088 of the European Parliament and of the Council of 27 November 2019 on sustainability-related disclosures in the financial services sector [2019] OJ L317/1.

32 European Commission, 'Proposal for a Directive of the European Parliament and of the Council on Corporate Sustainability Due Diligence and amending Directive (EU) 2019/1937' COM(2022) 71 final. For the relevance of the CSDDD proposal for sustainable and responsible contracting, see also Section 2.4.

identify and, where necessary, prevent, end or mitigate adverse impacts not only of their own and their subsidiaries' operations, but also of their business partners in their supply chains.

In addition to several more substance-related legislative proposals, such as proposals for a Nature Restoration Law[33] and a Regulation on Deforestation-Free Products[34], the EU has also created benchmarks, standards, and labels to help identify sustainable products. As the standards and labels are based on the EU Taxonomy, they will increase integrity and trust in the sustainable financial market and make it easier for investors to find sustainable investments. For example, the proposed European Green Bond Regulation sets a standard for high-quality green bonds.[35] Benchmarks are also useful tools for investors, as they allow them to measure and track the performance of assets and set allocations accordingly.[36]

Despite the growing need for sustainability information, the results of a European Commission study have shown that this demand is not being met.[37] Sustainability information is not easily accessible and digitally usable by public authorities in their supervisory and regulatory role, or by investors, financial professionals, consumers and other audiences. While new disclosure requirements, such as the EU Taxonomy, SFDR and CSRD, will increase the transparency of sustainability information, they will also increase the need for information accessibility. With its proposal for the European Single Access Point (ESAP) Regulation, the European Commission aims to bring 'simplification and improved efficiency' to sustainability information, by streamlining disclosure channels. The ESAP will be a

33 European Commission, 'Proposal for a Regulation of the European Parliament and of the Council on nature restoration' COM(2022) 304 final.

34 European Commission, 'Proposal for a Regulation of the European Parliament and of the Council on the making available on the Union market as well as export from the Union of certain commodities and products associated with deforestation and forest degradation and repealing Regulation (EU) No 995/2010' COM(2021) 706 final.

35 European Commission, 'Proposal for a Regulation of the European Parliament and of the Council on European green bonds' COM(2021) 391 final.

36 European Commission, 'Action Plan: Financing Sustainable Growth' (Communication) COM(2018) 97 final, 4, 7.

37 European Commission, 'Impact Assessment Report' SWD(2021) 344 final, 18, recital 12.

central platform that gathers public information, including sustainability information, in one place.[38]

2.2. The Link between Better Business and Better Society

While climate and nature issues typically dominate in sustainability discussions, it is important to note that sustainability also has social and economic components. The key elements of sustainability are often described by the acronym ESG, which stands for Environmental, Social, and Governance.[39] Economic sustainability is necessary in order to have the resources to invest in other aspects of sustainability, such as companies looking after their supply chains. Accordingly, better business and a better society are intrinsically linked.

Sustainability goals cannot be achieved without adequate financing. According to the Green Deal, the private sector is the key to financing the green transition.[40] The EU has given sustainable finance a central role in achieving its sustainability goals. There is a huge need for additional investment to meet the targets, and the Sustainable Finance Framework aims to help with this. The Framework consists of three building blocks: 1) a classification system, or 'taxonomy', of sustainable activities, 2) disclosures that provide investors with the necessary information on sustainability, and 3) tools, such as benchmarks and standards.[41] The goal of these is to prevent greenwashing. Because of the business value of sustainability, companies can gain undeserved advantages by making false sustainability claims.[42] This, in turn, can reduce the motivation of other companies to act sustainably. So false sustainability claims can actually lead to worse business and a worse society.

38 European Commission, 'Proposal for a Regulation of the European Parliament and of the Council establishing a European single access point providing centralised access to publicly available information of relevance to financial services, capital markets and sustainability' (ESAP proposal) COM(2021) 723 final, 5, recital 2.

39 See, e.g., European Commission, 'Strategy for Financing the Transition to a Sustainable Economy' (Communication) COM(2021) 390 final, 7.

40 COM(2019) 640 final, 16–17.

41 COM(2021) 390 final, 1–2.

42 See, e.g., COM(2019) 640 final, 8.

Accurate information and standardised definitions are therefore at the heart of the EU's efforts to promote sustainability. However, transparency alone cannot solve all sustainability problems, and there are many new obligations related to more concrete actions, such as greenhouse gas reduction and energy efficiency. In the following Sections, we will explore how sustainability disclosures and reporting, as well as sustainable and responsible contracting, can promote sustainability. Easy access to reliable sustainability information can greatly facilitate sustainable investment decisions. Sustainability requirements can also be incorporated into commercial contracts.[43]

2.3. Sustainability Reporting and Investor Disclosures to Promote Sustainable Investment

Investors need reliable sustainability information in order to make investment decisions that promote sustainability. Companies will also benefit from sustainability information because it can help them access financial capital and manage their own sustainability risks and opportunities. In addition, it can serve as a basis for better communication between companies and their stakeholders.[44] Most sustainability information is derived from companies' sustainability reporting and disclosures.

Despite the new EU legislation, sustainability reporting is not a new phenomenon. EU companies have been required to report on sustainability under the Non-Financial Reporting Directive 2014/95/EU.[45] However, the term 'non-financial' is confusing and imprecise, giving the impression that sustainability information has no financial relevance.[46] The CSRD makes sustainability reporting both broader and more standardised than before. It also aims to ensure the comparability of sustainability information and disclosure of all the relevant information. Machine-readability is an important objective as well, as it will facilitate the use of the future ESAP platform.

---

43 See also Salo-Lahti, Ranta and Haapio (n 16).

44 CSRD (n 27) recital 12.

45 Directive 2014/95/EU of the European Parliament and of the Council of 22 October 2014 amending Directive 2013/34/EU as regards disclosure of non-financial and diversity information by certain large undertakings and groups [2014] OJ L330/1.

46 CSRD (n 27) recital 8.

The SFDR requires financial market participants and financial advisors to disclose specific sustainability information to end investors. Identifying clients' sustainability preferences is now part of the duties of investment advisors. This should make sustainability more visible in the advisory process and increase the demand for sustainable investment products. The new EU legislation also aims to help investors identify sustainable investments. Therefore, the term 'sustainable investment' is harmonised in the SFDR. According to Article 2, sustainable investments contribute to environmental objectives as measured, for example, through key resource efficiency indicators on energy use, waste generation and greenhouse gas emissions. Sustainable investments can also contribute to social objectives, such as reducing inequality or promoting social inclusion.

In financial market law, the typical way to protect retail investors is to impose information requirements on those who have superior knowledge – typically companies and financial firms, as is also the case with sustainability information. This approach implicitly assumes that people are fairly rational and will read and digest the information they receive. It also homogenises retail investors, lumping them together as one large group of investors who all benefit from the same type of information.

Financial literacy studies can provide some insight into the average person's ability to use investment disclosures. These studies have shown that people's financial literacy is generally low. According to the OECD's definition, financial literacy consists of three main components: knowledge, behaviour and attitudes – i.e., it encompasses the aspects from thinking to doing.[47] The OECD has also measured financial well-being – a state of being in which individuals have control over their day-to-day finances, are able to cope with financial shocks, are able to achieve their financial goals and have the freedom to make choices that enable them to enjoy

47 OECD, 'OECD/INFE 2020 International Survey of Adult Financial Literacy' (2020) 3 <www.oecd.org/financial/education/launchoftheoecdinfeglobalfinancialliteracysurveyreport.htm> accessed 1 March 2023. See also Tiina Koskelainen, Panu Kalmi, Eusebio Scornavacca and Tero Vartiainen, 'Financial Literacy in the Digital Age – A Research Agenda' (2023) The Journal of Consumer Affairs 1, 3 <https://doi.org/10.1111/joca.12510> accessed 1 March 2023. Koskelainen and others note that, contrary to the OECD definition, behaviour is typically an outcome variable influenced by financial literacy rather than a component of literacy.

life.[48] The OECD found that financial well-being also scored low (below 50 % of the maximum), meaning that financial situation does not contribute positively to well-being, but rather causes stress and worry. There are also especially vulnerable investor groups that have been shown to have more difficulty with financial literacy and financial well-being. For example, young people (aged 18–29) scored lower on financial literacy. They had lower levels of financial knowledge and less prudent financial behaviour. At the other end of the spectrum, seniors (age 60 and over) also had lower financial literacy and financial well-being scores.[49]

High levels of financial literacy are associated with better economic outcomes and help people make day-to-day financial decisions as well as in long-term financial activities.[50] The perspectives of financial literacy and financial well-being are consistent with the goals of legal literacy, legal well-being, and legal design. They take into account the 'thinking to doing' approach and differences among individuals, and they focus on well-being rather than problems. However, these goals and perspectives have not yet materialised in investor disclosures and company reporting. Loughran and McDonald noted that investors do not read company annual reports. In fact, usually, they do not even open them.[51]

The core problem may be that reports and disclosures are typically written in a way that does not encourage or entice us to read them. The European Commission found in its study that the current investor disclosure framework is limited in what it can achieve, as current disclosures are not 'engaging'.[52] According to the Commission, engagement

---

48 Consumer Financial Protection Bureau, 'Financial Well-Being: The Goal of Financial Education' (January 2015) 5.

49 OECD (n 47) 9.

50 Koskelainen and others (n 47) 1–2.

51 Tim Loughran and Bill McDonald, 'The Use of EDGAR Filings by Investors' (2017) 18(2) Journal of Behavioral Finance 231, 231–232. Loughran and McDonald studied the 10-K filings of US companies, and how often they were accessed from the EDGAR (Electronic Data Gathering and Retrieval) filings. Although the EDGAR server log cannot capture all the possible views and downloads of the reports, it is virtually the primary source of this type of information. EDGAR is administered by the US Securities and Exchange Commission (SEC).

52 European Commission, Directorate-General for Financial Stability, Financial Services and Capital Markets Union, Daniela Uličná, Máté Vincze, Marius Mosoreanu, Maxime Hayet, Raphaël de Landsheer, Osmo Järvi, Véronique Bruggeman, Julija

is a precondition for reading and understanding disclosures, and making decisions based on them. While attention is paid to the availability and accessibility of information, the current framework does not help to make the documents engaging enough to capture the attention of users. Although standardisation of terms and measures will help to improve understanding, it cannot overcome the difficulties arising from the complexity of the terminology used. The European Commission states that even when this complexity is presented in a standardised way, it still does 'inhibit understanding'.[53] Later in this paper, we propose strategies and tools to solve this problem.

2.4. Sustainable and Responsible Contracting

The CSDDD proposal mentioned in Section 2.1 as an example of the flood of EU legislation on sustainability notes the critical role that contracts and procurement practices play in promoting sustainability throughout global value chains.[54] Its proposed Article 7 in its original form required companies to seek 'contractual assurances' from their direct business partners that they will comply with the company's code of conduct and that such 'assurances' may also be sought from the business partners of business partners that are part of the company's value chain.

It has been suggested that companies could fulfil many of their obligations under the originally proposed CSDDD by simply including clauses in their contracts requiring suppliers to follow their Code of Conduct. There has been wide criticism that this is going to lead to 'tick-the-box compliance' and that the required 'contractual assurances' would have allowed companies to pass on their responsibilities to their suppliers.[55]

Sproge, Sarah Fialon, Willem Pieter De Groen, Cosmina Amariei, Inna Oliinyk and Jelmer Nagtegaal, 'Disclosure, Inducements, and Suitability Rules for Retail Investors Study. Final report' (Publications Office of the European Union 2023) 14.

53 ibid.

54 Salo-Lahti, Ranta and Haapio (n 16) 203.

55 See, e.g., European Parliament Committee on Legal Affairs, 'Draft Report on the proposal for a directive of the European Parliament and of the Council on Corporate Sustainability Due Diligence and amending Directive (EU) 2019/1937 (COM(2022)0071 – C9-0050/2022 – 2022/0051(COD))' <www.europarl.europa.eu/doceo/document/JURI-PR-738450_EN.pdf> accessed 13 February 2023; and

In December 2023, the Council and the European Parliament reached a provisional agreement on the CSDDD. The wording of Article 7 in this version of the CSDDD has changed somewhat, but it contains a similar obligation to seek and establish contractual assurances.[56]

The discussion around the CSDDD proposal has brought today's procurement practices and contracts to the fore and drawn attention to how contracts are currently used and how they could be used in the future. Contracts have been seen in a new light, and growing attention has been paid by scholars and practitioners to the various purposes and functions of contracts. A similar discussion had already started, particularly among the promoters of proactive legal thinking, before sustainable and responsible contracting became a thing.[57]

Despite all the potential benefits that contracts can offer, research and practice tell us that contracts do not always work for the purposes they are expected to serve. The contract law duty to read contracts is not realistic. In commercial practice, contracts are not necessarily read – and

---

Susan Maslow, 'No Safe Harbor in the "Contract Assurances" Required in the EU Directive Proposal' (*AMM Blog*, 28 March 2022) <www.ammlaw.com/blog/no-safe-harbor-in-the-contract-assurances-required-in-the-eu-directive-proposal.html> accessed 13 February 2023.

56 Council of the EU, 'Corporate sustainability due diligence: Council and Parliament strike deal to protect environment and human rights' <www.consilium.europa.eu/en/press/press-releases/2023/12/14/corporate-sustainability-due-diligence-council-and-parliament-strike-deal-to-protect-environment-and-human-rights/> accessed 31 January 2024. See also Part 2 in Richard Gardiner, 'Only One Item on the Agenda for Today's Meeting of the Council of the European Union #CompanyLaw Working Party' [2024] LinkedIn <www.linkedin.com/feed/update/urn:li:activity:7157652239174483968/> accessed 31 January 2024.

57 See, e.g., Berger-Walliser, Shrivastava and Sulkowski (n 22). See also Anna Hurmerinta-Haanpää, *The Many Functions of Contracts: How Companies Use Contracts in Interorganizational Exchange Relations* (Doctoral Dissertation, University of Turku 2021); IACCM, *The Purpose of a Contract: An IACCM Research Report* (2017) <www.worldcc.com/Portals/IACCM/resources/files/9876_j18069-iaccm-purpose-of-contract-a4-2017-11-14-v1-webready.pdf> accessed 13 February 2023; and Marcelo Corrales Compagnucci, Helena Haapio and Mark Fenwick (eds), *Research Handbook on Contract Design* (Edward Elgar 2022), where Parts II and III include several chapters dedicated to 'Why contract design matters: rethinking the business and legal purpose and functions of contracts' and 'Designing better contracts for business and legal purposes'.

are even less likely to be understood by people who lack legal training.[58] This problem has been known for quite some time, especially in the context of consumer contracts: they are not engaging, and readers give up before starting to read. The problems and their causes are well known and widely researched.[59] Yet they persist in practice. The world of contracts – or contract research – does not change quickly. Apart from the proponents of proactive legal thinking and design, there has been much more academic work on the problems than on the solutions.

Contracts can be a powerful tool to promote, measure and monitor sustainability in supply chains. But if contracts remain unread, they fail to achieve this goal. This is where design comes in. The fields of legal design and contract design help legal and business professionals improve communications, services and solutions by applying design mindsets, tools and methods.

3. Strategies and Tools to Promote Sustainability

3.1. Possibility-Driven Design Solutions

According to the European Commission, disclosure is 'a necessary but insufficient means to support retail investors in making their choice', for reasons that were explained in Section 2.3.[60] Possibility-driven design can make a significant contribution to overcoming these challenges. It is

---

58 Mattias Rättzén, 'Automated Contract Review: Challenges and Outcomes of a Data Annotation Framework' (2022) 62 Jurimetrics Journal 225, 236. See also Berger-Walliser and others (n 19) 56: 'too many contracts that are much too long require more reading time than most managers can afford.... So business people may enter into contracts every day without examining them.' See also Simkins (n 19).

59 See, e.g., Uri Benoliel and Shmuel I Becher, 'The Duty to Read the Unreadable' (2019) 60 Boston College Law Review 2255; Wendy Wagner and Will Walker, *Incomprehensible!: A Study of How Our Legal System Encourages Incomprehensibility, Why It Matters, and What We Can Do About It* (CUP 2019); and Wendy E Wagner, 'Rethinking Legal Requirements: A Case Study of Incomprehensible Consumer Contracts in the United States' in Marcelo Corrales Compagnucci, Helena Haapio and Mark Fenwick (eds), *Research Handbook on Contract Design* (Edward Elgar 2022).

60 European Commission, Directorate-General for Financial Stability, Financial Services and Capital Markets Union and others (n 52) 14.

not enough for users of sustainability information to pay more attention to sustainability – sustainability needs to be moved from thinking to doing, taking action, in order to advance the goals of the Green Deal.

In this Section, we introduce some of the more prominent tools and give examples of how they can be used. First, we will discuss design patterns, which provide solutions for communicating complex information more clearly and in a way that is more likely to be read, understood and acted upon.[61] Templates and models can also facilitate the task of communicating effectively. In addition, responsible use of AI can help address the challenges of sustainability communication and contracting. For example, it can help draft summaries and explanations and present key information in a more engaging way. It can also make it easier to find information in large amounts of data. So, AI can help both readers and writers of contracts, sustainability reports and disclosures. However, the limitations and risks related to AI tools must also be taken into account, and they will be discussed later.

One of the problems with investor disclosures identified in the European Commission study mentioned above is that there is typically little focus on the environment and context in which the disclosure is used. Taking these into account would encourage investors to use and act on the information.[62] Possibility-driven design and AI tools can help contextualise and personalise sustainability information, for example, by changing its mass formatting or tone of voice to a personalised version, adjusting to the knowledge level of an individual and adapting the content and presentation accordingly.[63]

As one of the aims of this paper is to move from vision to action – from (design) thinking to doing – in order to genuinely promote sustainability, we argue for the need to move from merely drafting communications to designing communications and to consider the needs of different user groups. This is also a prerequisite for better legal literacy and self-care.

61 For contracts, see WorldCC Foundation, Stefania Passera and Helena Haapio, 'Contract Design Pattern Library' <https://contract-design.worldcc.com/> accessed 31 January 2023.

62 European Commission Directorate-General for Financial Stability, Financial Services and Capital Markets Union and others (n 52) 14.

63 See also Haapio, Barton and Corrales Compagnucci (n 6) 72.

In summary, we argue that design solutions have the potential to close the 'engagement' gap identified in the context of contracts and other complex information, such as disclosures. Legal design is based on the vision of a legal system that is more straightforward, more engaging, and more user-friendly, including the way information is presented.[64] Together with AI, possibility-driven legal design can help to overcome the communication challenges of sustainability information and serve as a foundation for sustainable action.

3.2. Design Patterns

Design patterns and pattern libraries have been used in various fields, including architecture, software engineering and UX design, as a way to share design knowledge. Design patterns can be defined as reusable models of a solution to frequently occurring problems in a domain. They also exist in the domains of legal design and contract design.[65] The use of patterns can help communicate design concepts and provide effective solutions to design problems.

In the context of contracts, the WorldCC Contract Design Pattern Library[66] provides design principles and real-world examples of how the patterns have been implemented. A design pattern is not a ready-made

---

64 ibid.

65 For examples and references, see, e.g., Helena Haapio and Margaret Hagan, 'Design Patterns for Contracts' in Erich Schweighofer, Franz Kummer, Walter Hötzendorfer and Georg Borges (eds), *Networks. Proceedings of the 19th International Legal Informatics Symposium IRIS 2016* (Österreichische Computer Gesellschaft OCG/books@ocg.at 2016); Rossi and others (n 14) 79; Helena Haapio and Stefania Passera, 'Contracts as Interfaces: Visual Representation Patterns in Contract Design' in Daniel M Katz, Ron Dolin and Michael J Bommarito (eds), *Legal Informatics* (CUP 2021); Arianna Rossi and Helena Haapio, 'Proactive Legal Design: Embedding Values in the Design of Legal Artefacts' in Erich Schweighofer, Franz Kummer and Ahti Saarenpää (eds), *Internet of Things. Proceedings of the 22nd International Legal Infomatics Symposium IRIS 2019* (Editions Weblaw 2019). Examples of Legal Communication Design Pattern Libraries can be found at <https://legaltechdesign.com/communication-design/legal-design-pattern-libraries/>, which includes a Know Your Rights Design Pattern Library, Contract Design Pattern Library and Privacy Design Pattern Library.

66 WorldCC Foundation, Passera and Haapio (n 61).

template or a finished design, but rather a model approach that provides guidance and examples for identifying a problem and developing a solution. The design pattern should not be strictly followed – instead, it should be adapted to meet the needs of the designer, the context and the audience.

Let's take an example: different readers and contexts can be accommodated with layering, which can be used both online and offline. With layering, the same information is presented in different ways, depending on the needs and capabilities of the audience. Creative Commons Licences are an early example of layering. Their three-layer design consists of the Legal Code layer – the typical 'lawyer-readable' version of the text; the Commons Deed – the 'human readable' version of the licence; and finally, the 'machine readable' version, which allows search engines and other technologies to 'understand' and interact with the licence terms.[67] With layering, it is possible to help readers avoid information overload: key information is quickly and easily findable, while details are available 'on demand' for those who want or need them. Layering is a good practice to support strategic reading.[68] A layered layout with multiple headings can help make the content easier to understand by breaking it down into smaller, more digestible sections. In this way, layering can promote transparency and facilitate acting upon information.

Adding explanations or summaries is particularly promising in our context. However, not everyone is enthusiastic about them. In a 2018 study, Uri Benoliel and Samuel Becher examined 500 widely-used websites' sign-in-wrap agreements and found that 22 included explanations or clarifications of the agreement or some of its terms, and 19 provided a summary just before the full contract terms. While such approaches may make the terms less tedious to read and arguably more memorable,

67 Creative Commons, 'About the Licences' <https://creativecommons.org/licenses/?lang=en> accessed 31 January 2023.

68 For contracts, see WorldCC Foundation, Stefania Passera and Helena Haapio, 'Layering' (*Contract Design Pattern Library*) <https://contract-design.worldcc.com/library/layering> accessed 1 March 2023. The Library currently contains ten different 'pattern families' that each have several patterns. There are currently eight different patterns in the layering 'pattern family', namely accordion, clause summaries, exemplar, guidance notes, skimmable headings, swim lanes, term sheet and user guide format, all with examples from real-world contracts. WorldCC Foundation, Passera and Haapio (n 61).

they raise several concerns, according to the authors. First, readers may be unsure about what they are supposed to read: the formal terms, the annotations, or both, and what parts of the text are legally binding. In the event of a legal dispute, should courts favour one type of text over another? Moreover, the authors ask, might such a text cause consumers to become less vigilant and not fully aware of the legal risks and obligations of the contract?

While the concerns raised by Benoliel and Becher are valid in the context of consumer contracts, they may not carry the same weight in the context of this paper: B2B contracts, where parties typically have more experience with and understanding of contracts.[69] In addition, the Benoliel and Becher article discusses a specific and narrow (though common) category of consumer standard form contracts: sign-in-wrap contracts, where consumers are asked to agree to the terms and conditions of a website. Web wrap contracts and complex B2B contracts serve fundamentally different purposes and audiences. The latter type of contracts often include hundreds if not thousands of obligations and detailed business and financial terms that not only need to be understood by the parties but also adhered to and potentially passed along the supply chain.

Some organisations and lawyers may wish their contracts and terms to remain unread – proactive lawyers think and act differently, using explanations to achieve greater transparency, efficiency and understanding, and adding clarifications, interpretation clauses and other contractual devices to reduce potential confusion about what to read and what parts of the text are legally binding.[70] On the question of how courts

69 Still they may be reluctant to read contracts. See Section 2.4, with references.

70 For interpretation clauses, see Chapter 3 in Marcel Fontaine and Filip de Ly, *Drafting International Contracts: An Analysis of Contract Clauses* (Brill 2009). One possible solution is to design contracts where all of their component parts are intended to be equally valid and part of the legally binding contract. For Composite Comic Contracts, which consist of images, text and a voice-over, see Anne Ketola, Robert de Rooy and Helena Haapio, 'Comic Contracts 2.0 – Contracts that Have (and Give) a Voice' in this volume. For suggestions related to the interpretation of images in contracts, see also Vesa Annola, Helena Haapio and Merja Koskela, 'Interpreting Images in Contracts' in Marcelo Corrales Compagnucci, Helena Haapio and Mark Fenwick (eds), *Research Handbook on Contract Design* (Edward Elgar 2022); Helena Haapio, Vesa Annola and Merja Koskela, 'Ten Ways to Make the Interpretation of Images More Predictable' *Contracting Excellence Journal* (5 November 2020)

should interpret the different types of text, it is important to note that in most jurisdictions the interpretation of contracts involves looking at the intention of the parties. Clear explanations can help demonstrate the intention behind certain provisions, particularly in cases where traditional legal language may be ambiguous.

3.3. Templates and Models

Contract drafting rarely starts with a blank sheet of paper. Rather, it begins with a template, form or model, or with a clause library. In today's contract practice, clauses and Codes of Conduct that address sustainability issues are frequently used. Where companies choose not to negotiate such clauses individually with each supplier, the clauses can be made part of standard terms and conditions. These tend to favour the buyer, due to the fact that there is often a major imbalance in the bargaining power between the buying companies and their suppliers. A new approach has been taken in the Model Contract Clauses known as ABA MCCs 2.0[71] produced by a Working Group of the Business Law Section of the American Bar Association. The same Working Group has also produced a model Buyer Code of Conduct called the 'Responsible Purchasing Code of Conduct'.[72] Based on these models, the leading members of the Working Group established the Responsible Contracting Project (RCP) in 2022, with the mission to improve human rights in global supply chains through innovative contracting practices. Following its mission, the RCP develops and disseminates 'practical contractual tools to support more cooperative relations between supply chain firms and better

---

<www.worldcc.com/Resources/Content-Hub/View/ArticleID/10897> accessed 13 February 2023.

71 American Bar Association, 'Contractual Clauses Project' <www.americanbar.org/groups/human_rights/business-human-rights-initiative/contractual-clauses-project/> accessed 13 February 2023. See also David Snyder, Susan Maslow and Sarah Dadush, 'Balancing Buyer and Supplier Responsibilities: Model Contract Clauses to Protect Workers in International Supply Chains, Version 2.0' (2021) 77 The Business Lawyer 115.

72 Working Group of the American Bar Association (ABA) Business Law Section, 'Responsible Purchasing Code of Conduct: Schedule Q Version 1.0' <www.americanbar.org/content/dam/aba/administrative/human_rights/contractual-clauses-project/scheduleq.pdf> accessed 13 February 2023.

human rights outcomes for workers'.[73] It has developed a toolkit, 'the Responsible Contracting Toolkit', seeking to operationalise and implement the Responsible Contracting Principles, which challenge the shortcomings of traditional contracting, such as supplier-only responsibility.[74]

Templates, guidance and model clauses are expected to be provided by the EU as well. In order to improve the comparability of sustainability disclosures, the European Commission has already formulated standardised disclosure templates in its Delegated Regulation (EU) 2022/1288[75], which specifies the SFDR. Articles 12 and 13 of the CSDDD state that the Commission will provide guidance for model contract clauses and may also issue guidelines for specific sectors or specific adverse impacts.

A European working group has recently published a draft of European Model Clauses (EMCs) for supply chains and has sought input on these clauses. Building on the ABA MCCs 2.0, their goal is to adapt the clauses to the European context and ensure that they comply with EU law and national contract law systems.[76] Adaptations may be required for some countries, but the European working group intends to develop general EMCs in order to accommodate the desire of many companies to use the

73 Responsible Contracting Project, 'The Mission' <https://responsiblecontracting.org> accessed 27 June 2023.

74 Responsible Contracting Project, 'The Toolkit' <https://www.responsiblecontracting.org/toolkit> accessed 6 November 2023. In addition to the MCCs 2.0 and the Responsible Purchasing Code of Conduct (the Buyer Code), the Toolkit also includes the recently published Supplier Model Contract Clauses (SMCs 1.0) for the apparel and textile sector.

75 Commission Delegated Regulation (EU) 2022/1288 of 6 April 2022 supplementing Regulation (EU) 2019/2088 of the European Parliament and of the Council with regard to regulatory technical standards specifying the details of the content and presentation of the information in relation to the principle of 'do no significant harm', specifying the content, methodologies and presentation of information in relation to sustainability indicators and adverse sustainability impacts, and the content and presentation of the information in relation to the promotion of environmental or social characteristics and sustainable investment objectives in pre-contractual documents, on websites and in periodic reports [2022] OJ L196/1.

76 Daniel Schönfelder, Bettina Braun and Martijn Scheltema, 'Contracting for Human Rights: Experiences from the US ABA MCC 2.0 and the European EMC Projects' (*Nova Centre on Business, Human Rights and the Environment Blog*, 1 November 2022) <https://novabhre.novalaw.unl.pt/contracting-for-human-rights-experiences-from-the-us-aba-mcc-2-0-and-the-european-emc-projects> accessed 13 February 2023.

same clauses across Europe: the EMCs are expected to indicate where specific legal systems require specific adaptations.[77]

Other initiatives in the area of model contract clauses include the Chancery Lane Project[78] for climate-aligned clauses and the Sustainable Terms of Trade Initiative (STTI)[79], a manufacturer-driven initiative focused on creating fairer purchasing practices in the textile and garment industry. Further initiatives are underway. However, many of these model clauses tend to be written by lawyers for other lawyers[80] and would benefit from a more user-centric design.

Reading, writing and (re)designing these templates and models is not an easy task. Next, we will look at how AI tools such as GPT-4 or ChatGPT could help, and how we could implement these tools responsibly.

3.4. Responsible Use of AI tools for Sustainability

3.4.1. Managing the Challenges of Generative AI

In its Sustainable Finance Strategy, the European Commission states that digital technologies can provide 'essential solutions for citizens, investors and SMEs to carry out their transition to sustainability'. The Commission encourages the use of innovative solutions to support retail investors' understanding of the sustainability of investment products. Therefore, technological innovation, including AI, has an important role to play in sustainable finance.[81] Similarly, the Commission's White Paper on Artificial Intelligence states that digital technologies, such as AI, are critical enablers for achieving the goals of the Green Deal. At the same time, AI poses risks, such as opaque decision making and different types of discrimination.[82] New innovations will also put more pressure on people's

77 ibid.

78 Chancery Lane Project, <www.chancerylaneproject.org/> accessed 29 June 2023.

79 Sustainable Terms of Trade Initiative, <www.sustainabletermsoftradeinitiative.com/> accessed 29 June 2023.

80 See Berger-Walliser and others (n 19) and Simkins (n 19).

81 COM(2021) 390 final, 8. See also Koskelainen and others (n 47) 2. The authors note that digital tools present both opportunities and challenges, and that today's digitised financial landscape is more complex than it was in the 'analogue' world.

82 European Commission, 'White Paper on Artificial Intelligence – A European Approach to Excellence and Trust' COM(2020) 65 final, 1–2, 19.

digital financial literacy. Investors and other users will need some technical knowledge and skills to understand and use new technologies.[83]

ChatGPT and GPT-4 are part of generative AI, which is a subset of AI that generates content such as text, images, audio, or video, resembling closely human-created content.[84] Applications based on generative AI are already widely used. For instance, ChatGPT became the fastest growing digital service ever, reaching 100 million users two months after launching.[85] AI-based applications affect people everywhere, from social media postings to the decisions about who will receive state benefits. If AI contains biases, it might have negative consequences even for our fundamental rights, if significant decisions are made based on algorithms that are biased against certain groups of people.[86]

Despite its great popularity and potential, generative AI has its risks and challenges. In addition to potential biases, the Norwegian Consumer Council divides the harms and challenges of generative AI into several categories: structural challenges; manipulation; discrimination, and content moderation; privacy and data protection; security vulnerabilities and fraud; replacing humans in consumer-facing applications with generative AI; environmental impacts; labour impacts; and intellectual property challenges.[87]

Intellectual property challenges relate both to image-generating tools and large language models (LLMs). According to *Strowel*, there are already at least five cases, mostly class actions, filed in the US and UK against generative AI. These cases mainly involve tools for creating graphic material.[88] In LLMs, training data can include copyrighted materials. Some models are transparent regarding their training data sources,

---

83 Koskelainen and others (n 47) 2, 4.

84 Norwegian Consumer Council, 'Ghost in the Machine – Addressing the Consumer Harms of Generative AI' (2023) 7.

85 Dan Milmo, 'ChatGPT Reaches 100 Million Users Two Months After Launch' *The Guardian* (2 February 2023) <www.theguardian.com/technology/2023/feb/02/chatgpt-100-million-users-open-ai-fastest-growing-app> accessed 26 June 2023.

86 European Union Agency for Fundamental Rights, 'Bias in Algorithms – Artificial Intelligence and Discrimination' (2022) 7.

87 Norwegian Consumer Council (n 84) 14–39.

88 Alain Strowel, 'ChatGPT and Generative AI Tools: Theft of Intellectual Labor?' (2023) 54 IIC – International Review of Intellectual Property and Competition Law 491, 492.

while others do not provide source information. Now, some solutions to this problem have been developed, such as the Kelvin Legal DataPack, which obtains data only from sources with clear intellectual property rights that explicitly allow the reuse of data for commercial purposes.[89] Microsoft, which is currently integrating its Copilot AI assistant into many of its software offerings, has announced that it has content filters and other technology in place to reduce the likelihood of copyright infringement, and has promised to defend its Copilot enterprise customers against copyright lawsuits.[90]

In addition to intellectual property rights, the risks associated with the practical use of GPT models include hallucinations and errors, inconsistent responses, lack of metacognition and statistical understanding, and lack of verifiability and reasoning. [91] Data privacy and the protection of minors have also been important concerns.[92] Age verification tools would prevent underage users from accessing generative AI models. In regard to privacy concerns, for example, Microsoft Azure[93] and ChatGPT Enterprise[94] promise to provide data privacy for their AI tools.

The widely cited challenges have not deterred us from exploring generative AI tools and encouraging others to do so. For us, the challenges

89 Jillian Bommarito, 'Why We Built the Kelvin Legal DataPack' (*Kelvin Legal Data OS*, 21 August 2023), <https://kelvin.legal/why-kelvin-legal-datapack/> accessed 30 August 2023.

90 'We are charging our commercial customers for our Copilots, and if their use creates legal issues, we should make this our problem rather than our customers' problem.' Brad Smith and Hossein Nowbar, 'Microsoft Announces New Copilot Copyright Commitment for Customers' (*Microsoft Blog*, 7 September 2023) <https://blogs.microsoft.com/on-the-issues/2023/09/07/copilot-copyright-commitment-ai-legal-concerns/> accessed 10 September 2023.

91 Srini Pagidyala, 'WARNING: This Paper Contains Model Outputs...' [2023] LinkedIn <www.linkedin.com/feed/update/urn:li:activity:7077400934682685447/> accessed 27 June 2023.

92 See, e.g., Garante Per La Protezione Dei Dati Personali, Provvedimento dell'11 aprile 2023 [9874702] <www.garanteprivacy.it/web/guest/home/docweb/-/docweb-display/docweb/9874702#english> accessed 30 August 2023.

93 Microsoft, 'Azure Customer Data Protection' (31 December 2022) <https://learn.microsoft.com/en-us/azure/security/fundamentals/protection-customer-data> accessed 30 August 2023.

94 OpenAI, 'Introducing ChatGPT Enterprise' <https://openai.com/blog/introducing-chatgpt-enterprise> accessed 8 September 2023.

mean that we need to be aware of the potential risks and challenges and act accordingly, primarily by having a knowledgeable human expert review and editing the output before it is accepted, distributed, and acted upon.[95] We have used generative AI under the close control and supervision of a human. The role of humans as users of AI tools and as reviewers and editors of input (prompts) and output is critical, and typically not well recognised when discussing the use of AI tools. In prompts, users can significantly guide the output, for example by asking for references and indicating what type of output is preferred and what is not. Rather than automating decision making or producing final versions, we have successfully used AI to suggest topics, headings and ideas, and to provide initial drafts. Used in this way, we have found that generative AI can greatly increase efficiency, while human oversight helps to address challenges such as bias and error.

Regulation is also an important response to the challenges of AI. Legislation on generative AI is emerging, and some of the existing EU legislation may also be applicable, depending on the context. For example, the General Data Protection Regulation (GDPR)[96] applies to generative AI applications in relation to personal data, and the Unfair Commercial Practices Directive (UCPD)[97] may address misleading or aggressive commercial practices using generative AI. Among the emerging EU regulations, the proposed AI Act is also important from a generative AI perspective.[98] The Parliament's position on the AI Act, which was adopted in June 2023, includes so-called foundation models in the proposal. Providers of foundation models, including GPT, would be required to ensure the protection of fundamental rights, health and safety and the environ-

95 See also Pagidyala (n 91).

96 Regulation (EU) 2016/679 of the European Parliament and of the Council of 27 April 2016 on the protection of natural persons with regard to the processing of personal data and on the free movement of such data, and repealing Directive 95/46/EC (General Data Protection Regulation) [2016] OJ L119/1.

97 Directive 2005/29/EC of the European Parliament and of the Council of 11 May 2005 concerning unfair business-to-consumer commercial practices in the internal market and amending Council Directive 84/450/EEC, Directives 97/7/EC, 98/27/EC and 2002/65/EC of the European Parliament and of the Council and Regulation (EC) No 2006/2004 of the European Parliament and of the Council [2005] OJ L149/22.

98 Norwegian Consumer Council (n 84) 42–44.

ment, democracy and the rule of law. Providers would also have to adequately assess and mitigate risks, comply with design, information and environmental requirements and register with the EU database. There are specific obligations for providers of foundation models of generative AI. These specific obligations relate to transparency, training, design and development of the model so that it does not generate illegal content. A sufficiently detailed summary of the use of copyrighted training data must also be published.[99] In this way, once applied, the AI Act can make AI tools more accurate and safer. However, the role of users in terms of the input and output will remain critical.

3.4.2. Examples of Using Generative AI Tools

AI, including machine learning, enables the processing of legal information, disclosures and contracts as data. While it can analyse massive amounts of data, it can also provide valuable information about what is typical, 'standard' or 'average' in a given set of circumstances. For example, there are AI tools designed to assist in the analysis of contracts and identify terms that deviate from what is considered customary or desirable in a particular industry or jurisdiction. Contract analysis and review tools can scan contracts and flag unusual or undesirable clauses for review. Such AI tools have been commercially available for several years, while generative AI tools are of more recent origin.[100] Whether the work is done by humans or AI, the contracting parties will benefit, when contract terms and disclosures are better read and understood. From a preventive standpoint, this can lead to a reduction in misunderstandings, disputes and litigation.[101] From a promotive perspective, it can also lead to more sustainable investments, better contracts and better business – all of which contribute to a better society.

99 European Parliament, 'Draft Compromise Amendments on the Draft Report Proposal for a regulation of the European Parliament and of the Council on harmonised rules on Artificial Intelligence (Artificial Intelligence Act) and amending certain Union Legislative Acts (COM(2021)0206 – C9 0146/2021 – 2021/0106(COD))' recital 60g, art 28b.

100 See, e.g., Russ Edelman, 'The Practicalities of AI and Contract Management' *Contracting Excellence Journal* (6 June 2023) <www.worldcc.com/Resources/Blogs-and-Journals/Contracting-Excellence-Journal/View/ArticleId/11552/The-Practicalities-of-AI-and-Contract-Management> accessed 11 September 2023.

101 Rättzén (n 58) 227, 235–37.

Recently, there has been a significant shift in AI's ability to process text. Arbel and Becher explored the capabilities of GPT-3 models to act as 'smart readers' of contracts, disclosures, and privacy policies. They identified four core capabilities of smart readers: they can simplify and summarise complex legal text; personalise the text based on the characteristics of the reader; interpret contract terms; and benchmark and rank contracts based on their quality.[102]

We have been testing OpenAI's GPT models in the field, particularly in the context of contracts and sustainability reporting. Figure 1 shows the potential we have found that generative AI such as Open AI's ChatGPT already has in the context of contract planning and design. In addition to providing translations from one language to another, it seems to be able to provide overviews and suggestions based on available information and help us to draft, summarise, explain and present contracts and contract clauses.

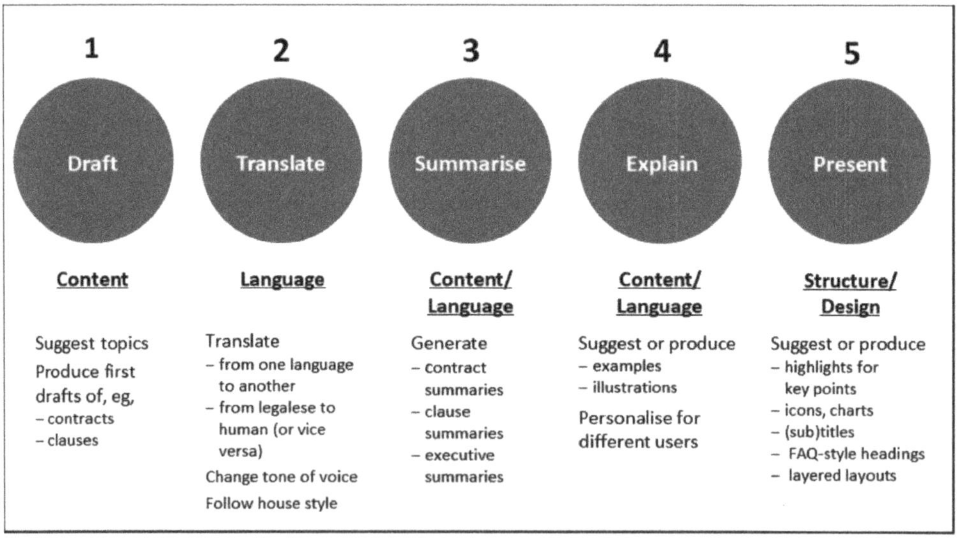

Fig. 1. AI-powered contract planning and design: what generative AI can already do. © 2023 Helena Haapio. Licensed under CC BY-NC 4.0

102 Yonathan A Arbel and Shmuel I Becher, 'Contracts in the Age of Smart Readers' (2022) 90 George Washington Law Review 83, 83, 89.

In the following, we present examples of our testing of OpenAI's GPT-4's ability to help us navigate sustainability legislation, suggest contract topics and ideas, and present initial drafts of contract content and presentation.

> The European Union has recently finalized the Corporate Sustainability Reporting Directive (CSRD) that will introduce more detailed sustainability reporting requirements for companies operating within the EU, as well as non-EU companies that meet certain criteria related to their net turnover in the EU and companies with securities listed on a regulated EU market. The CSRD came into force on January 5, 2023, and the rules will be gradually implemented starting from January 1, 2024, for certain large EU and EU-listed companies, with the aim of applying to all in-scope companies by January 1, 2028.
>
> The CSRD is part of a larger legislative package aimed at promoting corporate sustainability and a green economy, with other major European initiatives including the EU Taxonomy Regulation and the EU Sustainable Finance Disclosure Regulation. Further progress is expected in 2023 regarding related legislative and regulatory initiatives, including the Directive on Corporate Sustainability Due Diligence and the EU Green Bond Standard.
>
> Under the CSRD, companies must disclose how sustainability-related factors, such as climate change, affect their operations and how their business model impacts sustainability factors. The scope of required reporting covers environmental, social and human rights, and governance factors. Specifically, environmental factors include climate (including Scopes 1, 2 and 3 greenhouse gas emissions), water/marine resources, circular economy, pollution, and biodiversity. Companies are also required to disclose their plans to ensure that their business models and strategies are compatible with the goal of limiting global warming to 1.5 °C in line with the Paris Agreement and the EU's own European Climate Law, which aims to achieve climate neutrality by 2050.
>
> Regarding supplier contracts, the CSRD requires companies to disclose information about their value chain, including their own operations, products and services, business relationships, and supply chain where applicable. Companies are also required to disclose the due diligence processes they have implemented concerning sustainability matters, including any actions they have taken to prevent or mitigate any actual or potential adverse impacts related to their activities. However, I was unable to find more detailed information about the specific impact of these regulations on contracts with suppliers during this search.
>
> In summary, the EU's new sustainability legislation imposes substantial new disclosure and compliance requirements on companies, which could influence their business relationships and contracts, including those with suppliers. However, more research would be needed to detail these impacts more specifically.

Fig. 2. GPT-4 using Bing (Beta) summarising recent and forthcoming sustainability legislation and its impact on contracts with suppliers. Powered by OpenAI, used with ChatGPT Plus May 25, 2023 version. References omitted. Licensed under CC BY-NC 4.0.

Figure 2 shows an extract from the results of GPT-4, using its built-in browser and Bing (Beta), when asked to summarise recent and forthcoming EU legislation and its impact on contracts with suppliers.[103] This simple example demonstrates how AI can be used as an ideation and reading tool: it can help simplify and summarise text and find the most relevant information.[104] This example also illustrates how at the time of this test, the GPT-3 knowledge cut-off date, September 2021, was not a limiting factor: more recent information could be found in the output. Here GPT-4 correctly stated that the CSRD came into force on January 5, 2023. It also discussed some of the legislative changes expected in 2023. The 'Finished browsing' button allowed the viewer to see what kind of references were 'clicked' during the process. The 'Browse with Bing' feature, previously removed, has now been reinstated, enhancing the verification process and addressing some of the prevalent concerns with generative AI. GPT-4 also 'acknowledges' its shortcomings, noting that 'more research would be needed to detail these impacts more specifically'.

In our next test, again using OpenAI's GPT-4 with Bing (Beta), we first asked GPT-4 to summarise EU reporting requirements related to companies' and their value chains' carbon footprint and then, after receiving the summary, we asked it to explain how it did this, including which website it visited.[105] After receiving a step-by-step description of its search process, we asked it to suggest what about these reporting requirements a company should include in its contracts with its suppliers

103 We used the following prompt: 'I am writing an article about new EU sustainability legislation and how it impacts (and hopefully improves) investment decision-making and contracts. Can you help me by summarizing how the recent and forthcoming EU legislation impacts on contracts with suppliers, with references, please?' The full chat, with references, can be viewed at <https://chat.openai.com/share/ba37afce-387d-4602-aea3-3f47a1a67f8e>. ChatGPT named this chat of 21 June 2023 'EU Sustainability Impact on Contracts'.

104 For the opportunities and challenges of using GPT-3 as a reading tool in the context of contracts, see also Arbel and Becher (n 102).

105 For this purpose, we used the following prompt: 'Can you summarise EU reporting requirements related to companies' and their value chains' carbon footprint, please?' The full chat, including the response, can be viewed at <https://chat.openai.com/share/3ef10bc8-2198-45e4-9527-dba91582b383>.

and customers.[106] In the response, ChatGPT identified six key points to consider. These are shown in Figure 3.

As for what a company should include in its contracts with suppliers and customers, it's critical to include provisions that ensure compliance with the forthcoming requirements. Here are some points that could be considered:
Compliance with Regulations: Clauses should be included that require all parties to comply with applicable regulations, including the new sustainability reporting requirements. This includes any future amendments or additions to these requirements.
Data Collection and Reporting: Since the reporting requirements might need information from suppliers (such as Scope 3 emissions data), contracts should specify the obligations of suppliers to provide necessary data in a timely and accurate manner. The same applies to customers if their activities are relevant to the company's reporting requirements.
Auditing and Verification: To ensure the accuracy of the data provided by suppliers and used in reports, contracts may include the right to audit suppliers or require third-party verification of data.
Liability for Non-compliance: The contracts should clearly outline the consequences of non-compliance with the reporting requirements, including potential termination of the contract, financial penalties, or other remedial actions.
Cooperation in Case of Regulatory Inquiry: In case of any regulatory inquiries or investigations related to these reporting requirements, the contracts could include clauses requiring cooperation between the parties.
Confidentiality and Data Protection: Given that data sharing is involved, contracts should include robust confidentiality and data protection clauses to ensure compliance with privacy laws and regulations.
This is a complex issue, and companies should seek legal advice to ensure that their contracts are comprehensive and comply with all relevant laws and regulations. The exact requirements may also vary depending on the specific circumstances of the company and its value chain.

Fig. 3. GPT-4 with Bing (Beta) suggesting topics to include in contracts with suppliers and customers. Powered by OpenAI, used with ChatGPT Plus May 25, 2023 version. Licensed under CC BY-NC 4.0.

106 For this purpose, we used the following prompt: 'What should a company include about these forthcoming requirements in its contracts with its suppliers and customers?' The full chat can be viewed at <https://chat.openai.com/share/3ef10bc8-2198-45e4-9527-dba91582b383>.

Next we asked GPT-4 to generate a first draft of a clause to be included in a contract with suppliers related to item 2 on the list, 'Data Collection and Reporting'.[107] The clause it generated can be found in Figure 4 under the heading 'Full Contractual Clause Text'. As already noted, our tests were meant to generate first drafts, with a human reviewing, verifying and editing the output and AI acting as an assistant. For our test purposes, we did not evaluate the output in more detail.

Finally, we asked GPT-4 to suggest a way to put the contents of the clause into a table-type format and present it in a layered layout with FAQ-type headings, a summary or explanation in business language, and the original full text.[108] The result can be found in Figure 4. GPT-4 also warned us: 'this table is a guide and may need to be adjusted based on the specifics of your situation. It's always a good idea to consult with a legal professional if you have questions'.

FAQ-Type Heading	Explanation in Business Language	Full Contractual Clause Text
What data do I need to collect?	You need to gather data about your business's environmental, social, and governance (ESG) impacts. This could include things like your greenhouse gas emissions.	The Supplier shall collect and maintain all data necessary to comply with the environmental, social, and governance (ESG) reporting requirements as outlined in the Corporate Sustainability Reporting Directive (CSRD) of the European Union, or any other applicable law or regulation.

107 Our prompt and the output it generated can be viewed at <https://chat.openai.com/share/3ef10bc8-2198-45e4-9527-dba91582b383>. In its response, GPT-4 included the typical caveat: 'Please note that this is a generic draft and might need to be customised to fit the specific circumstances and legal requirements of your organisation and location. Always consult with a legal professional before implementing any legal documents or clauses'.

108 Our prompts and the respective outputs, including the table shown in Figure 4, can be viewed at <https://chat.openai.com/share/3ef10bc8-2198-45e4-9527-dba91582b383>.

How should I report the data?	Make sure the data is accurate and complete. Give it to your customer in a timely manner, so they have enough time to include it in their reports.	The Supplier shall ensure the accuracy, completeness, and reliability of all data collected and reported under this Agreement. The Supplier shall also ensure that the data is reported to the Company in a timely manner, consistent with the Company's reporting schedule and enough in advance of any reporting deadlines to allow the Company to include this data in its own reports.
In what format should I provide the data?	Provide the data in a way that your customer can easily understand and use. They might tell you how they want it presented.	The data shall be provided in a format and manner that is easily understandable and usable by the Company. The specific format may be determined by the Company and communicated to the Supplier from time to time.
What if something changes?	If something changes that could affect the data (like if you change your business practices), you need to tell your customer as soon as possible. You may also need to help them correct the data.	The Supplier shall promptly notify the Company of any changes or updates to the data that may affect the Company's reporting obligations. The Supplier shall also cooperate with the Company in making any necessary corrections or adjustments to the data.
What if the laws change?	If the laws or regulations change, you need to update the way you collect and report data to make sure you're still in compliance with the new rules.	In the event of any updates or changes to the CSRD or other relevant regulations, the Supplier shall update its data collection and reporting practices as necessary to comply with the updated regulations.

Fig. 4. GPT-4 suggesting a contract clause in a table-type format with FAQ-style headings and a layered layout. Powered by OpenAI, used with ChatGPT Plus May 25, 2023 version. Licensed under CC BY-NC 4.0.

This example shows how generative AI tools can be used as writing and document design tools – again, to prepare initial drafts. In this example, different layers are displayed for different reader needs: FAQ-type headings for quick skim reading; the explanation layer for a deeper understanding; and the full text (generated by GPT-4 in our earlier test) for those who are interested in the details. In a similar manner, generative

AI Tools can generate text and a layout that can be used as a draft for sustainability reports, disclosures or other documents.

The opportunities offered by AI-powered web translators such as Google Translate and DeepL Translator[109] and writing assistants such as DeepL Write[110] are already widely used by many writers. AI-assisted translations, explanations and summaries can be used as first drafts in layering information, in a fraction of the time and and with less effort than would be required otherwise.[111] We expect future AI tools to be able to generate timelines, flowcharts, swimlanes and other typical visual design patterns to explain contract clauses.[112] While AI tools cannot take the lead, their outputs can serve as a helpful starting point.

3.4.3. Generative AI in the Field of Legal Language

Large language models, such as Open AI's GPT-4, Google's BERT[113] and Cohere's language models[114] are trained on large amounts of data. However, because the training data contains very general texts, these models do not always capture the language used in some specific domains. A significant advantage, though, is that large language models can be fine-tuned with a relatively small sample of labelled texts. For example, FinBERT is tuned for financial texts. Huang, Wang and Yang performed an additional fine-tuning, which resulted in the FinBERT-ESG model. This model is specialised for ESG-related discussions. The model was trained

109 Google Translate <www.translate.google.com/>; DeepL Translator <www.deepl.com/translator>.

110 DeepL Write <www.deepl.com/write>.

111 For early layering experiments with GPT-3 by one of the authors of this paper, see Marcelo Corrales Compagnucci, Mark Fenwick and Helena Haapio, 'Digital Technology, Future Lawyers and the Computable Contract Designer of Tomorrow' in Marcelo Corrales Compagnucci, Helena Haapio and Mark Fenwick (eds), *Research Handbook on Contract Design* (Edward Elgar 2022); Robert Waller, Stefania Passera and Helena Haapio, 'Layered Contracts: Both Legally Functional and Human-Friendly' in Kai Jacob, Dierk Schindler, Roger Strathausen and Bernhard Waltl (eds), *Liquid Legal – Humanization and the Law* (Springer 2022).

112 Similarly Waller, Passera and Haapio (n 111).

113 Jacob Devlin, Ming-Wei Chang, Kenton Lee and Kristina Toutanova, 'BERT: Pre-training of Deep Bidirectional Transformers for Language Understanding' (v2, 24 May 2019) <www.arxiv.org/abs/1810.04805> accessed 1 February 2023.

114 Cohere, 'Making NLP Part of Every Developer's Toolkit' <www.cohere.com/> accessed 29 June 2023.

by manually labelling sentences from company disclosures into four categories: 1) environmental, 2) social, 3) governance, and 4) non-ESG issues.[115]

The specificity of legal language can be seen as a challenge to the application of generative AI in the legal field. Common words can be used with very specific meanings, and legal language often also uses words that do not exist in natural language. This means that legal experts are needed in the development of the AI models.[116] However, this challenge can be overcome, as shown by FinBERT and its subsequent development. A number of commercial AI tools are available as well, such as ContractPodAi's Leah Legal Copilot, which can, among other things, review and summarise legal documents and provide first drafts, redlines and extracts.[117] Spellbook by Rally can suggest new clauses and entire sections for contracts, detect aggressive terms, list missing clauses and definitions and make negotiation suggestions.[118] Codify AI, in turn, is a GPT-4 based tool that is trained to find answers about legislation, so that legal information can be found and understood quickly and with ease.[119] It can also suggest follow-up questions and gives the citation information used in its answers.

In addition to monitoring and supervising AI tools and auditing the algorithms, human experts are also needed to train the tools. This typically involves building a model and analysing and labelling thousands of contracts or other documents, depending on what a particular tool is being asked to perform.[120] Even with careful testing, AI tools can still contain biases and errors. These can be difficult to identify and correct. Tools that use machine learning are typically 'black boxes' – the logic of their thinking and learning is not visible to their users, and it is difficult to

115 Allen H Huang, Hui Wang and Yi Yang, 'FinBERT: A Large Language Model for Extracting Information from Financial Text' (2022) Contemporary Accounting Research 1, 3, 7, 13, 25 <https://doi.org/10.1111/1911-3846.12832> accessed 1 March 2023.

116 Rättzén (n 58) 230.

117 ContractPodAi, 'Generative AI Legal Assistant, Leah Legal Copilot' <https://contractpodai.com/leah-copilot-ai-legal-assistant> accessed 9 September 2023.

118 Spellbook by Rally, 'Draft Contracts 3x Faster with AI' <www.spellbook.legal> accessed 1 February 2023.

119 Codify AI, <www. codifyai.com> accessed 30 August 2023.

120 Rättzén (n 58) 227.

understand how they make predictions.[121] When it comes to using AI in expert tasks, its trustworthiness is at the core. In addition to technological means, trust can be built through legislation, such as the forthcoming AI Act, discussed above.

4. Conclusions

With its flood of new legislation on sustainability, the EU wants to make it clear that sustainability is no longer voluntary. It affects both society and business. The EU's Sustainable Finance Strategy highlights the importance of sustainable investment in achieving sustainability goals. It also considers the role of day-to-day business activities and contracts throughout the whole value chain. Sustainability and business are thus linked in a meaningful way. Better business can foster a better society.

With many new legal requirements, the EU is using law as an important tool to achieve sustainability goals. However, conventional contracts and legal documents are written primarily to allocate and manage risk and liability. This often results in dense texts full of legalese – complex legal language written by lawyers for other lawyers. Studies have shown that such contracts and documents are not necessarily read or understood. So, they do not contribute to better business or a better society.

The proactive approach reverses the mindset. It focuses on future possibilities rather than past failures. Combined with possibility-driven design and responsibly used AI tools, it helps move from design thinking to doing. In the context of sustainability, possibility-driven, AI-assisted design can help navigate the plethora of sustainability legislation and overcome many of the problems associated with disclosures, reports and contracts. These are typically not engaging and are therefore often ignored by the intended audience. If sustainability information is not accessed, read and understood, it cannot promote sustainability.

---

121 Amy McGovern, Ryan Lagerquist, David John Gagne II, G Eli Jergensen, Kimberly L Elmore, Cameron R Homeyer and Travis Smith, 'Making the Black Box More Transparent: Understanding the Physical Implications of Machine Learning' (2019) 100(11) Bulletin of the American Meteorological Society 2175, 2176.

In the financial context, the importance of financial well-being and financial literacy is already well recognised.[122] Similarly, we should shift the focus from a problem-oriented approach to legal well-being and legal literacy. In this paper, we have explored how possibility-driven, AI-assisted design can improve sustainability reporting and disclosure, as well as sustainable and responsible contracting. Using design patterns, templates, models and AI tools, information can be transformed and communicated more effectively, taking into account different user needs. One-size-fits-all solutions are not sufficient to promote sustainable actions.

To address the challenges and risks associated with AI tools, we emphasise the role of responsible use of AI tools. Even if the future brings us 'perfect' AI regulation and fully compliant AI tools, user risk will remain. When used responsibly, AI tools make it possible to generate, present and interact with information in ways that were not possible before. This opens up significant opportunities for both readers and writers of sustainability information, and possibility-driven legal design can provide a framework for balancing the needs and expectations of people, businesses and society at large.

Bibliography

American Bar Association, 'Contractual Clauses Project' <www.americanbar.org/groups/human_rights/business-human-rights-initiative/contractual-clauses project/> accessed 13 February 2023

Annola V, Haapio H and Koskela M, 'Interpreting Images in Contracts' in Marcelo Corrales Compagnucci, Helena Haapio and Mark Fenwick (eds), *Research Handbook on Contract Design* (Edward Elgar 2022)

Arbel YA and Becher SI, 'Contracts in the Age of Smart Readers' (2022) 90 George Washington Law Review 83

Benoliel U and Becher SI, 'The Duty to Read the Unreadable' (2019) 60 Boston College Law Review 2255

122 See Koskelainen and others (n 47) 1; OECD (n 47).

Berger-Walliser G, Shrivastava P and Sulkowski A, 'Using Proactive Legal Strategies for Corporate Environmental Sustainability' (2016) 6 Michigan Journal of Environmental and Administrative Law 1

—, Bird RC and Haapio H, 'Promoting Business Success through Contract Visualization' (2011) 17 Journal of Law, Business & Ethics 55

Bommarito J, 'Why We Built the Kelvin Legal DataPack' (*Kelvin Legal Data OS*, 21 August 2023), <https://kelvin.legal/why-kelvin-legal-datapack/> accessed 30 August 2023

Chancery Lane Project, <www.chancerylaneproject.org/> accessed 29 June 2023

Codify AI, <www. codifyai.com> accessed 30 August 2023

Cohere, 'Making NLP Part of Every Developer's Toolkit' <www.cohere.com/> accessed 29 June 2023

Commission Delegated Regulation (EU) 2022/1288 of 6 April 2022 supplementing Regulation (EU) 2019/2088 of the European Parliament and of the Council with regard to regulatory technical standards specifying the details of the content and presentation of the information in relation to the principle of 'do no significant harm', specifying the content, methodologies and presentation of information in relation to sustainability indicators and adverse sustainability impacts, and the content and presentation of the information in relation to the promotion of environmental or social characteristics and sustainable investment objectives in precontractual documents, on websites and in periodic reports [2022] OJ L196/1

Consumer Financial Protection Bureau, 'Financial Well-Being: The Goal of Financial Education' (January 2015)

ContractPodAi, 'Generative AI Legal Assistant, Leah Legal Copilot' <https://contractpodai.com/leah-copilot-ai-legal-assistant> accessed 9 September 2023

Corrales M, Fenwick M, Haapio H and Vermeulen EPM, 'Tomorrow's Lawyer Today? Platform-Driven Legal Tech, Smart Contracts & the New World of Legal Design' (2019) 22(10) Journal of Internet Law 3

Corrales Compagnucci M, Fenwick M and Haapio H, 'Digital Technology, Future Lawyers and the Computable Contract Designer of Tomorrow' in Marcelo Corrales Compagnucci, Helena Haapio and Mark Fenwick (eds), *Research Handbook on Contract Design* (Edward Elgar 2022)

—, Haapio H and Fenwick M (eds), *Research Handbook on Contract Design* (Edward Elgar 2022)

Council of the EU, 'Corporate sustainability due diligence: Council and Parliament strike deal to protect environment and human rights' <www.consilium.europa.eu/en/press/press-releases/2023/12/14/corporate-sustainability-due-diligence-council-and-parliament-strike-deal-to-protect-environment-and-human-rights/> accessed 31 January 2024

Creative Commons, 'About the Licences' <https://creativecommons.org/licenses/?lang=en> accessed 31 January 2023

Delft Institute of Positive Design, 'Our Mission' <https://diopd.org/about-us/mission/> accessed 12 February 2023

Devlin J, Chang M-W, Lee K and Toutanova K, 'BERT: Pre-training of Deep Bidirectional Transformers for Language Understanding' (v2, 24 May 2019) <www.arxiv.org/abs/1810.04805> accessed 1 February 2023

Directive 2005/29/EC of the European Parliament and of the Council of 11 May 2005 concerning unfair business-to-consumer commercial practices in the internal market and amending Council Directive 84/450/EEC, Directives 97/7/EC, 98/27/EC and 2002/65/EC of the European Parliament and of the Council and Regulation (EC) No 2006/2004 of the European Parliament and of the Council [2005] OJ L149/22

Directive 2014/95/EU of the European Parliament and of the Council of 22 October 2014 amending Directive 2013/34/EU as regards disclosure of non-financial and diversity information by certain large undertakings and groups [2014] OJ L330/1

Directive (EU) 2022/2464 of the European Parliament and of the Council of 14 December 2022 amending Regulation (EU) No 537/2014, Directive 2004/109/EC, Directive 2006/43/EC and Directive 2013/34/EU, as regards corporate sustainability reporting (CSRD) [2022] OJ L322/15

Doherty M, Corrales Compagnucci M, Haapio H and Hagan M, 'A New Attitude to Law's Empire: the Potentialities of Legal Design' in Marcelo Corrales Compagnucci, Helena Haapio, Margaret Hagan and Michael Doherty (eds), *Legal Design: Integrating Business, Design and Legal Thinking with Technology* (Edward Elgar 2021)

Doyle P and Passera S, 'Contract Design and Simplification – Is This Now a Must-do?' (2021) 14(56) International In-house Counsel Journal 7243

Edelman R, 'The Practicalities of AI and Contract Management' *Contracting Excellence Journal* (6 June 2023) <www.worldcc.com/Resources/Blogs-and-Journals/Contracting-Excellence-Journal/View/ArticleId/11552/The-Practicalities-of-AI-and-Contract-Management> accessed 11 September 2023

European Commission, Directorate-General for Financial Stability, Financial Services and Capital Markets Union, Uličná D, Vincze M, Mosoreanu M, Hayet M, de Landsheer R, Järvi O, Bruggeman V, Sproge J, Fialon S, De Groen WP, Amariei C, Oliinyk I and Nagtegaal J, 'Disclosure, Inducements, and Suitability Rules for Retail Investors Study. Final report' (Publications Office of the European Union 2023)

European Commission, 'Action Plan: Financing Sustainable Growth' (Communication) COM(2018) 97 final

European Commission, 'Proposal for a Directive of the European Parliament and of the Council on Corporate Sustainability Due Diligence and amending Directive (EU) 2019/1937' COM(2022) 71 final

European Commission, 'White Paper on Artificial Intelligence – A European Approach to Excellence and Trust' COM(2020) 65 final

European Commission, 'Impact Assessment Report' SWD(2021) 344 final

European Commission, 'Proposal for a Regulation of the European Parliament and of the Council establishing a European single access point providing centralised access to publicly available information of relevance to financial services, capital markets and sustainability' (ESAP proposal) COM(2021) 723 final.

European Commission, 'Proposal for a Regulation of the European Parliament and of the Council on European green bonds' COM(2021) 391 final

European Commission, 'Proposal for a Regulation of the European Parliament and of the Council on the making available on the Union market as well as export from the Union of certain commodities and products associated with deforestation and forest degradation and repealing Regulation (EU) No 995/2010' COM(2021) 706 final

European Commission, 'Strategy for Financing the Transition to a Sustainable Economy' (Communication) COM(2021) 390 final

European Commission, 'Proposal for a Regulation of the European Parliament and of the Council on nature restoration' COM(2022) 304 final

European Commission, 'The European Green Deal' (Communication) COM(2019) 640 final

European Parliament, 'Draft Compromise Amendments on the Draft Report Proposal for a regulation of the European Parliament and of the Council on harmonised rules on Artificial Intelligence (Artificial Intelligence Act) and amending certain Union Legislative Acts (COM(2021)0206 – C9 0146/2021 – 2021/0106(COD))'

European Parliament Committee on Legal Affairs, 'Draft Report on the proposal for a directive of the European Parliament and of the Council on Corporate Sustainability Due Diligence and amending Directive (EU) 2019/1937 (COM(2022)0071 – C9-0050/2022 – 2022/0051(COD))' <www.europarl.europa.eu/doceo/document/JURI-PR-738450_EN.pdf> accessed 13 February 2023

European Union Agency for Fundamental Rights, 'Bias in Algorithms – Artificial Intelligence and Discrimination' (2022)

Finnegan M, *User-Centered Design: A Key to Contract Simplification* (University of Vaasa 2021)

Fontaine M and de Ly F, *Drafting International Contracts: An Analysis of Contract Clauses* (Brill 2009)

Garante Per La Protezione Dei Dati Personali, Provvedimento dell'11 aprile 2023 [9874702] <www.garanteprivacy.it/web/guest/home/docweb/-/docweb-display/docweb/9874702#english> accessed 30 August 2023

Gardiner R, 'Only One Item on the Agenda for Today's Meeting of the Council of the European Union #CompanyLaw Working Party' [2024] LinkedIn <www.linkedin.com/feed/update/urn:li:activity:7157652239174483968/> accessed 31 January 2024

Goetz LH and Schork NJ, 'Personalized Medicine: Motivation, Challenges, and Progress' (2018) 109(6) Fertility and Sterility 952

Haapio H, 'Quality Improvement through Proactive Contracting: Contracts Are Too Important to Be Left to Lawyers!' in *Proceedings of Annual Quality Congress (AQC), American Society for Quality (ASQ)*, vol 52 (American Society for Quality 1998)

—, *Next Generation Contracts: A Paradigm Shift* (Lexpert Ltd 2013)

—, Annola V and Koskela M, 'Ten Ways to Make the Interpretation of Images More Predictable' *Contracting Excellence Journal* (5 November 2020) <www.worldcc.com/Resources/Content-Hub/View/ArticleID/10897> accessed 13 February 2023

—, Barton TD and Corrales Compagnucci M, 'Legal Design for the Common Good: Proactive Legal Care by Design' in Marcelo Corrales Compagnucci, Helena Haapio, Margaret Hagan and Michael Doherty (eds), *Legal Design: Integrating Business, Design and Legal Thinking with Technology* (Edward Elgar 2021)

— and Hagan M, 'Design Patterns for Contracts' in Erich Schweighofer, Franz Kummer, Walter Hötzendorfer and Georg Borges (eds), *Networks. Proceedings of the 19th International Legal Informatics Symposium IRIS 2016* (Österreichische Computer Gesellschaft OCG /books@ocg.at 2016)

— and Passera S, 'Contracts as Interfaces: Visual Representation Patterns in Contract Design' in Daniel M Katz, Ron Dolin and Michael J Bommarito (eds), *Legal Informatics* (CUP 2021)

—, de Rooy R and Barton TD, 'New Contract Genres' in Erich Schweighofer, Franz Kummer, Ahti Saarenpää and Burkhard Schafer (eds), *Data Protection / LegalTech. Proceedings of the 21st International Legal Informatics Symposium IRIS 2018* (Editions Weblaw 2018)

Huang AH, Wang H and Yang Y, 'FinBERT: A Large Language Model for Extracting Information from Financial Text' (2022) Contemporary Accounting Research 1 <https://doi.org/10.1111/1911-3846.12832> accessed 1 March 2023

Hurmerinta-Haanpää A, *The Many Functions of Contracts: How Companies Use Contracts in Interorganizational Exchange Relations* (Doctoral Dissertation, University of Turku 2021)

IACCM, *The Purpose of a Contract: An IACCM Research Report* (2017) <www.worldcc.com/Portals/IACCM/resources/files/9876_j18069-iaccm-purpose-of-contract-a4-2017-11-14-v1-webready.pdf> accessed 13 February 2023

Jevremovic N, 'Enforcing Sustainability Clauses in Global Supply Chains with a Focus on Proactive and Relational Contract Theory: Case of SDG 12' (2022) 25 ZEuS Zeitschrift für Europarechtliche Studien 393

Ketola A, de Rooy R and Haapio H, 'Comic Contracts 2.0 – Contracts that Have (and Give) a Voice' in Rossana Ducato, Alain Strowel, and Enguerrand Marique (eds), *Design(s) for Law* (Ledizioni 2024)

Koskelainen T, Kalmi P, Scornavacca E and Vartiainen T, 'Financial Literacy in the Digital Age – A Research Agenda' (2023) The Journal of Consumer Affairs 1 <https://doi.org/10.1111/joca.12510> accessed 1 March 2023

The Legal Design Alliance, 'What is legal design?' <www.legaldesignalliance.org/> accessed 31 August 2023

Loughran T and McDonald B, 'The Use of EDGAR Filings by Investors' (2017) 18(2) Journal of Behavioral Finance 231

Maslow S, 'No Safe Harbor in the "Contract Assurances" Required in the EU Directive Proposal' (*AMM Blog*, 28 March 2022) <www.ammlaw.com/blog/no-safe-harbor-in-the-contract-assurances-required-in-the-eu-directive-proposal.html> accessed 13 February 2023

McGovern A, Lagerquist R, Gagne DJ (II), Jergensen GE, Elmore KL, Homeyer CR and Smith T, 'Making the Black Box More Transparent: Understanding the Physical Implications of Machine Learning' (2019) 100(11) Bulletin of the American Meteorological Society 2175

Microsoft, 'Azure Customer Data Protection' (31 December 2022) <https://learn.microsoft.com/en-us/azure/security/fundamentals/protection-customer-data> accessed 30 August 2023

Milmo D, 'ChatGPT Reaches 100 Million Users Two Months After Launch' *The Guardian* (2 February 2023) <www.theguardian.com/technology/2023/feb/02/chatgpt-100-million-users-open-ai-fastest-growing-app> accessed 26 June 2023

Norwegian Consumer Council, 'Ghost in the Machine – Addressing the Consumer Harms of Generative AI' (2023)

OECD, 'OECD/INFE 2020 International Survey of Adult Financial Literacy' (2020) <www.oecd.org/financial/education/launchoftheoecdinfeglobalfinancialliteracysurveyreport.htm> accessed 1 March 2023

OpenAI, 'Introducing ChatGPT Enterprise' <https://openai.com/blog/introducing-chatgpt-enterprise> accessed 8 September 2023

Opinion of the European Economic and Social Committee on 'The proactive law approach: a further step towards better regulation at EU level' [2009] Official Journal of the European Union C175/26

Pagidyala S, 'WARNING: This Paper Contains Model Outputs...' [2023] LinkedIn <www.linkedin.com/feed/update/urn:li:activity:7077400934682685447/> accessed 27 June 2023

Passera S, *Beyond the Wall of Contract Text: Visualizing Contracts to Foster Understanding and Collaboration within and across Organizations* (Aalto University 2017)

Pohjonen S, 'Johdanto' ['Introduction'] in Soile Pohjonen (ed), *Ennakoiva sopiminen – liiketoimien suunnittelu, toteuttaminen ja riskien hallinta* [*Proactive Contracting – Planning, Implementing and Managing Risk in Business Transactions*] (WSOY Lakitieto 2002)

Regulation (EU) 2016/679 of the European Parliament and of the Council of 27 April 2016 on the protection of natural persons with regard to the processing of personal data and on the free movement of such data, and repealing Directive 95/46/EC (General Data Protection Regulation) [2016] OJ L119/1

Regulation (EU) 2019/2088 of the European Parliament and of the Council of 27 November 2019 on sustainability-related disclosures in the financial services sector [2019] OJ L317/1

Regulation (EU) 2020/852 of the European Parliament and of the Council of 18 June 2020 on the establishment of a framework to facilitate sustainable investment, and amending Regulation (EU) 2019/2088 [2020] OJ L198/13.

Regulation (EU) 2021/1119 of the European Parliament and of the Council of 30 June 2021 establishing the framework for achieving climate neutrality and amending Regulations (EC) No 401/2009 and (EU) 2018/1999 ('European Climate Law') [2021] OJ L243/1

Responsible Contracting Project, 'The Mission' <https://responsiblecontracting.org> accessed 27 June 2023

—, 'The Toolkit' <https://www.responsiblecontracting.org/toolkit> accessed 6 November 2023

Rossi A, Ducato R, Haapio H and Passera S, 'When Design Met Law: Design Patterns for Information Transparency' (2019) (122–3) Droit de la Consommation – Consumenterecht 79

— and Haapio H, 'Proactive Legal Design: Embedding Values in the Design of Legal Artefacts' in Erich Schweighofer, Franz Kummer and Ahti Saarenpää (eds), *Internet of Things. Proceedings of the 22nd International Legal Infomatics Symposium IRIS 2019* (Editions Weblaw 2019)

Rättzén M, 'Automated Contract Review: Challenges and Outcomes of a Data Annotation Framework' (2022) 62 Jurimetrics Journal 225

Salo-Lahti M, Ranta M and Haapio H, 'AI Tools for Sustainability – Actionable Information for Both Humans and Machines' in Erich Schweighofer, Jakob Zanol and Stefan Eder (eds), *Legal Informatics as Science of Legal Methods. Proceedings of the 26th International Legal Informatics Symposium IRIS 2023* (Editions Weblaw 2023)

Saloranta J and Hurmerinta-Haanpää A, 'Proactive Contract Theory in the Context of Corporate Sustainability Due Diligence' (2022) 6 Journal of Strategic Contracting and Negotiation 221

Schönfelder D, Braun B and Scheltema M, 'Contracting for Human Rights: Experiences from the US ABA MCC 2.0 and the European EMC Projects' (*Nova Centre on Business, Human Rights and the Environment Blog*, 1 November 2022) <https://novabhre.novalaw.unl.pt/contracting-for-human-rights-experiences-from-the-us-aba-mcc-2-0-and-the-european-emc-projects> accessed 13 February 2023

Simkins C, 'L2L Contracts: Thinking beyond B2C and B2B' (*Improving Contracts. Blog*) <https://improvingcontracts.com/l2l-contracts-thinking-beyond-b2c-and-b2b/> accessed 5 September 2023

Smith B and Nowbar H, 'Microsoft Announces New Copilot Copyright Commitment for Customers' (*Microsoft Blog*, 7 September 2023) <https://blogs.microsoft.com/on-the-issues/2023/09/07/copilot-copyright-commitment-ai-legal-concerns/> accessed 10 September 2023

Snyder D, Maslow S and Dadush S, 'Balancing Buyer and Supplier Responsibilities: Model Contract Clauses to Protect Workers in International Supply Chains, Version 2.0' (2021) 77 The Business Lawyer 115

Soto M, Xue H and Tsekleves E, 'Design for Balance: Wellness and Health' (2022) 7(6) Base, Diseño E Innovación 4

Spellbook by Rally, 'Draft Contracts 3x Faster with AI' <www.spellbook.legal> accessed 1 February 2023

Strowel A, 'ChatGPT and Generative AI Tools: Theft of Intellectual Labor?' (2023) 54 IIC – International Review of Intellectual Property and Competition Law 491

Sulkowski A and Jebe R, 'Evolving ESG Reporting Governance, Regime Theory, and Proactive Law: Predictions and Strategies' (2022) 59 American Business Law Journal 449

Sustainable Terms of Trade Initiative, <www.sustainabletermsoftradeinitiative.com/> accessed 29 June 2023

Tamminen P, *Possibility-Driven Design in Design-Oriented Communities* (Aalto University publication series Doctoral dissertations 235/2016, 2016)

Thaler RH, 'From Cashews to Nudges: The Evolution of Behavioral Economics' (2018) 108(6) American Economic Review 1265

— and Sunstein C, *Nudge: Improving Decisions about Health, Wealth, and Happiness* (Yale University Press 2008)

United Nations, 'Transforming Our World: the 2030 Agenda for Sustainable Development' (Resolution adopted by the General Assembly on 25 September 2015, A/RES/70/1, 21 October 2015)

Utterback J, Vedin B-A, Alvarez E, Ekman S, Walsh Sanderson S, Tether B and Verganti R, *Design-Inspired Innovation* (World Scientific Publishing Co. 2006)

Wagner WE, 'Rethinking Legal Requirements: A Case Study of Incomprehensible Consumer Contracts in the United States' in Marcelo Corrales Compagnucci, Helena Haapio and Mark Fenwick (eds), *Research Handbook on Contract Design* (Edward Elgar 2022)

— and Walker W, *Incomprehensible!: A Study of How Our Legal System Encourages Incomprehensibility, Why It Matters, and What We Can Do About It* (CUP 2019)

Waller R, Passera S and Haapio H, 'Layered Contracts: Both Legally Functional and Human-Friendly' in Kai Jacob, Dierk Schindler, Roger Strathausen and Bernhard Waltl (eds), *Liquid Legal – Humanization and the Law* (Springer 2022)

Working Group of the American Bar Association (ABA) Business Law Section, 'Responsible Purchasing Code of Conduct: Schedule Q Version 1.0' <www.americanbar.org/content/dam/aba/administrative/human_rights/contractual-clauses-project/scheduleq.pdf> accessed 13 February 2023

WorldCC Foundation, Stefania Passera and Helena Haapio, 'Contract Design Pattern Library' <https://contract-design.worldcc.com/> accessed 31 January 2023

—, Passera S and Haapio H, 'Layering' (*Contract Design Pattern Library*) <https://contract-design.worldcc.com/library/layering> accessed 1 March 2023

7. EXPLORING THE DIMENSIONS OF PARTICIPATION IN LEGAL DESIGN

Nina Toivonen and Santiago de Francisco Vela

Abstract
This article discusses the 'paradox of participation' in legal design and how to address it in practice. Law as a special social function needs multi-level participation, not only to fulfill its duty in society, but also for its own reflection and inner development. However, the legal culture, including classical legal analysis and many legal practices tend to reject anything 'non-legal', making it challenging for both lawyers, users and other professionals to initiate legal design projects and to engage in them. As described in design literature, putting multi-level participation into effect is a challenge also in design contexts other than law, and requires special mindfulness and methods to succeed. This paper shows how the model of five critical questions by Joseph Giacomin, the design matrix by Elizabeth Sanders and Pieter Stappers, and the participation ladder model by Frans Geilfus can be used to frame legal design projects from the perspective of participation, and to decide how to incorporate a more participatory approach to them, if desired.

1. Introduction

For Legal Design to establish itself as a unique field of design with a mission to improve legal systems, it is necessary to develop design methods that serve the specific purposes and features of law.[1] This paper argues for the fundamental role of participatory design practices[2] in Legal De-

1 Michael Doherty, Marcelo Corrales Compagnucci, Helena Haapio and Margaret Hagan, 'A new attitude to law's empire: the potentialities of legal design' in Marcelo Corrales Compagnucci, Helena Haapio, Margaret Hagan and Michael Doherty (eds), *Legal Design. Integrating Business, Design and Legal Thinking with Technology* (Edward Elgar Publishing 2021) 1.

2 Also understood as 'co-design', 'collaborative design' or 'participatory innovation', see Elizabeth BN Sanders and Pieter J Stappers, 'Co-creation and the new landscapes of design' (2008) 4 International Journal of CoCreation in Design and the Arts 5-18; Jacob Buur and Ben Matthews, 'Participatory innovation' (2008) 12 International Journal of Innovation Management 255-273.

sign building on two main insights introduced and discussed in previous research. The first insight is that designing legal artifacts that are part of complex social systems requires a multi-level understanding of the various functions, meanings, and values that the artifacts must gratify to be usable.[3] Such an understanding is best acquired by working together with users and other stakeholders, as they can not only help build the technical solution, but also its meaning, acceptability, and effects.[4] This participatory approach goes beyond 'user-centricity' or 'human-centricity', as it regards users as decision-makers, validators and agents of the design, not just as information providers.[5] The second insight is that although multi-level participation would be a must, engaging lawyers, designers and other stakeholders to design legal artifacts together can be a particular challenge.[6] That may be due to the different - sometimes opposite - expectations, understandings and attitudes of lawyers and other stakeholders towards problem solving, knowledge formulation and the value of co-work.[7] In particular, the legal profession is characterized by its legal-centric and somewhat exclusive working models.[8] Students at law

---

3 Petra Hietanen-Kunwald, Helena Haapio and Nina Toivonen, 'Systems Theory as a Research Framework for Dispute Prevention and Resolution by Design' in Rossana Ducato and Alain Strowel (eds), *Legal Design Perspectives - Theoretical and Practical Insights from the Field* (Ledizioni 2021) 86; Andrés Polanía and Santiago de Francisco Vela, 'Designing Interfaces for Legal Artifacts. Using Storytelling to Enhance Digital Legal Experiences' in N Martins and D Brandão (eds), *Advances in Design and Digital Communication III,* DIGICOM, 27 Springer Series in Design and Innovation (Springer 2022).

4 Lucy Kimbell, 'Design-as-practice and designs-in-practice' (CRESC Conference, Manchester 2009) 9; Ezio Manzini, *Design When Everybody Designs. An introduction to Design for Social Innovation* (MIT Press 2015) 45.

5 Elisabeth B. N. Sanders, 'From user-centered to participatory design approaches' in Jorge Frascara (ed), *Design and the social sciences: Making connections* (Taylor & Francis Books Limited 2002) 1-8.

6 Michael Doherty, 'The relationship between legal and design cultures: tension and resolution' in Marcelo Corrales Compagnucci, Helena Haapio, Margaret Hagan and Michael Doherty (eds), *Legal Design. Integrating Business, Design and Legal Thinking with Technology* (Edward Elgar Publishing 2021) 32; Margaret Hagan, 'Participatory Design for Innovation in Access to Justice' (2019) 148 Dædalus, Journal of the American Academy of Arts and Sciences 120, 122.

7 Doherty (n 6) 32, and Amanda Perry-Kessaris, 'Legal Design for Practice, Activism, Policy and Research' (2019) 46 Journal of Law and Society 185.

8 Doherty (n 6) 45; Perry-Kessaris (n 7) 185; Richard Susskind and Daniel Susskind,

schools are traditionally trained to analyze and solve problems on their own, normalizing the expectation of an independent and self-sufficient legal expert. Also, when practicing their special expertise, to interpret what is 'legal' or 'illegal,' lawyers can only turn to authoritative legal information sources, such as regulations or court rulings. Anything non-legal has little to no value in classical legal analysis.[9] Therefore, the idea of participation embedded in legal design, that legal problems could be solved with the help of non-legal experts and their non-legal knowledge, may seem counterintuitive or even irrational for some lawyers.[10] If not adequately addressed and unraveled, this discrepancy between ideals and reality, or as we call it 'the paradox of participation', may hamper the practice of design in the field of law.

This paper explores participation in legal design from two field-specific perspectives – those of law and design. In section 2 we first explain why a participatory approach to designing law and legal artifacts matters, and secondly, what may hinder the use of participatory methods in legal contexts. This overview is built on system-scientific, behavioral and socio-legal theories, with a twist of our personal experiences and project descriptions from the legal design field. As noted in previous legal design studies, systems sciences provide a useful analytical lens to understand complex human phenomena, such as the relationship between legal systems and society.[11] Systems sciences also support the development of

The Future of the Professions (OUP 2015) 136.

9 Steven Barkan, Barbara Bintliff and Mary Whisner, *Fundamentals of Legal Research, Tenth Edition* (Foundation Press 2015); Kaarlo Tuori, *Critical Legal Positivism* (Routledge 2002) 285; Hietanen-Kunwald, Haapio and Toivonen (n 3) 79.

10 Similarly Margaret Hagan, 'A Human-Centered Design Approach to Access to Justice: Generating New Prototypes and Hypotheses for Intervention to Make Courts User-Friendly' (2018) 6 Indiana Journal of Law and Social Equity 199, 202; Perry-Kessaris (n 7) 3.

11 Hietanen-Kunwald, Haapio and Toivonen (n 3); Joaquin Santuber and Lina Krawietz, 'User Research Methodologies in Legal Design Projects: Lessons from Practice' in Rossana Ducato and Alain Strowel (eds), *Legal Design Perspectives - Theoretical and Practical Insights from the Field* (Ledizioni 2021) 93. See also Santiago De Francisco Vela and Laura Guzman-Abello, 'Systemic design of justice: Transdisciplinary approach to access to justice' in this Volume.

design philosophy more generally, as design itself is a systemic method, seeking to create systemic impacts.[12]

In section 3 we continue our exploration with a more practice-oriented focus. As the design literature describes, there are multiple ways to understand 'human- 'or 'user-centric' design, but only some of the methods and solutions created under these concepts are participatory in the sense of letting users and other stakeholders have a say about the design outcomes. In this section we discuss how the model of five critical questions by Joseph Giacomin,[13] the matrix of design by Elizabeth Sanders and Pieter Stappers,[14] and the participation ladder model by Frans Geilfus[15] can help legal designers frame their projects from the perspective of participation and decide how to incorporate a more participatory approach to them, if desired. To demonstrate the potential of these models, we use method and solution examples from three legal design projects: the SMS tool created by the Eviction Prevention Learning Lab at Stanford University in San Francisco, USA,[16] the digital 'Entutela' tool created by Labjusticia at the University of los Andes, Colombia,[17] and the Legal Service Design Toolkit created by Háptica legal design consultancy in Colombia.[18] Our exploration will be concluded in the fourth section with a summary of our main findings, their possible uses in legal design practice, and ideas for future research.

---

12 Richard Buchanan, 'Systems Thinking and Design Thinking: The Search for Principles in the World We Are Making' (2019) 5(1) She Ji: The Journal of Design, Economics, and Innovation, 85, 86.

13 Joseph Giacomin, 'What is human centered design?' (2014) 17 The Design Journal 4, 606.

14 Sanders and Stappers (n 2).

15 Frans Geilfus, 80 Tools for Participatory Development: Appraisal, Planning, Follow-Up and Evaluation (IICA 2008).

16 Sarah Verschoor, 'How can text messages help prevent evictions?', <https://medium.com/legal-design-and-innovation/how-can-text-messages-help-prevent-evictions-77d477135bb4> accessed 8 February 2023.

17 Camila Padilla Casas and Santiago de Francisco Vela, 'Entutela. A digital tool to facilitate the drafting and creation of tutelas in Colombia' in Advances in Design and Digital Communication III - Proceedings of the 6th International Conference on Design and Digital Communication (Digicom 2023).

18 Angelica Flechas, Jorge García and Sofia Escobar, 'Aplicación de la metodología de Legal Service Design de cara a contextos de derecho público vs. derecho privado' (2021) 6 RChD: creación y pensamiento 11, 1-23.

2. The Paradox of Participation in Legal Design

Just like any other everyday objects invented by humans, legal artifacts have specific functions that satisfy human needs that no other artifact satisfies in a similar way.[19] In this paper we understand 'legal artifacts' in a broad sense as anything tangible or abstract that belongs to or is closely connected to the legal system by its functions, and which make law visible and something that can be experienced by its human users. The problem, however, as addressed by the legal design movement, is that legal artifacts are seldom designed to fit their *actual* purpose of use, at least not from the perspective of their laymen users.[20] Design as a practice-oriented philosophy is interested in promoting the well-being of people by satisfying their basic needs,[21] but the common design of legal artifacts often leaves these needs unsatisfied. Therefore, the question of purpose is closely connected to the question of *whom* the design solution is intended for and, therefore, whose needs, capabilities and motivations should be considered when designing legal artifacts.[22] The artifact's purpose also raises the question of *how* it should be designed and *by whom* to optimize its functionality. When seeking to understand the role of participation in legal design, it may therefore be helpful to start with a few ontological questions: What is law really for? What are legal artifacts really for?

2.1. Why Law Needs Participation

As understood in modern legal thinking, law as a human invented system can have many functions, depending on which perspective this system is viewed from. Law can be used to solve conflicts, to protect the vulnerable, to satisfy human needs, to allocate resources, to provide services, to enforce political ideas, or even to ensure a living for lawyers, to name a

19 Herbert A Simon, *The Sciences of the Artificial* (MIT Press 2019) 111.
20 Hagan (n 10) 202; Doherty, Corrales Compagnucci, Haapio and Hagan (n 1) 3.
21 Kimbell (n 4).
22 Gerlinde Berger-Walliser, Thomas Barton and Helena Haapio, From Visualization to Legal Design: A Collaborative and Creative Process (2017) 54 American Business Law Journal 2, 11.

few.[23] These purposes can also manifest in different ways in the form of legal artifacts. The legal artifacts that serve the purpose of conflict solving, for example, can be the procedural regulations that guide a litigation process, the litigation documents, the litigation process happening at a courthouse, the courthouse itself, and the final court ruling that seeks to solve the conflict.[24] From a purely legal point of view, it may also seem logical that lawyers are the primary users of these artifacts, and therefore their needs should be considered when designing these objects. However, as socio-legal theories help us understand, both the scope of users and the purposes of use for legal artifacts are more diverse due to the specific function that law has in society.

If we accept the idea that law has a unique function in society, it follows that the artifacts that are part of that system also share the same function. According to established legal and socio-legal theories, particularly the theory of social systems by late sociologist Niklas Luhmann, the specific purpose of law is to guide human behavior by establishing *normative expectations.*[25] Normative expectations, communicated for example in the form of legislation or court rulings, tell people how they are supposed to ('ought to') behave to satisfy interests that society considers worthy of protection, such as resolving conflicts or taking care of the vulnerable. Normative expectations also tell us what kind of behavior people are entitled to anticipate from others, thus helping people to plan their future activities and prevent possible conflicts of interest.[26] Only behaviors that meet the normative expectations set by the law can enjoy legal protection. This is also the core requirement of *legal certainty*, the central element of the rule of law.[27] From this viewpoint it becomes clear that law and legal things are intended for all members of society, or at least for everyone who needs to use them to access

23 Niklas Luhmann, *Law as a Social System* (KA Ziegert tr, OUP 2004) 149; Joseph Raz, *The Authority of Law, Essays on Law and Morality* (OUP 1979) 164-179; Tuori (n 9) 135.

24 Luhmann (n 23) 30.

25 Luhmann (n 23) 148; Raz (n 23) 164; Hans Kelsen, *The Pure Theory of Law* (Max Knight tr, University of California Press 1967) 31.

26 Raz (n 23) 169.

27 Aulis Aarnio, *The Rational as Reasonable. A Treatise on Legal Justification* (D Reidel Publishing Company 1987) 3.

the legal system and exercise their rights and obligations. As discussed by Michael Doherty, the purpose of law in guiding human behavior can therefore be seen as a justification for the application of human-centric approaches to designing better functioning legal artifacts.[28]

It is needless to say that guiding human behavior is a complex phenomenon, perhaps too complex for just lawyers to take care of it. If the purpose of legal artifacts is to communicate normative information about what kind of behavior the legal system expects from its users, ideally this communication and the way it is communicated should be based on a non-biased, scientific and context-related understanding of human behavior. This understanding can be acquired from various experts in behavioral and other human sciences, but also from the target end-users and other stakeholders themselves. According to a behavioral scientific theory called 'the COM-B model', there are three central components, 'capability,' 'opportunity,' and 'motivation,' that are all needed for any behavior to occur.[29] For example, if a person needs to represent herself at a court, to succeed in her task she needs the knowledge, skills, and stamina ('capability'), as well as time, money, and physical access to the necessary materials ('opportunity') and enough interest to take such action ('motivation') in order to succeed at the task.[30] This information about users' capabilities, opportunities, and motivations can be considered subjective and context-related.[31] Therefore, the best way to collect it is from the target people whose behavior the design primarily seeks to influence.[32]

While participatory design methods can help gather the necessary information about the behaviors the legal artifact should support, they may also have other benefits regarding guidance of behavior. Users of le-

28 Michael Doherty, 'Comprehensibility as a Rule of Law Requirement: The Role of Legal Design in Delivering Access to Law' (2020) 8(1) Journal of Open Access to Law 2.

29 Susan Michie, Lou Atkins and Robert West, *The Behaviour Change Wheel. A Guide to Designing Interventions* (Silverback Publishing 2014) 59; Susan Michie, Maartje van Stralen and Robert West, 'The behaviour change wheel: A new method for characterizing and designing behaviour change interventions' (2011) 6 Implementation Science 1, 42.

30 Michie, Atkins and West 2014 (n 29) 59.

31 Similarly Sanders and Stappers (n 2) 7.

32 Michie, Atkins and West (n 29) 66.

gal artifacts are the best experts in their own matters. Involving users in the legal design process as problem solvers and co-designers allows them to pursue agency and autonomy, the right to decide for themselves.[33] The democratic policy making process as well as the participatory design for policy movement are grounded in this very idea.[34] According to a behavioral scientific self-determination theory, the need for self-regulation and control is also one of the fundamental human needs and core factors for motivation.[35] Legal artifacts that fail to support their users' basic need for self-determination hardly bring out the best results. As described by Margaret Hagan in the context of self-represented litigants navigating inside the court system, if people experience that they have no chance to influence their own case or they have only bad options to choose from, they may become passive or reluctant to comply with the given circumstances and eventually lose their 'chances for taking the full advantage of the legal system.'[36] Participatory design methods that engage users as the contributors to the design outcome can improve users' experience of ownership and agency in the design solution and, therefore, give them a reason to comply with the behavioral models that the design proposes.[37]

User and stakeholder participation in legal design projects also enable a learning curve for all participants, not just for the users, but also for the lawyers, whose learning outcomes can eventually contribute to the inner development of the legal system.[38] This view is well adopted ia. in socio-legal and legal realism research traditions,[39] but also discussed in

33 Sanders and Stappers (n 2) 12.

34 Margaret Hagan, 'Prototyping for policy' in Marcelo Corrales Compagnucci, Helena Haapio, Margaret Hagan and Michael Doherty (eds), *Legal Design. Integrating Business, Design and Legal Thinking with Technology* (Edward Elgar Publishing 2021) 9.

35 Edward L Deci and Richard M Ryan, 'The "What" and "Why" of Goal Pursuits: Human Needs and the Self-Determination of Behavior' (2000) 11 Psychological Inquiry 4.

36 Hagan (n 10) 209.

37 Berger-Walliser, Barton and Haapio (n 22) 352.

38 David Johnson, 'Design for Legal Systems' (2020) 33 Singapore Academy of Law Journal, 434.

39 Amanda Perry-Kessaris, 'Doing Socio-Legal Research in Design Mode (Routledge 2021) 25; Perry-Kessaris (n 7) 8; Shauhin Talesh, Elizabeth Mertz and Heinz Klug,

modern legal theories, where lawyers are seen to have a dual role both as the interpreters and the creators of the legal system.[40] When engaging with different viewpoints on legal matters through participatory practices, legal drafters themselves have the potential to learn something new that benefits their legal thinking and lawyerly practices, and eventually the whole system.[41] Learning is therefore a fundamental element of positive change. As Buur and Matthews point out, 'When presented with an account of an exotic foreign mindset, we are compelled to view our natural assumptions and practices in a new light'.[42] If lawyers did not encounter different, outsider viewpoints to law (and to life!), the legal system would not receive the necessary information to reflect its internal biases and to imagine, test and build better working legal concepts and artifacts - for the sake of its own well-being.[43] Human-centric and participatory design methods can therefore work as practical tools to gather and analyze legally relevant information for the internal use of the legal system.

Participatory methods also have the potential to gather knowledge of, and make visible, the other different social systems and purposes that influence the legal design solution. As noted in previous legal design research, artifacts recognized inside the legal system as 'legal artifacts' can also have different uses outside the legal system.[44] Contracts are one example. If contracts are understood merely as 'legal documents', it is natural to expect them to be written by lawyers using specific 'legalese' language and clauses that prepare parties for a possible legal dispute.[45] From a business perspective, however, contracts can be seen as tools that,for example, help manage business commitments, create

'Introduction to the Research Handbook on Modern Legal Realism' in Shauhin Talesh, Elizabeth Mertz and Heinz Klug (eds), *Research Handbook on Modern Legal Realism* (Edward Elgar Publishing 2021) 1.

40 Tuori (n 9) 285.

41 Perry-Kessaris (n 7) 26-27.

42 Buur and Matthews (n 2) 4.

43 Perry-Kessaris (n 7) 3.

44 Hietanen-Kunwald, Haapio and Toivonen (n 3) 79.

45 Helena Haapio, 'Business Success and Problem Prevention Through Proactive Contracting' in P Wahlgren (ed), *Scandinavian Studies in Law Volume 49: A PROACTIVE APPROACH* (Stockholm Institute for Scandinavian Law 2006).

and protect value, and realize financial benefits.[46] If contracts were only designed from the legal perspective, the other purposes might remain unsatisfied. The difficult-to-understand legal text might even give rise to misunderstandings and the neglect of one's legal obligations,[47] risking the contractual relationship and its importance for the business. Participatory approaches can help recognize the artifacts' different uses in different social environments and create solutions that make sense in all of them.[48]

2.2. ...and Why It is a Particular Challenge for Legal Design

The aims and philosophy behind participatory legal design are easy to accept. In reality, however, based on our impressions and experiences as legal designers in legal design projects, and as described in the legal design literature,[49] putting the idea of participation into practice is trickier. The 'paradox of participation' may not only be due to the legal culture and the possible tensions that arise when it encounters the cultures of other disciplines or professions.[50] Successful communication and decision-making with other people, especially when there are many, who all represent different backgrounds, knowledge and ideals, is a universal human challenge – and sometimes a mission impossible.[51] We all perceive and interpret the world from our own unique inner perspective, without the possibility of fully experiencing what it is to be 'the other'. The way we see the world and intuitively trust our own perceptions can sometimes mislead us,[52] making multi-level collaboration a task that requires particular mindfulness, special methods and persistence in order to succeed.

---

46 Anna Hurmerinta-Haanpää, *The Many Functions of Contracts: How Companies Use Contracts in Interorganizational Exchange Relations* (University of Turku 2021) 37.

47 Robert Waller, 'Designing contracts for human readers' in Marcelo Corrales Compagnucci, Helena Haapio and Mark Fenwick (eds), *Research Handbook on Contract Design* (Edward Elgar Publishing 2022) 66.

48 Manzini (n 4) 35.

49 Comprehensively Doherty (n 6) 46; Hagan (n 6) 120.

50 Doherty (n 6) 32.

51 Geilfus (n 15) 1.

52 Emily Pronin, 'How We See Ourselves and How We See Others' (2008) 320 *Science*, 1177-1180.

Also, despite the popular interest that design thinking has gained during recent years, the participatory methods and techniques of design are not well known. If organizing multi-level co-work is a challenge as such, it can be a bigger challenge when participants need to first be introduced to the mindset, principles and methods of co-design. Although the design literature suggests that 'design' can be seen as a common language or as a connecting factor between different disciplines and stakeholders,[53] in reality, if people do not understand this language, it can connect them in a counterproductive way, such that it becomes the 'common enemy'. One reason for this could also be the way in which design as a systemic and holistic approach challenges common thinking models. The holistic and 'free' creative space that participatory design offers may not be the environment where people feel comfortable to operate, as it is not organized by similar mental frameworks, nor does it follow the deterministic, linear logic that many classical professions are taught to use.[54] If participants do not recognize the way the design process frames the problem solving, or how it can manage opposite viewpoints and understandings and eventually help create something coherent and sense-making out of them, they may experience the design process as not at all organized, and lose interest in participating.[55]

Then there are of course our all-time favorite excuses – time and money.[56] If doing a research interview or a stakeholder workshop adds the expenses of a project, people with tight budgets and busy schedules like to think that those things can be omitted and that by doing so they can save time and money. The ability to communicate the fundamental role of multi-level participation in a design process then becomes critical.

The above-mentioned reasons are already enough to overwhelm a legal designer who wants to successfully engage users and other stakeholders in a legal design process. As we like to suggest in the following, however, the concept of 'legal' and the different expectations and meanings that lawyers and society in general associate with it can give participatory legal design projects an extra twist. In our view that is because

53 Marc Stickdorn and others, *This is Service Design Doing* (O'Reilly 2018) 21.

54 Fritjof Capra and Pier Luigi Luisi, *The Systems View of Life. A Unifying Vision* (CUP 2014) 4; Doherty (n 6) 46; Berger-Walliser, Barton and Haapio (n 22) 18.

55 Geilfus (n 15) 1.

56 ibid.

the legal system and the traditional legal culture around it tend to foster a rather narrow understanding of what a 'legal' problem is and when a lawyer is needed to solve it. The multi-disciplinary and creative design process rebels against this narrowness and challenges both lawyers and others to think differently about law and the role of lawyers, causing confusion about how to react to this challenge.

From the perspective of the legal system only matters that have already been coded as 'legal' by the legal system itself – such as a question of ownership, the right to compensation or the due process of litigation – are proper 'legal' questions.[57] Traditionally people have approached lawyers with their legal matters when a problem has already actualized, or is about to actualize, and a legal analysis is needed to solve the conflict between the parties and their interests. This human tendency to react to problems only once they have occurred has created a culture where reactive problem solving is normalized, and preventive or proactive problem solving is perceived as its 'alternative' (or abnormal).[58] Against this traditional or reactive style of lawyering it is understandable that some lawyers may find it irrational to 'embrace a designer mindset', ideate and prototype with stakeholders in a joint co-creation process. Solving legal problems from a pragmatic and 'human-centric' viewpoint together with the users of the law differs significantly from the methods that lawyers traditionally use, but also from what the society in general has learned to expect from interaction with law and legal experts, as well as from legal problem solving in general. Therefore, especially in the beginning of a legal design project, there might be some confusion about everyone's role in the project, not just amongst the legal experts, but also amongst the other participants.

But what is the 'legal' work that lawyers are familiar with and what do people expect them to do? Lawyers' particular skill is legal interpretation, that is, the ability to determine from various facts what is 'legal' and distinguish it from what is 'illegal' using information sources that have authoritative value inside the legal system, such as legislation, case

57 Luhmann (n 23) 17.

58 Gerlinde Berger-Walliser, 'The Past and Future of Proactive Law: An Overview of the Development of the Proactive Law Movement' in Gerlinde Berger-Walliser and Kim Østergaard (eds), *Proactive Law in a Business Environment* (Djøf Publishing 2012) 24.

law, or established legal principles.[59] According to the above-described Luhmannian socio-legal understanding, this is how normative expectations are created.[60] Law school curricula, theories on legal analysis, and the practice of jurisprudence have developed around mastering this skill and the duty to the legal system that it involves.[61] Luhmann calls this the *autopoiesis* of the legal system, a self-regulation process that recreates and maintains the system.[62] Lawyers must follow the rules of legal analysis and interpretation, 'the laws of the law,' to maintain the coherence and unity of the system and the trust it enjoys in society.[63] In a legal design project, this knowledge is also crucial. However, it is applied from a different point of view, or together with other different points of view, and at a different moment on 'a legal problem escalation axis', often to prevent legal problems or to promote 'legal wellbeing'.[64]

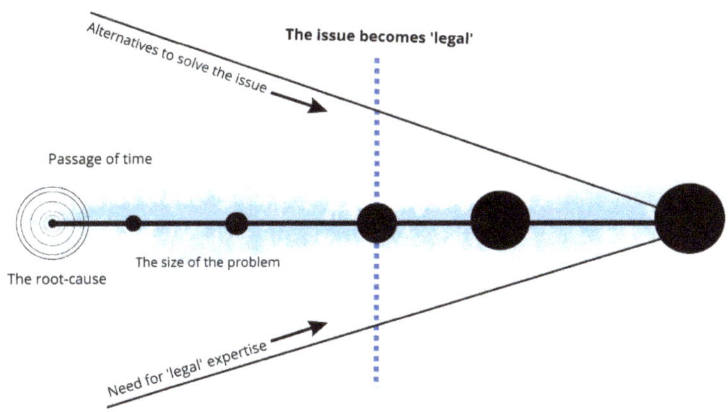

Fig. 1. The legal problem escalation axis.

59 Luhmann (n 23) 17.

60 ibid.

61 ibid 44.

62 ibid 18.

63 Aarnio (n 27) 3; Perry-Kessaris (n 7) 3; Roger Cotterell, *Sociological Jurisprudence: Juristic thought and social inquiry* (Routledge 2018) 31-33.

64 Legal Design Alliance, 'The Legal Design Manifesto' (v2) <www.legaldesignalliance.org/#v2> accessed 8 February 2023; Helena Haapio, 'Introduction to Proactive Law: A Business Lawyer's View' in P Wahlgren (ed), *Scandinavian Studies in Law Volume 49: A PROACTIVE APPROACH* (Stockholm Institute for Scandinavian Law, 2006).

The unusual roles and setting of a legal design project and the way it requires lawyers to practice their expertise beyond the traditional borders of law may therefore explain why some lawyers feel confused and unmotivated when invited to participate in design projects. Legal design in its essence is not about solving acute legal conflicts or reacting to a past event with legal consequences.[65] Legal design, just like design in general, operates in a space of many potentials, where things may not yet be definitely 'legal' or 'illegal', but perhaps have the potential to become such.[66] When operating inside the legal system lawyers do not have to deal with such open uncertainty and lack of structure when solving problems, especially if they are called to action when an issue has already become 'legal', as there often is a due legal process and rules regarding how to proceed with it, and therefore, less alternatives regarding how to deal with the issue.[67] This moment is illustrated below in figure 1.

As David Johnson points out, however, lawyers also know how to deal with uncertainty, as they use their knowledge in a certainty-seeking way.[68] This supports the purpose of law, which is to create normative expectations, in other words certainty, predictability and continuum in society. The challenge for the legal design movement is to make lawyers and anyone interested in improving the legal system understand that design can offer effective tools for this purpose, but from a different perspective, at a different moment of time, in different spaces, and especially – as we like to highlight in this paper - with different people.

3. From Human-Centric to Participatory Legal Design

As discussed above, multi-level participation differs from what law as a profession and a discipline has traditionally excelled in. It can thus be a real practical dilemma for a designer or a design team to engage lawyers

65 ibid.
66 Johnson (n 36), 392.
67 Helena Haapio, 'Introduction to Proactive Law: A Business Lawyer's View' (2010) 49 A Proactive Approach, Stockholm: Stockholm Institute for Scandinavian Law 1999-2010, 29; Petra Hietanen-Kunwald, Mediation and the Legal System. Extracting the Legal Principles of Civil and Commercial Mediation (Unigrafia Helsinki 2018) 33.
68 Johnson (n 52) 392; Doherty (n 6) 48.

in multidisciplinary co-work, facilitate it, and bring out satisfactory results. However, as the design literature shows, participation is a universal challenge in all design contexts, not just in law.[69] To address this issue, designers have developed alternative ways to understand and practice stakeholder involvement.

The participatory design approach, which emphasizes design *with* or *by* users rather than designing *for* users, first emerged in Northern Europe in the 1970s as a method to increase the value of industrial production.[70] The participatory approach put together the expertise and knowledge of designers and engineers and the situated expertise of the people whose work was to be impacted by the design outcome. However, participatory design shares the same philosophy of human-centered design (HCD), or user-centered design (UCD), and the different approaches have recently started to influence each other.[71] They both focus on understanding the needs of the people who use a solution or a design and propose that people (as 'humans' or as 'users') should be involved in the design process.[72] HCD and UCD have their origins in industrial engineering and computer sciences.[73] Donald Norman and Stephen Draper suggested in 1986 that technology and design should be molded to the user's capabilities and needs and not the other way around.[74] In his various works, Norman has also emphasized designers' need to understand human behavior and the psychology that supports (or does not support) the functionality of everyday things.[75] Recently Norman has raised the idea of shifting the design conversation from humans or users to humanity.[76] This shift promotes systemic changes that impact the societal level rather than the

69 Geilfus (n 15) 1.

70 Sanders and Stappers (n 2) 7.

71 Sanders and Stappers (n 2) 13; Buur and Matthews (n 2) 2. Despite the difference in terminology, there is no essential methodological difference between human-centered design and user-centered design.

72 ibid.

73 Buur and Matthews (n 2) 4.

74 Donald Norman and Stephen Draper, *User centered system design: New perspectives on human-computer interaction* (L. Erlbaum Associates 1986).

75 Donald Norman, *Design of Everyday Things* (Basic Books 2013) 7; Donald Norman, *The Psychology of Everyday Things* (Basic Books 1988) 57.

76 Donald Norman, *Design for a Better World. Meaningful, sustainable, humanity centered* (MIT Press 2023).

individual level. It responds to the criticism of the HCD and UCD models, that they have a narrow approach to people without considering individuals' relationship with social systems, regulations, or life itself. [77]

What the HCD and UCD approaches also put less focus on is the potential of transformation, innovation and learning that participation in the design process has.[78] The enhancement of users' skills and knowledge is one of the distinctive elements that distinguishes participatory design (or 'innovation') from the HCD and UCD approaches.[79] As we suggest in this paper, focusing on the quality of human-centric methods, rather than just approaching law with a 'human-centric' or 'user-centric' mindset or 'design thinking', may be more useful for the purposes of law and legal design.

In the following we introduce three frameworks to implement participatory design: 1) Giagomin's five critical questions, 2) Sanders' and Stappers' matrix of design, and 3) Geilfus' ladder of participation, and explain how they can help legal designers frame their project understanding from the perspective of participation, and how to incorporate a more participatory approach to them. We also demonstrate the frameworks using the participatory methods applied in the creation of three legal design solutions, as described in their published project reports:

1. The SMS system created by Eviction Prevention Learning Lab (EPLL) at the Legal Design Lab at Stanford University[80];
2. The digital 'Entutela' tool by Labjusticia at the University of Andes, Colombia[81] ; and
3. Legal Service Design Toolkit (LSDT) by Háptica legal design consultancy[82].

77 The Interaction Design Foundation, 'What is humanity-centered design?' <https://www.interaction-design.org/literature/topics/humanity-centered-design> accessed 8 February 2023.

78 Sara Beckman and Michael Barry, 'Innovation as a learning process: Embedding design thinking' (2007), 50 California Management Review 1, 25-56; Sanders (n 5).

79 Buur and Matthews (n 2) 4.

80 Verschoor (n 16).

81 Padilla Casas and de Francisco Vela (n 17).

82 Flechas, García and Escobar (n 18), Háptica is a Legal Service Design consultancy based in Columbia, <https://haptica.co> accessed 8 February 2023.

The Stanford Legal Design Lab's Eviction Prevention Learning Lab used an SMS strategy to help tenants get helpful information when facing eviction. For the development of the system EPLL used different sessions and interviews with legal aid experts, tenant advocacies and universities to understand best practices regarding using text messages to empower people in different stressed situations related to legal issues.[83] SMS messaging was used for three primary purposes: first, for outreach and intake for eviction help and informing people about their legal status; second, for ongoing engagement and participation of tenants by sending reminders and updates; and third, for tracking outcomes by monitoring tenants after they had received assistance.[84]

'Entutela,' developed by Labjusticia at the University of the Andes, Colombia, is a digital tool that helps citizens draft and create a 'tutela', a legal form for accessing fundamental rights in Colombia,[85] without the help of legal assistance. For the development of Entutela, explorations were made with citizens, lawyers, law students and judges. In each interaction with these users, the design team sought to validate the conceptual and functional elements of the tool. Once the prototype had been created and developed in an application to create forms, it was launched live to understand its scope and impact. With the results of this exploration, more than 100 tutelas were created in 4 months. The second iteration round of the design process focused more on the tool's user experience, its interface (no longer on a form), and the way the situations that make up the body of the tutela should be written. These latter validations were only done with the users of the Legal Clinic of the University of los Andes.

The Legal Service Design Toolkit (LSDT) by Colombian legal design consultancy Háptica is a compendium of tools and methodologies for de-

83 Verschoor (n 16).

84 ibid.

85 The tutela is the primary mechanism for safeguarding fundamental rights in Colombia. It was introduced in the 1991 Political Constitution and was intended to be expeditious, informal and subsidiary. According to the Constitution, a citizen residing in Colombia can file tutelas without legal assistance and free of charge. However, most people who want to file a tutela need the help of a lawyer, which implies a charge for the drafting and filing. In addition, tutelas are a case of congestion in the judicial branch. Today, 30 years later, more than 9 million tutelas have been filed in Colombia, see Padilla Casas and de Francisco Vela (n 17).

veloping projects in the legal field. A designer, lawyer or innovator can take this toolbox and use the cards that best suit their project. For the development of the LSDT, Háptica used Beckman and Barry's four phases of innovation[86] as a reference to define methodologies, tools or activities that allowed them to investigate the projects they had developed.[87] The toolkit is divided into four phases: Discover, Interpret, Delimit, and Propose. For each phase, a series of activities comprise the organization's know-how.[88]

3.1. Five Critical Questions to Frame the Design Challenge

Based on our experiences as legal designers, when facilitating multidisciplinary legal design work, it is necessary to pay attention to the legal context and the language that is used to describe the context to different stakeholders and make the roles that different stakeholders have clear and visible. When the different components of a design challenge are illustrated holistically as a starting point for the project, all of the stakeholders can better understand their unique role and the value of multi-level participation.[89] Framing the design challenge from different perspectives is especially useful to highlight how different stakeholders are connected to the 'legal' problem, although they may understand it differently.

One way to do this visualization is to use Giacomin's list of five critical questions: 'who,' 'what,' 'when,' 'how,' and 'why' as its basis.[90] The five questions help identify the connections between the different activities for a design strategy. In legal design, the model can help identify the desired behaviors and the people whose behavior the legal design solution should seek to influence and who should be involved in the legal design process. We evaluated the three projects under Giacomin's questions to understand the connections between their design decisions and the

86 Beckman and Barry (n 78).
87 Flechas, García and Escobar (n 18).
88 ibid.
89 Stickdorn and others (n 65) 10.
90 Giacomin (n 13).

legal designer's desired outcomes (for a summary of the projects see table 1).

The first and most important question is 'who'. It focuses on the people or parties involved in the design process, especially the target users. For example, in the EPLL's SMS project, the target users were tenants about to be evicted. In the Entutela case, the scope of the stakeholders was broader, ranging from citizens to judges to lawyers and legal-aid help providers.[91] The target users of the Legal Service Design Toolkit were Háptica's clients, typically other lawyers.[92]

'What' describes the type of desired activities, behaviors and functions that the design solution should support. In the case of the EPLL, the desired outcome was to support tenants in making more informed choices throughout an eviction process and empower them to take action for their own cause. If a tenant does not respond to an eviction notice, they are more likely to be evicted and face a more complicated legal situation.[93] In the Entutela case the 'what' is to help and educate citizens to draft a proper tutela without legal assistance, but it is also about giving them information about the legal system and how they can navigate within it. Háptica's toolkit aims at educating their clients about design methodologies. When clients contract the design consultancy to develop a legal services project, they must involve their organization's collaborators to understand and propose ideas. The toolbox helps them as a means to integrate their vision with the employees' experiences.

	Who?	What?	When?	How?	Why?
EPLL's SMS system	*Tenants who are being evicted*	*Receive legal information about the rights of a tenant*	*Before, during and after an eviction*	*SMS strategy*	*To help tenants represent themselves throughout an eviction process; improvement of a legal process*

91 Padilla Casas and de Francisco Vela (n 17).

92 Flechas, García and Escobar (n 18).

93 Verschoor (n 16).

Entutela	*Citizens, judges and law-yers who use tutelas*	*Know how to structure a tutela*	*During the drafting of a tutela*	*Digitally struc-tured template*	*To help citi-zens represent them right; improvement of the tutela process*
Legal Ser-vice Design Toolkit	*Clients / different stake-holder groups*	*Learn legal design methodolo-gies*	*During legal design workshops*	*Tools and fa-cilitation methods*	*Education, skills improve-ment; sociali-zation of legal service design methods*

Table 1. Giacomin's critical questions applied to legal design solutions

The 'when' is about the interaction's form and timing.[94] In the EPLL project the understanding was that there are three critical phases when the SMS system must provide guidance to tenants: before, during, and after the eviction. The timing question is more challenging to frame in the Entutela project, as there are many possible reasons, and therefore times and places, to file a tutela. The Entutela solution that enables citizens to make their tutela forms online using a digital platform solves the problem of accessibility, at least for users who can access the internet. The Háptica's toolkit is intended to be used during legal design workshops with clients and stakeholders.[95]

The question of 'how' refers to semiotics, communication, and design discourse.[96] The EPLL's solution uses an SMS strategy to send information that guides a tenant through an eviction process. SMS are also useful for monitoring and tracking how the tenant's legal process is proceeding. The SMS's also uses easy to comprehend language. Entutela uses a digitally structured template that guides the user throughout the experience of drafting a tutela. The tool is divided into sections that are navigable back and forth. Each section has easy-to-comprehend instructions and guidelines to complete the information.[97] The LSDT is composed of

94 Giacomin (n 13).
95 Flechas, García and Escobar (n 18).
96 Giacomin (n 13).
97 Padilla Casas and de Francisco Vela (n 17).

different activities according to the design phase. These activities have descriptions and examples of how to use them. Also, the toolkit requires a facilitator to provide guidance and respond to questions while participants use the tools.[98]

The 'why' refers to the purpose of the design. In the context of legal design, it is important to address the legal purpose of the artifact, while acknowledging that artifacts can also have many other purposes that can have value in creating a functionable outcome. Like in the example cases, the purpose can be guiding tenants or Colombian citizens through a legal process while informing them about their legal rights, so that they can base their decisions on actual options that the legal system provides them. The 'why' can also refer to an objective that supports other objectives, like training stakeholders to understand design methodologies, so that they can start to implement them more independently and thus socialize the legal design thinking and methodologies to their organization and beyond.

3.2. The Matrix of Design to Understand your Approach to Users

Sanders and Stappers originally proposed 'the landscapes of design,' a four-quadrant matrix, to identify new emerging design practices and understand the variations of human-centered design.[99] According to Sanders and Stappers, there are four different ways to categorize the practice of design: 1) research-led with an expert mindset, 2) research-led with a participatory mindset, 3) design-led with a participatory mindset, and 4) design-led with an expert mindset. Research-led refers to design practices dedicated to understanding design contexts, either involving (participatory mindset) or not involving (expert mindset) users. On the other hand, design-led can be understood as design practices dedicated to implementing solutions for (expert mindset or participatory mindset) users.[100] In legal design work, this matrix can help reflect whether the approach taken in the project is ideal considering the project's purpose and the need to involve users in fulfilling that purpose. However, as the

98 Flechas, García and Escobar (n 18).
99 Sanders and Stappers (n 2) 2.
100 ibid.

exercise below will show, not all legal design projects can be placed in just one quadrant of the matrix; they can apply the different approaches simultaneously. It is also useful to say that legal design projects can opt for many different ways of approaching their users, and that applying more of 'an expert-mindset' rather than a 'participatory mindset' may not make their results less effective.

The EPLL's eviction project could be placed in the first quadrant of Sanders and Stappers' matrix (see figure 1), 'research-led with an expert mindset'. As described in the project report, the project involved several consultations with different professionals who had expertise about managing eviction cases, and for example about how to use SMS as an intervention strategy, as well as the use of research data on typical pain points in eviction procedures.[101] Although it is not possible to evaluate all of the details of the design methods used in the project based on available data, it seems that end-user understanding was created by using more research-lead and expertise approaches than by engaging users as actual co-creators in the project. The need to understand the impact of SMS messages and the phases of the eviction process and their legal and behavioral effects supports the approach taken.

101 Verschoor (n 16).

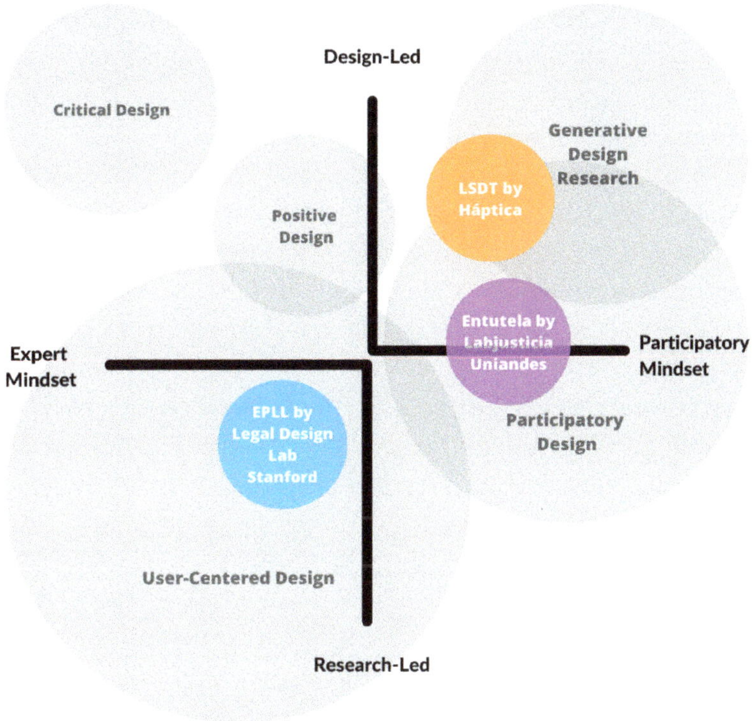

Fig. 2. Examples of Legal Design projects mapped on a design matrix introduced by Sanders and Stappers in 'Co-creation and the new landscapes of design', International Journal of CoCreation in Design and the Arts, 4, 5-18, 2008. © Sanders and Stappers, 2008. Reproduced with permission.

The approach taken in the Entutela project could be placed in the second quadrant of the matrix, 'research-led with a participatory mindset', but between the 'design-led' and 'research-mindset' quadrants. In the project it was necessary to understand profoundly the various experiences of different users and create common language and communication tools to reach that understanding. The project team used different generative tools, such as low and high-resolution prototypes, to dynamically understand and meet the needs of different stakeholders.[102] The project team also conducted several interview studies with

102 Padilla Casas and de Francisco Vela (n 17).

citizens to understand their experiences in drafting tutelas, as well as with law students, lawyers, and judges to understand their perspective in the process.[103] Although the user groups had a possibility to influence the design outcome, the design team made the necessary decisions to guide and manage the design process.

The case of Háptica differs from the two previously mentioned projects, because it itself is a tool to engage and activate different stakeholders and groups to design for themselves. Therefore, it could be placed within the quadrant in the corner, 'design-led with a participatory mindset'. It was designed by legal design experts to socialize legal service design methods and understanding, and therefore not only aims at improving people's participation in projects but also provides them with opportunities for learning and self-improvement. The toolkit could also be categorized as generative design research.

3.3. Ladder of Participation to Choose your Methods

Geilfus' ladder of participation identifies seven levels of participation determined by the degree of decision-making that participants have in the process (see table 2).[104] The first two levels 1) passivity and 2) information providing refer to low user involvement in the design process, especially to the level of agency and decision-making they have in the process. Users may be asked to participate for a certain period of the process, or to fill in surveys or questionnaires, but they have no say in how the information they have provided should be used.[105] The next two levels are 3) consultative participation, and 4) incentive-based participation. Design methods that consult users and hear their opinions to create the outcome, yet do not give users the power to make that decision, can be called consultative. EPLL's design methods could be categorized as consultative. EPLL developed a prototype for sending SMS messages to inform people who are about to face eviction. After the implementation phase, workshops were organized to identify the good practices of each actor involved. Virtuous cases were identified during these ses-

103 Padilla Casas and de Francisco Vela (n 17).
104 Geilfus (n 15) 3.
105 ibid.

sions where SMS had had a more significant impact.[106]

Incentive-based participation methods involve users or stakeholders who supply labor or other resources in exchange for certain incentives. A good example could be an organization that provides a test environment for a prototype and does not get to directly decide how the prototype is improved due to the testing, but as an exchange gets useful information about the test to improve its own operations, or a possibility for learning.[107]

7	**Self-development**	
6	**Interactive participation**	**Entutela by Labjusticia Uniandes** *Methods: Paper prototyping sessions, mockup navigation, prototype evaluation, functionalities hierarchy*
5	**Functional participation**	**LSDT by Háptica** *Method: Working sessions with facilitator with multiple stakeholders*
4	**Incentive-based participation**	
3	**Consultative participation**	**EPLL by Legal Design Lab Stanford** *Method: Interviews with experts upon SMS strategy results*
2	**Information provider**	
1	**Passivity**	

Table 2. Examples of how legal design methods can be located on Geilfus' ladder of participation.[108]

The last three steps on the ladder are 5) functional participation, 6) interactive participation, and 7) self-development. The methods mostly used in the Entutela project could be defined as functional participation.

106 Verschoor (n 16).
107 Geilfus (n 15).
108 ibid.

The project involved different stakeholder groups to meet pre-established project objectives, but they had little to no role in the project design. For example, lawyers and law students were invited to experiment, navigate and evaluate the prototype of the Entutela. Judges helped identify the elements they considered essential for a tutela to be understood, and once the online version was launched in collaboration with a courthouse, the results were analyzed with the help of some of the users who had sent their tutela through the system.[109]

Háptica's toolkit can be viewed as supporting interactive participation, or even self-development. Interactive participation solutions help organize stakeholders to participate in project design, and its implementation and evaluation. They also involve a systemic and structured teaching and learning process, as well as a progressive transition toward control and management by the stakeholders.[110]As in Háptica's case, it is important for a design agency to create their own tools and methods that support the specific needs their clients have in design projects, so that they can re-apply them if needed in future projects. To support this aim Háptica has also launched its own legal design courses under the name Háptica Academy, where people interested in mastering legal design methods can train their skills using the toolkit.[111] Both the toolkit and the courses support stakeholders' possibility to take their own initiative in legal design projects, without waiting for an external input from an expert. At this level of participation the roles of the designer-experts and the users have flipped: it is the expert that is being consulted, not the other way around.

What is noteworthy is that all of the example legal design cases represent a relatively high level of user and stakeholder engagement. This may be due to the social and systemic nature of the design projects, as well as the use of various design methods that as such require active participation from stakeholders. This supports the view of legal design as a genuinely participatory design approach.

---

109 Padilla Casas and de Francisco Vela (n 17).

110 Geilfus (n 15) 3.

111 Háptica (n 73).

4. Discussion and Implications

Our exploration in this paper has shown that the central idea in legal design, to make legal systems more human-centric and participatory, is more multi-layered than the everyday discussion about legal design often implies. First of all, there are multiple ways to reason this approach. The most important, and well acknowledged, reason is that the legal system itself needs information from multiple perspectives to function better. Different stakeholder groups and the end-users of the law can help lawyers, legal scholars, government officials and other caretakers of the legal system to reveal its internal biases and develop artifacts and systems that are more in line with the purpose of law. One purpose of the law, as understood in contemporary legal thinking, is to guide human behavior by creating normative expectations. This behavioral aspect of law also necessitates that the people whose lives are being influenced by the results also get to take part in the knowledge formulation and decision-making processes regarding the design, not just by providing information, but also through having agency and validating the meaning and acceptability of the result.

There are also multiple reasons why participation is easier said than done. Participation is a challenge in all design projects, and various authors in the design literature have provided their understanding of the phenomenon. However, in this paper we have focused on the special features of the legal context that can make collaboration in design projects trickier. Law, both as a professional culture and as a method of problem solving, tends to reject anything 'non-legal'. It is easy to understand that the legal system can only define, recreate and sustain itself in society with its own communicational codes ('legal'/'illegal') and its own communicators (lawyers, courts, legislation etc.) for the purposes of legal certainty and rule of law. However, proper lawyering does not only have to refer to reactive style problem-solving, working 'with an expert-mindset', or solving problems alone using only legal facts and legal information sources. If more lawyers, but also more people in general, understood that aside from the traditional and somewhat exclusive styles of lawyering there is space for human-centric, participatory and creative problem solving, perhaps more people would feel welcomed to be involved in it. As we have discussed above, both of these approaches aim to fulfill the same purpose of legal certainty.

The third dimension explored in this paper is the concept of 'participatory design' itself. Although the concept has its origins in human-centric and user-centric design approaches, it goes beyond understanding the user to providing them with decision-making power and experiences of learning and innovation. The design literature reports several frameworks and methods to plan and reflect the participatory approaches to be taken. In this paper we introduced three of them. Giacomin's five rhetorical questions can help break the design challenge into areas of 'who', 'what', 'how', 'when' and 'why', and answering them will show what direction and level of participation might be needed to ensure working results. Framing the project with these core questions at the beginning of a workshop, for example, will also show the participants what information and perspectives are needed from them, as well as from others.

Once the desired scope of the project has been defined, legal designers can use the Sanders' and Stappers' design matrix to reflect what type of approach to users, as subjects ('expert') or as partners ('participatory'), and design tools, tools to understand ('research') or to implement ('design'), to take. This exercise can help legal designers understand their own role in the project (a 'designer-expert' or a 'facilitator') and the pros and cons of their approach and create awareness about which type of tools and methods would support reaching the desired outcomes.

The third framework, Geilfus' ladder of participation, completes the matrix exercise and can be used to choose concrete participatory methods. Each level on the ladder refers to a certain type of a method. In the case of legal design it is useful to be aware that the higher the ladder, the more the methods on it give agency to the users and other stakeholders. For instance, if a legal design project has elements of research-led and expert mindset approaches, we would recommend looking for 'functionally participatory' methods that create a collective understanding about the topic, but also have elements that make users' point of view visible and give them a chance to analyze what the solution would mean for them. In practice this could mean conducting interviews with experts in the field, but also with users, for example using social cartographies as tools. [112] Social cartographies help multi-disciplinary teams create a common understanding about the topic or challenge they need to solve by formulating visual and tangible maps.

The exploration journey taken in this paper was a brief one. More research would be needed to better understand the elements and tensions of participation in legal design, especially from practical perspectives. The question of who should be allowed to design law and legal artifacts is provocative which reveals how important it is to have an ongoing discussion about the topic. If legal design has a specific purpose in improving the legal system, it should be about inviting different disciplines and users of the law to be part of legal design teams. This also calls for mindfulness about not fostering a too narrow understanding of 'the legal' when it comes to legal design. A brief look into the participants' backgrounds at legal design events, seminars, workshops and social media discussion threads shows that the idea of applying design in the contexts of law seems to attract and engage mostly other lawyers. Although it is only natural for legal experts to be interested in topics related to their own profession, it seems, however, that there is still a way to go for legal design to be a truly multidisciplinary approach. If not mindfully addressed, there is a risk of legal design becoming a mere fragmentation inside the legal system, not an approach that can connect people and generate impact and change. It should therefore be the collective aim of the legal design movement to create and promote alternative and easier-to-access spaces for multi-level collaboration in legal contexts.

There are many initiatives, projects, labs and working groups that are leading by their example.[113] More research would be needed to map their goals, methods and insights on multi-disciplinary approaches to law. One example can be found from Latin America. Labjusticia at the University of Andes in Bogotá, Colombia, connects an interdisciplinary team of designers, lawyers and engineers to approach real-life problems of access to justice from a systemic design perspective.[114]

112 Miguel Navarro-Sanint, 'Social cartography for social innovation: A design approach', in *Proceedings of the XVII Conference of the Iberoamerican Society of Digital Graphics* (SIGraDi: Knowledge-based Design 2013).

113 Some examples mentioned by Hagan (n 9) 122.

114 Santiago De Francisco Vela, Laura Guzman-Abello, Santiago de Pardo Rodriguez (2021) 'Design for Justice Lab: Interdisciplinarity in Times of Virtual Education' in

Bibliography

Aarnio A, *The Rational as Reasonable. A Treatise on Legal Justification* (D Reidel Publishing Company 1987)

Barkan S, Bintliff B and Whisner M, *Fundamentals of Legal Research, Tenth Edition* (Foundation Press 2015)

Beckman SL and Barry M, 'Innovation as a learning process: Embedding design thinking' (2007) 50(1) California Management Review 25

Berger-Walliser G, Barton T and Haapio H, 'From Visualization to Legal Design: A Collaborative and Creative Process' (2017) 54 American Business Law Journal 2

Berger-Walliser G, 'The Past and Future of Proactive Law: An Overview of the Development of the Proactive Law Movement' in Gerlinde Berger-Walliser and Kim Østergaard (eds), *Proactive Law in a Business Environment* (Djøf Publishing 2012)

Buchanan R, 'Systems Thinking and Design Thinking: The Search for Principles in the World We Are Making' (2019) 5(1) She Ji: The Journal of Design, Economics, and Innovation 85

Buur J and Matthews B, 'Participatory innovation' (2008) 12 International Journal of Innovation Management 255-273

Capra F and Luisi P L, *The Systems View of Life. A Unifying Vision* (Cambridge: CUP 2014)

Cotterell R, *Sociological Jurisprudence: Juristic thought and social inquiry* (Routledge 2018)

De Francisco Vela S and Guzman-Abello L, 'Systemic design of justice: Transdisciplinary approach to access to justice' in Rossana Ducato, Alain Strowel and Enguerrand Marique (eds), *Design(s) for Law* (Ledizioni 2024)

De Francisco Vela S, Guzman-Abello L and Pardo Rodríguez S, 'Design for Justice Lab: Interdisciplinarity in Times of Virtual Education' in Erik Bohemia and others (eds), *Proceedings of the DRS Learn X Design 2021: 6th International Conference for Design Education Researchers* (2 Design Research Society 2021)

Erik Bohemia and others, *Proceedings of the DRS Learn X Design 2021: 6th International Conference for Design Education Researchers*, 2 (Design Research Society 2021); Santiago De Francisco Vela and Laura Guzman-Abello, 'Systemic design of justice: Transdisciplinary approach to access to justice' in this Volume.

Doherty M, Corrales Compagnucci M, Haapio H and Hagan M, 'A new attitude to law's empire: the potentialities of legal design' in Marcelo Corrales Compagnucci, Helena Haapio, Margaret Hagan and Michael Doherty (eds), *Legal Design. Integrating Business, Design and Legal Thinking with Technology* (Edward Elgar Publishing 2021)

—, 'The relationship between legal and design cultures: tension and resolution' in Marcelo Corrales Compagnucci, Helena Haapio, Margaret Hagan and Michael Doherty (eds), *Legal Design. Integrating Business, Design and Legal Thinking with Technology* (Edward Elgar Publishing 2021)

—, 'Comprehensibility as a Rule of Law Requirement: The Role of Legal Design in Delivering Access to Law' (2020) 8(1) Journal of Open Access to Law 2

Flechas A, García J and Escobar S, 'Aplicación de la metodología de Legal Service Design de cara a contextos de derecho público vs. derecho privado' (2021) 6 RChD: creación y pensamiento 11, 1-23

Geilfus F, *80 tools for participatory development: appraisal, planning, follow-up and evaluation* (IICA 2008)

Giacomin J, 'What is human centered design?' (2014) 17(4) The Design Journal 606

Haapio H, 'Introduction to Proactive Law: A Business Lawyer's View' in P Wahlgren (eds), *Scandinavian Studies in Law Volume 49: A PROACTIVE APPROACH* (Stockholm Institute for Scandinavian Law 2006)

—, 'Business Success and Problem Prevention Through Proactive Contracting' in P Wahlgren (eds), *Scandinavian Studies in Law Volume 49: A PROACTIVE APPROACH* (Stockholm Institute for Scandinavian Law 2006)

Hagan M, 'Prototyping for policy' in Marcelo Corrales Compagnucci, Helena Haapio, Margaret Hagan and Michael Doherty (eds), *Legal Design. Integrating Business, Design and Legal Thinking with Technology* (Edward Elgar Publishing 2021)

—, 'Participatory Design for Innovation in Access to Justice' (2019) 148 Dædalus, Journal of the American Academy of Arts and Sciences 120

—, 'A Human-Centered Design Approach to Access to Justice: Generating New Prototypes and Hypotheses for Intervention to Make Courts User-Friendly' (2018) 6 Indiana Journal of Law and Social Equity 199

Hietanen-Kunwald P, Haapio H and Toivonen N, 'Systems Theory as a Research Framework for Dispute Prevention and Resolution by Design' in Rossana Ducato and Alain Strowel (eds), *Legal Design Perspectives - Theoretical and Practical Insights from the Field* (Ledizioni 2021)

Hietanen-Kunwald P, *Mediation and the Legal System. Extracting the Legal Principles of Civil and Commercial Mediation* (Unigrafia Helsinki 2018)

Hurmerinta-Haanpää A, *The Many Functions of Contracts: How Companies Use Contracts in Interorganizational Exchange Relations* (University of Turku 2021)

Johnson D, 'Design for Legal Systems' (2020) 33 Singapore Academy of Law Journal

Kelsen H, *The Pure Theory of Law* (Max Knight tr, University of California Press 1967)

Kimbell L, 'Design-as-practice and designs-in-practice' (CRESC Conference, Manchester 2009)

Legal Design Alliance, 'The Legal Design Manifesto' (v2) <www.legaldesignalliance.org/#v2> accessed 8 February 2023

Luhmann N, *Law as a Social System*, (KA Ziegert tr, OUP 2004)

Manzini E, *Design When Everybody Designs. An introduction to Design for Social Innovation* (MIT Press 2015)

Michie S, Atkins L and West R, *The Behaviour Change Wheel. A Guide to Designing Interventions* (Silverback Publishing 2014)

Michie S, van Stralen M and West R, 'The behaviour change wheel: A new method for characterizing and designing behaviour change interventions (2011) 6 Implementation Science 1

Navarro-Sanint M, 'Social cartography for social innovation: A design approach', in *Proceedings of the XVII Conference of the Iberoamerican Society of Digital Graphics* (SIGraDi: Knowledge-based Design 2013)

Norman D, *Design for a Better World. Meaningful, sustainable, humanity centered* (MIT Press 2023)

—, *Design of Everyday Things* (Basic Books 2013)

—, *The Psychology of Everyday Things* (Basic Books 1988)

Norman D and Draper S W, *User Centered System Design; New Perspectives on Human-Computer Interaction* (L Erlbaum Associates Inc 1986)

Padilla Casas C and de Francisco Vela S, 'Entutela. A digital tool to facilitate the drafting and creation of tutelas in Colombia'(2023), in *Advances in Design and Digital Communication III, Proceedings of the 6th International Conference on Design and Digital Communication*, Digicom 2022, November 3–5, 2022, Barcelos, Portugal

Perry-Kessaris A, 'Legal Design for Practice, Activism, Policy and Research' (2019) 46 Journal of Law and Society 185

Polanía A and de Francisco Vela S, 'Designing Interfaces for Legal Artifacts. Using Storytelling to Enhance Digital Legal Experiences' in N Martins and D Brandão D (eds) *Advances in Design and Digital Communication III,* DIGICOM 2022, 27 Springer Series in Design and Innovation (Springer 2022)

Pronin E, 'How We See Ourselves and How We See Others' (2008) 320 Science 1177

Raz J, *The Authority of Law, Essays on Law and Morality* (OUP 1979)

Sanders EBN and Stappers P, 'Co-creation and the new landscapes of design' (2008) 4 International Journal of CoCreation in Design and the Arts 1

Sanders EBN, 'From user-centered to participatory design approaches' in Jorge Frascara (ed), *Design and the social sciences: Making connections* (Taylor & Francis Books Limited 2002)

Santuber J and Krawietz L, 'User Research Methodologies in Legal Design Projects: Lessons from Practice' in Rossana Ducato and Alain Strowel (eds), *Legal Design Perspectives - Theoretical and Practical Insights from the Field* (Ledizioni 2021)

Simon HA, *The Sciences of the Artificial* (MIT Press 2019)

Susskind R and Susskind D, *The Future of the Professions* (OUP 2015)

Stickdorn M, Hormess M, Lawrence A and Schneider J, *This is Service Design Doing* (O'Reilly 2018)

Talesh S, Mertz E and Klug H, 'Introduction to the Research Handbook on Modern Legal Realism' in Shauhin Talesh, Elizabeth Mertz and Heinz Klug (eds), *Research Handbook on Modern Legal Realism* (Edward Elgar Publishing 2021)

Tuori K, *Critical Legal Positivism* (Routledge 2002)

The Interaction Design Foundation, 'What is humanity-centered design?' <https://www.interaction-design.org/literature/topics/humanity-centered-design> accessed 8 February 2023

Verschoor S, 'How can text messages help prevent evictions?', <https://medium.com/legal-design-and-innovation/how-can-text-messages-help-prevent-evictions-77d477135bb4> accessed 8 February 2023

Waller R, 'Designing contracts for human readers' in Marcelo Corrales Compagnucci, Helena Haapio and Mark Fenwick (eds), *Research Handbook on Contract Design* (Edward Elgar Publishing 2022)

8. SYSTEMIC DESIGN OF JUSTICE: TRANSDISCIPLINARY APPROACH TO ACCESS TO JUSTICE

Santiago de Francisco Vela and Laura Guzmán-Abello

Abstract
Access to justice is one of the most critical issues in law. The legal justice system needs a transdisciplinary approach to ensure better access to justice. This article presents a methodology that combines the principles of Legal Systems, Legal Design, and Systemic Design to be applied to the context of access to justice. This methodology has been developed through an undergraduate course for law, design, and engineering students at Universidad de los Andes in Bogota, Colombia. It considers three primary contexts: legal, social, and users. We have developed a methodological guide that starts with the definition of the regulatory framework, then identifies users´ perspective, followed by the interaction between users to build the social system. The conjunction of these three elements defines the boundary and requirements of prototypes, which are iterated and validated with potential users. The application of this iterative methodology has allowed students to reframe the problem, present a robust diagnosis, and propose solutions to the studied situation. In the end, we present one successful case of the application of this methodology: the reduction of pro-bono cases that remain untaken by lawyers.

1. Introduction

The legal justice system is complex. This complexity arises from the variety of individual actors and public or private organisations, with their interests and goals, that interact and intervene in it.[1] From this perspective, situations and problems presented by the legal justice system fall under the definition of complex problems. Complex problems do not have a single solution; therefore, the approach to solving them must be systemic. Thinking about the improvement of the administration of

1 Camilo Olaya and Juliana Gomez-Quintero, 'Conceptualization of Social Systems: Actors First' (Curran Associates Inc 2016).

justice invites for a synergy between engineering, law, and design. This combination of disciplines has made it possible to explore the social systems surrounding justice administration and design solutions that improve its performance.

To develop this idea, we will begin by exploring why access to justice should be understood as a transdisciplinary activity. Within that transdisciplinary exploration, we will review the connections that design, law, and engineering have and how that led us to think about the methodology we use. That methodology is based on Legal Design,[2] Systemic Design,[3] and Legal Systems[4] (See figure 1). These synergies result in the Systemic Design of Justice (SDJ) proposal. However, for this methodology to work within the educational and project field, it is essential to define the transdisciplinary tools we develop and use at different project moments such as understanding the challenge, designing solutions, and challenge management.

2 Colette R Brunschwig, 'Visual Law and Legal Design: Questions and Tentative Answers' in Erich Schweighofer and others (eds), *Proceedings of the 24th International Legal Informatics Symposium IRIS 2021* (Editions Weblaw 2021); Margaret Hagan, 'Legal Design as a Thing: A Theory of Change and a Set of Methods to Craft a Human-Centered Legal System' (2020) 36 Design Issues 3.

3 Alex Ryan, 'A Framework for Systemic Design' (2014) 7 FormAkademisk - forskningstidsskrift for design og designdidaktikk <https://journals.oslomet.no/index.php/formakademisk/article/view/787> accessed 26 February 2023; Peter H Jones, 'Systemic Design Principles for Complex Social Systems' in Gary S Metcalf (ed), *Social Systems and Design*, vol 1 (Springer Japan 2014).

4 David Howarth, *Law as Engineering: Thinking about What Lawyers Do* (Edward Elgar 2013).

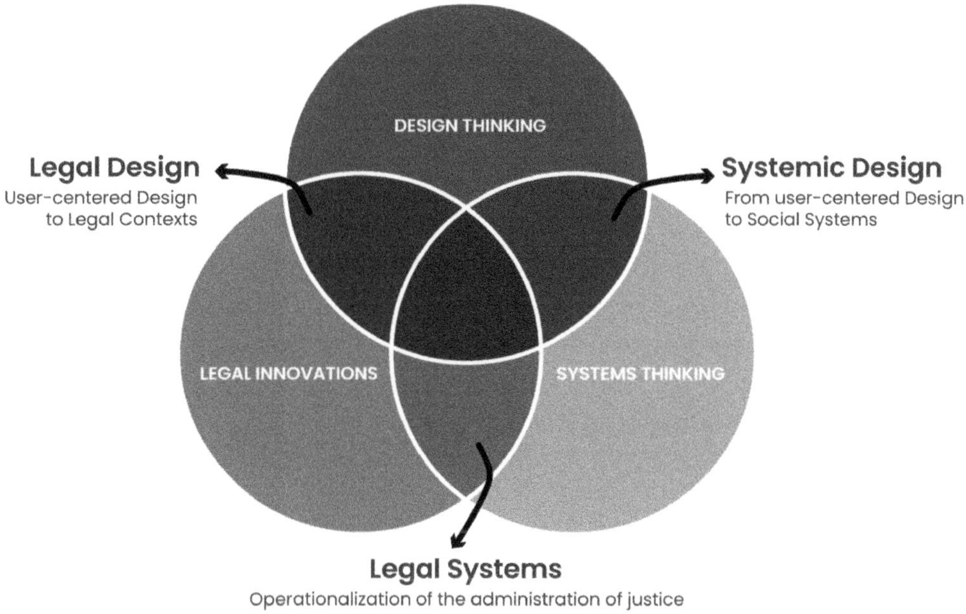

Fig. 1. Intersections of design, law and engineering disciplines

In the end, we present a successful case developed by students on the course, using the methodology in question; and we put forward some reflections on the future of these disciplines and the work with organisations that ensure access to justice.

2. Transdisciplinary Dimension to Justice

The "wicked problems" concept defined by Rittel[5] perfectly describes what is involved in working within the legal justice system. Justice systems, like most systems, are composed of people, which makes them a social system. Specifically, in the justice system, the improvement

5 Rittel's first definition of wicked problems was presented by C West Churchman, 'Wicked Problems' (1967) 14(4) Management Science B-141. In that definition, he posited that wicked problems were a "class of social system problems which are ill-formulated, where the information is confusing, where there are many clients and decision makers with conflicting values, and where the ramifications in the whole system are thoroughly confusing."

challenges take time to be identified. In some cases, we talk about the implementation of technology; in other cases, we talk about the improvement of administrative management. In essence, many possible points of intervention can be attacked. However, for each intervention point, there are multiple types of users whose motivations are not always aligned. We can have judges, who want to administer justice best, and citizens who want their rights to be respected. However, in trying to achieve both points, we encounter barriers (regulatory, informational, access, etc.) that prevent designers from having a clear idea of what to do. In an exercise between the Liquid Legal Institute and the School of Design Thinking at the Hasso Plattner Institute, where a design exercise was proposed to respond to the Common Legal Platform, Kohlmeier and Santuber[6] reflected on and reinforced the idea of "wicked problems" in legal design.

Designing for access to justice is a wicked problem, requiring the intervention of different disciplines. This interaction of different disciplines is known as cross-disciplinary. Within cross-disciplinarity, three dynamics are recognised: multidisciplinary, interdisciplinary, and transdisciplinary. According to Chew,[7] multidisciplinarity provides independent inputs from each intervening discipline without needing knowledge integration. Interdisciplinarity proposes an interaction between disciplines where particular dynamics are shared, generating collective agreements. Transdisciplinarity takes advantage of interdisciplinarity to investigate complex issues, generating synergies that transcend the domain of a single discipline. Chew also opened a debate on the operational challenges of generating cross-disciplinary curricula, highlighting the need for more alignment between disciplines, generating fewer synergies, and creating more distance between disciplines.[8]

6 Astrid Kohlmeier and Joaquin Santuber, 'Is the Common Legal Platform a Wicked Problem?: A Legal Design Approach. Case Study' in Kai Jacob, Dierk Schindler and Roger Strathausen (eds), *Liquid Legal* (Springer International Publishing 2020).

7 Jia Ying Chew, 'Siloed in Breaking Silos: A Case Study of Interdisciplinary Curriculum (Mis)Alignment', *LearnxDesign 2021: Engaging with challenges in design education* (Design Research Society 2021) <https://dl.designresearchsociety.org/learnxdesign/learnxdesign2021/researchpapers/36> accessed 24 February 2023.

8 ibid.

Since the emergence of Design Thinking, design has evolved as a cross-disciplinary practice. On the one hand, Buchanan[9] broadened the spectrum of design by proposing four areas in which the designer can intervene. These areas involve the subjects of (1) communication, (2) materialities, (3) services, and (4) complex systems. On the other hand, Kimbell[10] made an interesting distinction between design-as-practice and design-in-practice. Design-as-practice speaks of a designer's processes and methodologies to develop a project.

In contrast, Design-in-practice speaks of the multiple results or implementations of these exercises, understood as tools, prototypes, and proposals. Also, this evolution of the design discipline has led it to adopt a transversal position. For example, design and medicine have given rise to Medising;[11] design and psychology to Positive Design;[12] and design and anthropology to Design Anthropology;[13] and recently, design and law have given origin to Legal Design.

2.1. Design + Law = Legal Design

For Brunschwig,[14] Legal Design is as much about process (design-as-practice) as it is about the outcome (design-in-practices). She states that Legal Design comprises four elements: processes, products, actors, and contexts, and that it can also have sub-areas such as graphic design, product design, and service design, among others. Brunschwig's vision implies a transversality between design (and its areas) and law. Likewise, from Stanford's Legal Design Lab, Hagan[15] defines Legal Design as applying User-Centred Design approaches, typical of Design Thinking, to the legal or

---

9 Richard Buchanan, 'Wicked Problems in Design Thinking' (1992) 8 Design Issues 5.

10 Lucy Kimbell, 'Rethinking Design Thinking: Part II' (2012) 4 Design and Culture 129.

11 Richard Goossens, Johan Lange and Gert-Jan Kleinrensink, 'MEDISIGN: Educating Designers for the Operating Room' (2004) 13 Minimally Invasive Therapy & Allied Technologies 185.

12 Pieter Desmet and Anna Pohlmeyer, 'Positive Design An Introduction to Design for Subjective Well-Being' (2013) 75.

13 Wendy Gunn, Ton Otto and Rachel Charlotte Smith (eds), *Design Anthropology: Theory and Practice* (Bloomsbury 2013).

14 Brunschwig (n 2).

15 Hagan (n 2).

justice context. For Hagan, this has allowed the exploration of different design dimensions, such as communication, product, services, spaces, and policies, all under the scope of technology. Both Brunschwig and Hagan recognise that Legal Design has wide application as a design practice and a response to different situations that arise in legal contexts.

The rise of Legal Design has allowed more universities, research labs, and law firms to adopt its visions, methodologies, and tools. More and more courses, publications, and events bring together different professionals to build on Legal Design. Complementing Brunschwig's vision, Legal Design has begun to expand its boundaries to enrich itself with Systems Thinking. Including Systems Thinking or Systems Theory in Legal Design allows for approaching legal problems from a broader perspective, generating a framework of analysis that identifies critical elements to develop solutions to legal problems.[16] However, Design Thinking and Systems Thinking also have a practice in common, Systemic Design.

2.2. Design Thinking + Systems Thinking = Systemic Design

Ryan[17] has made a proposal that combines the holistic views of Systems Thinking with the user-focused approaches of Design Thinking. In his vision of Systemic Design, there are three levels: Mindset, Method, and Methodology. These three levels interconnect, allowing systemic designers to bring to the table the values, criteria, and practices (mindset) to apply tools (method) in a process (methodology). With this idea, Systemic Design is intended to approach highly complex contexts. However, to define complexity, Jones[18] defines principles to differentiate a systemic problem from a traditional design problem. The principles are idealisation, wickedness, purpose, boundary framing, requisite variety, feedback coordination, ordering, generative emergence, continuous adaptation, and self-organising. It should be noted that when Jones talks about these differences,

16 Petra Hietanen-Kunwald, Helena Haapio and Nina Toivonen, 'Systems theory as a research framework for dispute prevention and resolution by design' in Rossana Ducato and Alain Strowel (eds), *Legal Design Perspectives: Theoretical and Practical Insights from the Field* (Ledizioni 2021).

17 Ryan (n 3).

18 Jones (n 3).

he also references the four areas proposed by Buchanan.[19]

Systemic Design is also on the rise. On the one hand, the Design Council launched a methodology called Beyond Net Zero.[20] This methodology seeks to consolidate the visions of Design Thinking and Systems Thinking. On the other hand, in 2021, a group of researchers led by Van Ael, Ryan, and Jones[21] launched the Systemic Design toolkit. The methodology addresses tools from systemic thinking, such as zoom out, and design thinking, such as zoom in. These tools alternate to give relevance and perspective to this more comprehensive approach.

2.3. Engineering + Law = Legal Systems

It is common to think that the intersection between engineering and law is in the design of technology for the administration of justice. In many cases, it is a resource that uses engineering to solve problems in addition to justice issues. However, this intersection goes beyond a specific product. Howarth[22] says that Law and Engineering are similar in answering what engineers and lawyers do.

> The characterisation of lawyers that best fits what lawyers actually do is not hero, or statesman, or trickster, or hired gun – all of which in some way relate back to litigation – but engineer. Clients come to lawyers, as they come to engineers, with problems that they cannot solve themselves. The service both engineers and lawyers provide is the solving of those problems. But more than that, although both lawyers and engineers might solve clients' problems merely by offering advice and guidance, the central instrument for solving problems that both use is a device of some kind – usually a physical device in the case of engineers and a document in the case of lawyers, although, as we shall see, it is less the physical embodiment of a device that matters as how it alters the system within which it operates.[23]

19 Buchanan (n 9).

20 Design Council, 'Beyond Net Zero. A Systemic Design Approach'.

21 Sabrina Tarquini, Stefanos Monastidiris and Koen Peters, 'Systemic Design Toolkit' <https://www.systemicdesigntoolkit.org/> accessed 26 February 2023.

22 Howarth (n 4).

23 ibid.

They are alike in their purpose of producing solutions to problems and in considering the social implications of those solutions. The latter is rooted in engineering practice, as engineers must constantly test and validate their designs. To be more precise, this intersection stems from our understanding of legal systems as social systems. These are systems where different actors and organisations, public and private, interact and produce justice (or injustice). Thus, the law is responsible for designing legal instruments that solve access to justice problems. From engineering, it is complemented with the analysis of how this legal solution could be correctly inserted into that social system so that it produces the desired results. Thus, legal innovation is complemented by a systemic vision of its implementation in a complex system.

3. Design + Law + Engineering = Systemic Design of Justice

So far, we have discussed that merging two disciplines can broaden the approach to a specific topic. For instance, engineering and law can optimise the processes of justice administration. Law and Design can improve the experiences around legal services. Design and Engineering can generate a more holistic vision of the contexts, from the human to the systemic scale. In this article, we want to present a methodology that combines the principles of Legal Systems, Legal Design, and Systemic Design to be applied in the context of access to justice. We have been prototyping, iterating, and evolving this methodology since 2019 through an undergraduate course for students of the three disciplines: Design for Justice Lab. This class is structured around challenge-based learning. For the different versions of the course, we have looked for public organisations with challenges that can be addressed from the law, design, and engineering perspectives. One of the biggest challenges has been finding a balance between the contributions the disciplines can make. After five versions, we have arrived at this methodology called Systemic Design of Justice (SDJ). This transdisciplinary methodology is where the three disciplines share knowledge and combine tools to develop projects considering the legal context, the social context, and the people within the contexts (see figure 2).

Fig. 2. Abstraction of the contexts of interest for design for justice

The legal context addresses the regulatory framework. The social context allows for representing the social system(s) bounded by the legal context. Furthermore, the user perspective allows for identifying the people and organisations that interact within the social context through legal and non-legal artefacts. In the Design for Justice course, we have approached projects starting from the legal context and regulatory framework. However, we envision that the model can be approached from any point, as it has a cyclical property. In that order of ideas, we first address the understanding of the current regulation or norm in which the project will be developed, in other words, to define the regulatory framework. This regulation delimits the legal restrictions and defines a contextual framework for the project. This definition of the legal limits allows for identifying the users, artefacts, and organisations that use these laws. A process of observation and information gathering defines the identification of users. Identifying actors gives us the starting point to build a social system model. This model identifies the decisions and interactions of the different actors playing different roles in the system; their interactions produce feedback loops that determine the system's performance. With the social system, we identify system archetypes and leverage points. These leverage points allow for modelling and the evaluation of user and system proposals. Next, we begin an ideation process of prototyping. The process includes evaluating how the interventions affect the system's dynamics (feedback loops ans system's structure) and which is the best option based on these results. Finally, we validate whether the proposed solution responds to the studied regulatory framework. If yes, the proposal could be implemented; if not, it would be necessary to see if there is an option to propose an adjustment of the regulatory framework (see figure 3).

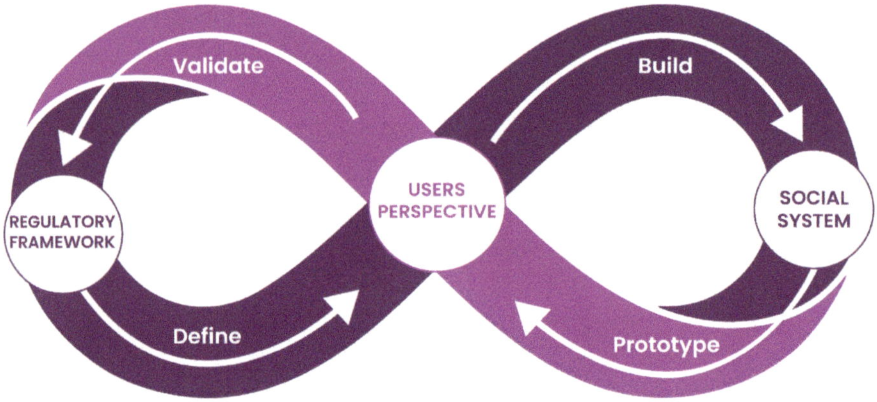

Fig. 3. The Mobius strip inspires the SDJ. It aims to create a research loop so that all the elements integrate smoothly into the projects.

In the first step, lawyers translate the regulatory framework elements so that designers and engineers can use them. In the second step, designers are responsible for carrying out information-gathering activities so that engineers and lawyers can conceptualise the social system. In the third step, engineers are responsible for building the social system model so that designers and lawyers can visualise the context. In the fourth step, engineers and designers define points of intervention. In the fifth step, designers and lawyers propose solutions to implement. Furthermore, in the sixth step, lawyers and engineers validate the impact of the solutions. We have begun to validate this tool through work with students from the three disciplines and research projects for the construction of new products and services for access to justice.

4. Tools for Transdisciplinary Solutions

To apply the methodology described previously, we use different types of tools that we organise according to the project moment in which we use them: understanding the challenge, designing solutions and challenge management. The first two moments occur in a consecutive way and the third one is transversal throughout all of the process. Some tools already exist and are commonly used in each discipline (disciplinary), some are common across two disciplines (interdisciplinary), and we have also created our tools that articulate elements from different disciplines (transdisciplinary).

4.1. Tools for Understanding the Challenge

Understanding the challenge is where we aim to grasp its legal, social and user context (as shown in figure 2). Most of the tools we use at this stage are specific to each discipline and some are interdisciplinary.

- Analysis of problem environment (interdisciplinary – design and engineering): As a first approximation to the problem, we invite students to develop a PESTEL analysis, which consists in identifying political, economic, social, technological, environmental, and legal aspects that are relevant to the challenge. This analysis allows students to see the challenge holistically and identify potential barriers and facilitators for its solution.
- Regulatory framework (disciplinary – law): Students must identify the regulatory framework relevant to the challenge. This is an exercise in critical legal analysis where the gaps or barriers between what the law says and what happens in reality, are identified. Groups should refer to the relevant norms, identify the gap or barrier that prevents that rule from being effective, and identify regulatory facilitators that can be used to reduce the gaps identified. This tool mainly defines the legal aspects of the challenge; hence leadership from law students is expected.

- User perspective (disciplinary – design): We ask students to identify at least 20 different actors that interact with the challenge for which they must define: names, relevant characteristics, needs, motivations, and interests. We then ask them to organise them in a 2x2 matrix[24] using their needs or motivations as exes. Finally, we ask them to describe profile personas[25] [26] according to the results of the 2x2 matrix analysis. This user analysis is an activity mainly led by design students.
- Social system (interdisciplinary – design and engineering): As a final task for understanding the challenge, we ask students to build a stakeholder map where they identify actors (individuals and organisations), the roles they play, and the interactions they have;[27] [28] we have developed a guideline for building these types of maps. We also ask them to build a systemic model (Causal Loop Diagram - CLD) based on the decisions made by the stakeholders they have identified. This CLD must include all decisions relevant to the challenge and feedback loops that determine the problem.[29] Building this type of model is taught in a previous course for industrial engineering students called "System Dynamics." Industrial engineering students mainly lead this exercise.

4.2. Tools for Designing Solutions

Designing solutions consists of a process of devising, iterating and validating different proposals that arise from the understanding of the challenge and that can provide a solution to it. These tools are mainly disci-

24 Natalia Agudelo and Silvia Lleras, 'Mapa de Actores', *Para el salón: herramientas para el diseño centrado en el usuario* (Primera edición, Universidad de los Andes, Facultad de Arquitectura y Diseño 2015).

25 Natalia Agudelo and Silvia Lleras, 'Personas', *Para el salón: herramientas para el diseño centrado en el usuario* (Primera edición, Universidad de los Andes, Facultad de Arquitectura y Diseño 2015).

26 Irawan Nurhas, Stefan Geisler and Jan Pawlowski, 'Positive Personas: Integrating Well-Being Determinants into Personas' <https://dl.gi.de/handle/20.500.12116/3299> accessed 26 February 2023.

27 Olaya and Gomez-Quintero (n 1).

28 Agudelo and Lleras (n 19).

29 John Sterman, 'Causal Loop Diagrams'. In Business Dynamics (Irwin McGraw-Hill 2000).

plinary from design and engineering.

- Systemic archetypes and leverage points (disciplinary – engineering): Systemic models are helpful to visualise the system as a whole and to explore potential places to intervene with a systemic perspective. Identifying systemic archetypes [30]-[31] enables the identification of feedback dynamics that can potentially be intervened to leverage the system's performance.
- Critical thinking (disciplinary - engineering): We encourage students to reflect on the ethical implications of their proposals. For this, we use the Critical Heuristics of Social Systems Design[32]-[33] from which students must address questions about four sources: motivation, power, expertise, and legitimacy.
- Creativity exercises (disciplinary - design): To encourage creativity, we carry out ideation exercises such as "the cat and the fridge," "what if?", "10x10", "Brainwriting," "WOW-POW-HOW Matrix." These exercises are intended to produce as many ideas as possible that allow students to think "outside the box" while producing innovative solutions to the challenge.
- Prototyping (interdisciplinary – design and engineering): Once students have at least three options for solving the challenge, we ask them to select one and develop the idea further. We do not expect complete functional prototypes but ask them for at least mock-ups of how it would work.
- Implementation manual (transdisciplinary – design, engineering, law): Once the prototyping is done, we ask students to develop an implementation manual, where they justify their design, explain its functionalities, and also come up with a plan of how the organisation can implement the solution taking into account the system in which it will be embedded.

30 Daniel H Kim, *Systems Archetypes* (Pegasus Communications 1994).

31 William Braun, 'The System Archetypes. System' 1 <https://www.albany.edu/faculty/ gpr/PAD724/724WebArticles/sys_archetypes.pdf> accessed 26 February 2023.

32 Werner Ulrich, 'Critical Heuristics of Social Systems Design' (1987) 31 European Journal of Operational Research 276.

33 Werner Ulrich, 'A Brief Introduction to Critical Systems Heuristics (CSH)' [2005] ECOSENSUS project site.

4.3. Tools for Challenge Management

The last group of tools is used transversally throughout the entire process. These tools are mainly focused on project management and group work.

- Group work (interdisciplinary – design and engineering): Each group is composed of students from three different disciplines (law, design, and engineering); there is a need to encourage communication, teamwork, and shared understanding. For this, we use the Marshmallow challenge[34] to break the ice among students who do not know each other. Each group has to build the highest tower with limited resources in 18 minutes and keep the marshmallow on top of the tower. While building the towers, groups use different strategies: have the most spaghetti tied and put it together in the shape of a tower, others use a trial and error strategy to start with low towers and ensure the marshmallow holds before building any further, and others use all available resources to raise the tower by any means necessary. We have found that this tool illustrates what is expected from students in the class: they have to deliver a design that accomplishes the objective and makes the best use of available resources. This exercise is also an opportunity to reflect on group leadership, the ability to listen to others, and the way they organise and delegate their tasks.
- Project management (disciplinary – engineering): we have developed a methodological guide with different tools for effectively managing the challenge.[35] [36] The guide develops three stages of project management: Planning, Execution, and Validation. For the Planning stage, the guide suggests activities and questions for defining the scope and objective, group roles and activities, and strategies for effective qual-

34 Hend S Al-Khalifa, 'Applying the Marshmallow Challenge in a Research Methods Course: Lessons Learned', 2017 16th International Conference on Information Technology Based Higher Education and Training (ITHET) (IEEE 2017) <http://ieeexplore.ieee.org/document/8067793/> accessed 26 February 2023.

35 Project Management Institute (ed), *A Guide to the Project Management Body of Knowledge (PMBOK Guide)* (4th ed, Project Management Institute, Inc 2008).

36 Tom Kendrick, *The Project Management Tool Kit: 100 Tips and Techniques for Getting the Job Done Right* (Third Edition, AMACOM, American Management Association 2014).

ity management and risk management. For the Execution stage, the guide focuses on prototyping, iteration, and trial and error management recommendations. Finally, the Validation stage focuses on stakeholder management and project documentation.

5. Case Study: How to Increase the Selection of Legal Cases at the ProBono Foundation?

As mentioned, we have applied this methodology and tools in our undergraduate course at Universidad de los Andes. Last year we had a case with the ProBono Foundation, where we could track the results beyond the course.

5.1. Challenge

The ProBono Foundation in Colombia is an organisation that offers free legal advice to people who do not have the possibility of hiring a lawyer. Their model connects people with a legal need with lawyers from firms linked to the Foundation interested in dealing with the case. Of all the cases that the Foundation receives, some "orphan cases" are not selected by any lawyer. In particular, cases that have to do with Family Law (divorces, inheritance, alimony, and child custody problems, among others) are those with a lower lawyer selection rate. The Foundation had noticed that in the past, the number of Family Law cases incoming had increased. However, the number of these cases that any lawyer did not select also increased. The Foundation wanted the number of cases of Family Law that are not selected to decrease. Hence the challenge was: how to sustainably reduce the number of Family Law cases that lawyers do not select (see figure 4).

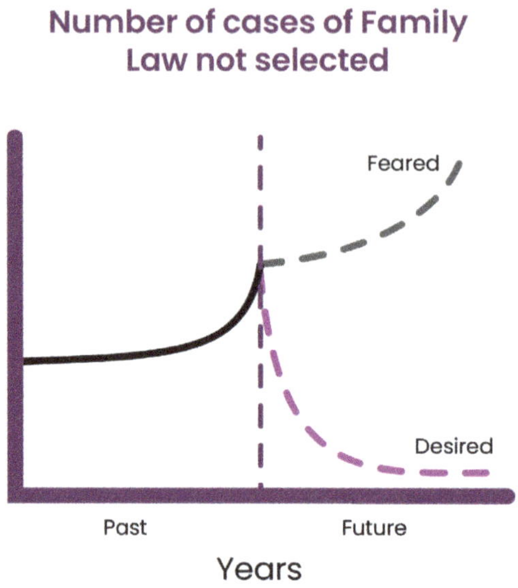

Fig. 4. Visualisation of the current scenario and the desired and feared scenario.

5.2. Understanding the Challenge

The team working on this project defined the legal context within the Social Function of Law. In Colombia, ProBono work is not regulated. Therefore, it is directly related to the social function of the legal profession and the possibility for everyone to access the judicial system. This lack of regulation means that there are no incentives to carry out ProBono work. The lack of incentives means that there are insufficient staff to meet the legal needs of the population without legal representation. Within this normative analysis, they found two valuable opportunities. The first was to make clear the need for ProBono work to fulfil the social function of the lawyer to promote the effective implementation of justice. The second was related to the formative value that these cases could have and thus connect the practice of the Foundation with the Legal Aid Clinics in order to increase the possibility of accepting and receiving cases that are left out.

From the user perspective, the team conducted interviews with 16 people within the context of the ProBono Foundation. The result of the interviews allowed them to construct a 2x2 matrix where the affinity of the users with the selected cases (family area) and the number of cases that the lawyers select were taken into account. By classifying the users, they realised that most had little affinity with cases in the family area, but many more took ProBono cases from other areas. This classification allowed them to identify that family cases are not sought after by lawyers who take ProBono cases due to their legal complexity. Attorneys taking ProBono cases look for cases that are easy to resolve, with family cases being among the most time and resource consuming.

The matrix analysis also allowed them to construct four profiles representing users in each quadrant. The first profile is a law student that collaborates with the ProBono Foundation doing judicial oversight of the processes. The second profile is a firm lawyer who handles different cases and has a flexible schedule for meeting with clients. The third profile is an independent lawyer who does consultancies for different entities. The fourth profile is a full-time intern in a law firm whose role is to support senior lawyers in handling their cases. These four profiles represent different ways in which lawyers and users interact with ProBono cases and should be taken into account during the design process to ensure that the solution considers their particular interests, i.e. consider that law students can be of support for cases that firm lawyers take.

The development of the social system model (CLD) led them to understand two moments of intervention within the system. The first was related to the information provided by ProBono for the offer of cases and the conversion indicators for case intake. Although the information was widely disseminated, family cases were orphaned due to the need for more timely information. The reinforcement loop involved modifying the newsletter to detail case information and provide more understanding of the cases. The second moment was related to the incentives to take the cases. Somehow, since they do not exist, there is no way to connect them with the productive indicators of the firms; hence, there is no motivation to take cases.

These understandings from the legal, user and social system perspective reframed the challenge in three main aspects: information, communication, and evaluation. In terms of information, the team identified the need to filter the information that the Foundation delivers to the different users according to the interests of the firms. In relation to communication the team identified a need to communicate cases more effectively so they would not be orphaned. And in regard to evaluation the team identified a need to generate mechanisms to measure the satisfaction and user experience of the lawyers after having accepted the case.

5.3. Designing Solutions

The proposed solutions were structured around the redesign of newsletters (information and communication), the integration of an incentive model (evaluation), and the creation of a support network. Newsletter, graphic and content changes were proposed for the weekly newsletter to provide complete information on the types of cases. The modifications give lawyers the necessary information to decide whether or not they are interested in the case. The incentive system was devised as a strategy to assign differential points to each case that law firms or attorneys can acquire by taking the case. In this way, it will avoid benefiting the firms or lawyers that take the most cases during the year, but the one that accumulates the most points; since the objective is to reduce Family Law "orphan cases", this type of cases were given more points to incentive their selection. The legal assistance network proposed a free service for firm and independent lawyers allied to the ProBono Foundation called "ProAsistencia." The network is built through alliances with the legal aid clinics of the universities to help with the follow-up and development of cases.

5.4. Implementation Results

Recently, the Foundation informed us that in 2022 case selection increased substantially. This increment was due to a series of implementations they made after receiving the students´ proposal. Within the aspects proposed by the students (information, communication, and evaluation), the ProBono Foundation implemented a "direct assignment" strategy where they modified the information content of their newsletter. The modifications include: more detail on the case, the area of the law, and the documents needed to start working on it. This strategy has facilitated the understanding of the case by the firm or attorney and is a more helpful definition for taking the case. Due to technical issues, they have not yet made any graphic modifications.

Regarding the incentive model, they implemented a strategy called "Formula Pro," a system of points awarded to the firms for their performance in taking cases, closing them to satisfaction and customer service. In addition, the formula has extra points and badges that are awarded for taking cases in areas such as labour, family, and judicial representation. Furthermore, in terms of the legal assistance network, they created a strategy called "Profe ProBono," in which they have the assistance of professors in the family area who offer advice to volunteer lawyers who take cases in this area. This network is to reduce the fear among the network of lawyers of taking cases that are outside their expertise.

6. Discussion and Conclusions

Future professionals need to be able to understand and propose alternatives for their disciplinary challenges, but also to articulate with other disciplines. This articulation is what Chew[37] calls inter or transdisciplinary education. However, inter or transdisciplinarity has challenges, mainly when disciplines are rooted in a different ethos. The main goal of inter and transdisciplinarity is to use the best of each discipline to deliver an intervention that creates value. This crossover of disciplines does not mean that professionals should change their nature.

In other words, if lawyers, designers, and engineers work together to improve access to justice, designers must not become lawyers, lawyers, engineers, or engineers designers. They have to be able to understand their disciplinary strengths to create synergies. They need to potentialise their practice and expand the disciplinary frontiers while acknowledging their role in a transdisciplinary project.

Since 2019, when Labjustica started, we have had this same transdisciplinary concern. Labjusticia is a transdisciplinary proposal to prepare lawyers, designers, and engineers to address access to justice issues. However, beyond thinking of this space as a design, law, or engineering

37 Chew (n 4).

course, we think of it as a platform to visualise the future of these professions. That is why we have reflected upon the strengths and weaknesses of transdisciplinary education. For example, projects that could be solved by generating decrees of law would leave out the design or engineering work. More importantly, it would make the power of combining disciplines invisible. Likewise, if the result were the transformation of a document into a graphic piece, the contribution of engineering and law would be reduced. The good news is that these three disciplines have already managed to have interdisciplinary spaces between them. Design and engineering have given way to Systemic Design; engineering and law to Legal Engineering; and finally, law and design to Legal Design. However, what happens when the three disciplines are combined? Should one of the disciplines be given priority over the other two, or should one seek to blur the disciplinary boundaries to implement solutions that respond to the challenge rather than the disciplines? While these questions may seem simple to resolve, they are not.

Over the years, we have defined, reflected on, and redefined our approach. According to Chew, we have moved from interdisciplinary to transdisciplinary, working on five pillars: real problems approach, user-centredness, systemic thinking, empirical exploration, and disciplinary synergy.[38] One of the crucial elements of these pillars is respect for the other disciplines. The leadership dynamics represent the respect that the disciplines must have concerning the project phase. We presented an evolved model that alternates between different practices while exploring particularities from each discipline. Legal practices frame the social system, and the social system frames the actors involved. Legal practices, or legal contexts as we call them, are related to the regulatory framework, which sets the guidelines for people to behave. Social systems comprise the social context within the regulatory framework. The perspective of actors, or users as we call them, is related to the people and organisation within the social system. These actors have roles, in-

38 Santiago De Francisco Vela, Laura Guzman-Abello and Santiago Pardo Rodriguez, 'Design for Justice Lab: Interdisciplinarity in Times of Virtual Education', *LearnxDesign 2021: Engaging with challenges in design education* (Design Research Society 2021) <https://dl.designresearchsociety.org/learnxdesign/learnxdesign2021/researchpapers/41> accessed 26 February 2023.

tentions, and motivations.[39] In the legal context, law students or lawyers lead to identify the regulatory constraints for people to behave. From the user's perspective, design students or designers lead on understanding and discovering the motivations, interactions, and interests of those actors, people, or organisations. In social contexts, engineering students or industrial engineers lead on building the social system to understand and identify possible opportunities for intervention.

Despite all of this disciplinary reflection, we have encountered other types of challenges related to transdisciplinarity, such as teamwork. Transdisciplinary teamwork faces information asymmetry, disciplinary jargon, differences in thinking processes, and types of deliverables. To address these issues, we decided to use bonding activities before introducing any justice challenge. These previous activities taught us that creating a smaller challenge would allow students to learn how their peers behave while developing a project, so now, we dedicate three weeks to team bonding before entering into any transdisciplinary approach. We have used the Marshmallow Challenge because it helps to set the expectations of what these students will face in a larger project. Another challenge is the relationship with organisations. We have tried different ways in which organisations have the tools to draft their challenges. However, we still need to ensure that these challenges contemplate topics that can be addressed from all disciplines. In the end, we have to set up multiple meetings with the organisations to refine the scope of the projects. For example, if the scope is too narrow, students will only have the chance to explore some of the contexts. Also, they will need help to alternate leadership among the project. If the scope is too broad, students will not have the time to narrow it down or will be lost most of the time. For future methodology developments, we will improve the relationship with organisations.

39 Olaya and Gomez-Quintero (n 1).

Bibliography

Agudelo N and Lleras S, 'Mapa de Actores', *Para el salón: herramientas para el diseño centrado en el usuario* (Primera edición, Universidad de los Andes, Facultad de Arquitectura y Diseño 2015)

—, 'Personas', *Para el salón: herramientas para el diseño centrado en el usuario* (Primera edición, Universidad de los Andes, Facultad de Arquitectura y Diseño 2015)

Braun W, 'The System Archetypes' (2002) <https://www.albany.edu/faculty/gpr/PAD724/724WebArticles/sys_archetypes.pdf> accessed 26 February 2023

Brunschwig CR, 'Visual Law and Legal Design: Questions and Tentative Answers' (2021) in Erich Schweighofer and others (eds), Proceedings of the 24th International Legal Informatics Symposium IRIS 2021 (Editions Weblaw 2021)

Buchanan R, 'Wicked Problems in Design Thinking' (1992) 8 Design Issues 5

Chew JY, 'Siloed in Breaking Silos: A Case Study of Interdisciplinary Curriculum (Mis)Alignment', *LearnxDesign 2021: Engaging with challenges in design education* (Design Research Society 2021) <https://dl.designresearchsociety.org/learnxdesign/learnxdesign2021/researchpapers/36> accessed 24 February 2023

De Francisco Vela S, Guzman-Abello L and Pardo Rodriguez S, 'Design for Justice Lab: Interdisciplinarity in Times of Virtual Education', *LearnxDesign 2021: Engaging with challenges in design education* (Design Research Society 2021) <https://dl.designresearchsociety.org/learnxdesign/learnxdesign2021/researchpapers/41> accessed 26 February 2023

Desmet PMA and Pohlmeyer AE, 'Positive Design: An Introduction to Design for Subjective Well-Being' (2013) 7 5 <http://www.ijdesign.org/index.php/IJDesign/article/view/1666>

Design Council, 'Systemic Design Framework - Beyond Net Zero by Design Council - Issuu' (1 April 2021) <https://issuu.com/designcouncil/docs/systemic_design_framework_-_beyond_net_zero> accessed 26 February 2023

Gunn W, Otto T and Smith RC (eds), *Design Anthropology: Theory and Practice* (Bloomsbury 2013)

Hagan M, 'Legal Design as a Thing: A Theory of Change and a Set of Methods to Craft a Human-Centered Legal System' (2020) 36 Design Issues 3

Hietanen-Kunwald P, Haapio H and Toivonen N, 'Systems Theory as a Research Framework for Dispute Prevention and Resolution by Design' in Rossana

Ducato and Alain Strowel (eds) *Legal Design Perspectives: Theoretical and Practical Insights from the Field* (Ledizioni 2021)

Howarth D, *Law as Engineering: Thinking about What Lawyers Do* (Edward Elgar 2013)

Jones PH, 'Systemic Design Principles for Complex Social Systems' in Gary S Metcalf (ed), *Social Systems and Design*, vol 1 (Springer Japan 2014)

Kendrick T, *The Project Management Tool Kit: 100 Tips and Techniques for Getting the Job Done Right* (Third Edition, AMACOM, American Management Association 2014)

Kim DH, *Systems Archetypes* (Pegasus Communications 1994)

Kimbell L, 'Rethinking Design Thinking: Part II' (2012) 4 Design and Culture 129

Kohlmeier A and Santuber J, 'Is the Common Legal Platform a Wicked Problem?: A Legal Design Approach. Case Study' in Kai Jacob, Dierk Schindler and Roger Strathausen (eds), *Liquid Legal* (Springer International Publishing 2020)

Nurhas I, Geisler S and Pawlowski J, 'Positive Personas: Integrating Well-Being Determinants into Personas' <https://dl.gi.de/handle/20.500.12116/3299> accessed 26 February 2023

Olaya C and Gomez-Quintero J, 'Conceptualization of Social Systems: Actors First' (Curran Associates Inc 2016)

Project Management Institute (ed), *A Guide to the Project Management Body of Knowledge (PMBOK Guide)* (4th ed, Project Management Institute Inc 2008)

Ryan A, 'A Framework for Systemic Design' (2014) 7 FormAkademisk - forskningstidsskrift for design og designdidaktikk <https://journals.oslomet.no/index.php/formakademisk/article/view/787> accessed 26 February 2023

Sterman J, 'Causal Loop Diagrams' in Business Dynamics (Irwin McGraw-Hill 2000)

Tarquini S, Monastidiris S and Peters K, 'Systemic Design Toolkit' <https://www.systemicdesigntoolkit.org/> accessed 26 February 2023

Ulrich W, 'Critical Heuristics of Social Systems Design' (1987) 31 European Journal of Operational Research 276

9. DESIGNING FOR POSTHUMAN LEGALITIES: LEGAL DESIGN(ING) AND THE ONTOLOGICAL TURN

Joaquin Santuber and Pablo Hermansen

Abstract
Designing for posthuman legalities explores ways of projecting new human-nature-technology relations within the frame of legal rights. We do so, addressing the problematic notions of human, nature, and technologies – all three of which are hallmarks of modernity. In times of a global climate crisis and accelerated digitalisation, the legal system needs to shift the human-centred paradigm to consider other ontologies that account for our posthuman condition. Problematising the current human-centred design practices, this paper explores other ways of designing beyond the Anthropocentric worldview. This demands a reworking, on both the epistemic and ontological levels —ways of knowing and ways of being— of the design part as much as the legal part. Against this context, we explore the designing of the rights of nature and the rights of machines. We elaborate five propositions regarding ways of designing for the posthuman in the realm of law and justice. The propositions are 1) prototyping as a way of disclosing worlds, 2) posthuman legalities as trans-ontological liminality, 3) from explanations to describing, performing, and becoming, 4) posthuman solicitations, affectivity, and attunement, and 5) posthuman co-incidences, resonances, and frictions. At the end of each one of the propositions we share experiences from our projects on designing for the posthuman. The propositions are not meant to be a checklist, but to provide possibilities for action to the reader. Thus, fellow researchers and practitioners will find in this paper a rich conceptual reference, as well as strategies to explore and disclose other worlds. It will also serve as an invitation and encouragement to delve into the complexities of the emergent posthuman legalities.

1. Introduction

The challenges the world is facing in the 21st century pose tough questions for our modern concepts and disciplines, yet the tools we have can only provide weak answers.[1] The big issues of today, digitalisation,[2] climate change, and recently having to live with a virus, are forcing us to question how we coexist in this world.[3] In this regard, posthuman approaches have addressed this by placing the focus not on discrete entities, but on their relationship with other beings. This approach intends to shift the centre from the human, overcoming human-nature and human-machine dualities, by conceiving of them as relational ontologies. Yet, the law still has a one-world world paradigm, focusing on the regulation of purely human action, i.e., human action on the environment.[4] The posthuman stream of research has called for a legal ontological turn to place the sphere of action of the law beyond the human to deal with environmental issues.[5] In a similar direction, a proposal for a *cosmolegal* approach aims to account for the agency of other-than-human in the current challenges, and the consideration of them in law-making processes.[6] The need to rethink the human-nature relation has also been addressed from the way in which environmental law is designed with an emphasis on socio-ecological resilience.[7] In this chapter, we address Designing for Posthuman Legalities in the context of climate change and digitalisation, the two most pressing issues of our times.

---

1 Boaventura de Sousa Santos, *Epistemologies of the South: Justice Against Epistemicide* (Routledge 2015).

2 Roger Brownsword, *Law, Technology and Society: Re-Imagining the Regulatory Environment* (Routledge 2019).

3 Bruno Latour, *After Lockdown: A Metamorphosis* (Julie Rose tr, Polity Press 2021); R Braidotti, '"We" Are In This Together, But We Are Not One and the Same' (2020) 17 Journal of Bioethical Inquiry 465.

4 Emille Boulot and Joshua Sterlin, 'Steps Towards a Legal Ontological Turn: Proposals for Law's Place beyond the Human' (2022) 11 Transnational Environmental Law 13.

5 Emille Boulot and others, 'Editorial Posthuman Legalities: New Materialism and Law beyond the Human' (2021) 12 Journal of Human Rights and the Environment 1.

6 Elena Cirkovic, 'The Cosmolegal Proposal' (19 June 2020) <https://papers.ssrn.com/abstract=3631056> accessed 28 October 2022; Elena Cirkovic, 'The Next Generation of International Law: Space, Ice, and the Cosmolegal Proposal' (2021) 22 German Law Journal 147.

7 Brita Bohman, *Legal Design for Social-Ecological Resilience* (CUP 2021) <https://www.cambridge.org/core/books/legal-design-for-socialecological-resilience/68AA86B6BB09BED7E3DAE6FAEB11214C> accessed 25 October 2022.

Despite the grandiose narrative around these anthropocentric issues i.e., climate change and artificial intelligence, the micro-dynamics that constitute them touch our daily lives. Wildfires burning large extensions of woodlands and displacing non-human animals and human population are becoming commonplace—even if it takes so little to forget about them. Moreover, heavy rainfall leading to flooding and landslides has led to towns and neighbourhoods being buried. And paradoxically, year after year we are confronted with historical droughts that risk traditional means of agricultural food production, extending the agony of rural villages. While a human-centric body of legal literature has created concepts such as the *force majeure* to deal with such situations, it does not address the need for a reciprocally respectful and sustainable relation, in which humans and more-than-human beings have mutual rights and obligations.

In the context of the digitalisation of private and public spaces, the story is no different. The digital knows no boundaries and captures every aspect of our social life, exercising novel forms of control.[8] Our work, social, family, and sexual relationships are increasingly mediated by digital technology, and thus coordinated and regulated by it. Many of the constitutive activities of our lives such as teaching –at both schools and universities– are now carried out in private spaces, digital spaces owned by big tech companies, which are replacing public spaces. This is also the case for public services, including courts of justice, which are increasingly moving to platforms and interfaces, in which the references of our social organising are replaced by shiny buttons, dropdown boxes, and clicks[9].

Recent design research has problematised the limitations of human-centred approaches in relation to digital technologies and smart cities.[10] This criticism has extended to placing humans and users at the centre of design to solve the planetary challenges of our time.[11] The alter-

---

8 Gilles Deleuze, 'Postscript on the Societies of Control' (1992) 59 October 3.

9 Joaquin Santuber, 'Designing for Digital Justice' (Doctoral Thesis, Universität Potsdam 2023) <DOI: 10.25932/publishup-60417>.

10 Laura Forlano, 'Decentering the Human in the Design of Collaborative Cities' (2016) 32 Design Issues 42; Laura Forlano, 'Posthumanism and Design' (2017) 3 She Ji: The Journal of Design, Economics, and Innovation 16.

11 Martin Tironi, Camila Albornoz Novoa and Marcos Chilet, 'Problematizing Hu-

native to that shortcoming of human-centredness in the social sciences and philosophy has been framed under the posthuman discourse and approaches.[12] In the field of designing, the ontological turn(ing) to the posthuman has been positioned as a reaction to the Anthropocene,[13] as the terminal phase of capitalist modernity.[14] This has also been fostered by the idea of designing for a pluriverse, in which many worlds are possible.[15] The use of the verb designing over the noun design is especially relevant in the context of posthuman ontologies and legalities. Design as an object or noun suggests a fixed structure that is adapted to be applied in a particular case. On the contrary, by focusing on designing, we relieve the performative dimension, we open ourselves to intra-action, and we question the hegemony of the word as a strategy for categorising, predicting, and regulating relationships. Design is a properly humanistic-modern-Western discipline, while designing is a doing —a political action— whose performative dimension allows us to apprehend[16] other-than-humans, re-know-us and trans-form-us into/with other ontologies[17].

In line with previous work in design research, addressing the posthuman is to overcome human-centeredness and embrace the social and material complexity of a model in crisis, projecting more "respon-

man-Centred Design: Notes on Planet- Oriented Design Open Debate' (2022) 77 diid 12.

12 Karen Barad, 'Posthumanist Performativity: Toward an Understanding of How Matter Comes to Matter' (2003) 28 Signs: Journal of women in culture and society 801; Rosi Braidotti, 'Critical Posthuman Knowledges' (2017) 116 South Atlantic Quarterly 83; Silvia Gherardi, 'A Posthumanist Epistemology of Practice' in Cristina Neesham (ed), *Handbook of Philosophy of Management* (Springer International Publishing 2020).

13 Cameron Tonkinwise, 'Before Design, More-than-Design: Elucidating "Ontological Design"' (2022) 14(3) Design and Culture 341; Anne-Marie Willis, 'Ontological Designing' (2006) 4 Design Philosophy Papers 69.

14 On this we refer to the critical perspectives from Zizek, Preciado, Haraway, Bautista, among others.

15 Arturo Escobar, 'Worlds and Knowledges Otherwise' (2007) 21 Cultural Studies 179; Arturo Escobar, *Designs for the Pluriverse: Radical Interdependence, Autonomy, and the Making of Worlds* (Duke University Press 2018).

16 Judith Butler, *Bodies That Matter: On the Discursive Limits of Sex* (Routledge 1993).

17 Martín Tironi and others, *Design For More-Than-Human Futures: Towards Post-Anthropocentric Worlding* (1st edn, Routledge 2023).

sible, accountable, and ethical ways of engaging with emerging technologies".[18] From this we frame our contribution as foregrounding the human-nature-machines legal entanglements. We do this by exploring *posthuman legalities,* within the frame of rights of nature and machines.

Recently, legal design has emerged as an interdisciplinary practice, at the intersection of law and justice, and design.[19] Despite its brief history, its foundations in human-centred design have been questioned, urging for an "expanded practice of inquiry".[20] Answering that call, legal design has also been addressed from critical design perspectives,[21] speculative design,[22] radical imagination,[23] cosmopolitical design,[24] and designing with theories via diffraction.[25] In doing so, together with fellow researchers, we have taken a critical—yet affirmative—stance on the injustices and inequalities meditated by the law and its design.

---

18 Forlano, 'Decentering the Human in the Design of Collaborative Cities' (n 10) 42; Carl DiSalvo and Jonathan Lukens, 'Nonanthropocentrism and the Nonhuman in Design: Possibilities for Designing New Forms of Engagement with and through Technology' in Marcus Foth and others, *From Social Butterfly to Engaged Citizen* (MIT Press 2011).

19 Margaret Hagan, 'Legal Design as a Thing: A Theory of Change and a Set of Methods to Craft a Human-Centered Legal System' (2020) 36 Design Issues 3.

20 Dan Jackson and others, 'What Legal Design Could Be: Towards an Expanded Practice of Inquiry, Critique, and Action' [2022] DRS Biennial Conference Series <https://dl.designresearchsociety.org/drs-conference-papers/drs2022/editorials/32>.

21 Phoebe Walton, 'James v Birnmann: The Potential of Critical Design for Examining Legal Issues' [2022] DRS Biennial Conference Series <https://dl.designresearchsociety.org/drs-conference-papers/drs2022/researchpapers/106>.

22 Karma Dabaghi, 'Beyond Design Thinking and into Speculative Futures in Legal Design' [2022] DRS Biennial Conference Series <https://dl.designresearchsociety.org/drs-conference-papers/drs2022/researchpapers/70>.

23 Hallie Jay Pope, 'Liberatory Legal Design and Radical Imagination' [2022] DRS Biennial Conference Series <https://dl.designresearchsociety.org/drs-conference-papers/drs2022/researchpapers/254>.

24 Pablo Hermansen and Martín Tironi, 'Cosmopolitical interventions: prototyping inter-species encounters' in Jennifer Roberts-Smith and others (eds), *Prototyping Across the Disciplines* Bristol (Intellect Books 2020).

25 Joaquin Santuber and Jonathan Edelman, 'Designing with Theories: Producing Legal Design Diffractively in Courts of Justice' [2022] DRS Biennial Conference Series <https://dl.designresearchsociety.org/drs-conference-papers/drs2022/researchpapers/259>.

In this paper, we build on that communal effort and offer theoretical and practical insights into a posthuman approach to legal design. This approach places the emphasis on the human-machines and human-nature ontologies and their possible novel forms of co-existence. After a brief literature overview on designing and the posthuman legalities— within the frame of the rights of natures and rights of machines— we elaborate on five propositions for the practice and research. These propositions are: 1) prototyping as a way of disclosing worlds, 2) posthuman legalities as trans-ontological liminality, 3) from explanations to description, from description to performing different worlds, 4) posthuman solicitations and embodied attunement, and 5) posthuman co-incidences, resonances, and frictions. For each of these we provide short accounts of our own experiences of doing design research on interspecies relations and digital logic in courts of justice.

2. Related Work

While the topic of posthuman designing and legalities is novel, there is already a basis of literature stemming from critical design and legal theory. In the following pages, we cover part of it to provide a frame and justify the need for Legal Design to embrace an ontological turn into posthuman legalities.

Posthuman Designing and the Problem with Human-Centred Design

> *it is often ethically appropriate and morally important to do design that does not align with the status quo of governing, or for that matter, with industry. It is a responsibility of academic designers to ask questions and pursue lines of thinking and doing that are at odds with our standard forms of government and governmentality and that are at odds with free-market ideologies.*[26]

We take this call to action as our opening statement. Designing outside the dominant canon, the logic of industrial production and the endless pursuit of efficiency, cost reduction, and profit seems an impossible en-

26 Carl DiSalvo, *Design as Democratic Inquiry: Putting Experimental Civics into Practice* (MIT Press 2022) 9.

deavour. Trying to do so questions the very core of our modern condition of humans. Our social life is shaped —after all— by the same rules and values as the production chains in a factory, from education to labour. And while it is hard to imagine the end of the capitalist system,[27] we see hope in contemporary critical understanding of design as a posthuman practice.[28] In this regard, design's sources and beneficiaries exceed the all-mighty *consumer* of products and services. Design accomplishes its goals by orchestrating and serving a myriad of actors ranging from other ways of being people, to other living species, bacteria, and technologies.[29]

However, while a refreshed perspective on design is welcomed, we need to be wary of the long-term commitments of design to industrial production, relentless innovation and novelty and the universality of its application, which can render contemporary forms of imperialism, and design-powered authority and dominion.[30]

This phenomenon, described by design researcher DiSalvo, is even more true for human-centred design due to its large adoption in industry and the public sector. This has turned *the human* into a marketable being, often referred to as the *user*. Where traditionally there was a citizen, now there is a user. Where there was a voter, now there is a user. The modern condition of being human is inextricably compounded with that of being a user — a *homo usus:* to be is to use. Thus, placing a market type of human at the centre for the design activity justifies the reproduction of systems by placing the spark or inspiration for new products and services in the human-user-consumer.

In the field of law and justice, and in politics and democracy the unquestioned adoption of human-centred design approaches is even more problematic. The adoption of such practices in policy and legal design has served as a trojan horse to impose market values over those of democ-

27 Boaventura de Sousa Santos, 'Más allá de la imaginación política y de la teoría crítica eurocéntricas' [2017] Revista Crítica de Ciências Sociais 75.

28 Forlano, 'Posthumanism and Design' (n 10); Ron Wakkary, 'Nomadic Practices: A Posthuman Theory for Knowing Design' (2020) 14 International Journal of Design 117.

29 Marzia Mortati, 'New Design Knowledge and the Fifth Order of Design' (2022) 38 Design Issues 21, 21.

30 DiSalvo (n 26) 1.

racy, justice, and equality. The alliance between design and the market, via human centred design, has surpassed its dominant influence in the private sector and industry and has been embraced with determination and enthusiasm in government, public offices and civil society.[31] This can be seen as another manifestation of the citizen-consumer paradigm.[32] Similarly, critical voices have raised the concern that access to justice projects has been captured by logics of globalisation and neo-liberalism since it is instrumental to the global market's operation and the safeguarding of foreign investment.[33]

The popular statement from design theorists that now everybody designs[34] is inscribed in the notion that design recreates and reproduces elements of the systems we live in –industrialised production, mass consumption, and a global system of labour. On this, Design Thinking, a methodology which popularised human-centred design in corporate settings, has been characterised as part of a strategy in which consultancy firms have ensured that Anglo European design remains at the "apex of global hierarchies of labour and creativity",[35] in a global context of manufacturing power that is being taken over by China and India. This strategy is easy to spot on any of the digital hardware coming from Silicon Valley, as they proudly announce on the back of Apple products: *Designed in California. Assembled in China*. When competition on expertise with the raising Chinese and Indian economies was no longer possible, Design Thinking helped western corporate leaders to move from expertise to empathy and mysticism, entitling themselves as the only ones capable of translating the needs of humanity.[36] By doing that, Design Thinking and

31 ibid 1.

32 Margaret Scammell, 'The Internet and Civic Engagement: The Age of the Citizen-Consumer' (2000) 17 Political Communication 351.

33 Yash Ghai and Jill Cottrell, 'The Rule of Law and Access to Justice: Findings of an ABA Project on Access to Justice' (2008) 3 <https://www.semanticscholar.org/paper/The-Rule-of-Law-and-Access-to-Justice%3A-Findings-of-Ghai-Cottrell/bb4d3cb44300b5c8da7c717edd7fe3b22224507c> accessed 20 June 2022.

34 In different forms throughout the last century, this message has been propagated by many design researchers, from Simon, Papanek, and Cross, tot the more popular business oriented IDEO's CEO Tim Brown and David Kelley.

35 Lilly Irani, '"Design Thinking": Defending Silicon Valley at the Apex of Global Labor Hierarchies' (2018) 4 Catalyst: Feminism, Theory, Technoscience 1, 1.

36 Rebecca Ackermann, 'Design Thinking Was Supposed to Fix the World. Where

human centred design have helped corporations to perpetuate the epistemic injustice around creativity and inventiveness that is intertwined with technological progress dependencies between the North and the South.

Summarising the three problems with human-centred design:

1. Placing the human as the source of needs, and only a *certain* human as the creative one
2. The human as the only recipient of the benefits of design
3. Homologising the human and the user, turning the human into a market-consumer entity

However, there is hope. Placing ourselves in the realm of legal design comes with the deep belief in, and commitment to, the notion that the legal system is a valid and powerful vehicle for social transformation and change.[37] Specifically, legal design practice is bounded to the betterment of the rule of law, access to justice, and ultimately social peace.[38] That is valid, even acknowledging that the way it is currently done serves the interests of a dominant way of being and knowing and excludes others.[39] However, this acknowledgement should not lead to surrender and hopelessness; instead it should lead to a revitalised approach to our legal systems and the drive to change from within[40], even if that means dismantling part of it. In this direction, in the context of designing for law and justice, it is important to first acknowledge the

---

Did It Go Wrong?' (*MIT Technology Review*) <https://www.technologyreview.com/2023/02/09/1067821/design-thinking-retrospective-what-went-wrong/> accessed 10 February 2023; Irani (n 35).

37 Joaquin Santuber and Lina Krawietz, 'The Sociomateriality of Justice: A Relational Ontology for Legal Design (La Sociomaterialidad de La Justicia: Una Ontología Relacional Para El Diseño Legal)' (2021) 6 RChD: creación y pensamiento 1; Joaquin Santuber and Lina Krawietz, 'User Research Methodologies in Legal Design Projects: Lessons from Practice' in Rossana Ducato and Alain Strowel (eds), *Legal Design Perspectives. Theoretical and Practical Insights from the Field* (Ledizioni 2021).

38 Amanda Perry-Kessaris, 'Legal Design for Practice, Activism, Policy, and Research' (2019) 46 Journal of Law and Society 185; Amanda Perry-Kessaris, *Doing Sociolegal Research in Design Mode* (Routledge 2021); Santuber and Krawietz (n 37).

39 Santuber and Krawietz (n 37).

40 Michael Doherty and others, 'A New Attitude to Laws Empire: The Potentialities of Legal Design' in Marcelo Corrales Compagnucci and others (eds), *Legal Design* (Edward Elgar Publishing 2021).

role of law in creating systems of subordination and reworking them from within towards liberatory expressions of the law as a joint effort of radical transformation.[41] It is, however, necessary to overcome the anthropocentric limitations of the law and designing a legal system for a more-than-human world.

3. Posthuman Legalities: the Rights of Nature

As a major source of structure and coordination of our social life, law and the design of legal systems project a defined worldview and leave others out.[42] In relation to nature, the worldview and commitments represented by the legal system are in-line with those of production-based progress, massive extraction of earthly goods, and infinite consume-powered growth.[43] This projected worldview of the anthropocentric legalities—or the regulation and coordination of a unique anthropocentric world—could be otherwise. Such an alternative has been conceptualised in legal scholarship as an expression of a lifeway, in the context of indigenous legalities and an "earth-centric 'rooted' form of constitutionalism".[44] This represents an alternative to the dominant western constitutional tradition because it is not the same practice with a different object (i.e., nature); instead it represents a whole novel form of doing constitutional law, which represents *a* lifeway, a way of being in the world.

In the human-nature ontology, the field of environmental law plays a significant role. Based on previous research, law should move from accounting for human action as harmful to the environment to a mutually enhancing relationship, conceived of as posthuman legalities.[45] In the study "Towards an EU Charter of the Fundamental Rights of Nature", evidence and recommendations are provided for the implementation of

41 Pope (n 23) 4.
42 Santuber and Edelman (n 25); Santuber and Krawietz (n 37).
43 Boulot and others (n 5) 3–4.
44 Aaron James (Waabishki Ma'iingan) Mills, 'Miinigowiziwin: All That Has Been given for Living Well Together: One Vision of Anishinaabe Constitutionalism' (Thesis, 2019) iii <https://dspace.library.uvic.ca/handle/1828/10985> accessed 9 February 2023.
45 Boulot and others (n 5).

the rights of nature at the legislative and policy level in the EU.[46] This study emphasises the

> *need to reframe rights from adversarial to synergistic, moving us* from "rights" to "right relationship"*, a "right relationship" being one that supports the wellbeing of the whole*[47]

From a constitutional perspective on environmental issues, the Constitutions of Bolivia and Ecuador consider Nature a subject of rights. In the same direction, the rejected constitutional project in Chile granted rights to nature.

To conceive the Rights of Nature, we argue that an ontological turn is necessary. The reason is that the mobilising capacity of our current legal instruments towards a regenerative human-nature relation are limited by the condition that our current legal paradigm is at the root of the degenerative practices of production, enabling and protecting them.[48] This is at odds with nature's generative power, as in the case of plants, which turn into life everything that they touch, because plants make the world.[49] A challenge for western legal systems is the one-world world paradigm.[50] The one-world reference builds on a critical account of mononaturalism and multiculturality, which states that there is just one way of being and knowing, while differences can be explained simply as cultural differences.[51] In contrast, the invitation is to design for/from a pluriverse[52] or fractiverse,[53] in which many worlds fit in the world. This is also what legal pluralism has fostered, be it intended or unintended [54].

---

46 European Economic and Social Committee and others, *Towards an EU Charter of the Fundamental Rights of Nature: Study* (Publications Office 2020) <https://data.europa.eu/doi/10.2864/25113> accessed 25 January 2023.

47 ibid 5.

48 ibid.

49 Emanuele Coccia, *The Life of Plants: A Metaphysics of Mixture* (English edition, Polity 2019).

50 Boulot and Sterlin (n 4).

51 John Law, 'What's Wrong with a One-World World?' (2015) 16 Distinktion: Journal of Social Theory 126.

52 Escobar (n 15).

53 Law (n 51).

54 John Griffiths, 'Legal Pluralism' in Neil J Smelser and Paul B Baltes (eds), *International Encyclopedia of the Social & Behavioral Sciences* (Pergamon 2001).

An important case of posthuman legal issues has to do with interspecies justice and non-human consent.[55] Moreover, the notion of the consent of other-than-humans has also been addressed by design research, as an exploration of ways in which stones and trees say no.[56] Far from being a pretentious account of trees and stones in biology and geology, it seeks local stories in which posthuman legalities are made explicit and visible. Those new materialisations of legal concepts, rights and duties in our legal systems need to be designed, prototyped, and implemented. The role of design in (pre)figuring those relationships has been addressed as designing and prototyping a cosmopolitical practice, a doing.[57] In this, through design intervention, the team of designers propitiated inter-species' encounters with animals in a Chilean Zoo.[58].

The issue with the current legal system's paradigm is its intrinsic human centredness—if not exclusivity. In this regard, the exclusivity we refer to is not only human activity as the only source of law-making and regulating, but that the human is its unique beneficiary, and thus it has a self-imposed constraint to remain in the realm of the Anthropos.[59] Put differently, under this logic, nature or the environment is worth protecting because it provides a value to the human, and not because it has a value on its own. The design practices that deal with posthuman legalities should be wary of reproducing such a problematic tradition. An

55 Richard Healey and Angie Pepper, 'Interspecies Justice: Agency, Self-Determination, and Assent' (2021) 178 Philosophical Studies 1223.

56 Franca López Barbera, 'When a Stone Says No' (*Futuress*, 6 April 2022) <https://futuress.org/stories/when-a-stone-says-no/> accessed 9 February 2023; Franca López Barbera, 'When a Tree Says No' (*Futuress*, 21 April 2021) <https://futuress.org/stories/when-a-tree-says-no/> accessed 9 February 2023.

57 Pablo Hermansen and José Neira, 'The Prototype as a Cosmopolitical Place: Ethnographic Design Practice and Research at the National Zoo in Santiago, Chile' [2016] DRS Biennial Conference Series <https://dl.designresearchsociety.org/drs-conference-papers/drs2016/researchpapers/46>; Martin Tironi and Pablo Hermansen, 'Prototyping Multispecies Environments: Attentiveness and Friction as Modes of Knowing' [2018] DRS Biennial Conference Series <https://dl.designresearchsociety.org/drs-conference-papers/drs2018/researchpapers/57>.

58 Martín Tironi and Pablo Hermansen, 'Prototipando la coexistencia: Diseños para futuros interespecie' (2020) 106 ARQ (Santiago) <https://dx.doi.org/10.4067/S0717-69962020000300038>.

59 Anna Grear, 'Deconstructing Anthropos: A Critical Legal Reflection on "Anthropocentric" Law and Anthropocene "Humanity"' (2015) 26 Law and Critique 225, 225.

issue that arises from engaging with other ontologies is the lack of communication mechanisms of such beings in a written or oral human language. In legal theory, the role of Nature's guardian has been proposed, as someone or a group that speaks for the trees; yet alternatives have been proposed in the direction of eco-feedback, as a form of expression of the fundamental right of free speech of nature to prevent acts that silence nature's voice.[60]

However, engaging with posthuman legalities demands an ontological shift, overcoming human pride and opening the space for other ways of being and relations, beyond the human. In this regard, a reconsideration of the legal ontology implies that...

> *animals and plants, then, as well as robots, should have rights not because they are like humans, but because of what they are.*[61]

Thus, when designing for posthuman legalities, it is crucial to resist the temptation to humanise things and to ascribe them qualities that were thought and refined to fit the human way (more specifically western-European) of being in the world. We should not attempt to ascribe intention and free will to posthuman legalities. Instead, this is an opportunity to rethink our role in the world, moving the human from the driver's seat to the role of a passenger who finds itself in a world and tries to make sense of it. Reformulating our set-in-stone legal building blocks is important to prevent us from transposing human hierarchies and inequalities that our societies have failed to solve to posthuman relations, amplifying existing inter-species inequalities.[62]

4. Posthuman Legalities: the Rights of Machines

While machines and even very sophisticated digital technology are not considered to have human capabilities, media equation research has

---

60 Matt Harvey and Steve Vanderheiden, '"For the Trees Have No Tongues": Eco-Feedback, Speech, and the Silencing of Nature' (2021) 12 Journal of Human Rights and the Environment 38.

61 Phil McNally and Sohail Inayatullah, 'The Rights of Robots: Technology, Culture and Law in the 21st Century' (1988) 20 Futures 119, 122.

62 Grear (n 59).

shown how people treat technology like real people and places, in a comparable way to how people relate to other people.[63] This research emphasises the idea that in our intuitive conduct of everyday practices the distinctions between us and them are blurry, and the human-machine gap vanishes at times (or has never really been there).

Already in the 1980s, researchers in the foresight studies division of the Hawaii Judiciary speculated about 21st century robots having legal rights and duties.[64] Already, 20 years into the new century such a futuristic scenario has not entirely become true. Nevertheless, a world with increasing agency of technologies and nature (often (mis)understood in the form of natural disasters) sets a path to rethink the relation, and the responsibilities that one and the other have. In this regard,

> *the expansion of rights to robots may promote a new appreciation of the interrelated rights and responsibilities of humans, machines and nature. With such a holistic extension of rights to all things in nature, from animals and trees to oceans, comes a renewed sense of responsibility, obligation and respect for all things.* [65]

While some argue that HCD approaches should play a vital role in the design of AI,[66] the need for an expanded practice of inquiry is necessary. The complexity of human-digital relations is posing new challenges to the capacity of law to regulate and coordinate our social life.[67] Moreover, the waves of digitalisation of our daily practices, digital infrastructure, are displacing traditional forms of regulation and coordination, in a phenomenon characterised as the digital undertow.[68] This challenges the human

63 Byron Reeves and Clifford Ivar Nass, *The Media Equation: How People Treat Computers, Television, and New Media like Real People and Places* (1 paperback ed, [reprint], CSLI Publ 1996).

64 McNally and Inayatullah (n 61).

65 ibid 120.

66 Jan Auernhammer, 'Human-Centered AI: The Role of Human-Centered Design Research in the Development of AI' [2020] DRS Biennial Conference Series <https://dl.designresearchsociety.org/drs-conference-papers/drs2020/researchpapers/89>.

67 Brownsword (n 2); Richard Mohr and Francesco Contini, 'Reassembling the Legal' (2011) 20 Griffith Law Review 994.

68 Susan Scott and Wanda Orlikowski, 'The Digital Undertow: How the Corollary Effects of Digital Transformation Affect Industry Standards' (2022) 33 Information

hierarchy of the regulator and coordinator, and places digital technologies as both the regulated and regulators. In this direction, technologies constitute a competing regulative regime that rivals traditional legal and policy instruments.[69] As such, we are no longer —or perhaps we never have been—in the position to regulate digital technologies. The question is not whether certain technology (think of AI) needs to be regulated, it has always been regulated. The real question here is by whom it is being regulated, and whether we humans are regulating or being regulated by technology. Taking a posthuman approach situates us within the human-machine entanglement; thus this regulation is no longer an interaction, but rather an intra-action. In this scenario, the human-machine relation also needs to be understood as a posthuman legality.

Moreover, machines and their digital programming operate in a logic of omnipresence, in which every aspect of social and material life can be captured in the form of data.[70] This logic has been further characterised into two goals: capturing the world and its realities in bites and datapoints (digital omniscience), and the control of social and organisational life via information technologies and systems.[71] Thus, digital technologies are not just a means to perform a task but are pervasive and ubiquitous in our lives. Even if they become invisible (we cannot see algorithms), they have politics that click by click, scroll by scroll are invisibly enacted in our societies.[72] In this regard, in designing technological infrastructures, engineers, developers, and designers project their norms, values and worldviews,[73] and have the capacity to shape behaviour on a large scale

Systems Research 311.

69 Jannis Kallinikos, 'The Regulative Regime of Technology' in Francesco Contini and Giovan Francesco Lanzara (eds), *ICT and Innovation in the Public Sector: European Studies in the Making of E-Government* (Palgrave Macmillan UK 2009).

70 Vern L Glaser, Neil Pollock and Luciana D'Adderio, 'The Biography of an Algorithm: Performing Algorithmic Technologies in Organizations' (2021) 2 Organization Theory 26317877211004610.

71 Henri Schildt, 'The Institutional Logic of Digitalization' in Thomas Gegenhuber and others (eds), *Digital Transformation and Institutional Theory*, vol 83 (Emerald Publishing Limited 2022) 235.

72 Laura Forlano, 'Invisible Algorithms, Invisible Politics' (*Public Books*, 12 February 2018) <https://www.publicbooks.org/invisible-algorithms-invisible-politics/> accessed 9 February 2023.

73 Bob Hinings, Thomas Gegenhuber and Royston Greenwood, 'Digital Innovation

by means of their codes and software.[74] In the design of digital technologies, theories about the world are embedded in their infrastructures and are thus adopted through their use, performing the world.[75] The modern illusion of the machine subjugated to the human starts to fade, and we observe all around configurations of human-machine ensembles in which the boundaries are hard to point at. These hybrid bodies made up of human-machine configurations have been the subject of Science and Technology Studies as hybrid ontologies in the form of cyborgs.[76] This is not a matter only of corporations and private life but has reached the very court of our legal institutions.

Previous research in the digitalisation of courts has called to account more-than-human agencies in the design of courts' e-Proceedings,[77] and more recently the effect of AI in transforming the relation between humans and technologies in courts of justice [78]. The materiality of the legal and justice systems has always been there – the bench, the coat of arms, and the columns.[79] That materiality is now being replaced, augmented and transformed by algorithms and their interfaces. It is an invisible materiality, but yet so material, so political. These hybrid ontologies have also been considered under the rubric of *technolegalities* i.e., in DNA profiling in criminal justice and forensics.[80]

As such, law and justice can leverage the current developments in design, philosophy and the social sciences to account for more than human agencies and capture new forms of coexistence. An example of that is

---

and Transformation: An Institutional Perspective' (2018) 28 Information and Organization 52, 54.

74 Laurence Diver, 'Digisprudence: Code as Law Rebooted', *Digisprudence: Code as Law Rebooted* (Edinburgh University Press 2022).

75 Glaser, Pollock and D'Adderio (n 70).

76 Donna Haraway, *Simians, Cyborgs, and Women: The Reinvention of Nature* (Routledge 1990).

77 Francesco Contini and Giovan Francesco Lanzara (eds), *The Circulation of Agency in E-Justice: Interoperability and Infrastructures for European Transborder Judicial Proceedings* (Springer Netherlands 2014).

78 Francesco Contini, 'Artificial Intelligence and the Transformation of Humans, Law and Technology Interactions in Judicial Proceedings' (2020) 2 Law, Tech & Hum 4.

79 Mohr and Contini (n 67).

80 Victor Toom, Amade M'charek and Matthias Wienroth (eds), *Law, Practice and Politics of Forensic DNA Profiling: Forensic Genetics and Their Technolegal Worlds* (Routledge 2023).

our relation to things and their right to be repaired. In a recent publication, the "more-than-human-right to repair" is presented as a design opportunity to rethink the relation with things and artificial intelligence.[81] Starting from a legal change, introduced by the right-to-repair in a briefing in the European Parliament,[82] there has been a shift in the focus on purely human needs to the relations of humans and our everyday things, such as a toaster and all the unremarkable and small smart things around us (Internet of Things).[83]

5. Ontological Clashes in Public Space: The Case of Climate Activism and the Case Techno-Judicial Entanglements

To highlight the relevance of taking an ontological turn in Legal Design practice and research, we ground our methodological proposal in two cases of ontological clashes in public spaces: climate non-violent activism by the German group Letzte Generation, and their practices of gluing their bodies to public spaces. The second case is the digitalisation of Chilean courts, especially the hosting of judicial hearings online via Zoom.[84]

5.1. Climate Activism in Public Space

For the still-influential Habermasian idea of the public sphere, public spaces are those where rational discussion and deliberation for the common good occurs spontaneously without state interference, market

---

81 Michael Stead and Paul Coulton, 'A More-than-Human Right-to-Repair' [2022] DRS Biennial Conference Series <https://dl.designresearchsociety.org/drs-conference-papers/drs2022/researchpapers/269>.

82 'Right to Repair | Think Tank | European Parliament' (2022) <https://www.europarl.europa.eu/thinktank/en/document/EPRS_BRI(2022)698869> accessed 28 October 2022.

83 Stead and Coulton (n 81).

84 Santuber and Krawietz (n 37); Joaquin Santuber, Reem Abou Refaie and Christoph Meinel, 'Delivering Digital Justice: Liminal Innovation & Permanence in Courts', *ACIS 2021 Proceedings* (2021); Joaquin Santuber, Reem Abou Refaie and Christoph Meinel, 'Interrogating E-Justice: Lessons from Digitalizing Courts in Chile' [2022] EGOV-CeDEM-ePart 2022 54.

regulations, or media influence. This idealisation of public space omits or naturalises the different norms that these spaces materialise and impose on the bodies that move and unfold there.[85] The regulations that make up public spaces become especially evident when citizen groups demonstrate in streets, squares, and parks to publicly make visible what they consider to be situations or unjust power relations. Since 2011, the massive mobilisations and demonstrations of social discontent that have developed in various parts of the world have once again put on the scene the political and citizen character of public space. [86]

Fig. 1a. A climate activist glued his hand to the asphalt on a public street as a form of nonviolent protest, while police agents observed without being able to clear the space. The photo by Letzte Generation, available on Pressebilder - Letzte Generation • and Pressefotos [EXTERN FREIGEGEBEN] - Google Drive, is marked with CC0.

85 *Scales of Justice: Reimagining Political Space in a Globalizing World* (Repr, Polity Press 2012).

86 Judith Butler, *Notes toward a Performative Theory of Assembly* (Harvard University Press 2015); Manuel Castells, *Networks of Outrage and Hope: Social Movements in the Internet Age* (Second edition, Polity Press 2015); Roberto Fernández, 'El Espacio Público En Disputa: Manifestaciones Políticas, Ciudad y Ciudadanía En El Chile Actual' (2013) 12 Psicoperspectivas 28.

Fig. 1b: A group of climate activists glued themselves to the asphalt using their bodies as a form of protest by occupying a public space like a street. The action was captured by other members of the group and uploaded to the website for diffusion. © Nele Fischer, available on Pressebilder - Letzte Generation • and Pressefotos [EXTERN FREIGEGEBEN] - Google Drive, is licensed under CC-BY 4.0.

One of the constituent elements of any citizen manifestation in the public space is that, to make visible what is claimed, those who demonstrate performatively overflow the configuration, the programme, the daily uses and the materialities of the space where they manifest themselves. As a space of appearance and encounter or to question the power relations that constitute the polis,[87] those who protest occupy the public space aiming to be seen through actions that allow them to make visible their contested bodies, slogans, and demands. This visibility dialogues creatively with multiple counterparts. At the same time, it constitutes an adversary while affirming as a collective those who demonstrate; it calls for the definition of others with respect to what is claimed while temporarily displacing the usual practices of the place where it is performed.[88] As seen in Images 1 and 2, the activists appear with their faces, posing for the camera to capture their actions (see Image 1b). In short, by overflowing the configuration, the programme, the daily uses and the

---

87 Hannah Arendt, *Eichmann and the Holocaust* (Penguin Books 2006); Butler (n 86).

88 Pablo Hermansen and Roberto Fernández, 'Photo-Ethnography and Political Engagement: Studying Performative Subversions of Public Space' [2020] Dearq 100.

materialities of public spaces, its normativity and the power relations that we exercise daily when making *normal* use of it become evident. In the antipodes of the Habermasian idea, we observe that it is performative frictions – not discussion and rational deliberation in pursuit of the common good – that evidence the political character of public spaces, opening the possibility of reflection and critical action.[89]

Fig. 2. Two climate activists glued their hands to the wall after throwing porridge on a Monet painting worth several millions at the Barberini Museum in Potsdam, Germany. The photo by LetzteGeneration, available on Pressebilder - Letzte Generation • is marked with CC0.

89 Fraser (n 85); Hermansen and Fernández (n 88).

For example, as we can see in images 1a, 1b and 2, the narrative tension of the scene emerges from the contrast between the protesters and their background – the museum as an institution and the street as a normative infrastructure. Those who protested at the museum (image 2) challenged the sacredness of Art and the radical indifference of institutionalised culture regarding the urgent problems that the protesters claimed, stressing the republican imaginary, government architecture and cultural symbols of power. The possibility of demonstrating is limited by time, spatial and material conventions: the bars and the security personnel define the space that can be occupied, and that which cannot. The transgressive character of those who protest is that, through their staging, they overflow and appropriate the infrastructures of power, cultural symbols and limits of political action – certainly for a limited time, as we see in image 3, but that lasts through the publication of its photographic record.

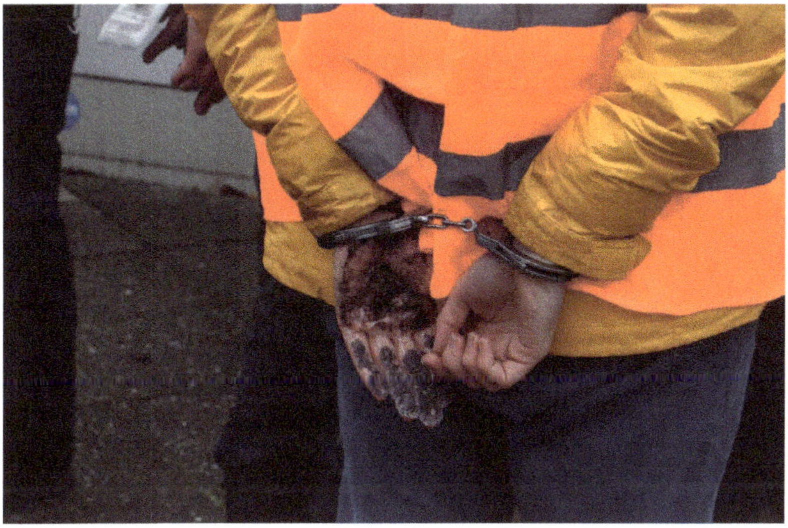

Fig. 3. A handcuffed climate activist with asphalt leftovers on his/her hand resulting from glueing him/herself to the pavement on a street and the following removal by police agents. The photo by Letzte Generation, available on Pressebilder - Letzte Generation • is marked under CC0.

Their performances are at odds with the historicist republican imaginary of the transcendental stillness of the museum, its guards, the masterpieces and, in general, its symbolical power. The set, efficiently made, creates a perfect contrast against the materiality of the museum. In turn, the protesters' use of their equipment and clothing demands a dexterity that is difficult to improvise. So, we can affirm that the scene is not the product of an outburst, but of careful planning. And in turn it demands dexterity from the police forces to clear the area without harming the bodies of the protesters glued to the pavement (image 3).

Those who register (image 1b) are simultaneously protesters and communicators. The mass media have lost the monopoly over the publication of images: it is increasingly common for individuals, social movements and citizens in general to generate and disseminate their own photographs and videos.[90] The images they produce while demonstrating circulate both in their intimate sphere and in their social networks and independent media, collapsing the usual separation between those who demonstrate and the mass media, and challenging the monopoly that they have historically held. In the case of the climate activist group Letzte Generation, they have a gallery with all of their images on their website and a cloud-stored Google Drive folder that is open to every person who would like to use the images.[91] Moreover, this dual role amplifies its relevance since the image can circulate in real time.[92]

In this way, streets, squares and parks are public spaces to demonstrate *off* and *online* through the visual registration of demonstrators and their practices, which usually operate with full awareness of social actors, who are increasingly conscious of this visual dimension and make strategic use of it. Moreover, streets as a space for demonstration acquire political status and the potential for transformation if what is happening on the street is being socialised via the press or cotemporary social media platforms and the internet.[93] The activity of sharing becomes a constitutive

90 Pablo Hermansen and Marcos Chilet, 'Ciudad Virtual, Ciudad Real: Conflicto y Emergencia de Un Nuevo Entorno Urbano' (2010) 2 Diseña 40.

91 'Pressebilder' (*Letzte Generation* •) <https://letztegeneration.de/presse/pressebilder/> accessed 16 March 2023; 'Pressefotos [EXTERN FREIGEGEBEN] - Google Drive' <https://drive.google.com/drive/folders/1xaq6DXe-_yQaHuk9XeEAl2kqp-pCNkOxj> accessed 16 March 2023.

92 Hermansen and Chilet (n 90).

93 Castells (n 86) 95.

action of the political movement.[94] The staging of those who manifest themselves supposes a visuality capable of being registered and disseminated, in order to transmit messages, but also generate affections and interpellations.[95] Beyond its capacity for dissemination, this dynamic of the registration and publication of political manifestations in the public space performatively configures many of the visibility actions that these same demonstrators-communicators develop, since they are deployed in dialogue with the visual register and to enhance the memorability of this once it is published. The way in which bodies express themselves in public spaces is intricately connected to the communication and technological tools -devices- they utilise to convey information about the events occurring in the streets.[96]

5.2. Technologies in Public Spaces

Dialoguing with the Habermasian idea of public space, the court can be described as the place where a rational discussion and deliberation takes place, inscribed in the constitution and laws, and conducted by a group of experts in doing justice, to resolve differences between private parties whose conflicts exceed in intensity or complexity what they can resolve directly and spontaneously.

Following the Habermasian ideal, for this mediation to occur without the interference of other powers of the State, the market, or the influence of the media, the staging of judicial procedure – with its order and hierarchy – is considered a constitutive dimension of the exercise of justice. This is especially relevant given the public access to the judicial process. Consequently, in its staging, the court incorporates a section of public space into its structure, but a highly regulated one. The court scene and the area for the public are clearly and materially separated by a bar or rail. In the same way that in government buildings i.e., the Presidential Palace or Congress, metal barriers and police personnel are arranged to contain the citizen overflow within the executive power, inside the room a half-height wall —known as the bar— with a door in

94 Butler (n 86).

95 Diana Taylor, *The Archive and the Repertoire: Performing Cultural Memory in the Americas* (Duke University Press 2003).

96 Butler (n 86).

its centre materialises the separation between the public space and the judiciary. In Chilean criminal courtrooms the litigator scene is divided into two sectors, the bench and the lower stage (for the litigators), and together it must have a size (52 m2), equipment and invariable distribution, which are organised to ritualise the roles, positions and flows of those who lead the process. On the contrary, the size of the spectator public area within the room is relative. When considered necessary, two capacities are suggested: for 32 people (30 mts 2) and for 16 (16 mts^2). The bench and litigator area are materially distinguished. The floor of the judge's bench is 32 centimetres higher than the rest of the room and the three judges who are located there face the rest of the participants, sitting in a closed front with wooden panels. Wood, especially in courts where modern materials such as concrete prevail, symbolically inscribes the judges in the institutional tradition, suggesting that their authority takes root and continues the history of this power.

The two sectors have differentiated access, but while the judicial scene has six access points – four for officials and two for security personnel – the public have only one entrance door to their sector, which is controlled by a security officer who is subject to a strict protocol. The distribution of judicial officials at the scene clearly shows their inscription in the institutional hierarchy, while their location and equipment facilitate their agency and manifest their role. For its part, the spectator or public area is designed for those who occupy it to perform as non-participating observers. While the bleachers for the public only facilitate sitting and witnessing the judicial action (passive scrutiny), the equipment of the judge's bench and the litigation area is designed for experts to deploy their work devices and develop their tasks, such as taking notes or consulting documents. They *do* justice.

5.3. Zoomification of the Judicial Scene

The restrictions on movement imposed in the pandemic forced the administration of justice to take place within private spaces, more precisely within the *digital sphere*. This imposed on the judicial scene a new configuration, programming, modes of use and materialities. The courtroom, with the bench, the litigation area and spectators or public space were reduced to a latent image, to the memory of those who inhabited it.

What justice is emerging with the irruption of the digital sphere?

The algorithm behind the Zoom platform allocates the position of each participant in its own unknown and obscure logic. However, it provides each participant the same space in terms of pixels. This sense of horizontality in the relation happening in the digital courtroom breaks with the highly normative –century old model—distribution of the judges, parties, and audience in the courts. The hierarchy is flattened by the screen, without the depth of a shared space that provides the architecture of the courtroom. Moreover, the homogeneity forced by the software make invisible references to the identities of the participants. We cannot tell who the judges are, or the offender, or the victim. Furthermore, their role is limited to delivering information, as a vehicle constituting them as commodities in the process of delivering justice. The documentation, record, profiling, and storage of portraits of the participants is given by the videoconferencing platform possibilities. These profiling mechanisms, however, are outside of public scrutiny and critique by civil actors, communities and other public institutions because they are behind a wall of secrecy, which is justified in the property of the algorithm. This is an issue of the privatisation of public space and processes, in which the traditional agencies of regulation and coordination of the processes are replaced by human and more-than-human techno-power. These novel forms of techno-power are internal actors, however with different logics and values, as well as external actors that are inscribed in the digital sphere, which exceeds the self-imposed limits imposed by the judiciary to preserve its independence.

We use the expression *digital sphere* instead of digital technologies to highlight the scope, complexity, and particularity of the globalised *maraña* that constitutes the digital networks of information, interaction, and communication.[97] Given the field we are dealing with, it is especially important to distinguish the already mentioned digital sphere from the public sphere, the environment that confers legitimacy on the judiciary. It is dangerous not to problematise the fact that justice being a constitutive part of the public sphere, the digital platforms on which justice

97 Pablo Hermansen and José Guerra Solano, 'Furrowing the Maraña: Designing to Sail out of the Anthropocene' in Martin Tironi and others (eds), *Design for more than human futures* (Routledge 2023).

rested during the pandemic are private collective spaces, over which the State has a discreet influence. The private infrastructures for the exercise of justice tend to be at odds with the materialities, practices, postulates, and principles that have made the law and justice. This makes it problematic to suggest without criticism that, for example, these platforms improve access to justice, since they could tend to change what justice is.

The digital sphere, as a private infrastructure for collective life, works mainly on privacy regulations designed to guarantee the profit of its owners. Consequently, when used for exercising citizenship, they often come into conflict with national laws and public interests. At the same time, the increase in discretionary solutions with which members of the judiciary face the adaptation of their practices to the new digital platforms also increases the influence that the logic of the digital sphere has on the practice of justice. When acting tactically, each official reproduces a way of doing things that they have naturalised in their everyday experience of social networks, which constitutes a hotspot or access door for the logic of the digital sphere. The point is that besides the spontaneous individual agency underlies the logic of social networks, opening a new flank for the irruption of their influence.

In turn, responding to the tireless search for surplus value with which their owners overcome the hectic flows of capital, these regulations and their "terms of use" evolve at a frenetic pace, which contrasts with the slow pace with which the laws respond to social changes. Due to the already mentioned differences –in materiality, power relations, goals, principles, adaptability, etc.– the places that make up the digital sphere –Zoom, Facebook, YouTube, Instagram, etc.– are ontologically different from those of the public sphere –squares, courtrooms, streets, parliament, etc. In other words, the distance between these private digital places of collective meeting and the halls of the justice buildings is greater than the difference between a public square and a shopping mall.

While the public is supposed to be a collective space for a dialogue regarding the common where private interests and the power relations that regulate our coexistence in private environments are put on hold, the digital sphere privatises the common, and organises the collective in business spaces where the exercise of what is public must be submitted to the extraction of surplus value. In each sphere, citizenship means radically different things.

6. Methodological Propositions for Designing for Posthuman Legalities

Due to its early development and its fundamentally exploratory spirit, we present in the following section five propositions for the practice of, and research into designing for posthuman legalities. This propositions, as they stand, are better understood as lines on a sketch, projections of something that is becoming a gestalt. They are also to be thought of as steppingstones from which to delve into the posthuman legalities. The propositions are: 1) prototyping as a way of disclosing worlds, 2) posthuman legalities as trans-ontological liminality, 3) from explanations to describing, performing, and becoming, 4) posthuman solicitation, affectivity, and attunement, and 5) posthuman co-incidences, resonances, and frictions.

6.1. Prototyping as a Way of Disclosing Worlds

Designing for posthuman legalities demands a radically different approach to the scenarios we are designing. In this context prototyping is never an end-result, or as in human-centred design a tool to validate assumptions regarding user needs. In contrast to prototypes aimed at matching an actual need or desirability, prototyping posthuman legalities aims at revealing a world that is hidden. This is different from speculating about a possible future through prototyping;[98] this is about disclosing a present that already exists, yet is invisible to us— epistemologically and ontologically. In other words, by prototyping we do not bring to the present a future or aim at predicting it;[99] instead we unearth and shed light on something that is already here - we disclose an aspect of the world that our ways of knowing and creating knowledge have prevented us from seeing.

---

98 Anthony Dunne and Fiona Raby, *Speculative Everything: Design, Fiction, and Social Dreaming* (MIT Press 2013).

99 Sohail Inayatullah, 'Deconstructing and Reconstructing the Future: Predictive, Cultural and Critical Epistemologies' (1990) 22 Futures 115.

In this way, the embodied process of building or sketching a prototype, together with the gestures and stories that are part of it, serves as a scaffold to the unfolding scenarios we are designing.[100] The emphasis in prototyping is on practices, ways of doing, which in turn open up ways of being in a world (in contrast to results). Processes and practices can be found in an account of experiencing a line, in which the line is not the connection between two points, but rather is the embodied experience of the pen's friction against a sheet of paper.[101] A line *is* in the multiple experiences of "walking, weaving, observing, storytelling, singing, drawing and writing" a line.[102] It is the process of becoming a line, not the line as an output, a result, a number. Similarly, in an exploration of the interstice of posthuman ontologies, free from human-centred epistemic constraints, practices can be enacted in "walking, flowing, listening, differentiating, processing salt, reading, photosynthesising, thinking, flocculating, writing, infecting, revising, or filter-feeding".[103]

This is particularly relevant in working with plants, since in plants doing and being are inextricably entangled.[104] The way plants *are* in the world is by making the world because plants do not have other worlds to escape to. In this regard, beyond the human ways of creating by means of our hands, plants are a great example of shaping the world like no other actor, yet they do not have hands.[105] Likewise, from the famous "for the trees have no tongue" by The Lorax, trees do not need translators nor representatives that speak up for them; they are expressive in their own ways, just not our human centred ways. The way in which different worlds are disclosed is far from being a well-defined process or objective; they look more like tales of something that happens.

During my research on the digitalisation of courts, I set up a research apparatus to collect data on the social media activity of the Chilean

100 Jonathan Edelman, 'Understanding Radical Breaks: Media and Behavior in Small Teams Engaged in Redesign Scenarios' (2011) 79–80 <https://purl.stanford.edu/ps394dy6131> accessed 29 January 2019.

101 Tim Ingold, *Lines: A Brief History* (Routledge 2016).

102 ibid.

103 Kate Judith, *Exploring Interstitiality with Mangroves: Semiotic Materialism and the Environmental Humanities* (Routledge 2022) 8.

104 Coccia (n 49).

105 ibid 12.

courts.[106] To perform the data collection I registered my personal account to use the API of social media platforms such as Facebook, YouTube, Twitter, and Instagram. The moment of revelation came when I was in bed, before falling asleep on social media scrolling past photos of friends, and suddenly I found myself engaging with the content of Chilean court trials. That situation disclosed a set of relations in which --without actively consenting-- I was part of the judiciary's communication machinery by consuming their content, liking posts, sharing and reposting, all from my bedroom thousands of kilometres away from Chile. The entanglement of courts' activity and social media algorithms became a substantial part of my doctoral work and a departure point for posthuman legalities.

In the work on cosmopolitical prototyping, the doing poses questions about the status that would otherwise not be asked. Prototyping in this sense questions and dis-locates without having the answers and does not even aim at them. By prototyping a form of more-than-human relationship, the very conditions of that relationship and the entities that participate in it are tested, revealed, and become.[107] As we discussed, it is a challenge for the law to incorporate prototyping and its vocation of failure or failure as a speculative or test form for the construction of legal bodies for relationships that exceed the scope of the word. Prototyping allows us to test the relationship conditions for which we have no empirical background to predetermine a norm, such as the relationships between ecosystems and algorithms, such as the release of water from a reservoir or dam by an algorithm.

6.2. Posthuman Legalities as Trans-Ontological Liminality

The approach to posthuman legalities is always trans-ontological.[108] The designer cannot grasp another ontology without leaving the boundaries of its own worldview. This transit between ontologies and the indeterminacy of the process can be better characterised using liminal theory.

---

106 Joaquin Santuber and others, 'Building an Apparatus: Disclosing Affectivity in Sociomaterial Research' [2020] ICIS 2020 Proceedings <https://aisel.aisnet.org/icis2020/adv_research_methods/adv_research_methods/9>.

107 Barad (n 12).

108 We take this concept from the work of the economist and theologist Franz Hinkelammert.

At the beginning of the 20th century, the book Rites of Passage pointed out the hallmark transitions and their rituals in different communities, across time and space, that are performed to ease the passage from one state to another, childhood-adulthood, life-death, and marriage.[109] The stage of liminality was then further explored, the liminal phase, the "betwixt and between" state.[110] From their original application in small-scale societies and groups, liminality has also been studied in more extensive contexts.[111]The recent COVID-19 pandemic and the climate crisis we are in have been characterised as a form of global liminality.[112] In the context of digitalised judicial practices, liminality has been used to make sense of the governance (or the lack of it) of digital technologies in public services.[113]

Across contexts and scales, a key element for liminality is suspended normativity, in a transitional and transformative space with blurred boundaries.[114] Designing from a trans-ontological place lifts the century old legal structures and concepts and opens a space to re-imagine fundamental positions, and by imagining them we become them. This process is characterised by blurring boundaries, distinctions and positions, and even the suspension of societal values and principles.[115] Moreover, liminal processes bring opportunities as well as risks to modern organisations, cultures, and societies.[116] On one side, liminality creates a temporary space for generativity, disruption and creativity,[117] while on the

109 Arnold van Gennep, *The Rites of Passage* (Psychology Press 1960).

110 Victor Witter Turner, *The Ritual Process: Structure and Anti-Structure* (Penguin Books Limited 1974).

111 Bjørn Thomassen, 'The Uses and Meaning of Liminality' (2009) 2 International Political Anthropology 5.

112 Tom Boland, 'Global Liminality: The Pandemic as Anti-Structure. Introduction to the Special Issue' (2020) 13 International Political Anthropology 5; Tom Boland and Marius Ion Bența, 'Special Issue: Crisis, Liminality and Performance' (2020) 13 International Political Anthropology 3.

113 Santuber, Abou Refaie and Meinel (n 84).

114 Turner (n 110).

115 Boland (n 112).

116 A Horvath, *Modernism and Charisma* (Palgrave Macmillan UK 2013).

117 Barbara Czarniawska and Carmelo Mazza, 'Consulting as a Liminal Space' (2003) 56 Human Relations 267; Mayli Mertens, 'Liminal Innovation Practices: Questioning Three Common Assumptions in Responsible Innovation' (2018) 5 Journal of Responsible Innovation 280.

other, the capacity of liminality to become permanent generates constant uncertainty and disintegration.[118] Designing for posthuman legalities is not about solving the trans-ontological paradoxes (as a human-centred solution fixed approach would aim for) but working the liminal condition through. We should not attempt to define this trans-ontological, as we should not fruitlessly try to explain it, but we can start by moving our practices from describing to performing posthuman legalities.

In the project in the Chilean courts, conducting design research on non-human agency, the liminality came from many sides. Trying to account for digital, physical, legal, judicial, institutional, and individual agency, at times it felt like the language was missing, or falling short. At times it felt like the methodology needed many hacks and walks around. Regarding the data, while interviews served as the steppingstone, soon I realised it was a very human account of things, and I needed to go back to disclose the non-human doings in the courts. I then reconstructed a genealogy of the practice by putting little parts of a trans-ontological mosaic of data points. It was, nevertheless, fascinating and rewarding.

6.3. From Explanations to Describing, Performing, and Becoming

While there is a temptation to stay in the realm of what has been explained by our fellow natural scientists, in these interstices, liminal places in which posthuman legalities enfold the demand for scientific certainty may lead to stagnation. Even worse, seeking explanations will put us *back on track* towards reproducing the inequalities that science has created. Breaking from the scientific exclusivity allows us to transit to other places and put them in a trans-ontological dialogue. Latour's approach put forward descriptions as a more satisfactory approach to social phenomena than explanations.[119] However, as designers and researchers we are not outside the world we are observing, because observing a world is at the same time producing that world. In the engagement with post-

118 Árpád Szakolczai, 'Permanent (Trickster) Liminality: The Reasons of the Heart and of the Mind' (2017) 27(2) Theory & Psychology 231; Horvath (n 116); Boland and Bența (n 112).

119 Bruno Latour, *Reassembling the Social: An Introduction to Actor-Network-Theory* (1st Edition, OUP 2007).

human legalities, when designing we are already performing those ontologies differently.

Non-human are a substantial part of the *world making* process. From the perspectives of plants and nature "to be in the world necessarily means to *make world*: every activity of living beings is an act of design upon the living flesh of the world".[120] In these practices of becoming in relation to other-more-than-human ontologies, a key element is the search for a meaningful and reciprocally value laden relationship. In performing this ontology the invitation is to embrace values beyond the exclusive benefit and centrality of the human, co-constituting these relations in a process that is "more like filter-feeding".[121] Humans, in this sense, do not play a central role in such a performance but are part of a thick mesh of relations of humans and more than humans [122].

From a methodological perspective, designing is understood as the performance of the people, media and tools we work with.[123] Put otherwise, designing is already a performance of things, tools, and the people they work with. Performing different ontologies implies a rearticulation of objects, behaviours, and narratives to adhere to the rules and principles of a world. In this relation, it is not clear who is using whom, the tools the people, or the people the tools. [124] Performing those ontologies, we need to *do* differently. The differentiation capacity of practices as world making follows from the notion that "different realities are enacted in different practices".[125]

In the project on courts digitalisation in Chile my goal was never to explain what was happening; rather, we transited from looking for and then drafting stories about what I was seeing in the emerging digitalised practices in courts. After a long time dealing with the phenomena, we could not but acknowledge that we too were part of it. We spent hours and hours watching, scrolling down, attending virtual hearings, and talk-

120 Coccia (n 49) 74.
121 Judith (n 103) 8.
122 Hermansen and Guerra Solano (n 97).
123 Jonathan Edelman and others, 'Designing as Performance: Bridging the Gap Between Research and Practice in Design Thinking Education' (2021).
124 Donna Jeanne Haraway, *ModestWitness@SecondMillennium.FemalemanMeetsOncomouse: Feminism and Technoscience* (Routledge 1997).
125 Law (n 51) 130.

ing to court personnel. We were playing our part; we were performing with others - human and non-human - in the digital courts in Chile.

6.4. Posthuman Solicitations, Affectivity, and Attunement

Our design practices, as mentioned above with prototyping, are our ways of, and vehicles to disclosing different worlds. For that an openness to that world is required. Here the concept of solicitations is useful. Solicitations are situated experiences in which an agent feels the inclination to act in a certain way; it is the/a world calling to act on it.[126] This are a certain type of affordances that stand out as relevant to the situated individual, in a landscape rich with affordances as our modern life is.[127] This is not just a possibility for action, but to be drawn by the particularities of a situation, called to act upon a matter.[128]

In designing for posthuman legalities, as being and existing in a trans-ontological liminality, we adopt strategies, or leverage from artefacts, behaviours and narratives to be open to solicitations. This is a form of disposition to be moved, to be touched by something and with that gain a glimpse of the trans-ontological liminality. To be part of it, designers need to develop a sensibility to the regularities of the environment, the ability to be affectively open to these encounters – to affect and be affected by something as in Spinoza's *affectus.*[129] Moreover, on Spinoza's *affection* it is about, an "encounter between the affected body and a sec-

126 Hubert Dreyfus and Sean D Kelly, 'Heterophenomenology: Heavy-Handed Sleight-of-Hand' (2007) 6 Phenomenology and the Cognitive Sciences 45.

127 Erik Rietveld, Damiaan Denys and Maarten Van Westen, 'Ecological-Enactive Cognition as Engaging with a Field of Relevant Affordances' in Albert Newen, Leon De Bruin and Shaun Gallagher (eds), *The Oxford Handbook of 4E Cognition* (OUP 2018); Erik Rietveld and Julian Kiverstein, 'A Rich Landscape of Affordances' (2014) 26 Ecological Psychology 325.

128 Joaquin Santuber and others, 'Towards an Enactive-Ecological Approach to Sociomateriality in Information Systems Research', *AMCIS 2020 Proceedings* (2020) <https://aisel.aisnet.org/amcis2020/meta_research_is/meta_research_is/9>.

129 Gilles Deleuze and Felix Guattari, *A Thousand Plateaus: Capitalism and Schizophrenia* (Brian Massumi tr, 2nd Edition, University of Minnesota Press 1987). The quote comes from a definition provided by the translator Brian Massumi in the foreword to A Thousand Plateaus.

ond, affecting, body".[130] The reference to bodies is, in its broadest sense, human and more-than-human, i.e., a body-without-organs. The capacity to affect and to be affected is tightly connected to the ability to solicit and to be solicited by something.

A solicitation, as affection, is not a thought, an emotion, or a decision, it is being part of a constant flux, an attunement with the regularities of different worlds. It is us responding to the movement of the waves in the sea, as the Oysters loyally respond to the proposals of the tidal rhythms in the mangroves.[131] When our anthropocentric ways of communicating fail, the door to other worlds is to return to the attunement of the *vibrant matter.*[132] Moreover, things do not affect us because some philosophers granted them some sort of human agency, but because they are part, as much as we are, of the dynamic flow and currents of the lifeworld.[133] While this is usually invisible to our way of knowing, it is a matter of a bodily attunement of our sensing bodies to the currents of that other lifeworld.

While studying the digitalisation of courts' practices, we had the chance to interview a lawyer working with victims of sexual abuse and rape. Inquiring about the tensions of interviewing victims via videoconference, he reflected on the importance of "breathing the same air" during an interview face-to-face - sharing the same space and connecting through the invisible medium of air that surrounded and permeated the lawyer and victim. In remote interviews, the shared breaths were missing, and so was the ability to generate trust.

In the project on Interspecies Encounters at the Chilean Zoo,[134] the team of designers was engaged with Judy and Gombe while they were playing with a rope. Suddenly, one of the chimpanzees took away the rope from the other. In that moment, she turned around and asked one of the designers to solicit something to restore the rope. The perception

130 Brian Massumi, *Notes to the Translation*, ibid xvi.
131 Judith (n 103).
132 Jane Bennett, *Vibrant Matter: A Political Ecology of Things* (Duke University Press 2010).
133 Tim Ingold, 'Materials against Materiality' (2007) 14 Archaeological Dialogues 1, 1.
134 Pablo Hermansen and Martín Tironi, 'Designing and Worlding: Prototyping Equivocal Encounters' [2022] DRS Biennial Conference Series <https://dl.designresearchsociety.org/drs-conference-papers/drs2022/researchpapers/78>.

of such a subtle change in the currents of the play by the designers was a way of the chimpanzee acting on him, revealing that all the time he was observing their play, he was being part of it already. It was not that the chimpanzees invited him, but that through bodily participation the designers were already performing that world, even if he was not yet aware of it.

6.5. Posthuman Co-Incidences, Resonances, and Frictions

By decentring the human from the world, attunement is not a matter of will and intentions but of concurrence. Thus, in posthuman legalities we seek co-incidences, resonances and frictions as modes of trans-ontological affectivity.

Co-incidences have to do with a shared world making, and a shared becoming. We co-make the world and thus we co-exist in it, and our fate is bounded to that of nature and machines. Even if we are not all the same, "we are all in this together".[135] By co-incidences we emphasise the posthuman notion of having a shared incidence in the world's destiny. With the capacity to influence the situation comes at the same time the responsibility of humans and non-humans to create a caring world. Caring is understood as providing the conditions for the possibility of other relationships to emerge, in a way that new forms of being in the world are fostered.[136] In the case of plants' immersion, action is not necessarily bounded to consciousness, but to compenetrating posthuman ontologies.[137] Paying attention to posthuman co-incidences is the human taking a humble position and accepting that far from being at the centre of creation, we have come late to a world already in the making, which exceeds our generativity in space and time.[138] Life on earth was there before humans, and will last beyond our existence, we are just playing our part.

135 Braidotti, '"We" Are In This Together, But We Are Not One and the Same' (n 3).

136 María Puig de la Bellacasa, '"Nothing Comes Without Its World": Thinking with Care' (2012) 60 The Sociological Review 197, 200.

137 Coccia (n 49).

138 Braidotti, '"We" Are In This Together, But We Are Not One and the Same' (n 3) 468.

Posthuman resonances resemble the physical phenomenon of an increased amplitude of a wave or frequency. In the trans-ontological affection, resonances are amplifications resulting from the alignment between worlds, their rules and values. Differently, frictions relate to the resistance of the motion of other surfaces. This is two worlds that are in conflict, or worlds that do not touch each other, that do not overlap. Resonances and frictions are part of a trans-ontological coexistence.[139] The inspiration for resonances as a category comes from the project "Tectonic Resonances" presented by Chile in the London Design Biennale 2021.[140] One of the authors (Hermansen) was part of the curator team of that project.[141] In this project, resonances were used to refer to the natural sound of stones extracted from the Chilean Andes. By foregrounding the voice of the stones regarding the impact of extractivism and highly techno-mediated life, the installation reactivated the potential for more-than-human forces in dealing with the current issues of the Anthropocene.[142]

The notion of friction has been worked in design, with an optimistic connotation, in which frictions, as tensions, conflicts and disagreement move the design inquiry forward, arising as possibilities, turnings, and dead-ends demanding to be worked through via prototyping.[143]

7. Discussion

If in human-nature-technology relations, these two non-human ontologies were transformed into subjects of law, then the relations between

139 Hermansen and Tironi (n 134).

140 *Resonancias Tectónicas- Bienal de Diseño de Londres 2021* (Directed by British Council Chile, 2021) <https://www.youtube.com/watch?v=VKqL27lAB_M> accessed 3 November 2022.

141 The designers of the Tectonic Resonances project are Macarena Irarrázaval, Sistema Simple Studio, Design Systems International, and Valentina Aliaga. The curators are Marcos Chilet, Martin Tironi, Carola Ureta Marín, and Pablo Hermansen.

142 'Tectonic Resonances inaugura en la Bienal de Diseno de Londres' <https://diseno.uc.cl/2021/06/tectonic-resonances-inaugura-en-la-bienal-de-diseno-de-londres/> accessed 12 February 2023.

143 Laura Forlano and Anijo Mathew, 'From Design Fiction to Design Friction: Speculative and Participatory Design of Values-Embedded Urban Technology' (2014) 21 Journal of Urban Technology 7, 1.

natural and technological entities would be between subjects of law. Taking a design research stance, such a body of law covering these relationships must be prototyped, not drafted a priori. Such explorations via designing and prototyping reveal new questions that we cannot formulate without digging into those posthuman ways of being. Speculating in this direction, the nature-human-technology trio leaves out a constitutive ontology of Latin America: non-corporeal or spiritual beings. For example, Mapuche[144] cosmology considers that nature, humans, technologies, and spirits (deities, ancestors, earth beings, etc.) live on a continuum. In other words, spiritual entities are not transcendent (like the Christian God) but immanent (a la Spinosa). If they are immanent, they live with us and their existence depends on certain material conditions (e.g., earth beings), could they become subjects of law?

In this sense, facing the current challenges with the old habits and references, which were instrumental to creating our current condition, can only render more of the same[145]. Considering this context, aggravated by the current global climate crisis, we take on the challenge that embracing the complexity of our time, we need to creatively look for theories and concepts that can help us make sense of the challenges that lie ahead in a fast-changing and highly technologically mediated world.[146] This is true, even when those theories and concepts are resisted and lie at the periphery of scientific and political knowledge creation.

The ontological turn addresses the exclusions performed by modern concepts that are widely accepted in the western world: human, nature, and technologies. Designing for the human is problematic – not to say unethical because the modern dominant concept of humans as a normative category excludes the sexualised, racialised, and naturalised bodies, grouped under the less-than-human others.[147] Similarly, the dominant modern notion of nature places it in fundamental opposition

144 Mapuche , means people of the earth, and is the denomination of a group of indigenous inhabitants in the southern and central regions in Chile and Argentina.

145 Rosi Braidotti, 'Writing as a Nomadic Subject' (2014) 11 Comparative Critical Studies 163, 163.

146 ibid.

147 Braidotti, '"We" Are In This Together, But We Are Not One and the Same' (n 3); Boaventura de Sousa Santos, 'The Resilience of Abyssal Exclusions in Our Societies: Toward a Post-Abyssal Law' (2017) 22 Tilburg Law Review 237.

to humans, defined by the exclusion of what-is-not-human.[148] This essentialist European notion of nature differs from older historic meanings in the European tradition, as well as other non-European meanings that take a relational approach to it.[149] Similarly with the concept of technology, as modern neologism it was adopted to make invisible all kind of inventiveness from less-than-human others (their creations are labelled as handcrafts and hacks, stemming out of hobbies).[150] Thus, from a critical stance, technology, as a term, has been instrumental to picturing a modern male authority and the North's superiority in industrial production and scientific knowledge creation, as a male-led technologically advantaged region.[151]

Doing post-anthropocentric design[152] demands not only a shift in the object of our design practice and research moving beyond the modern concepts of human, nature, and technology, but also the expansion of the methodologies we use, for example prototyping for multi-species coexistence in a Zoo.[153] In this case, prototyping —relationally and performatively— redefines the power relations between human and non-human animals and, therefore, there is a reciprocal construction of para-rights. This is the power of prototyping as an instance to empirically redefine our legal bodies. Furthermore, this has been extended to knowledge creation which in design research and practice has also been theorised under posthuman ontologies.[154]

8. Closing Remarks

This paper delves into the potential of a posthuman approach to legal

---

148 Frédéric Ducarme and Denis Couvet, 'What Does "Nature" Mean?' (2020) 6 Palgrave Communications 1.

149 ibid.

150 Ruth Oldenziel, *Making Technology Masculine: Men, Women, and Modern Machines in America, 1870-1945* (Amsterdam University Press 1999).

151 ibid 20.

152 Li Jönsson and others, 'Doing and Undoing Post-Anthropocentric Design' [2022] DRS Biennial Conference Series <https://dl.designresearchsociety.org/drs-conference-papers/drs2022/editorials/17>.

153 Hermansen and Tironi (n 24).

154 Wakkary (n 28).

design in the human-machine, and human-nature relationship, considered as mutually constituting ontologies. Fellow researchers will find in this paper novel concepts, frameworks and theorical perspectives to enrich the repertoire of legal design research and practice. Legal design practitioners will benefit from this contribution, as it contains examples and references regarding how posthuman approaches to legal design can be carried out and implemented in practice. A call for posthuman legal design does not oppose HCD approaches, yet it positions itself outside of them to critically assess their potential, and most importantly their limitations. Furthermore, to tackle the grand challenges of our time, fostering access to justice and the rule of law, requires a critical assessment of our legal design practices. By doing that we can embrace new forms of understanding the world we are co-designing together with more-than-human agencies.

Acknowledgements

This work was supported by the National Fund for Scientific and Technological Development (Fondecyt), Grant No. 1210006, Chile; and the German Academic Exchange Service (DAAD), Grant ref. no. 91837827, Germany. Access to data and participants affiliated to the Chilean Judiciary was possible thanks to a research cooperation agreement with the Administrative Corporation of the Judiciary, Chile.

Bibliography

Ackermann R, 'Design Thinking Was Supposed to Fix the World. Where Did It Go Wrong?' (*MIT Technology Review*) <https://www.technologyreview.com/2023/02/09/1067821/design-thinking-retrospective-what-went-wrong/> accessed 10 February 2023

Arendt H, *Eichmann and the Holocaust* (Penguin Books 2006)

Auernhammer J, 'Human-Centered AI: The Role of Human-Centered Design Research in the Development of AI' [2020] DRS Biennial Conference Series <https://dl.designresearchsociety.org/drs-conference-papers/drs2020/researchpapers/89>

Barad K, 'Posthumanist Performativity: Toward an Understanding of How Matter Comes to Matter' (2003) 28 Signs: Journal of women in culture and society 801

Bennett J, *Vibrant Matter: A Political Ecology of Things* (Duke University Press 2010)

Bohman B, *Legal Design for Social-Ecological Resilience* (CUP 2021)

Boland T, 'Global Liminality: The Pandemic as Anti-Structure. Introduction to the Special Issue' (2020) 13 International Political Anthropology 5

Boland T and Bența MI, 'Special Issue: Crisis, Liminality and Performance' (2020) 13 International Political Anthropology 3

Boulot E and others, 'Editorial Posthuman Legalities: New Materialism and Law beyond the Human' (2021) 12 Journal of Human Rights and the Environment 1

Boulot E and Sterlin J, 'Steps Towards a Legal Ontological Turn: Proposals for Law's Place beyond the Human' (2022) 11 Transnational Environmental Law 13

Braidotti R, 'Writing as a Nomadic Subject' (2014) 11 Comparative Critical Studies 163

—, 'Critical Posthuman Knowledges' (2017) 116 South Atlantic Quarterly 83

—, '"We" Are In This Together, But We Are Not One and the Same' (2020) 17 Journal of Bioethical Inquiry 465

Brownsword R, *Law, Technology and Society: Re-Imagining the Regulatory Environment* (Routledge, Taylor & Francis Group 2019)

Butler J, *Bodies That Matter: On the Discursive Limits of Sex* (Routledge 1993)

—, *Notes toward a Performative Theory of Assembly* (Harvard University Press 2015)

Castells M, *Networks of Outrage and Hope: Social Movements in the Internet Age* (Second edition, Polity Press 2015)

Cirkovic E, 'The Cosmolegal Proposal' (19 June 2020) <https://papers.ssrn.com/abstract=3631056> accessed 28 October 2022

—, 'The Next Generation of International Law: Space, Ice, and the Cosmolegal Proposal' (2021) 22 German Law Journal 147

Coccia E, *The Life of Plants: A Metaphysics of Mixture* (English edition, Polity 2019)

Contini F, 'Artificial Intelligence and the Transformation of Humans, Law and Technology Interactions in Judicial Proceedings' (2020) 2 Law, Tech & Hum 4

Contini F and Lanzara GF (eds), *The Circulation of Agency in E-Justice: Interoperability and Infrastructures for European Transborder Judicial Proceedings* (Springer Netherlands 2014)

Czarniawska B and Mazza C, 'Consulting as a Liminal Space' (2003) 56 Human Relations 267

Dabaghi K, 'Beyond Design Thinking and into Speculative Futures in Legal Design' [2022] DRS Biennial Conference Series <https://dl.designresearchsociety.org/drs-conference-papers/drs2022/researchpapers/70>

de la Bellacasa MP, '"Nothing Comes Without Its World": Thinking with Care' (2012) 60 The Sociological Review 197

de Sousa Santos B, 'The Resilience of Abyssal Exclusions in Our Societies: Toward a Post-Abyssal Law' (2017) 22 Tilburg Law Review 237

Deleuze G, 'Postscript on the Societies of Control' (1992) 59 October 3

Deleuze G and Guattari F, *A Thousand Plateaus: Capitalism and Schizophrenia* (Brian Massumi tr, 2nd Edition, University of Minnesota Press 1987)

DiSalvo C, *Design as Democratic Inquiry: Putting Experimental Civics into Practice* (The MIT Press 2022)

— and Lukens J, 'Nonanthropocentrism and the Nonhuman in Design: Possibilities for Designing New Forms of Engagement with and through Technology' in Marcus Foth and others (eds), From Social Butterfly to Engaged Citizen (MIT Press 2011)

Diver L, 'Digisprudence: Code as Law Rebooted', *Digisprudence: Code as Law Rebooted* (Edinburgh University Press 2022)

Doherty M and others, 'A New Attitude to Laws Empire: The Potentialities of Legal Design' in Marcelo Corrales Compagnucci and others (eds), *Legal Design* (Edward Elgar Publishing 2021)

Dreyfus H and Kelly SD, 'Heterophenomenology: Heavy-Handed Sleight-of-Hand' (2007) 6 Phenomenology and the Cognitive Sciences 45

Ducarme F and Couvet D, 'What Does "Nature" Mean?' (2020) 6 Palgrave Communications 1

Dunne A and Raby F, *Speculative Everything: Design, Fiction, and Social Dreaming* (MIT Press 2013)

Edelman J, 'Understanding Radical Breaks: Media and Behavior in Small Teams Engaged in Redesign Scenarios' (2011) <https://purl.stanford.edu/ps394dy6131> accessed 29 January 2019

—, 'Designing as Performance: Bridging the Gap Between Research and Practice in Design Thinking Education' (2021)

Escobar A, ‘Worlds and Knowledges Otherwise’ (2007) 21 Cultural Studies 179

—, *Designs for the Pluriverse: Radical Interdependence, Autonomy, and the Making of Worlds* (Duke University Press 2018)

European Economic and Social Committee and others, *Towards an EU Charter of the Fundamental Rights of Nature: Study* (Publications Office 2020) <https://data.europa.eu/doi/10.2864/25113> accessed 25 January 2023

Fernández R, ‘El Espacio Público En Disputa: Manifestaciones Políticas, Ciudad y Ciudadanía En El Chile Actual’ (2013) 12 Psicoperspectivas 28

Forlano L, ‘Decentering the Human in the Design of Collaborative Cities’ (2016) 32 Design Issues 42

—, ‘Posthumanism and Design’ (2017) 3 She Ji: The Journal of Design, Economics, and Innovation 16

—, ‘Invisible Algorithms, Invisible Politics’ (*Public Books*, 12 February 2018) <https://www.publicbooks.org/invisible-algorithms-invisible-politics/> accessed 9 February 2023

— and Mathew A, ‘From Design Fiction to Design Friction: Speculative and Participatory Design of Values-Embedded Urban Technology’ (2014) 21 Journal of Urban Technology 7

Fraser N (ed), *Scales of Justice: Reimagining Political Space in a Globalizing World* (reprint Polity Press 2012)

Ghai Y and Cottrell J, ‘The Rule of Law and Access to Justice: Findings of an ABA Project on Access to Justice’ (2008) <https://www.semanticscholar.org/paper/The-Rule-of-Law-and-Access-to-Justice%3A-Findings-of-Ghai-Cottrell/bb4d3cb44300b5c8da7c717edd7fe3b22224507c> accessed 20 June 2022

Gherardi S, ‘A Posthumanist Epistemology of Practice’ in Cristina Neesham (ed), *Handbook of Philosophy of Management* (Springer International Publishing 2020)

Glaser VL, Pollock N and D’Adderio L, ‘The Biography of an Algorithm: Performing Algorithmic Technologies in Organizations’ (2021) 2 Organization Theory 26317877211004610

Grear A, ‘Deconstructing Anthropos: A Critical Legal Reflection on “Anthropocentric” Law and Anthropocene “Humanity”’ (2015) 26 Law and Critique 225

Griffiths J, ‘Legal Pluralism’ in Neil J Smelser and Paul B Baltes (eds), *International Encyclopedia of the Social & Behavioral Sciences* (Pergamon 2001)

Hagan M, 'Legal Design as a Thing: A Theory of Change and a Set of Methods to Craft a Human-Centered Legal System' (2020) 36 Design Issues 3

Haraway D, *Simians, Cyborgs, and Women: The Reinvention of Nature* (Routledge 1990)

Haraway DJ, *Modest Witness@Second Millennium Femaleman Meets Oncomouse: Feminism and Technoscience* (Routledge 1997)

Harvey M and Vanderheiden S, '"For the Trees Have No Tongues": Eco-Feedback, Speech, and the Silencing of Nature' (2021) 12 Journal of Human Rights and the Environment 38

Healey R and Pepper A, 'Interspecies Justice: Agency, Self-Determination, and Assent' (2021) 178 Philosophical Studies 1223

Hermansen P and Chilet M, 'Ciudad Virtual, Ciudad Real: Conflicto y Emergencia de Un Nuevo Entorno Urbano' (2010) 2 Diseña 40

Hermansen P and Fernández R, 'Photo-Ethnography and Political Engagement: Studying Performative Subversions of Public Space' [2020] Dearq 100

Hermansen P and Guerra Solano J, 'Furrowing the Maraña: Designing to Sail out of the Anthropocene' in Martin Tironi and others (eds), *Design for more than human futures* (Routledge 2023)

Hermansen P and Neira J, 'The Prototype as a Cosmopolitical Place: Ethnographic Design Practice and Research at the National Zoo in Santiago, Chile' [2016] DRS Biennial Conference Series <https://dl.designresearchsociety.org/drs-conference-papers/drs2016/researchpapers/46>

Hermansen P and Tironi M, 'Cosmopolitical Interventions: Prototyping Interspecies Encounters for More than Human Futures' in J Roberts-Smith and others (eds), *Prototyping across the Disciplines* (Intellect Books 2021)

Hermansen P and Tironi M, 'Designing and Worlding: Prototyping Equivocal Encounters' [2022] DRS Biennial Conference Series <https://dl.designresearchsociety.org/drs-conference-papers/drs2022/researchpapers/78>

Hinings B, Gegenhuber T and Greenwood R, 'Digital Innovation and Transformation: An Institutional Perspective' (2018) 28 Information and Organization 52

Horvath A, *Modernism and Charisma* (Palgrave Macmillan UK 2013)

Inayatullah S, 'Deconstructing and Reconstructing the Future: Predictive, Cultural and Critical Epistemologies' (1990) 22 Futures 115

Ingold T, 'Materials against Materiality' (2007) 14 Archaeological Dialogues 1

—, *Lines: A Brief History* (Routledge 2016)

Irani L, '"Design Thinking": Defending Silicon Valley at the Apex of Global Labor Hierarchies' (2018) 4 Catalyst: Feminism, Theory, Technoscience 1

Jackson D and others, 'What Legal Design Could Be: Towards an Expanded Practice of Inquiry, Critique, and Action' [2022] DRS Biennial Conference Series <https://dl.designresearchsociety.org/drs-conference-papers/drs2022/editorials/32>

Jönsson L and others, 'Doing and Undoing Post-Anthropocentric Design' [2022] DRS Biennial Conference Series <https://dl.designresearchsociety.org/drs-conference-papers/drs2022/editorials/17>

Judith K, *Exploring Interstitiality with Mangroves: Semiotic Materialism and the Environmental Humanities* (Routledge 2022)

Kallinikos J, 'The Regulative Regime of Technology' in Francesco Contini and Giovan Francesco Lanzara (eds), *ICT and Innovation in the Public Sector: European Studies in the Making of E-Government* (Palgrave Macmillan UK 2009)

Latour B, *Reassembling the Social: An Introduction to Actor-Network-Theory* (1st Edition, OUP 2007)

—, *After Lockdown: A Metamorphosis* (Julie Rose tr, Polity Press 2021)

Law J, 'What's Wrong with a One-World World?' (2015) 16 Distinktion: Journal of Social Theory 126

López Barbera F, 'When a Tree Says No' (*Futuress*, 21 April 2021) <https://futuress.org/stories/when-a-tree-says-no/> accessed 9 February 2023

—, 'When a Stone Says No' (*Futuress*, 6 April 2022) <https://futuress.org/stories/when-a-stone-says-no/> accessed 9 February 2023

McNally P and Inayatullah S, 'The Rights of Robots: Technology, Culture and Law in the 21st Century' (1988) 20 Futures 119

Mertens M, 'Liminal Innovation Practices: Questioning Three Common Assumptions in Responsible Innovation' (2018) 5 Journal of Responsible Innovation 280

Mills AJ (Waabishki M, 'Miinigowiziwin: All That Has Been given for Living Well Together: One Vision of Anishinaabe Constitutionalism' (Thesis, 2019) <https://dspace.library.uvic.ca/handle/1828/10985> accessed 9 February 2023

Mohr R and Contini F, 'Reassembling the Legal' (2011) 20 Griffith Law Review 994

Mortati M, 'New Design Knowledge and the Fifth Order of Design' (2022) 38 Design Issues 21

Oldenziel R, *Making Technology Masculine: Men, Women, and Modern Machines in America, 1870-1945* (Amsterdam University Press 1999)

Perry-Kessaris A, ‘Legal Design for Practice, Activism, Policy, and Research’ (2019) 46 Journal of Law and Society 185

—, *Doing Sociolegal Research in Design Mode* (Routledge 2021)

Pope HJ, ‘Liberatory Legal Design and Radical Imagination’ [2022] DRS Biennial Conference Series <https://dl.designresearchsociety.org/drs-conference-papers/drs2022/researchpapers/254>

‘Pressebilder’ (*Letzte Generation*) <https://letztegeneration.de/presse/pressebilder/> accessed 16 March 2023

‘Pressefotos [EXTERN FREIGEGEBEN] - Google Drive’ <https://drive.google.com/drive/folders/1xaq6DXe-_yQaHuk9XeEAl2kqppCNkOxj> accessed 16 March 2023

Reeves B and Nass CI, *The Media Equation: How People Treat Computers, Television, and New Media like Real People and Places* (1 paperback ed., [reprint], CSLI Publ 1996)

Resonancias Tectónicas- Bienal de Diseño de Londres 2021 (Directed by British Council Chile, 2021) <https://www.youtube.com/watch?v=VKqL27lAB_M> accessed 3 November 2022

Rietveld E, Denys D and Van Westen M, ‘Ecological-Enactive Cognition as Engaging with a Field of Relevant Affordances’ in Albert Newen, Leon De Bruin, and Shaun Gallagher (eds), *The Oxford Handbook of 4E Cognition* (OUP 2018)

Rietveld E and Kiverstein J, ‘A Rich Landscape of Affordances’ (2014) 26 Ecological Psychology 325

‘Right to Repair | Think Tank | European Parliament’ (2022) <https://www.europarl.europa.eu/thinktank/en/document/EPRS_BRI(2022)698869> accessed 28 October 2022

Santos B de S, *Epistemologies of the South: Justice Against Epistemicide* (Routledge 2015)

—, ‘Más allá de la imaginación política y de la teoría crítica eurocéntricas’ [2017] Revista Crítica de Ciências Sociais 75

Santuber J, ‘Designing for Digital Justice’ (Doctoral Thesis, Universität Potsdam 2023) <DOI: 10.25932/publishup-60417>

—, ‘Towards an Enactive-Ecological Approach to Sociomateriality in Information Systems Research’, *AMCIS 2020 Proceedings* (2020) <https://aisel.aisnet.org/amcis2020/meta_research_is/meta_research_is/9>

—, 'Building an Apparatus: Disclosing Affectivity in Sociomaterial Research' [2020] ICIS 2020 Proceedings <https://aisel.aisnet.org/icis2020/adv_research_methods/adv_research_methods/9>

Santuber J, Abou Refaie R and Meinel C, 'Delivering Digital Justice: Liminal Innovation & Permanence in Courts', *ACIS 2021 Proceedings* (2021)

—, 'Interrogating E-Justice: Lessons from Digitalizing Courts in Chile' [2022] EGOV-CeDEM-ePart 2022 54

Santuber J and Edelman J, 'Designing with Theories: Producing Legal Design Diffractively in Courts of Justice' [2022] DRS Biennial Conference Series <https://dl.designresearchsociety.org/drs-conference-papers/drs2022/researchpapers/259>

Santuber J and Krawietz L, 'User Research Methodologies in Legal Design Projects: Lessons from Practice' in Rossana Ducato and Alain Strowel (eds), *Legal Design Perspectives. Theoretical and Practical Insights from the Field* (Ledizioni 2021)

—, 'The Sociomateriality of Justice: A Relational Ontology for Legal Design (La Sociomaterialidad de La Justicia: Una Ontología Relacional Para El Diseño Legal)' (2021) 6 RChD: creación y pensamiento 1

Scammell M, 'The Internet and Civic Engagement: The Age of the Citizen-Consumer' (2000) 17 Political Communication 351

Schildt H, 'The Institutional Logic of Digitalization' in Thomas Gegenhuber and others (eds), *Digital Transformation and Institutional Theory*, vol 83 (Emerald Publishing Limited 2022)

Scott S and Orlikowski W, 'The Digital Undertow: How the Corollary Effects of Digital Transformation Affect Industry Standards' (2022) 33 Information Systems Research 311

Stead M and Coulton P, 'A More-than-Human Right-to-Repair' [2022] DRS Biennial Conference Series <https://dl.designresearchsociety.org/drs-conference-papers/drs2022/researchpapers/269>

Szakolczai Á, 'Permanent (Trickster) Liminality: The Reasons of the Heart and of the Mind' (2017) 27(2) Theory & Psychology 231

Taylor D, *The Archive and the Repertoire: Performing Cultural Memory in the Americas* (Duke University Press 2003)

'Tectonic Resonances inaugura en la Bienal de Diseno de Londres' <https://diseno.uc.cl/2021/06/tectonic-resonances-inaugura-en-la-bienal-de-diseno-de-londres/> accessed 12 February 2023

Thomassen B, 'The Uses and Meaning of Liminality' (2009) 2 International Political Anthropology 5

Tironi M and others, *Design For More-Than-Human Futures: Towards Post-Anthropocentric Worlding* (1st edn, Routledge 2023)

Tironi M, Albornoz Novoa C and Chilet M, 'Problematizing Human-Centred Design: Notes on Planet- Oriented Design Open Debate' (2022) 77 diid 12

Tironi M and Hermansen P, 'Prototyping Multispecies Environments: Attentiveness and Friction as Modes of Knowing' [2018] DRS Biennial Conference Series <https://dl.designresearchsociety.org/drs-conference-papers/drs2018/researchpapers/57>

Tonkinwise C, 'Before Design, More-than-Design: Elucidating "Ontological Design"' (2022) 14(3) Design and Culture 341

Toom V, M'charek A and Wienroth M (eds), *Law, Practice and Politics of Forensic DNA Profiling: Forensic Genetics and Their Technolegal Worlds* (Routledge 2023)

Turner VW, *The Ritual Process: Structure and Anti-Structure* (Penguin Books Limited 1974)

van Gennep A, *The Rites of Passage* (Psychology Press 1960)

Wakkary R, 'Nomadic Practices: A Posthuman Theory for Knowing Design' (2020) 14 International Journal of Design 117

Walton P, 'James v Birnmann: The Potential of Critical Design for Examining Legal Issues' [2022] DRS Biennial Conference Series <https://dl.designresearchsociety.org/drs-conference-papers/drs2022/researchpapers/106>

Willis A-M, 'Ontological Designing' (2006) 4 Design Philosophy Papers 69

LEGAL DESIGN INTERVENTIONS AGAINST MISLEADING DESIGN AND MISINFORMATION ONLINE

10. DESIGNING PUBLIC SERVICES IN THE AGE OF BIG TECH. BEYOND GOVERNMENT-TO-CITIZEN SERVICE DESIGN TO INFRASTRUCTURE DESIGN

Margaret Hagan

Abstract
As more people go online to find help for their housing, family, and money problems, there is a large risk that they will find incorrect or unreliable information there. Just like with misinformation regarding elections, political news, and public health, online platforms like search engines and social media sites can strongly influence people's beliefs and choices. That means there is a huge opportunity to connect people with their rights and public services to help them resolve their life problems, as well as a huge risk that they will rely on incorrect information (or not find any help information) and their life problem will spiral into a larger crisis.
The problem is that public service design is usually predicated on a two-way public agency-to-user relationship that doesn't acknowledge the growing prominence and authority of private technology platforms like search engines and social media. As described in this paper's case study of the Better Legal Internet initiative, these platforms have growing control over what information people see, what they see as authoritative, and whether or how they connect with public services. As such, public service agencies must engage in more ambitious design interventions that go past traditional efforts of creating websites, applications, visual guides, and other agency-to-consumer services. Instead, they must also design infrastructure to understand what is happening with public services on big tech platforms, to spot misinformation problems and harms, and to engage with the platforms on improving their algorithms, interfaces, and other policies. This paper presents the detailed case study of how our team identified and designed these kinds of research, data, and expert infrastructure in the civil justice professional community. It also details the robust efforts in the voting and medical services domains, to improve public services through a mixture of adversarial and collaborative policy-making with big tech platforms that were enabled through extensive research, data, and organizational infrastructure in their professional communities.

1. A Different Kind of Misinformation Problem: Public Services

In the past decade, more government agencies and nonprofits have realized the threat misinformation and disinformation pose to a stable, democratic society. What information does the public see about elections, politics, pandemics, climate change, or other important policy topics? Misinformation (incorrect information spread unintentionally or intentionally) or disinformation (incorrect information spread intentionally by actors) must be a public policy concern. If people rely on false, deceptive, or misleading information on these topics, many harms might result. Conspiracy theories might spread; people might avoid important services and treatments; there might be increased distrust in institutions; and more people may participate in violence and antisocial behavior.[1]

But much of the misinformation coverage and research has been focused on these high-profile policy domains. When policymakers focus on the harms of online information, they are often discussing coordinated campaigns of bots, trolls, and other deliberate efforts to spread false or misleading information to the public.[2] This misinformation research points to an important new trend for policymakers: that more people are relying on information from the Internet, including search engines and social media, for important topics like health, politics, education, foreign affairs, and the justice system. But most frequently the conver-

1 Yasmine Green and others, 'Evidence-Based Misinformation Interventions: Challenges and Opportunities for Measurement and Collaboration' (2023) <https://carnegieendowment.org/2023/01/09/evidence-based-misinformation-interventions-challenges-and-opportunities-for-measurement-and-collaboration-pub-88661> accessed 3 February 2023.

2 ibid, Justin Farrell, Kathryn McConnell, and Robert Brulle, 'Evidence-Based Strategies to Combat Scientific Misinformation' (2019) 9 Nat Clim Change 191; Michael Golebiewski and Danah Boyd, 'Data Voids: Where Missing Data Can Easily Be Exploited' (2018) <https://datasociety.net/about/#funding.> accessed 13 February 2023; Laura Courchesne, Julia Ilhardt, and Jacob N Shapiro, 'Review of Social Science Research on the Impact of Countermeasures against Influence Operations' (2021) 2(5) Harvard Kennedy School Misinformation Review 1; Gordon Pennycook and others, 'The Implied Truth Effect: Attaching Warnings to a Subset of Fake News Headlines Increases Perceived Accuracy of Headlines without Warnings' (2020) 66 Management Science 4944.

sation is framed around how to counteract deliberate misinformation campaigns in political and health domains.

This paper highlights another concerning trend with the public's increasing reliance on Internet platforms for information: low-quality information about public services. What rights does a person have? What government programs can help them with housing, financial, family, and other problems? What nonprofit services can help them with complicated but important challenges like getting affordable housing, receiving unemployment benefits, clearing a criminal record, securing a restraining order, or getting an immigrant visa? These are all public services that can have a significant impact on an individual's well-being and stability, and taken as a whole can contribute to a more equitable, stable, and cohesive society.

Just like with the high-profile misinformation topics of health and politics, many people go to the Internet to find information on public services or the underlying problems that the services are meant to help with.[3] But there is no apparent coordinated misinformation problem with public services information online. Unlike with health, politics, or other high-profile topics, there are no reports of troll farms or misinformation campaigns trying to spread misleading information about how to submit a food assistance application or whether people have a right to a free lawyer if they are facing eviction.

Because of this lack of a coordinated misinformation campaign, public service actors like government agencies, legal aid groups, or nonprofits may assume that there is no need to focus on misinformation online. Why should public service agencies spend precious resources on how information spreads on the Internet when there are so many other challenges to tackle in delivering effective and impactful public services? The current misinformation discourse's focus on countering bots, influencers, rumors, and conspiracy theories doesn't have much to offer these

3 Pew Research Center, 'Information Searches That Solve Problems' (2007) <https://www.pewresearch.org/internet/2007/12/30/information-searches-that-solve-problems/> accessed 9 December 2019; Brooke Auxier and Monica Anderson, 'Social Media Use in 2021' (*Pew Research Center*, 7 April 2021) <https://www.pewresearch.org/internet/2021/04/07/social-media-use-in-2021/> accessed 20 January 2022; Elizabeth Sillence and Pam Briggs, 'Please Advise: Using the Internet for Health and Financial Advice' (2007) 23 Computers in Human Behavior 727.

agencies, which are not dealing with these kinds of coordinated misinformation problems with their public service information.

This paper proposes that public service agencies, including governments and nonprofits that offer services meant to help the public, all must have online misinformation strategies. Public service agencies should focus on whether and how people can get crucial information about rights, services, and processes on the Internet. And, at least as of 2023, this focus must also include the big tech platforms that most people use to search and prioritize information online. As detailed in this paper's case study, public services are not a simple two-party interaction of agency to citizens. Rather, technology platforms – especially search engines and social media sites – often now mediate whether and how public service agencies connect with the public.

This paper presents an example of this online public service information challenge, in the domain of civil justice. How can public agencies like courts, legal aid groups, bar foundations, and community navigator programs connect with the public, to inform them of their rights, legal processes, and free services available to help with civil justice matters like debt collection, eviction, divorce, restraining orders, or criminal record clearing? Our Stanford Legal Design Lab had begun to tackle this problem in 2015 with an initiative called Better Legal Internet, using a human-centered design process in collaboration with partner courts, legal aid groups, and government agencies. This paper profiles our initiative and distills the lessons we learned about how challenging it is to design effective interventions when private 'big tech' platforms play such a large role in the relationship between public service agencies and the public.

Based on this ongoing research and design project, this paper argues that public service agencies should be investing in deliberate, human-centered design efforts to create infrastructure in their professional community. This infrastructure includes:

1. **Research Infrastructure**: to understand how the public currently uses the Internet for the public service topic their agency is trying to provide, and the life problems the service is meant to address; and to profile how the search engine and social media tech platforms decide what information to show the public in this topic area and how these tech companies' policies are set; and

2. **Data Infrastructure**: to standardize the types of information that are relevant for users of public services, including what organizations can help them, what rules and guidance they should know about their problem area, and what official documents or tools they can rely on to address their problem;
3. **Expert Infrastructure**: to bring various officials, professionals, and experts (including community experts) in a policy domain together, so that there is a coherent approach to judge what information in this domain is authoritative and reliable, and what is misleading or harmful. Expert infrastructure also makes it easier for outside groups, like teams that work at big tech platforms, to understand this unique policy domain and build ongoing collaborations that get dedicated attention, policy-making, and engineering resources focused on this domain's problems.

This paper's case study of the Better Legal Internet design initiative raises several concerns from which other public service agencies and civic innovation researchers can build. First, this case study found that there is a particular misinformation problem with public services information online: of high-quality information from government and nonprofit agencies being obscured and drowned out by low-quality content from private actors. This misinformation problem is not one of the malicious campaigns trying to deceive the public, as has been profiled in the high-profile areas of vaccines or elections. Rather, this misinformation problem is about well-resourced for-profit companies trying to capture the Internet public's attention and engagement on search engine results pages and social media sites, and in the process diverting the public away from government and nonprofit agencies' information. This is a different type of misinformation problem, but still, one that should be a strong policy concern. The case study discusses this public services misinformation problem so that more government bodies and nonprofit agencies can explore their own information landscape on the Internet and how to address it.

Second, this paper highlights the need for new strategies to engage big tech platforms in the government-to-citizen service relationship. Even if there is more design work happening in public service agencies to make these services more accessible and equitable, traditional service design approaches do not work when trying to solve a challenge like public services online. Traditional service design techniques assume that public service agencies and members of the public are two parties in a relationship with each other.

Our design work found that technology platforms are actually an increasingly large third party in the government-to-citizen relationship and that these platforms' policies, interfaces, and algorithms play a huge role in how public service agencies can connect with the public. It is not enough for a public service agency to focus innovation efforts on its own communications, marketing, websites, or guides. Rather, to truly be discoverable and usable to the public, government and nonprofit agencies must also engage with technology platforms to change their policies and algorithms. This is a big shift, in acknowledging that even if an agency has formal authority as a government body or public interest designation -- a third-party technology platform might actually be more influential with the public.

This paper proceeds as follows. First, it gives an overview of the Better Legal Internet initiative, as a case study of how a university-based design team tried to lead public service agencies through a service design process to improve how they help the public with civil justice matters online. It then highlights the main challenges that this initiative encountered: the large role that tech platforms play in online public services, and the new kind of misinformation challenges that appeared. The paper discusses the methods that the Better Legal Internet initiative adapted into the traditional design process, including tech platform audits and public-private design workshops. The conclusion discusses what future researchers and public service agencies might do to build from this work, including more mixed carrot-stick approaches to tech platforms' policy-making, and coordinated interventions to improve the delivery of public services online.

2. A Design Effort to Improve Public Services Online

The Stanford Law School's Legal Design Lab is a justice innovation research and design group that works on reforming the United States civil justice system to be more human-centered, equitable, and accessible. In 2015, the Lab launched the Better Legal Internet initiative to conduct research and design new interventions regarding how people can find legal help and public services on the Internet.[4] The initiative's objective was to ensure that anyone searching for information on housing, debt, family, or other related legal issues on the Internet, was made aware of the public legal services, local laws, and the procedures to resolve their issues.

Our Lab chose to focus on Internet information and services because it came up regularly in our design workshops and user interviews.[5] When we spoke to people using the courts or legal aid offices, they regularly discussed how they tried to find information by searching online or going on forum sites to seek help.[6] From an initial set of Internet searches for legal help services, our team found that many government and nonprofits websites did a poor job in showing people's rights, the law, or legal procedures. We were concerned that these websites weren't created in a clear or accessible way, to serve the public. Our initial project goal was to improve people's ability to find helpful, authoritative information when they went online for a query like 'help with eviction' or 'how do I respond to a debt collection lawsuit'.

Notably, our Lab did not begin the Better Legal Internet initiative framed in the language of misinformation or disinformation. Though our team was aware of efforts in other policy domains to combat coordinated campaigns to spread misleading and deceptive information online,[7] we did not consider this relevant to the civil justice space. Our

---

4 Stanford Legal Design Lab, 'A Better Legal Internet | Increase People's Access to Justice Online' (2015) <https://betterinternet.law.stanford.edu/> accessed 14 February 2023.

5 Margaret D Hagan, 'A Human-Centered Design Approach to Access to Justice Generating New Prototypes and Hypotheses for Intervention to Make Courts User-Friendly' (2018) 6 Indiana Journal of Law and Social Equality 199.

6 See some of the specific concerning incidents in our working paper, Margaret D Hagan and Yue Li, 'Legal Help Search Audit: Are Search Engines Effective Brokers of Legal Information?' [2020] SSRN Electronic Journal <https://papers.ssrn.com/abstract=3623333> accessed 14 February 2023.

7 We were aware of a growing field of research and journalism highlighting misinformation in areas like health and politics, and that technology companies were being called out to address this, with reports like: Google, 'How Google Fights Disinformation' (2019) <https://kstatic.googleusercontent.com/files/388aa7d18189665e5f5579aef18e181c2d4283fb7b0d4691689dfd1bf92f7ac2ea6816e09c02eb98d5501b8e5705ead65af653cdf94071c47361821e362da55b> accessed 7 February

framing of the design was about the delivery of public services. The government and public interest groups had resources, experts, and guidance to give the public, to improve their housing, finances, and family outcomes. How could we better improve these public service agencies' ability to deliver services to the public?

3. Taking the Traditional Public Service Design Approach, and Hitting a Wall

We thought of the challenge as a typical service design challenge: a well-meaning public interest group wanted to serve its potential audience better.[8] How could we help them improve their communications, interfaces, and other strategies to better serve the public? Naively, we expected the design effort to be relatively straightforward: our Lab design team should help research people's needs and preferences, then craft better website designs through collaborative, creative sessions, and then work with government and nonprofit networks to scale these best practices to as many jurisdictions as possible.

This traditional service design approach that we began with is similar to what other public interest groups are embracing in their move towards more human-centered innovation. Government agencies, educational institutions, and nonprofits are increasingly focused on public interest technology and innovation in order to better serve individual people and improve all of society. White House issued an executive order directing federal agencies to have customer experience plans, to ensure that people can have accessible, understandable, and empowering government experiences.[9] Court systems like the California state Judicial Council have built design teams to research how people try to solve legal problems in the state courts, and then created new digital platforms that

---

2023; and Alexandre Bovet and Hernan Makse, 'Influence of Fake News in Twitter during the 2016 US Presidential Election' (2019) 10 Nature Communications.

8 See more about the traditional service design approach at Marc Stickdorn and others, *This Is Service Design Doing* (O'Reilly 2017).

9 Shalanda D Young and Dominic J Mancini, 'Memorandum for Heads of Executive Departments and Agencies on Improving Access to Public Benefits Programs through the Paperwork Reduction Act' (2022) <https://www.whitehouse.gov/omb/information-regulatory-affairs/federal-> accessed 10 November 2022.

are more user-friendly.[10] More governments have created design and innovation labs that are focused on improving people's journeys through a complicated, bureaucratic process.[11] These efforts have all been predicated on the belief that people should get these public resources in low-burden, empowering ways -- and that this improved process design will then build greater trust, authority, and confidence between people and government institutions.

Our Lab's earlier innovation projects in the civil justice space had been guided by the service design approach to good success. We used the human-centered design process to understand the user experience and systemic policies that affected a given challenge.[12] Our approach, like many other public interest innovation teams, followed a 'double diamond' design process that involved a first phase of user, system, and market research to uncover people's main frustrations and needs, and the main opportunities to improve the given system. In the second phase, we use creative techniques to brainstorm many different possible solutions with diverse stakeholders and gradually test, prototype, and refine them into pilots that our partner agencies can implement.

The double-diamond, empathy-driven service design approach worked for our team and partners in other civic justice challenges. These justice challenges ranged from improving traffic ticket courts, to how people apply for guardianships of children, to how to make the divorce process more efficient. We conducted design research and used user-focused insights to generate solutions for our government agency or non-profit partner to implement. These solutions were typically aimed at the public service agency or the public. For the public, we helped create us-

---

10 California Courts Judicial Council, 'California Courts Digital Services and Self Help Redesign - RFP' (2019) <https://www.courts.ca.gov/42412.htm> accessed 14 February 2023.

11 Lorenzo Allio, 'Design Thinking for Public Service Excellence' (2014) <http://www.undp.org/content/undp/en/home/librarypage/capacity-building/global-centre-for-public-service-excellence/DesignThinking.html>; Lucy Kimbell and Jocelyn Baile, 'Prototyping and the New Spirit of Policy-Making' (2017) 13 CoDesign 214; Matt Fuller and Anna Lochard, 'Public Policy Labs in European Union Member States' (2016) <http://kokeilevasuomi.fi/documents/1777665/1915666/final+report+w+identifiers.pdf/c99c823c-e125-491e-9734-0fbf3d379976>.

12 Margaret D Hagan and F Kürşat Özenç, 'A Design Space for Legal and Systems Capability' (2020) 36 Design Issues 61.

er-facing interventions for the agency to offer, like new handouts, fliers, guides, navigators, websites, or apps. For the agency, we created back-end system interventions, like changes to room layout or architecture, creation of new staffing positions, the establishment of new data exchanges, or changes to court rules or procedures.[13] Our team had gotten comfortable in this two-party service design approach. We could either encourage the system 'owners' (like court leadership, legal aid directors, government agency workers or nonprofit executives) to change how the system worked, or we could direct these agencies on how to make it easier for people to find and use the system. Inherent in both of these solution spaces is the assumption that the public service agencies held power and authority over the public's interactions with public services.

As we entered into the Better Legal Internet initiative, the Lab team assumed this two-party service design approach would be sufficient. We could follow the same basic double diamond process and rely on our usual strategies of user interviews, stakeholder workshops, journey mapping, and qualitative data-gathering to understand the current breakdowns and opportunities for legal help information online. After using these service design research methods, we would then be able to craft user-facing and back-end interventions for our court and legal aid partners to implement. Likely, our team predicted, we would end up with proposals to help public service agencies improve their legal help website interfaces, visuals, and content, so that more people could discover and use these sites to protect their rights and resolve their conflicts.

We began the project with a combination of user research and stakeholder workshops, as typical in a service design project. For user research, we conducted a structured survey of people online, to have them share their past experiences searching for legal help online and then go through a simulation exercise and share their experiences.[14] Through this survey of nearly 50 adults throughout the US, we began to uncover a trend that would reveal itself more prominently: many people began

13 See more detail on the front-end, back-end approach to service design at Margaret D Hagan, 'A Future Agenda', *Law By Design* (2018) <https://lawbydesign.co/ch-6-future-agenda/> accessed 14 February 2023.

14 Margaret D Hagan, 'The User Experience of the Internet as a Legal Help Service: Defining Standards for the next Generation of User-Friendly Online Legal Services' (2016) 20 Va JL & Tech 395.

their Internet problem-solving on a tech platform like Google Search or a social media site like Yahoo Answers. We also identified that many people never reached the website or content from a public service agency. People were starting on a private tech platform, expressing the need for help with a problem or asking about a certain service, but they were not ending up where they thought they would go. We had assumed most people online would go to a public service agency's website, like from a court, a government agency, or a nonprofit legal aid group. Rather, these organizations' information was rarely appearing to people. Even if our team thought of these organizations as authoritative and high quality, most people did not visit them online when seeking help.

We convened a stakeholder workshop in the autumn of 2015, to do more design research on the challenge topic. Our team invited approximately 25 court leaders, legal aid groups, civic technologists, and data experts together for a day-long session on the largest problems these groups saw with legal help services online, and what opportunities they proposed to work on as priorities.[15] This stakeholder workshop affirmed that the starting challenge of our initiative was worthwhile. The stakeholders agreed that the Internet held the potential to help courts and legal groups better deliver services to the public. Some use cases included helping immigrants through citizenship applications, helping people without lawyers to navigate the court process, or empowering consumers in submitting complaints to the department of justice. Stakeholders agreed that currently many people were not able to find or use these public services, but that it should be a priority to ensure they could.

During this workshop, our team realized that the Better Legal Internet challenge did not fit into the traditional service design framework. Our stakeholders, particularly those who worked in civic technology and data, flagged that our initial vision of possible solutions was overly limited -- and not likely to succeed. If we followed a traditional service design approach, our work would focus on improving public service agencies' communications, technology, and infrastructure. We might help them build better front-end experiences, with websites that have

15 Stanford Legal Design Lab, 'A Better Legal Internet Working Group: Scoping Meeting' (*A Better Legal Internet*, 28 November 2015) <https://betterinternet.law.stanford.edu/2015/11/28/a-better-legal-internet-working-group-scoping-meeting/> accessed 14 February 2023.

better interfaces, technology, and content. But, these civic technologist stakeholders warned us, even if our initiative led to more courts building these better websites, this would not solve a key problem: what the technology platforms would actually show to people.

Even if government agencies and nonprofit groups thought of themselves as authoritative, search engines and social media platforms did not necessarily grant them any authority. The public service agencies were not at the center of the challenge. If we wanted to have the desired policy impact, of connecting people online with high-quality public services information that helped them resolve their life problems, we needed to shift our focus from public service agencies to tech platforms. Our team would have to alter our design process to focus on the tech platforms' policies, data infrastructure, and business models, in addition to the government and nonprofits' policies, technology, and services. Our initiative would have to grapple with a different kind of policy and service design, this time with private, for-profit technology companies.

4. Tech Companies and Public Service Design

Our stakeholders' feedback led our team to begin a new research track, layered onto our traditional service design work: profiling and understanding the technology companies that operate the dominant platforms on the Internet. To solve our public service information challenge, we had to employ qualitative and quantitative design research methods to understand these companies' behaviors, needs, frustrations, and incentives.

To begin this process, we adapted our typical co-design methodology of convening workshops in which mixed stakeholder groups did process mapping, empathy maps, and brainstorming of new solutions for the design challenge. By 2016 and 2017, our team had done enough background research to identify leaders in big tech who had some interest in working on public service information challenges. By doing market research and organizational mapping of technology companies and secondary research of industry publications and conferences, our team could identify specific groups and leaders within search engine companies like Google and Microsoft, as well as social media companies like Reddit, that might have some interest in improving how people find public services help online. We also identified a cross-company nonprofit initiative, of Schema.org, that had a mission in line with ours. The Schema.org project, in which most of the big tech companies participated, aimed to build more common data structures and consistent labeling of information online, so that tech platforms could better match people to the content that could help them.

Our team convened another multi-stakeholder workshop in early 2017, this time with representatives from big tech companies like Google and Microsoft, industry initiatives like Schema.org, and public service agencies in the civil justice space, like courts and legal aid groups.[16] For this two-day workshop, our focus was more precise than our first one. Rather than explore many different needs, use cases, and possible solutions, we narrowed in on the central question of how technology platforms might alter their algorithms, policies, and interfaces to better deliver public service information to the public. Our team no longer framed the challenge as centered on the courts or legal aid groups. Rather, the framing now was on the search engines and social media sites at the center. What could they do, and what could the civil justice community do with them, in order to ensure that the public could find high-quality public service information when they looked online for help with evictions, debts, divorce, deportation, or the like?

5. Design Research into Tech Platform Policymaking

It was during this second round of work that we fully understood that our challenge might need to be framed as a misinformation problem. What we, from our civil justice perspective, had thought about as a public legal education problem (how do public agencies present information about complex legal topics in engaging and user-friendly ways) might need to be reframed as a technology platform policy problem, about how they sort and moderate information. This would change how we could run a human-centered design process to create impactful solu-

16 Stanford Legal Design Lab, 'Better Legal Internet Working Group Meeting' (*A Better Legal Internet*, 28 September 2017) <https://betterinternet.law.stanford.edu/2017/09/28/better-legal-internet-working-group-meeting/> accessed 14 February 2023.

tions. If we were to make an impact, we would need to understand what needs and preferences big tech companies had, as well as what kinds of interventions could work to change their information policies.

Our partners in the tech sector shared with us their outsider's view of our civil justice domain. This helped us to understand how for-profit, worldwide, big tech companies approach problems and policymaking. The design workshop helped us see our group of public service agencies and information challenges the way that tech platform teams might: as one more in a series of information domains. Though our court and legal aid stakeholders were thoroughly immersed in the challenges of getting people crucial information about housing, finances, family, and employment law, and valued this for the public interest impact it could have on society, this was not necessarily compelling to a tech company team. They had many similar professional communities coming to their companies, with complaints, demands, and proposals for how the tech platforms should deal with information in their domain. It was not just our group talking to them about a "Better Legal Internet" for civil justice problem-solving. There were similar teams of doctors, elections commissioners, political researchers, consumer advocates, reproductive rights specialists, and people working in other policy domains, all trying to get on the tech platforms' agenda to get the misinformation problems around their domain improved. The tech company teams did not necessarily know about each of these policy and information domains: what kinds of problems people were searching for, what a 'good' search results page would look like, and what harms or benefits could result.

During the workshop, they recommended that our civil justice community look to analogous professional communities, who had been able to realize changes to search engines and social media sites for misinformation problems in their domains. In particular, our stakeholders urged us to explore how the medical and public health community, and how the voting and elections community, had approached tech platform companies to work on information problems and solutions in their domain. If we wanted to engage in a collaborative design and policy process with the big tech platforms, then they pointed us toward these analogous areas to understand what we should do.

Our second workshop reaffirmed that engaging big tech platforms would be essential to improving public services on the platform. It did not give a step-by-step blueprint of exactly how to engage these companies in the reform of their platforms for civil justice information, in either a 'carrot' approach of collaborations and rewards or a 'stick' approach of accountability and criticisms. Instead, we left that second workshop with a mandate to explore how other analogous professional communities had reformed tech platforms' policies and to map out the levers that public service agencies could have in changing how tech platforms show and prioritize information to the public.

6. Strategies to Engage Big Tech in Public Service Challenges

Our project had now officially transformed into one focused on information. We began to explore the literature on how different policy communities had found misinformation or disinformation problems for topics related to their policies, and then how they worked to solve these information challenges on the Internet. This research was to help us scope possible solutions for our overarching design process. What could we learn from analogous efforts that could guide possible new communication, product, service, or policy designs? Much of the literature about addressing online information problems focused on intentionally misleading or deceptive information on tech platforms. The online information research and policy recommendations often focused on responding to trolls, bots, influencers, or foreign actors attempting to spread harmful information for political reasons or for profit.[17]

The strategies to respond to deliberate misinformation campaigns did not seem entirely relevant to the civil justice information problems online. In our workshops and discussions with legal aid and court experts, we asked lawyers and technologists if they had ever seen deliberate misinformation or disinformation in the civil justice space on the Internet. A few trends emerged. First, some for-profit law firms or legal services groups would label their websites in terms like "legal aid" or buy adwords with keywords like "legal aid" to attract people who were

17 For example, see health misinformation strategies at Vivek H Murthy, 'Confronting Health Misinformation: The U.S. Surgeon General's Advisory on Building a Healthy Information Environment' (2021) <https://www.hhs.gov/sites/default/files/surgeon-general-misinformation-advisory.pdf> accessed 13 February 2023.

seeking out free public services. This kind of misinformation was about mislabeling sites and misleading ads to direct people away from public services and towards private ones. The other misinformation trend we heard about was one without a deliberate actor behind it. We heard from legal aid website administrators who regularly saw search engines mislead people to their local website, with local legal information only relevant to residents of their state - -when the people were in another region or country altogether. This misinformation problem was more about big tech platforms being insensitive to the importance of jurisdiction, and thus mistakenly sending users to information that was wrong or harmful to them.

We thus began to focus on information challenges and misinformation strategies that were more akin to these problems: where big tech platforms may be showing misleading, deceptive, or low quality information to people who were trying to use the platforms to seek help with a life problem. Rarely were these the work of coordinated actors trying to use misinformation for profit or political influence. Rather, the concern was the quality and accuracy of the information the big tech platforms were spotlighting for people. Were the platforms' policies about what to recommend or refer people to ill-equipped to judge what was accurate and reliable? Was the localized, specialized knowledge in the civil justice domain too difficult for the big tech platforms to make sense of and produce quality results around?

7. Strategies to Tackle Misinformation in Voting & Elections Services

We began to frame our challenge as one of a peculiar kind of misinformation: for a complex, fractured topic area that had many special and local rules, services, and documentation, it seemed that big tech platforms built for national or global scale may struggle to know what information to show a person seeking help. For this kind of misinformation, we found some professional communities that could be models for the civil legal justice community and other public service agencies. Through the public-facing accounts of their misinformation research, creation of new information initiatives, and engagement with big tech platforms, we were able to identify strategies for our community to consider.

In the voting and elections domain, we found that professionals had organized a deliberate effort to collaborate with big tech platforms to counteract misinformation and promote authoritative information from public service agencies. This professional community engaged in a data-driven, multistakeholder process that brought government officials, big tech teams, and nonprofit foundations to collaborate on solutions. The Voting Information Project, developed as a collaborative effort between Pew Charitable Trusts, recent graduates of a university's public policy department, big tech platforms like Google, and local election officials.[18] It brought these groups together to create a coordinated, standardized, national dataset of election rules and procedures. This central database of information can be considered the 'authority' on voting information in the country. It provides specific procedures, locations, requirements, and other actionable information to help people ensure they can participate in elections in their local jurisdiction.

The database is accessible to big tech platforms like Google Search, Instagram, Facebook, or Twitter so that they can know reliably what local voting information to display to their users. Teams at the big tech platforms can take the verified, standardized data and then integrate it into special banner ads, search engine responses, voice assistant replies, or even as a reference point when another post is flagged for misinformation. The voting community's database provides a convenient authority for the big tech, to help their teams rely on this community to give detailed, accurate information when their users are seeking it, or when their users might be seeing incorrect or harmful information on this topic.

Building such a national, standardized database is a major effort. It entails working with local officials throughout thousands of jurisdictions around the country, to get their buy-in and participation, as well as their follow-through in providing their local information into the standardized data format. It also entails quality review, to ensure that the information is (and continues to be) reliable, so that the big tech platforms can rely on it without incident. It is an ongoing effort to maintain quality, as rules, contact points, hours, and other details may change.

18 Voting Information Project, 'VIP Projects' (2022) <https://www.votinginfoproject.org/projects> accessed 9 February 2022.

This database approach was not the only strategy that big tech companies took to combat elections-related misinformation. Currently, social media big tech like Meta have extensive suites of automated and human review of information about elections, particularly to deal with bots and coordinated disinformation campaigns.[19] The structured data about public services related to where to vote, how to vote, and what to bring, were more analogous to the civil justice space. We still took note of the extensive counter-misinformation strategies that search engines and social media sites used, but tended to focus in on the strategies to promote high quality, local, actionable information for a person with a query (rather than trying to spot and fight 'bad actors' trying to spread disinformation).

The elections community's misinformation strategies offered one blueprint for the civil justice community to follow. There could be a similar collaborative effort among technology companies, civic leaders, and legal subject matter experts to develop a system that identifies and vets authoritative information about how people can make use of their local court and legal aid systems to address their housing, money, family, and other problems. This information should be represented as structured data, in labeled databases that laid out what rules, documents, timelines, and services were relevant for which jurisdictions and problem types. Once the civil justice information was consistently structured and saved in one central place, then it could be opened as an API for big tech platforms to use. Search engines might use the standardized legal help data in call-outs or banners on search results pages, to flag authoritative and trustworthy answers. Social media could counter any possible misinformation with data from this API. People visiting these platforms would be connected with local, authoritative info -- perhaps without ever having to click on a court or legal aid website.

This strategy, to sum up, was about organizing the local leaders of the professional community, setting a common data standard, managing the community and automation techniques to get each local jurisdictions' information correctly recorded in the standard, and then establishing the legitimacy and governance apparatus of this new central database

19 Meta, 'Preparing for Elections' (2022) <https://about.meta.com/actions/preparing-for-elections-on-facebook/> accessed 14 February 2023.

and API. This strategy was collaborative and technocratic. The goal was to change big tech platforms' policies and behaviors by offering them a useful, authoritative API of structured data that helped the platforms serve their customers better, and that outsourced the granting of authority to the professional community so that the big tech platforms' teams did not have to make difficult decisions about who held authority on a topic. In this strategy, the onus was to make fractured, localized professional communities somewhat unified, at least about standardized procedural data and agreeing on the authority and importance of the central database and API.

8. Strategies to Tackle Misinformation in Medical Services

In the medical domain, professional communities have dedicated extensive research and implementation strategies to change how big tech platforms respond to people's health information queries and posts. Like with the elections domain, many of the strategies have been collaborative, with big tech teams working with medical institutions, individual experts, and government agencies to identify risks, harms, and better practices.

In 2015, Google Search team leaders shared that they worked with in-house medical doctors at Google and the Mayo Clinic institution to create a new intervention to prevent medical misinformation from appearing on the search results page.[20] Unlike with the voting, this intervention was not about sourcing a central database of structured, local procedural information. Rather, for medical information challenges, the big tech team had identified common diseases and problems, like concussions, celiac diseases, or pink eye. They then created customized content to display to people searching for these issues. Their team of experts compiled, curated, and reviewed the information that would be shown in special knowledge panels to users. In effect, people who searched for keywords that indicate a common health issue would not be shown the usual search results.

---

20 Prem Ramaswami, 'A Remedy for Your Health-Related Questions: Health Info in the Knowledge Graph' (*Google: The Keyword Blog*, 15 February 2015) 1 <https://blog.google/products/search/health-info-knowledge-graph/> accessed 26 April 2021.

In the medical domain, big tech platforms like Google decided to change their default policy, by not deferring to its standard search rank algorithm's prediction. Rather, they decided to give special treatment to this topic area, invest in expert content-creation and review (even including special medical illustrations they commissioned), and to give large amounts of the search results page's real estate to this curated knowledge panel rather than to ads or top results. Since 2015, big tech platforms have continued to build and expand on this strategy, by working with official institutions and experts as trusted partners to provide curated content about the given topic.[21]

Social media platforms like Facebook began to track pages and users who shared misinformation, including around vaccines, COVID-19, climate change, and elections, to create interventions that might slow or stop misinformation -- including context references linking to independent fact-checkers or warnings from the platform itself that posts might be false.[22] Twitter also instituted a medical misinformation policy to flag or contextualize tweets that may include misleading information about health.[23] This policy ended in November 2022, with the change in ownership of the tech platform.[24]

This amount of policy change and labor for the medical domain may have been a result of a combination of factors. It could be that the medical community created extensive research that showed how many people were seeking health information on the Internet, highlighting the scale of the problem.[25] Another reason for this policy activity may be

21 Google Search Help, 'Medical Information on Google ' (2023) <https://support.google.com/websearch/answer/2364942?hl=en#zippy=%2Cmedical-information-sources> accessed 14 February 2023.

22 Meta, 'Taking Action Against People Who Repeatedly Share Misinformation' (*Meta Newsroom*, 26 May 2021) <https://about.fb.com/news/2021/05/taking-action-against-people-who-repeatedly-share-misinformation/> accessed 14 February 2023.

23 The policy was at https://help.twitter.com/en/rulesand-policies/medical-misinformation-policy but it no longer exists there.

24 Associated Press, 'Twitter's COVID Misinformation Policy Will No Longer Be Enforced' (*NPR Technology*, 29 November 2022) <https://www.npr.org/2022/11/29/1139822833/twitter-covid-misinformation-policy-not-enforced> accessed 13 February 2023.

25 Lila J Finney Rutten and others, 'Online Health Information Seeking Among US

because of how many government officials, journalists, and researchers published on how dangerous health misinformation can be to individuals and to society, and how frequently this misinformation was appearing on big tech platforms.[26] This emphasis on the size of the misinformation problem, and the level of harm that misinformation could cause, was likely a key factor in the big tech platforms adjusting their algorithms, interfaces, and rules around medical information.

From our research and conversations about how the medical community had been able to change big tech platform's policies, we identified a few strategies. One was to create research and public discussion about exactly what was happening with user's use of the Internet, how big tech platforms provided information on these topics, what specific misinformation dynamics were occurring, and what harms could result. In order to get tech companies to change their policies, one strategy is to launch a coherent research agenda in a professional community that could give a handle on key breakdowns, issues, and behavior patterns. This research and discussion could then both help the tech teams understand what solutions might be possible, and also publicly pressure them to address the misinformation problems that had been officially documented and publicized.

A second strategy in the medical community mirrored that of the elections community: investing in common data standards for their community's topics. In the medical domain, experts worked directly with a nonprofit organization, Schema.org, whose members include leading big tech platforms like Google, Yahoo, and Microsoft. Medical leaders from universities like Harvard and Duke, along with government groups like the National Center for Biotechnology Information, worked with big tech platforms' teams through the Schema.org nonprofit apparatus and the World Wide Web Consortium (W3C) that focuses on Internet standards.[27] This collaboration between medical leaders and tech teams

---

Adults: Measuring Progress Toward a Healthy People 2020 Objective' (2019) 134 Public Health Reports 617.

26 See, for example, Murthy (n 17).

27 Aaron Brown, 'New Proposal: Health & Medical Extensions to Schema.Org from Aaron Brown on 2012-05-14 (Public-Vocabs@w3.Org from May 2012)' (*W3C*, 2012) <https://lists.w3.org/Archives/Public/public-vocabs/2012May/0057.html> accessed 14 February 2023.

led to new data standards to represent health and medical information, as a standardized schema. This health and medical schema could then be applied to authoritative resources (like government or hospital websites), so that search engines and social media could better identify and make sense of the information they were sharing, and match it to people's searches.[28] The schema provided an infrastructure to improve big tech platforms' ability to serve quality results to their users, avoid mismatches, and prevent other misinformation harms. The health/medical schema was formally integrated into the Schema.org standards, which the large search engines all use in their crawling of the Internet and their search rank policies. It is notable that no other professional communities have a specialized schema for their topics included in the Schema.org standard.[29] The medical community, though, was able to engage with the tech platform teams to create this extensive, coordinated data standard that could alter the platforms' policies around medical topics.

A third strategy was to present a coherent group of experts who could represent the professional community as 'authorities', who could create, review, and approve content for the big tech platforms to show to users. This effort in the medical community has been more extensive than in the voting community. Perhaps because of the huge number of health issues and complexity around symptoms and consequences, compared to the more straightforward and procedural information about elections, this community has had a different approach to preparing information for tech platforms to use. Rather than creating one central database with an API like the voting information project, the medical community instead has developed ongoing relationships between its private and public institutions and the tech companies themselves. They have an ongoing content review and creation relationship, to be able to create authoritative content and also to respond to possible misinformation.

28 Schema.org, 'Documentation for Health/Medical Types' (2023) <https://schema.org/docs/meddocs.html> accessed 14 February 2023.

29 See a high level overview of the schemas on Schema.org. https://schema.org/docs/schemas.html Most are general labels that could apply to most all kinds of organizations, services, creative works, or events. Of all the possible topic areas (like government services, politics, elections, education, the environment or beyond) only the health and medical field has its own specialized data standard within Schema.org.

These strategies taken from the medical domain might indicate that the civil justice community should invest in research about what kinds of misinformation problems are happening for their topics and users. The community might also try to make a more coherent network of experts who could advise the tech platforms. All of this points to more organization of the professional community, so that it would be easier to engage with the tech companies. Also, as we learned from the elections community, creating common data standards in partnership with big tech platform teams could also lead to collaborative new policy-making about what the platforms show to people and how they address misinformation.

More concrete data would be needed about what people are searching for in this domain, what the tech platforms show them, and what harms and information problems are occurring on the platforms. Only if there was reliable knowledge about the tech platforms' performance, and explanation of why it was meaningful, concerning or harmful, would there be a way to convince tech platform teams to be interested in this area.

9. Researching the Tech Platforms' Policies on Authority & Importance

Our research into analogous domains like voting and medical information helped us see professional communities' approaches to changing tech platforms' policies. These accounts of successful strategies could help us deduce how tech platforms' teams carried out policymaking. How did they decide which kinds of topics and services merited attention, labor by their company teams, and special treatment on their platform? How did they decide what kinds of information and sources to designate as high quality or authoritative on their platform? How did they choose to give some organizations or topic areas special treatment in their interface designs, or adjustment of their algorithm?

As many researchers have identified before, tech platforms like search engines and social media sites are political.[30] Even if the choice of what

30 Lucas D Introna and Helen Nissenbaum, 'Shaping the Web: Why the Politics of Search Engines Matters' (2000) 16 The Information Society 169; Laura Ann Granka, 'The Politics of Search: A Decade Retrospective' (2010) 26 Information Society 364.

Siri says back to a person, what Google Search ranks as the top, or what Instagram shows in a feed is governed by technical systems, the humans within the tech companies have designed the algorithms and interfaces to prioritize some organizations and topics as more important and authoritative than others. Our Better Legal Internet design team saw that some communities, like the medical and voting professional communities, had been able to use a mix of accountability and collaboration strategies to affect big tech platforms' policies. Their strategies led to changes in what was shown or spoken to users of big tech platforms on designated topics. It changed how possible harmful misinformation was flagged or removed. It changed how professionals could do outreach on important, timely topics like upcoming elections, vaccination campaigns, or masking mandates -- by having the tech platforms prioritize this information and proactively show it to their millions of users.

These public accounts of how and why big tech platform teams collaborated with professional communities helped us create some hypotheses of what the platforms' internal policies on authority and importance were. The accounts showed that the teams were often motivated about improving the quality of high-stakes information online, to prevent harm that could result if their platform users were shown misleading, false, or confusing information on a topic. They were also motivated to fix quality problems, where outside groups called out the platform for showing incorrect, irrelevant, or harmful misinformation to its users. In addition, they seemed to be motivated to collaborate with well-organized professional communities that could offer coherent decisions about what kinds of information were quality, authoritative, or harmful. It seemed that, especially on high-stakes public service matters, the tech teams wanted to be able to have a trustworthy, third-party organization make judgment calls about authority and quality, so that they would not have to make these specialized judgments and then possibly face reproach from users, journalists, or government institutions.

These policy values and motivations were all suppositions our team deduced. We could not know for sure about how big tech platforms' executives and product teams decided which topic areas to invest specialized resources in, when and how to change their algorithms or interfaces, or which organizations to engage as authorities. Private companies' policy-making happens within a black box, with little public transparency about how or why their decisions are made.

That said, our design team did find some documents from big tech platforms that laid out their information policies with some clarity: training manuals. Our team identified a publicly-available internal document used by Google Search teams to train new staff and contractors whose job it is to manually review websites and score them for quality.[31] This internal document gave clear insight into their official policies about what kinds of topics deserved greater attention, content curation, and engineering resources to prevent misinformation harms. The document encouraged website raters to use a "YMYL" or "Your Money Or Your Life" policy to evaluate the topics being discussed on a given website. The policy laid out that if the topic would strongly impact a person's finances, personal security, health, or other high-stakes interest, then any website should be evaluated with more scrutiny or care. The search engine results might also reflect this YMYL policy. If the company teams thinks that a given topic (like, vaccine information, or a possible eviction) is sufficiently "YMYL", then they might make the search engine results page more populated with public services, they might take all ads off, or they might manually put a hotline phone number at the top of the results in a call-out box.

The other key official policy we found, at least at Google Search, was that of E-E-A-T: expertise, experience, authoritativeness, and trustworthiness. Google Search trained its website rater teams to evaluate whether web content was created by people who could demonstrate these E-E-A-T factors, especially if the content was about a YMYL topic. The Google Search team gave the example of a user searching online about how to file their taxes.[32] The platform has a policy that this topic is YMYL because it will have major consequences for a person's finances and compliance with the law (as well as possible risks of financial pen-

31 Google Search, 'Search Quality Evaluator General Guidelines' (2022) <https://static.googleusercontent.com/media/guidelines.raterhub.com/en//searchqualityevaluatorguidelines.pdf> accessed 14 February 2023.

32 Google Developers, 'Our Latest Update to the Quality Rater Guidelines: E-A-T Gets an Extra E for Experience ' (*Google Search Central*, 15 December 2022) <https://developers.google.com/search/blog/2022/12/google-raters-guidelines-e-e-a-t> accessed 14 February 2023.

alties or criminal violations). Because the topic is YMYL, then the search raters should pay particular attention to content about tax filing, by rating content and sites higher if they can demonstrate higher E-E-A-T.

Internal policies like YMYL and E-E-A-T resonated with what our team identified in the medical and voting domains. The professional communities had gathered data and presented information about why their domain's topics were YMYL. They could demonstrate that misinformation problems were occurring on the platforms, and that incorrect, misleading or deceptive information in this topic area would have significant harm to people's money, life, and stability. Likely, the tech companies also had data about the volume of misinformation problems occurring on the platform, or they could find this data once the professional community published reports, held meetings, or approached them with misinformation concerns.

The professional community also organized their domain to better supply tech companies with E-E-A-T content. They organized experts from across many jurisdictions and sub-domains to increase the online content they were creating, to present this content in standardized and coordinated ways, and to engage with tech companies through official partnerships.

10. Public Service Design Focus on Infrastructure

With this design research into big tech platform policymaking, our Better Legal Internet team changed how we approached our typical human-centered design process to improve public services. Rather than focus our interventions solely on designing excellent websites and content with courts and legal aid groups, we prioritized the design of infrastructure. If our civil justice community was to reach its goals of building awareness and uptake of public services like legal aid, self-help guides, and court services, then the highest impact was likely to be in creating coherent research, information, and organizational infrastructure in our community. Following from the voting and medical communities, we needed to invest in making our professional community and policy domain more coherent. Coordinated infrastructure would not only strengthen our professional community, but it would give this community power to either hold big tech platforms accountable in an adversarial way, or to engage big tech platforms in collaborative policymaking and design interventions.

Our Better Legal Internet team ran several more workshops and stakeholder groups among civil justice professionals, in which we presented the strategies we had gleaned from analogous professional communities and from the tech companies' internal training documents. From these sessions, we then identified the infrastructure interventions to pilot in order to have an impact on public services on the Internet.

Research Infrastructure. We identified that the civil justice space had very little empirical research on what people were searching for online, what misinformation problems were occurring on big tech platforms, and what harms or risks were occurring. Thus, our Better Legal Internet team identified research methods to begin gathering this data. With the support of the Pew Charitable Trusts and collaboration with computer scientists who had previous experience with auditing tech platforms' political information policies, our team designed and launched legal help search audits. These audits involved thousands of searches on Google for common civil justice queries, like "help I've been evicted" or "how do I get a restraining order", from different zip codes. The audits record what Google shows to people in response to these queries, including the domain, the url, and the type of interface presentation.

These audits produce empirical evidence about what a platform is prioritizing for our topic areas, what misinformation problems are occurring and with what frequency, and what opportunities exist. For example, our search audits gave us evidence that Google was rarely showing public interest websites to the public, but was rather favoring national commercial entities for justice searches.[33] They also revealed that Google was frequently showing information from the incorrect jurisdiction, which could lead to people following the wrong rules, losing their case, and facing legal harm. More research is needed about people's behavior on big tech platforms, the platforms' behavior, harms, and opportunities, but the search audit research has given an initial set of evidence that

---

33 Margaret D Hagan and Nora Al Haider, 'Does Googling Justice Work: Auditing Search Engine Algorithm's Quality for Legal Help Searches (Forthcoming)' [2023] UCLA Journal of Law and Technology.

can be used to hold platforms accountable and also to encourage them to consider this domain as a priority, for possible special focus and labor.

Data Infrastructure. Our team compared the civil justice information landscape to that in the medical and voting space. We lacked a common machine-readable data standard to represent the different life problems that people experience, and which they might ask about on a search engine or social media site. To this end, our team designed the Legal Issues Taxonomy (LIST) to represent the many different civil justice problems and queries that people might have.[34] LIST built on top of many previous legal problem taxonomies that legal aid groups and funders used in order to manage their case systems or funding requirements.

In addition, our team designed another data infrastructure intervention: Legal Schema markup.[35] Following the medical community's example, we identified how legal information and services might need specialized markup in Schema.org, so that there could be accurate and consistent representations of legal topics that search engines and social media platforms could automatically understand. We integrated the LIST problem codes into the Legal Schema markup, so that tech platforms' automated systems could understand what specific problems certain government and legal aid websites could help with. We also communicated the Legal Schema Markup design to teams at Schema.org nonprofit, the W3C community, and Google Search teams directly, following the example of the medical community.

Our hope was that this data infrastructure would present our civil justice domain as coherent and accessible to the tech platforms, so they might prioritize new algorithmic policies and design interventions to improve the quality of information they showed to their users. The problem goes back to the black box of tech platforms' policymaking, though. Even if our community creates a data infrastructure and presents it to the platforms, we cannot know if and how they take note of it, or if they

34 Margaret D Hagan, 'Every Legal Problem That Exists: The Legal Help Taxonomy for Machine Learning' (*Legal Design and Innovation*, 4 September 2018) <https://medium.com/legal-design-and-innovation/every-legal-problem-that-exists-the-legal-help-taxonomy-for-machine-learning-3c9f2f75460> accessed 14 February 2023.

35 Stanford Legal Design Lab, 'Markup Your Site with Legal Schema' (*Better Legal Internet*, 2019) <https://betterinternet.law.stanford.edu/markup-your-site/> accessed 14 February 2023.

will ultimately engage in reform, redesigns, or other changes based on our intervention.

Expert Infrastructure. The final area for our infrastructure design was on creating a more coherent set of experts with which to create high-quality, authoritative content and also to interface with tech companies. Our team designed new expert cohorts, to begin building a clear national network out of the civil justice community's highly localized, fragmented organization.

First, we created a small cohort of legal aid groups to work with us on implementing data standards and running search audits.[36] We then expanded this informal cohort into two more formalized groups. The Legal Internet Steering Committee is an invite-only expert group of leaders from courts, government agencies, legal aid, university labs, nonprofit technology consultants, for profit technology providers, and others who have a demonstrated record of working on public interest justice innovation. The LISC group meets quarterly to discuss how civil justice issues are playing out on the Internet, what research is happening, what misinformation problems are arising, and what possible policies, technologies, or other interventions might improve how legal help is provided online. The LISC group is one that could potentially partner with big tech platforms' teams, like the voting and medical communities have. It could also issue reports, write editorials, and hold tech platforms accountable for how they perform on civil justice.

The second expert community is the Legal Help Online Cohort. This community is for the groups that administer public services websites for civil justice issues. This includes web administrators, technologists, designers, and content-writers. Our goal with this cohort is to educate them on tech companies' policies, and empower them to make the strongest possible websites to rank high on the platforms and effectively connect with their target audience. Even if we cannot officially get tech companies to change their policies around civil justice topics, the Legal Help Online Cohort can make the strongest possible content for the current policies -- with strong search engine optimization strategies, con-

36 Nora Al Haider, 'Using Schema.Org to Help People Find Legal Aid' (*Legal Design and Innovation*, 30 January 2023) <https://medium.com/legal-design-and-innovation/using-schema-org-to-help-people-find-legal-aid-8e92e0ff6d19> accessed 14 February 2023.

tent that can easily be excerpted by Siri or Google Knowledge Panels, or that can be shared on social media. This Cohort might also become a future source of official, authorized content, like has happened with the medical community's official content collaborations with Google.

11. Directions for Improving the Impact of Public Service Design

These three areas of infrastructure are ongoing, strategic design interventions. When we began our design effort to improve how people find public services information online about civil justice problems, we did not think this was the kind of intervention we would be designing. We had been following the service design framework that many other government agencies and innovation labs have -- about offering engaging, user-friendly apps, documents, and services to help a person through a complex system. Our team had expected to follow this pathway, and end up designing interventions like a user-friendly website, an intuitive interactive form-filling app, a supportive hotline text message flow, or a usable process map to explain people's rights and options.

From our design journey over the past 8 years, though, we advise other public services designers to prioritize infrastructure interventions in addition to these more traditional kinds of service, communication, and technology interventions. This is especially true as big tech platforms play a growing role as brokers of authority and information. One exchange from a Better Legal Internet design workshop is particularly enlightening. A state supreme court justice was speaking with a search engine platform engineer. The justice asked, why is my court's webpage not the first result on your search engine, if someone in my jurisdiction is searching for help with a lawsuit or their rights? The engineer responded that the court's webpage was likely not very good. If more people had clicked on it, spent time on it, and linked to it, then that would have demonstrated that the website had valuable content to users. The fact that the court's webpage rarely appeared on the first page of search results was proof to the search engine that it wasn't user-centered, and shouldn't be prioritized in the results. The justice replied, my court is the local authority, and you should be putting it at the top of the results by default. The engineer replied that they would only do so if the website proved valuable to users.

This exchange highlights some broader trends that government agencies, nonprofits, and other public service groups must be aware of. First, these public service agencies' authority is not always a given. Big tech platforms, especially search engines and social media sites, often are the place where people go to understand their problems, get information, and decide what is reliable. The private platforms thus have much of the authority, and they can decide which organizations or experts to delegate authority to. A court official cannot order a tech company to put their website as the first result. The tech platform has its own policy-making process that is largely opaque.

That said, there are strategies to engage big tech platforms' executives and product teams in improving how public services information appears to their users and in addressing misinformation harms that may occur. This paper summarizes many of these specific strategies and messaging frames that span the adversarial, that focus on accountability for misinformation frequency and harms, and the collaborative, that focus on ways that professional communities can work with private companies to improve information quality and benefit the public.

For those working in an area in which they are attempting to communicate with the public, to get them access to rights, services, documents, and other important public interest help, they might expand upon efforts to improve customer experience and usability. To have maximum impact, they might invest in three key areas of infrastructure -- empirical research, data standards, and expert organization -- so that they might pressure and collaborate with private technology companies to know the scope of their misinformation problems, have reliable and coordinated information to offer people online, and to have ongoing design work that responds to new technological advancements and misinformation threats. Infrastructure design is not easy or straightforward, but it will provide the basis for better policy-making and service designs in the future.

Bibliography

Al Haider N, 'Using Schema.Org to Help People Find Legal Aid' (*Legal Design and Innovation*, 30 January 2023) <https://medium.com/legal-design-and-innovation/using-schema-org-to-help-people-find-legal-aid-8e92e0ff6d19> accessed 14 February 2023

Allio L, 'Design Thinking for Public Service Excellence' (2014) <http://www.undp.org/content/undp/en/home/librarypage/capacity-building/global-centre-for-public-service-excellence/DesignThinking.html> accessed 13 February 2023

Associated Press, 'Twitter's COVID Misinformation Policy Will No Longer Be Enforced' (*NPR Technology*, 29 November 2022) <https://www.npr.org/2022/11/29/1139822833/twitter-covid-misinformation-policy-not-enforced> accessed 13 February 2023

Auxier B and Anderson M, 'Social Media Use in 2021' (*Pew Research Center*, 7 April 2021) <https://www.pewresearch.org/internet/2021/04/07/social-media-use-in-2021/> accessed 20 January 2022

Bovet A and Makse HA, 'Influence of Fake News in Twitter during the 2016 US Presidential Election' (2019) 10 Nature Communications

Brown A, 'New Proposal: Health & Medical Extensions to Schema.Org from Aaron Brown on 2012-05-14 (Public-Vocabs@w3.Org from May 2012)' (*W3C*, 2012) <https://lists.w3.org/Archives/Public/public-vocabs/2012May/0057.html> accessed 14 February 2023

California Courts Judicial Council, 'California Courts Digital Services and Self Help Redesign - RFP' (2019) <https://www.courts.ca.gov/42412.htm> accessed 14 February 2023

Courchesne L, Ilhardt J and Shapiro JN, 'Review of Social Science Research on the Impact of Countermeasures against Influence Operations' (2021) 2(5) Harvard Kennedy School Misinformation Review 1

Farrell J, McConnell K and Brulle R, 'Evidence-Based Strategies to Combat Scientific Misinformation' (2019) 9 Nat Clim Change 191

Finney Rutten LJ and others, 'Online Health Information Seeking Among US Adults: Measuring Progress Toward a Healthy People 2020 Objective' (2019) 134 Public Health Reports 617

Fuller M and Lochard A, 'Public Policy Labs in European Union Member States' (2016) <http://kokeilevasuomi.fi/documents/1777665/1915666/final+report+w+identifiers.pdf/c99c823c-e125-491e-9734-0fbf3d379976>

Golebiewski M and Boyd D, 'Data Voids: Where Missing Data Can Easily Be Exploited' (2018) <https://datasociety.net/about/#funding.> accessed 13 February 2023

Google, 'How Google Fights Disinformation' (2019) <https://shorturl.at/tCDN7> accessed 7 February 2023

Google Developers, 'Our Latest Update to the Quality Rater Guidelines: E-A-T Gets an Extra E for Experience ' (*Google Search Central*, 15 December 2022) <https://developers.google.com/search/blog/2022/12/google-raters-guidelines-e-e-a-t> accessed 14 February 2023

Google Search, 'Search Quality Evaluator General Guidelines' (2022) <https://static.googleusercontent.com/media/guidelines.raterhub.com/en//searchqualityevaluatorguidelines.pdf> accessed 14 February 2023

Google Search Help, 'Medical Information on Google ' (2023) <https://support.google.com/websearch/answer/2364942?hl=en#zippy=%2Cmedical-information-sources> accessed 14 February 2023

Granka LA, 'The Politics of Search: A Decade Retrospective' (2010) 26 Information Society 364

Green Y and others, 'Evidence-Based Misinformation Interventions: Challenges and Opportunities for Measurement and Collaboration' (2023) <https://carnegieendowment.org/2023/01/09/evidence-based-misinformation-interventions-challenges-and-opportunities-for-measurement-and-collaboration-pub-88661> accessed 3 February 2023

Hagan MD, 'Every Legal Problem That Exists: The Legal Help Taxonomy for Machine Learning' (*Legal Design and Innovation*, 4 September 2018) <https://medium.com/legal-design-and-innovation/every-legal-problem-that-exists-the-legal-help-taxonomy-for-machine-learning-3c9f2f75460> accessed 14 February 2023

—, 'A Future Agenda', *Law By Design* (2018) <https://lawbydesign.co/ch-6-future-agenda/> accessed 14 February 2023

—, 'A Human-Centered Design Approach to Access to Justice Generating New Prototypes and Hypotheses for Intervention to Make Courts User-Friendly' (2018) 6 Indiana Journal of Law and Social Equality 199

—, 'The User Experience of the Internet as a Legal Help Service: Defining Standards for the next Generation of User-Friendly Online Legal Services' (2016) 20 Va JL & Tech 395

— and Al Haider N, 'Does Googling Justice Work: Auditing Search Engine Algorithm's Quality for Legal Help Searches (Forthcoming)' [2023] UCLA Journal of Law and Technology

– and Li Y, 'Legal Help Search Audit: Are Search Engines Effective Brokers of Legal Information?' [2020] SSRN Electronic Journal <https://papers.ssrn.com/abstract=3623333> accessed 14 February 2023

– and Ozenc K, 'A Design Space for Legal and Systems Capability' (2020) 36 Design Issues 6

Introna LD and Nissenbaum H, 'Shaping the Web: Why the Politics of Search Engines Matters' (2000) 16 The Information Society 169

Kimbell L and Bailey J, 'Prototyping and the New Spirit of Policy-Making' (2017) 13 CoDesign 214

Meta, 'Preparing for Elections' (2022) <https://about.meta.com/actions/preparing-for-elections-on-facebook/> accessed 14 February 2023

–, 'Taking Action Against People Who Repeatedly Share Misinformation' (*Meta Newsroom*, 26 May 2021) <https://about.fb.com/news/2021/05/taking-action-against-people-who-repeatedly-share-misinformation/> accessed 14 February 2023

Murthy VH, 'Confronting Health Misinformation: The U.S. Surgeon General's Advisory on Building a Healthy Information Environment' (2021) <https://www.hhs.gov/sites/default/files/surgeon-general-misinformation-advisory.pdf> accessed 13 February 2022

Pennycook G and others, 'The Implied Truth Effect: Attaching Warnings to a Subset of Fake News Headlines Increases Perceived Accuracy of Headlines without Warnings' (2020) 66 Management Science 4944

Pew Research Center, 'Information Searches That Solve Problems' (2007) <https://www.pewresearch.org/internet/2007/12/30/information-searches-that-solve-problems/> accessed 9 December 2019

Ramaswami P, 'A Remedy for Your Health-Related Questions: Health Info in the Knowledge Graph' (*Google: The Keyword Blog*, 15 February 2015) 1 <https://blog.google/products/search/health-info-knowledge-graph/> accessed 26 April 2021

Schema.org, 'Documentation for Health/Medical Types' (2023) <https://schema.org/docs/meddocs.html> accessed 14 February 2023

Sillence E and Briggs P, 'Please Advise: Using the Internet for Health and Financial Advice' (2007) 23 Computers in Human Behavior 727

Stanford Legal Design Lab, 'A Better Legal Internet: Increase People's Access to Justice Online' (2015) <https://betterinternet.law.stanford.edu/> accessed 14 February 2023

—, 'Better Legal Internet Working Group Meeting' (*A Better Legal Internet*, 28 September 2017) <https://betterinternet.law.stanford.edu/2017/09/28/better-legal-internet-working-group-meeting/> accessed 14 February 2023

—, 'A Better Legal Internet Working Group: Scoping Meeting' (*A Better Legal Internet*, 28 November 2015) <https://betterinternet.law.stanford.edu/2015/11/28/a-better-legal-internet-working-group-scoping-meeting/> accessed 14 February 2023

—, 'Markup Your Site with Legal Schema' (*Better Legal Internet*, 2019) <https://betterinternet.law.stanford.edu/markup-your-site/> accessed 14 February 2023

Stickdorn M and others, *This Is Service Design Doing* (O'Reilly 2017) <https://www.thisisservicedesigndoing.com/methods> accessed 22 November 2018

Suarez-Lledo V and Alvarez-Galvez J, 'Prevalence of Health Misinformation on Social Media: Systematic Review' (2021) 23 Journal of Medical Internet Research

Voting Information Project, 'VIP Projects' (2022) <https://www.votinginfoproject.org/projects> accessed 9 February 2022

Young SD and Mancini DJ, 'Memorandum for Heads of Executive Departments and Agencies on Improving Access to Public Benefits Programs through the Paperwork Reduction Act' (2022) <https://www.whitehouse.gov/omb/information-regulatory-affairs/federal-> accessed 10 November 2022

11. A CRITICAL ASSESSMENT OF THE NOTION OF LEGAL DESIGN THROUGH THE CASE OF "LES SURLIGNEURS", A LEGAL-CHECKING MEDIA OUTLET

Vincent Couronne, Joachim Savin, Marie-Sophie de Clippele and Apolline Le Gall

Abstract

In the wake of numerous fact-checking initiatives, the association "*Les Surligneurs*", founded in France in 2017 and disseminating in Europe (Belgium), aims to carry out legal-checking, i.e. to verify the conformity with the law of statements made by public figures, particularly in the media. Legal-checking also aims to shed light on the political debate through legal issues. The project follows some clear design patterns (yellow colour, a recognisable logo, the structure of the short articles to be more readable, etc.) and could therefore be seen as part of the legal design movement. However, the project *Les Surligneurs* was created without knowing about the legal design movement. This movement only started to gain interest in France in 2018-2019. Moreover, the project did not really follow the canonical approach (inherited from design thinking) of a legal design project: it was not the result of a user-research approach. This case study therefore raises the following questions: to which academic field does design thinking belong, and which frame should we use to look at projects at the intersection of design and law? These issues will be critically assessed in this paper, paying attention to the rise of the legal design movement and the real improvement in terms of meeting users' needs.

1. Introduction

This article aims to provide an in-depth exploration and critique of the concept of legal design and its current utilisation in France. It stems from our experience as involuntary participants in legal design through the *Les Surligneurs* project. Our motivation to write this piece arises from our respective professional backgrounds—Marie-Sophie de Clippele and Vincent Couronne in law, and Joachim Savin and Apolline Le Gall in design—collaborating and offering diverse viewpoints on the methods and outcomes associated with this evolving practice.

Since 2017, we have observed a gradual proliferation of the term 'legal design' within our professional circles. While the legal domain has shown justified enthusiasm in embracing novel methodologies, catering to user interests, and acknowledging the human aspects and various touchpoints of law, the design sphere has not paralleled this same level of engagement. As an industrial designer with a background from a National High Education institution, Joachim Savin, one of the co-authors, noticed numerous constraints that prompted critical questions: Firstly, why has this approach gained significant traction in the legal field despite its evident design limitations? Secondly, how can we cultivate a professional culture in legal design that truly embodies the essence of design?

Drawing from the *Les Surligneurs* case, this paper will explore alternative methods of collaboration between lawyers and designers within legal design projects. Indeed, we noticed some limitations of legal design, some stemming from design thinking principles and some specific to its implementation in the French context. Finally, we will examine how *Les Surligneurs* unveils novel challenges that extend beyond the conventional boundaries of Design or Law.

2.* Les Surligneurs*: a Legal-Checking Media Outlet Designed for Public Debate

2.1. Genesis, Missions, and Design of Les Surligneurs

In the wake of numerous fact-checking initiatives, the association *Les Surligneurs* was founded in France in 2017 by flatmates Vincent Couronne, a researcher in law, and Joachim Savin, an industrial designer. Before that, Vincent Couronne had started a blog in August 2016 on "*Contre-vérités en droit européen*" ("Counter-truths in European law"). Playing with the idea of a radio station, Couronne and Savin eventually changed the blog to *Les Surligneurs* and aimed for a bigger scope: to refocus the public debate on the law, what it says, what it allows or forbids and how politicians should take the law into consideration and respect it when making statements in the media. *Les Surligneurs* started as a university website and found immediate success as the project was launched during the French presidential elections in 2017. It drew the attention of journalists, who were eager to use legal arguments to counter political statements. Yet, the project at that time attracted less attention from the larger public.

Les Surligneurs carries out legal-checking, i.e. checks on the conformity with the law of statements made by public figures, particularly in the media. Legal-checking also aims to shed light on the political debate through legal issues.

These two objectives are achieved through "legal highlighting" (*surlignages*) or "legal clarification" (éclairages) operations, in which law professors, or students under the supervision of professors, or legal practitioners, write short articles, which are easily accessible to the public. The legal issues are then clearly apparent: legally false, problematic, to be qualified, incomplete, etc. Statements are "highlighted", and politically debated subjects are "clarified" in law. These articles are then published online (https://lessurligneurs.eu/) and disseminated on social networks, all with a view to feeding the public debate. The association of *Les Surligneurs* has grown over the years and now has a full team with Vincent Couronne and Joachim Savin still involved as co-founders and Couronne also acting as publications director. Moreover, several enthusiasts have joined the board of directors, including Professor Jean-Paul Markus, who acts as editing director, Tania Racho, as training director, and Audrey Darsonville, Emma Cacciamani, and Juliette Toussaint, respectively acting as president, vice-president, and secretary-general of the association. *Les Surligneurs* has an Editing Committee (11 members currently) and a Technical Committee (4 members). The association also relies on more than one hundred legal students, researchers and practitioners who scout for and flag problematic statements in the media, post them on an internal Whatsapp Group, are then, guided by Jean-Paul Markus regarding whether or not this deserves legal-checking, draft the legal highlighting or clarification and publish it on the website and on social media.

Over time, the project has extended its offering, and, besides the articles, it currently develops podcasts, makes up quizzes to test users' knowledge of the political and legal arena, and hosts events, such as a legalthon or a webinar on promoting fact-checking on social media. *Les Surligneurs* also publishes interviews with actors in the field, such as with the Ukrainian journalist Alina Mosendz, who set up a media to fight fake news.[1] Members often take part in the public debate by collaborating with other media outlets (press, television, etc.), gaining strong recognition of the added value and importance of such legal checking in the broader – mostly French – media.

Building on this intensive media coverage (more than one thousand legal checking articles have been published, with millions of page views), *Les Surligneurs* has become more than a university collective and is now recognized as a media outlet. The association has been a signatory of the International Fact-Checking Network (IFCN) Code of Principles since July 2021.[2] *Les Surligneurs* also takes part in the Journalism Trust initiative, from Reporter Sans Frontières, and helped drafting a transparency report in that respect.[3] It is a member of the European Digital Media Observatory (EDMO)[4] and the French-speaking platform for the initiative of the fight against disinformation.[5]

Finally, the media outlet goes beyond national borders and is also present in Belgium, with a sister website.[6] In Belgium, Professor Pierre-Olivier de Broux is Editing Director with a team of three other professors in the Editing Committee: Christine Guillain, Jogchum Vrielink and Marie-Sophie de Clippele. They are all professors at the same university, Université Saint-Louis – Bruxelles and are partly involved in a class, following the format of a legal clinic, around the project *Les Surligneurs*. Students from the former year are still involved in the drafting of legal checkings.

With regard to legal design, the project is interesting as it follows some clear design patterns:

1 Les surligneurs, 'Les Surligneurs' (*Les Surligneurs*, 4 March 2022) < https://www.lessurligneurs.eu/alina-mosendz-la-desinformation-russe-en-ukraine-est-une-arme-de-guerre/> accessed 20 January 2023.

2 'IFCN Code of Principles' <https://www.ifcncodeofprinciples.poynter.org/profile/les-surligneurs> accessed 20 January 2023.

3 Active value GmbH, 'JTI:App' (*JTI:App*) <https://www.jti-app.com> accessed 20 January 2023.

4 'EDMO – United against Disinformation' <https://edmo.eu/> accessed 20 January 2023.

5 'La plateforme francophone des Initiatives de Lutte contre la désinformation' (*ODIL*) <https://odil.org/> accessed 20 January 2023.

6 'Les Surligneurs Belgique' <https://be.lessurligneurs.eu/> accessed 20 January 2023.

- A recognisable yellow colour,
- A recognisable logo,
- Yellow highlighting of a tag to show the problematic political statement according to the existing legal framework,
- Yellowing of a picture of the politician whose statement is highlighted but only showing the underpart of his face (mouth) without the eyes,
- The structure of the articles is made more readable (title – summary – short text),
- Language is used that is accessible to the general public.

All these elements were crafted at the project's onset, though some underwent subsequent adjustments, occasionally tailored to embody a more 'sophisticated' or 'professional' aesthetic characteristic of a media website. Consequently, the design of *Les Surligneurs* distinctly aligns with the ethos of the legal design movement.

Fig. 1. Screen shot website Les Surligneurs *with distinguishable design*

However, when designing the concept, Vincent Couronne and Joachim Savin were not aware of a specific movement around law and design.

They started with the conviction that in order to bring the law into the public debate more, it needed to be accessible to non-lawyers and this needed to be done in an attractive way. It was only a year or two later, in 2018-2019, that the legal design movement really emerged in France.

2.2. Beyond Design Thinking: Les Surligneurs *as a Mix of "Meaning Driven Design" and "Projective Design"*

The project *Les Surligneurs,* from its inception, did not follow the canonical approach to legal design, centred on design thinking, i.e. "a process" aimed at "formulating a 'problem" from a user's point of view and trying to solve it by creating desirable, viable and feasible experiences".[7]

In contrast to this multidisciplinary and user-centred approach of legal design thinking, *Les Surligneurs* has followed a different path. The project started in the mind of the designer and the lawyer, following their intention to highlight legal texts and their application to nourish the public debate.

In that respect, they elaborated what might be qualified as a "Meaning Driven Design", i.e. a traditional "art-based" design approach, where the intent of the designer – a new vision of the political and public debate scenery – was to create new meanings, without necessarily consulting the users beforehand.[8] *Les Surligneurs* could also qualify as "Information Design", which aims to visualise information following several criteria: accuracy, simplicity and clarity, as theorised, among others, by Per Mollerup.[9]

Moreover, *Les Surligneurs* also aimed to create and formalise devices "in order to spark debate" following a more critical design approach – the yellow highlighting of politicians making legally problematic statements was designed to be visible enough to critically react to such

7 Apolline Le Gall, 'Legal Design beyond Design Thinking: Processes and Effects of the Four Spaces of Design Practices for the Legal Field' in Rossana Ducato and Alain Strowel (eds), *Legal Design Perspectives: Theoretical and Practical Insights from the Field* (Ledizioni 2021) 41.

8 ibid.

9 Per Mollerup, *Data Design: Visualising Quantities, Locations, Connections* (Illustrated edition, Bloomsbury Visual Arts 2015).

statements.[10] This is what Apolline Le Gall and Sumi Saint-Auguste called a "Projective Design".[11]

Together with "Research-Design",[12] the Meaning Driven Design and the Projective Design constitute other spaces of legal design, besides the predominant Legal Design Thinking. Le Gall and Saint-Auguste drafted these four spaces of design practice, allowing for embracing "a broader comprehension of design, acknowledging its diversity of practices" and thereby drawing a design theory that is much more in line with designerly thinking than the only 'design thinking'.[13]

Other authors have also gone beyond legal design thinking to welcome legal design. Margaret Hagan insists on the fact that applying design to law is not only about the visual aspect of law, nor only about information being better designed; it could embrace product design, service design and organisation design. For her, "Legal design is the application of human-centered design to the world of law, to make legal systems and services more human-centered, usable, and satisfying".[14] This includes not only creating better front-ends and back-ends to the legal system, thereby helping the lay person and the legal profession, but also improving the design of the actual legal system, through incremental and breakthrough changes.[15] *Les Surligneurs* fits Hagan's purposes of better communication ("to communicate information – particularly complex legal information – in a clearer, more compelling, and more usable way") and of new products and services. As mentioned before, *Les Surligneurs* generates ideas of how to use the law in the public debate and improve it if need be.

Certainly, *Les Surligneurs* serves as a conduit for citizens to access authenticated, understandable information regarding legal matters under discussion in the public sphere (featured in headlines across media

10 'Où sont les Dragons' <https://ousontlesdragons.fr/publications/legal-design-roundtable/> accessed 20 January 2023.

11 ibid.

12 "Designers formulate a new and comprehensive vision of a topic or ecosystem, for example by building a state of the art review, organizing user research or stakeholders focus groups", ibid.

13 'Où sont les Dragons' (n 10).

14 Margaret D Hagan, '1. Legal Design' (*Law By Design*, 26 January 2015) <https://lawbydesign.co/legal-design/> accessed 20 January 2023.

15 ibid.

outlets, contentious subjects, etc.). This remains the primary objective that the project has steadfastly pursued: to communicate a lucid and approachable explanation of the existing legal framework. In the case of *Les Surligneurs*, legal design holds significance in engaging the public, stimulating the interest in participating in public discourse about policy decisions or broader political conversations. It transcends a mere simplification of the law; it encompasses an educational aspect, aiming to impart legal knowledge to the public. For these reasons, the project surpasses certain inherent limitations associated with legal design, as outlined in the next chapter.

3. Legal Design Limitations

Les Surligneurs serves as an interesting example of a *design project within the legal sphere*, which is different from *legal design* projects, thereby surpassing certain constraints within legal design and offering solutions to overcome them. It exceeds four particular limitations commonly associated with legal design (2.1). These limitations can be understood in the context of design thinking (2.2).

3.1. Four Limitations to Legal Design

3.1.1. Cultural Timidity: Hiding Design Production

The first limitation that struck us was the disproportion between the discourses (oral and written) held about legal design qualities and the lack of physical evidence of such achievements. In other words, we hear a lot about *legal design* but we do not see that much of it. However, from the design point of view, legitimacy is built precisely by being able to show and display projects. The presentation of the production and its criticism by teachers and peers is constitutive evidence of the training and the future professional culture of the practitioner.[16]

Thus, a designer's worth lies in what s/he does, not what s/he says. Even if discourse has taken an important place in some recent practices

---

16 Robin S Adams and others, 'Characterizing the Work of Coaching during Design Reviews' (2016) 45 Design Studies 30 <https://www.sciencedirect.com/science/article/pii/S0142694X15001155> accessed 27 November 2023.

(discursive design, fiction design...), a discourse relies on artifacts, material elements that are the support for the discourse or the narrative.[17] Of course, nowadays there are several counter-examples of famous designers who talk more than they design (or make their teams design for them), and some of these writings and speeches obviously contribute to the structure of the discipline (Raymond Loewy, Ettore Sottsass, Bruno Munari, Kenya Hara...). Nevertheless, for every design professional, the extent of their competence is measured by the object they create or its representation in photo or video.

Yet, since the first appearance of the term *legal design* in France, i.e., 10 years ago, there have been almost no images available to portray the works done, apart from the *legal design community* initiative by Ubisoft. A search on the internet mainly reveals diagrams inspired by those of Margaret Hagan or methodological representations inspired by *design thinking*.

Legal design practitioners frequently cite the confidentiality clause as the rationale behind this phenomenon. This explanation is not satisfactory; there are methods to anonymize or conceal elements without compromising "business secrecy". Notably, various French ministries or governmental agencies, such as the *Direction de l'information légale et administrative* (DILA, the Directorate for legal and administrative information) and *Commission nationale de l'informatique et des libertés* (CNIL, the National Commission on computing and liberties), have availed themselves of such services, yet traces of this work are seldom found.

Our assumption revolves around a conflict between two professional cultures, where legal experts tend to refrain from showcasing their work. This hesitation may stem from apprehensions about "failure" and poten-

17 Maxime Mollon, 'Design pour débattre : comment créer des artefacts dissonants, et leurs situations de communication, afin d'ouvrir des espaces de contestation mutuelle (agonisme) et d'expression des voix marginales (dissensus)' (phdthesis, Université Paris sciences et lettres 2019) <https://theses.hal.science/tel-03120398> accessed 12 December 2023.

tial criticism.[18] Additionally, their primary mode of communication leans towards text rather than visuals, contributing to this reluctance.[19]

In contrast to the cultural timidity and the emphasis placed on discussing legal design rather than the actual designed outcome, *Les Surligneurs* took a different approach by promptly introducing a tangible product: a website with recognisable design features. Essentially, as a public platform, *Les Surligneurs* inherently surpasses this initial limitation. Yet, its founders encountered internal debates concerning the editorial direction and making the analytical work visible at a 'non-academic' level. Convincing law professors, who typically have low visibility in the media, to participate in this project was crucial, leading to the need for visual and editorial compromises that satisfied all of the parties involved.

3.1.2. Methodological Rigidity: The User as the Only Goal

The second critique of French legal design centres on its methodological inflexibility, primarily relying on the almost exclusive use of the user-centred approach. This limitation becomes more pressing when considering the evolution of Design over time—a progression that has diversified the discipline, gradually freeing it from its original domains of industrial and graphic design. This expansion, described by Chanal, Le Gall, and Irrmann as the "extension of the fields of Design",[20] has notably spurred designers' interest in new realms of application and markets. This shift has also attracted new disciplines and practitioners intrigued by the impact of design within their respective fields, such as the service industry, digital engineering, public services, the medical sector, and prospective design. Consequently, this evolution has fuelled the emergence of design thinking.

18 Rae Morgan and Emily Allbon, 'Is Law Really That Special ?' in Rossana Ducato and Alain Strowel (eds), *Legal Design Perspectives: Theoretical and Practical Insights from the Field* (Ledizioni 2021).

19 Michelle Harner, 'The Value of "Thinking Like a Lawyer"' [2011] Faculty Scholarship <https://digitalcommons.law.umaryland.edu/fac_pubs/1031>.

20 Valérie Chanal and others, *Former par le design: principes, méthodes et outils pour préparer les étudiants aux enjeux du XXIe siècle* (Éditions EMS, management & société 2022).

In the subsequent section, we will delve into the dearth of knowledge and historical references, constituting the third limitation we aim to explore. Our objective is to emphasise that the current practice of legal design in France only captures a fraction of the practices and approaches inherited from design thinking. Le Gall's article further explores these facets in greater detail.[21]

The methodological rigidity generates a particular effect: it curtails the transformative potential of accomplishments, a point highlighted by Don Norman and Roberto Verganti.[22] The prevalent use of user-centred approaches tends to foster incremental advancements rather than radical innovations. In essence, it leads to enhancements in the existing situation without scrutinising the underlying problems or the flawed framework itself. There is improvement, but the fundamental aspects remain unchanged.

This specific limitation, when coupled with the first one, provokes certain repercussions: the standardised approach yields minimal alterations at the core, and significant changes are either minimal or concealed. Consequently, the representation of legal design, both internally (among actors) and externally (among sponsors), remains confined to standardised methodologies, limiting innovative strides and broader visibility.

To get back to *Les Surligneurs*, the project is not (only) user-centred, unlike most legal design initiatives. It is a mix of "Meaning Driven Design" and "Projective Design". However, this mix was unintentional when it was created by the founders; it came out as something outside of their respective fields of expertise. Following that approach, real innovation was possible when developing the product.

3.1.3. Notional Blur: Cut Off from Its Historical Roots

The third limitation, although it partly accounts for the methodological rigidity we just discussed, has been segregated deliberately. This segregation is essential as one limitation is contingent upon the examination of the other, leading to specific consequences.

---

21 Le Gall (n 7).

22 Donald A Norman and Roberto Verganti, 'Incremental and Radical Innovation: Design Research vs. Technology and Meaning Change' (2014) 30 Design Issues 78 <https://doi.org/10.1162/DESI_a_00250> accessed 27 November 2023.

As previously mentioned, Design as a discipline boasts its own autonomy and historical trajectory, dating back to the late 19th century. However, in the domain of legal design, a notable absence exists regarding references to its historical evolution and the concepts formulated by earlier professionals and theorists. Consequently, a variety of terminologies emerge from disparate spheres: terms like plain language, behavioural sciences, infographics, customer acquisition, and legal tech find common ground with terms borrowed from user-centred design and graphic design, such as UX/UI, user journey, and prototype. Strikingly absent are terms directly tied to the original practices of service design, like sketch, scale model, touchpoints, or references.

To illuminate the diverse "threads" interwoven within the contemporary legal landscape, we propose applying Verganti's framework.[23] This application aims to disentangle the conventional innovation approaches from the technical, marketing, and user-centric approaches. While the complete implementation of this framework remains a work in progress, we anticipate that it will, at the very least, help delineate the unique expertise inherent in each field. This delineation, in turn, will ideally clarify the trends driving legal innovation.

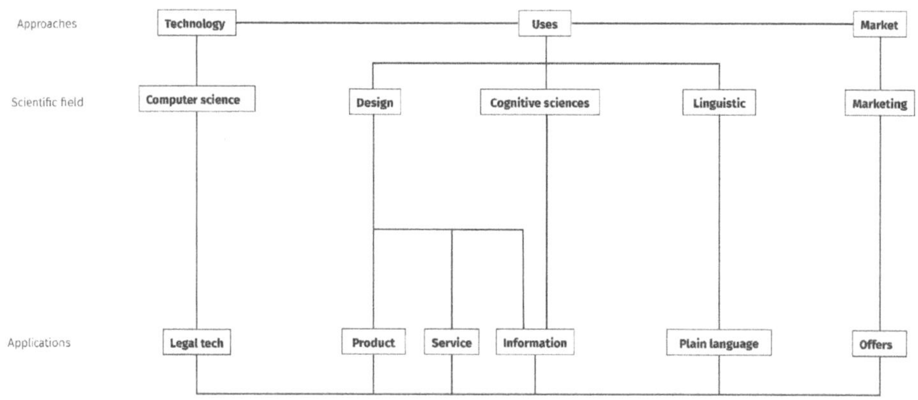

Fig. 2. Approaches to legal innovation by Joachim Savin, inspired by Verganti, 2009

23 Roberto Verganti, *Design Driven Innovation: Changing the Rules of Competition by Radically Innovating What Things Mean* (Harvard Business Review Press 2009).

The novelty of legal design as a practice does not inherently clarify the prevalent sense of amateurism or unfamiliarity observed in its utilisation of Design's intellectual and methodological tools. This becomes even more perplexing considering the clearly defined potential impacts of legal design, which owe much to the foundational work of Margaret Hagan.

This "notional blur" becomes especially paradoxical when wielded by professionals in an intensely specialised discipline characterised by enclosed domains that mandate adherence to established rules. It is somewhat ironic that lawyers, known for their specific attachment to the notion of "jurisdiction", end up challenging the "jurisdiction" in terms of the professional territory wielded by designers.[24] By contrast, *Les Surligneurs* has avoided conceptual ambiguity by relying from the start on specific design concepts especially in graphic, web and service design.

Our premise suggests that this situation arises from both the nature of the individuals involved and the professional and academic landscape of Design in France. On the one side, the majority of actors in legal design are lawyers, who naturally lack the broad references typically acquired through comprehensive training, which can span up to five years. Although some have either hired trained designers for specific tasks or pursued supplementary training, often resulting in shorter degrees, this remains limited.

On the other side, from an academic standpoint, Design lacks a robust structure in France. There is a notable absence of a unified university section dedicated to the discipline. Historically, collective representation, associations, and unions within the design realm have been weak. These entities encompass only a fraction of the design professionals due to various specialised statuses (for instance, graphic designers can join the Maison des Artistes, while the same is not applicable for industrial designers). Additionally, the individualistic culture prevalent among designers further contributes to this fragmentation.

Consequently, the lack of robust professional representation and the absence of an established legal design culture, combined with the disregard for the design profession, as noted by Rae Morgan and Emily

24 Claude Dubar, Pierre Tripier and Valérie Boussard, *Sociologie des professions* (3e éd, A Colin 2011).

Allbon,[25] perpetuate the conceptual ambiguity that undermines the credibility of this field.

3.1.4. Political Scope: Little to No Political Commitment

Concerning the various legal design initiatives in France, few prioritise or embody symbolic or political values. Discounting student or associative projects, the predominant showcase revolves around enhancing existing practices, neglecting to re-evaluate the significance and influence of law itself. Notably, nondisclosure agreements, corporate contracts, compliance measures, and organisational processes form the bulk of the accomplishments. However, the subject matter being manipulated is inherently political, governing the lives of both the city and its citizens.

While Design encounters its internal contradictions between the humanistic ideals it upholds and the consumption-driven society fostering its growth,[26] self-reflection remains pivotal. From William Morris to Designers éthiques, professionals have frequently interrogated their role in production and assumed political stances. Consequently, while not all designers today are politicised, they acknowledge the profound political implications intrinsic to their profession and practice. This is clear to the legal-checking project *Les Surligneurs,* which questions the law by sometimes going beyond mere checking - taking political assertions seriously - within the limits of the rule of law. Therefore, it critically assesses the law, and has a clear political scope, unlike other legal design projects.

In the current democratic climate, engaging with the law could have served as a potent avenue for advocacy, empowering collectives and individuals, and prompting scrutiny of institutions and legal frameworks. Yet, beyond seeking operational efficiency or, at best, ensuring consumer rights, it appears that legal design, rooted in a commercial context as a professional practice, only partially realises its concealed potential.

This limitation appears to stem not only from the absence of a critical historical consciousness among professionals and the methodological dominance of the user-centred approach, which constrains the conception process to the individual. It also seems to be connected to the manner in which legal design was introduced in France.

---

25 Morgan and Allbon (n 19).

26 Alexandra Midal, *Design - introduction à l'histoire d'une discipline* (Pocket 2009).

4. Limitations in the Context of Design Thinking and of the French Environment

In this section, our aim is to elucidate the emergence of these limitations by examining the almost epistemological connection between design and legal design via the framework of design thinking. Additionally, we will contextualise this connection within the local setting by providing a historical overview of its application.

4.1. The Design Thinking Heritage

This part revolves around the third and fourth limitations (methodological rigidity and political stakes). We believe that a big portion of the limitations we identified could be directly attributable to the direct filiation between *legal design* and *design thinking.*

Made popular by Tim Brown, one of the founders of the consulting agency IDEO, *design thinking* is a method inspired by the work and way of thinking of designers: It puts emphasis on the conception and design process and starts from a close comprehension of the user to develop a prototype and test solutions.[27] In its model, design thinking is a method that aims to develop a universal design method, which companies could seize upon. This approach by method, reproduced in *legal design*, is contrary to the logic-based approach that is proper to design, as defined by Stéphane Vial:[28]

"1. *Design is a project discipline as well as architecture and engineering.*
2. *Design is a project discipline based on a specific creative culture, which is not reducible to that of architecture, the decorative arts, engineering or marketing [...]*
3. *Design is a project discipline with its own mode of knowledge or understanding through which it contributes to the contemporary epis-*

27 Tim Brown, *Change by Design: How Design Thinking Transforms Organizations and Inspires Innovation* (HarperBusiness 2009).

28 Extract translated from Stéphane Vial, 'De la spécificité du projet en design : une démonstration' [2014] Communication et organisation. Revue scientifique francophone en Communication organisationnelle 17.

teme [...] it is not only a way to design and build artifacts but also, through them, a way of knowing and understanding the world [...]

4. *Design is a project discipline that is philosophically committed to an ideal for a better and sustainable future, whose goal is to improve the 'inhabitability of the world'*[29] *[...]*
5. *Design is a discipline of project in progress in which the concept of project changes over time [...]"*

This definition offers a favourable perspective on the earlier critiques: design is politically engaged (point 4), and its procedural methodology is continually advancing (point 5). Regarding this latter point, it is worth noting that designers are simultaneously progressing in terms of problem identification and solution formulation, engaging in a form of abductive reasoning: *"Abductive reasoning is "in opposition to deductive (from the general to the specific) and inductive (from the specific to the general) reasoning... [it is a] 'logical leap of the mind' or an 'inference to the best explanation' to imagine a heuristic for understanding the mystery".*[30]

Certainly, Schön illustrates that the practical execution of design hinges on a dynamic "conversation" between the designer and the context.[31] Some scholars even characterise "design as a conversation": the design proposition forms a middle ground between the designer's perspective, the viewpoint and objectives of the commissioning organisation, the intended users of the "object", and the various constraints (legal, technical, economic, etc.) that govern its creation.

The introduction of design thinking among novices highlights the crucial requirement for a successful project: the team's adeptness in han-

29 Alain Findeli, 'Searching for Design~Research Questions: Some Conceptual Clarifications' in Rosan Chow, Jonas Wolfgang and Joost Gesche (eds), *Questions, Hypotheses & Conjectures* (iUniverse 2010) 292.

30 Roger Martin, 'Design Thinking: Achieving Insights via the "Knowledge Funnel"' (2010) 38 Strategy & Leadership 37 <https://doi.org/10.1108/10878571011029046> accessed 12 December 2023.

31 Donald A Schön, *The Reflective Practitioner - How Professionals Think In Action* (Basic Books 1983). See also Donald A Schön and Vincent DeSanctis, 'The Reflective Practitioner: How Professionals Think in Action' (1986) 34 The Journal of Continuing Higher Education 29.

dling ambiguity—a challenging stance to adopt.[32] Consequently, the most effective groups in design thinking are those that do not adhere strictly to a sequential approach but continuously engage in "problem framing" exercises throughout the project.[33]

> Ultimately, achieving success in a project rooted in design thinking methods necessitates a certain detachment—a reflexive approach or, in simpler terms, an understanding of design as a process with its unique culture, reasoning, and practices.[34]

The teaching of design (as long as it is done several times, and taken with reflexivity) allows for experimenting with a succession of activities to make design decisions in the unknown and understand when one must hold back its judgement to move forward and know when to diverge and converge[35]. Design practices can thus navigate fluidly between the formulation of a design situation and the formalisation of innovative proposals, as Lawson has shown.[36] In other words, the problem and the solution are developed simultaneously, and that can look counterproductive for professionals who learned to first frame the problem and only then search for solutions and for those whose fields of knowledge are impermeable.

To better illustrate this process, Nigel Cross explains that the thinking in design is based on an emergency phenomenon, i.e., based on relevant characteristics that emerge from attempted solutions, which were not

---

32 "Facilitating the design thinking process involves helping teams develop a greater tolerance for, and ways of working through, this ambiguity", Victor P Seidel and Sebastian K Fixson, 'Adopting Design Thinking in Novice Multidisciplinary Teams: The Application and Limits of Design Methods and Reflexive Practices' (2013) 30 Journal of Product Innovation Management 19 <https://onlinelibrary.wiley.com/doi/abs/10.1111/jpim.12061> accessed 12 December 2023.

33 "However, high-performing teams did not discard this method later but continued needfinding in concept selection", ibid.

34 "The results during the concept generation phase suggest a model of design thinking in which it is not the adoption of individual methods themselves, but the early use of the methods in a reflexive manner that leads to successful innovation", ibid.

35 Bryan Lawson, *How Designers Think: The Design Process Demystified* (4th ed, Architectural Press 2005).

36 ibid.

formally expressed in the problem formulation in the first place.[37] It is a way of reasoning oriented to the making and production of material objects in order to avoid procrastination in the face of the immensity and variety of information needed to approach a complex problem. In other words, one can act before thinking, one can - and even must - act to think. This is what Schön describes with the concept of the professional as a reflective practitioner who constantly thinks in and about the situation and can thus exercise his own creativity.[38] That is something that lawyers find difficult to accept because often their profession (especially in the liberal or private sector) consists precisely of "risk management" and "documenting before acting", which is also related to the first limitation, cultural timidity.

When it comes to political engagement, regarding the problematisation of the user's "pain points", *legal design* reproduces an individualistic (a user) and utilitarian (a problem) view from *design thinking and* inevitably encloses its projects in a limited horizon, without thought about "what's desirable", when other design approaches allow for better questioning the core/sense of things,[39] systems,[40] and the desirability of possible futures.[41]

More widely speaking, for Banathy, the genesis of a design process relies on the fact that one either wishes to, or must, change a system or create a new one. It is a matter of going beyond the current state of the environment, of going beyond what exists and allowing the framework for the creative and the new to exist.[42] It is the transcendence of the existing situation that allows individuals to contemplate the field of possibilities and opportunities, such that the interpretation and problematisation of the existing situation is the first step in defining and structuring

37 Nigel Cross, *Design Thinking: Understanding How Designers Think and Work* (Berg Publishers 2011).

38 Schön (n 32).

39 Verganti (n 24).

40 Alain Findeli and Rabah Bousbaci, 'L'Eclipse de L'Objet Dans Les Théories Du Projet En Design (The Eclipse of the Object in Design Project Theories)' (2005) 8 The Design Journal 35.

41 Mollon (n 17).

42 Bela H Banathy, *Designing Social Systems in a Changing World* (Springer US 1996).

the problem of the future service. It is from this first phase of transcendence that a phase of imagination and exploration of possibilities begins.[43]

By turning Design into a method, *design thinking* follows the general movement of economics and companies of not being politically inclined, but like it or not, Design is a political activity, for by definition it is a prescribed activity: "designers may be seen to prescribe and to create the future".[44]

4.2. Specificities in the French Context

This section refers in particular to limits 1 (cultural timidity) and 3 (notional blur). In this section we will rely mostly on observations and encounters that took place at professional *legal design* events in France and our experience at "Lab Legal", which is the professional association that unites the actors of legal design in France today in view of the national salon dedicated to legal innovation. We also count with different documentary searches to try to retrace the conditions of appearance and diffusion of this practice in a synthetic and inevitably non-exhaustive way.

While the term "legal design" initially emerged in the US in 2013, its introduction to France occurred in 2015 through a publication by CNIL's prospective unit, LINC. Geoffrey Delcroix, was the leader of this unit, before being Head of Legal Innovation at Ubisoft in 2020. This initial publication, co-authored with Mylène Podvin during her time as a student at ENSCI, mapped initiatives linked to privacy design and legal design but did not directly reference Margaret Hagan. Another mention of the term appeared in an interview with Miroslav Kurdov and an article profiling Olivia Zarcate, a legal expert and founder of Imagidroit, but both omitted the perspective of design thinking, thus diverging from Margaret Hagan's interpretation of legal design. The CNIL holds significance in this history, primarily due to its influence in the realm of legal innovation.

The term gradually gained traction within professional associations, notably through ThinkLeD from OpenLaw, an influential association ad-

43 ibid.

44 Robert Farrell and Cliff Hooker, 'Values and Norms Between Design and Science' (2014) 30 Design Issues 29.

vocating open innovations in the legal sphere, and the establishment of Assas Legal Innovation within a major French law school. Concurrently, several legal experts and lawyers in the private sector, including Ghislaine Brenas of *Juste Cause*, Alexandra Sabbe-Ferri with *mesindemnites.com*, and Marie Potel-Saville, who later became the French ambassador for Finnish legal design company Dot in 2018 before founding her agency, *Amurabi*, displayed an interest in the subject.

Subsequently, the term began to surface in articles from major French legal publishers like Francis Lefebvre and Lefebvre-Sarrut. Sumi Saint-Auguste, then co-president of Open Law, supervised the R&D department, contributing to this increased exposure. The year 2018 witnessed a surge in interest from various entities, including the *Maison du Barreau de Paris* and an association of young legal professionals in corporations, leading to a rise in mentions of, and conferences on legal design.

In 2019, the third national salon dedicated to legal design expanded its programme to involve legal design actors in conferences and workshops. Concurrently, the Ecole Française des Barreaux, France's largest lawyer training school, introduced mandatory training modules on legal innovation, including a dedicated module on legal design.

Finally, in late 2019, multiple French legal design actors, including some of those previously mentioned, united within a professional association named Lab Legal, whose statutes were submitted in 2020. By October of the same year, the fourth legal design salon had been renamed *Rendez-vous de la Transformation du Droit*, signalling a certain maturity in approach towards various legal innovation actors, with a dedicated space and extensive programming for legal design.

This historical overview is only partial but it allows us to make an observation: aside from CNIL, the promotion of *legal design* in France is done essentially in private, particularly through lawyers, legal experts, companies' lawyers, and major legal publishers with structures dedicated to innovation. That means that in France, *legal design* has been promoted by individuals with little knowledge of Design and with a working culture that is not very consistent with the project and its presentation. Moreover, this emergence took place in a context of technological and commercial competition, driven by the *legal tech* sector, quite far from the ideal of the Legal Design Lab, directed by Margaret Hagan, whose academic projects are dedicated to the issues of access to and defence of rights, and the improvement of the American legal system.

5. Design of the Public Debate and the Fight Against Dis- and Misinformation Through Better Access to Information

5.1. Politics and the Law are More and More Complex

Politics and the law are becoming more and more complex, due to the complexification of global issues (climate, refugees, economy, terrorism, etc.). In 2015, the former President of the European Commission Jean-Claude Juncker declared that Europe was in the midst of a "polycrisis".[45] The situation is no better today, as historian Adam Tooze said in 2022.[46] Tooze underlines many of the stresses the world faces today, to which he adds the risk of nuclear escalation, inflation, shortages, the possible return of a Trumpist president in the US and many others. This analysis considers the fact that the current crises come with highly technical issues. Climate change makes us deal with carbon footprint, quotas, chemical substances, new kinds of taxations and social conflicts.

Inevitably, the law designed to address these crises is becoming more and more complex. In 2003, texts containing 1.87 million signatures were published in the French Official journal. In 2013, it was 3.2 million. In the last 20 years, the number of legislative acts has grown by 73%, and the number of decrees by 53%, according to a study by the French Government.[47] Their length has increased at the same time.

---

45 Speech by President Jean-Claude Juncker – European Parliament Plenary session (European Commission 19 January 2016). See also, 'Mireille Delmas-Marty : « Profitons de la pandémie pour faire la paix avec la Terre »' *Le Monde.fr* (17 March 2020) <https://www.lemonde.fr/idees/article/2020/03/17/mireille-delmas-marty-profitons-de-la-pandemie-pour-faire-la-paix-avec-la-terre_6033344_3232.html> accessed 12 December 2023..

46 Adam Tooze, 'Chartbook #130 Defining Polycrisis - from Crisis Pictures to the Crisis Matrix.' (*Chartbook*, 24 June 2022) <https://adamtooze.substack.com/p/chartbook-130-defining-polycrisis> accessed 12 December 2023.

47 Secrétariat Général du Gouvernement, Indicateur de suivi de l'activité normative (2022) <https://www.dalloz-actualite.fr/sites/dalloz-actualite.fr/files/resources/2022/04/indicateurs_de_suivi_de_lactivite_normative.pdf> accessed 5 March

In addition, the levels of government of becoming more complex. Decentralisation gives more powers to local governments; the building of the European Union makes it possible for more institutions to pass legislation and regulations. This situation makes it more difficult for journalists, politicians and, of course, citizens, to be able to ask for accountability. *Les Surligneurs* had to publish articles to tackle the idea according to which France's pensions reform is a requirement from the European Union.[48] From a legal point of view, the political majority in France since 2017 is the one pushing for the pensions reform, not the European Union, and *Les Surligneurs* has given evidence of this.

But who can blame the citizens? The making of the law has become so complex that it is almost impossible to know who is accountable for which reform unless you are an expert. François Ost and Michel van de Kerchove pointed out the slow change from a pyramid of norms to a network of norms involving governance instead of government.[49] It is no surprise that conspiracy theories are so popular nowadays since they allow a simplistic explanation to a complex issue.

5.2. A Paradox: It's Getting Harder to Find Reliable Sources

In the meantime, citizens, who are also voters, struggle more and more in finding intelligible information. Of course, access to information is meant to be easier thanks to digital platforms and search engines, but the proliferation of websites and sources has created a digital mess. The results of an online search are not based on how reliable the website is, but on other factors that eventually have to fulfil one of the search engine's goals: being profitable.[50] Hence, when searching the EU directive

---

2023.

48 Vincent Couronne, 'La réforme de notre système de retraite serait une "exigence" de l'Union européenne "en contrepartie du plan de relance"' (31 January 2023) Les Surligneurs, <https://www.lessurligneurs.eu/la-reforme-de-notre-systeme-de-retraite-serait-une-exigence-de-lunion-europeenne-en-contrepartie-du-plan-de-relance/> accessed 5 March 2023.

49 François Ost and Michel van de Kerchove, *De la pyramide au réseau? pour une théorie dialectique du droit* (Publications Fac St Louis 2002).

50 Shoshana Zuboff, *The Age of Surveillance Capitalism. The Fight for a Human Future at the New Frontier of Power* (PublicAffairs 2019).

on posted workers on the Google search engine, the EU official website eur-lex.eu does not necessarily come among the first results.

Some remarkable efforts have been made in these last years in France with official websites such as vie-publique.fr and service-public.fr. But these efforts are far from being sufficient to make sure that citizens can access reliable information, in a country where 17% of the population suffer from digital illiteracy.

Indeed, it seems that the business model of online platforms relies too much on getting more and more personal data, and therefore they are not able to make sure that the information that is displayed is reliable. Shoshana Zuboff shows how what she calls "radical indifference"[51] has shaped the algorithmic models of online platforms. She recalls this memo that Andrew Bosworth, then one of the top directors of Facebook and now president of Meta Virtual Reality, shared with his teams in 2016, in which he declared about Facebook that "*Maybe it costs a life by exposing someone to bullies. Maybe someone dies in a terrorist attack coordinated on our tools [...] The ugly truth is that we believe in connecting people so deeply that anything that allows us to connect more people more often is *de facto* good*".[52]

We know to what extent the attention economy has been instrumental to the growth of online platforms.[53] There is more and more evidence that disinformation is used to make the attention economy more efficient,[54] making disinformation part of the business model of online platforms, and eventually weakening the trust of citizens in democratic institutions. In this context, the work of actors such as law teachers and designers is crucial.

51 ibid 670.

52 Charlie Kantrowitz, Charlie Warzel and Ryan Mac, 'Facebook Executive In 2016: "Maybe Someone Dies In A Terrorist Attack Coordinated On Our Tools"' (*BuzzFeed News*, 29 March 2018) <https://www.buzzfeednews.com/article/ryanmac/growth-at-any-cost-top-facebook-executive-defended-data> accessed 12 December 2023.

53 Matthew B Crawford, *The World Beyond Your Head: On Becoming an Individual in an Age of Distraction* (Reprint édition, Farrar, Straus and Giroux 2016).

54 Camille D Ryan and others, 'Monetizing Disinformation in the Attention Economy: The Case of Genetically Modified Organisms (GMOs)' (2020) 38 European Management Journal 7.

5.3. Where Are the Law Teachers and the Legal Designers?

The difficulty of finding intelligible information is deepened by the polarisation of the debate and the massification of information sources (social networks, search engines, notifications, etc.). At the same time, lawyers and legal scholars, who can contribute to or enlighten the public debate, are scarcely heard in the public debate in France. In 1912, 30% of the members of the National Assembly were also lawyers. The number dropped to 5% in 1997.[55] Indeed, after the Second World War, law professors and lawyers were replaced by spin doctors and high ranking civil servants who studied political science or other disciplines, for example at the National School of Administration.[56] As a consequence, law professors and lawyers, who are not involved in the making of the law as they were before, tend to lose the skills to communicate the substance of the law to the public.

Legal designers are also usually absent from the political stage, as was previously shown in this paper.[57] Designers can be found in France in two public instances: first, in public administrations where they work on websites such as service-public.fr or vie-publique.fr; and second, in public innovation, under the leadership of the *Direction interministérielle à la transformation publique*, a department of the public modernisation ministry. Interestingly, there are no legal designers in these two services.

5.4. Les Surligneurs *as Public Debate Design*[58]

When drafting the "legal highlightings" and the "legal clarifications" the

---

55 'Répartition des députés par catégories socio-professionnelles' (Assemblée Nationale, 1997) <https://www.assemblee-nationale.fr/11/tribun/csp1.asp#P548_27168> accessed 5 March 2023.

56 Laureline Fontaine, *Qu'est-ce qu'un grand juriste ? Essai sur les juristes et la pensée juridique contemporaine* (LGDJ 2012) <https://www.lgdj.fr/qu-est-ce-qu-un-grand-juriste-9782359710656.html> accessed 12 December 2023.

57 See 1.1.4.

58 The following section and its several findings are based on a presentation given by Vincent Couronne and Jean-Paul Markus at the *Séminaire interdisciplinaire d'études juridiques* in Brussels on 10 May 2022. See Vincent Couronne and Jean-Paul Markus, *'Legal Checking. L'expérience Des Surligneurs' – SIEJ (10/05/2022)* (Directed by SIEJ, 2022) <https://www.youtube.com/watch?v=ro3loysBu1s> accessed

members of *Les Surligneurs* realised that the exercise was not that evident: proving that a statement is wrong by referring to an existing legal norm assumes that the law is clear in itself. But that is not always the case; the law itself is rarely black or white, and its application often depends on the single case and how you put things forward.[59] Therefore, the tags used to do a legal-check of the political statements sometimes become more nuanced (not simply 'wrong' or 'illegal' but 'problematic', 'difficult', 'misleading' or 'to be nuanced') indicating that the exercise is more complex. As a matter of fact, the law often travels in grey zones and providing a clear and accessible information of the current legal framework is more challenging than it seems. Moreover, the law may change and so what is considered illegal today might not be so tomorrow or vice-versa. Contributors to *Les Surligneurs* have therefore slowly switched their approach: it is not only about referring to the current legal texts to check a political statement but also about taking some statements seriously and examining how one statement would impact the existing legal framework if it were to be implemented. For instance, if Marine Le Pen (leader of a right wing party) were to declare that France was going to quit the energy market of the European Union, it could not be done according to the current legal framework, unless France left or modified the European Treaties. A political statement could however only be taken seriously if it fitted with the rule of law; that is the limit beyond which to legal-check politicians. This implies that the notion of rule of law is clear enough, which might also not be the case.[60]

The experience of *Les Surligneurs* also reveals other hurdles.[61] First, legal-checking should not be perceived as censoring: the political statement should not be overinterpreted or taken too literally, or even taken seriously when it was meant as a touch of humour. Politicians often use

---

23 January 2023.

59 Ost and van de Kerchove (n 50). See also, how to think further of this inherent equity in the application of the law: Jérémie Van Meerbeeck, 'Penser par cas... Et par principes' (2014) 73 Revue interdisciplinaire d'études juridiques 77.

60 For a more critical approach on the danger of the subjectivity of truth, especially in the public space, where everything then risks being dominated by the powerful, see Claudine Tiercelin, 'Métaphysique et philosophie de la connaissance' [2019] L'annuaire du Collège de France. Cours et travaux 415 <https://journals.openedition.org/annuaire-cdf/14294> accessed 23 January 2023.

61 Couronne and Markus (n 58).

registers other than rational law-centred phrasings and resort to emotions, symbols, philosophy, history and so on. For instance, when Paul Magnette, the president of the Socialist Party in the French-speaking community of Belgium, said that the liberal party's suggested measures for unemployment amount to forced labour and was therefore highlighted by *Les Surligneurs* as "excessive", he mentioned the following in his right of reply: "It's the entire difference between legal language and political expression, which is always made up of metaphors".[62]

Second, the articles might not be read, and thereby fail to participate, in the public debate. To avoid that risk, the editing focuses on staying concise, and avoiding legal jargon, as well as any sensationalism, arrogance, or simplism. Concerning the lectorate, about one third are lawyers and two thirds are journalists.[63] It remains difficult to reach the broader public and involve the layman citizen.

Third, one of the biggest hurdles is not being, or even not *being perceived as,* partial. When legal-checking political statements, there is an inherent subjective component to that exercise (the selection of the statement – not too much from one political party or movement – and the drafting of the checking), which should be as neutral as possible. To escape any political labelling, *Les Surligneurs* follows two bodies of deontological rules:

- academic deontology requires remaining independent and not subjecting these checking techniques to your own political opinions as well as going further than checking the current legal framework and going up in the hierarchy of norms;
- journalistic deontology requires abiding by a deontological code (allowing a right of reply…).

Fourth, even if the articles should remain concise and accessible, they may not contain any errors. There may be inaccuracies, which can

62 Pierre-Olivier de Broux, '"Pour le président du MR, la solution aux pénuries est le travail forcé", assène Paul Magnette' (*Les Surligneurs*, 23 November 2021) <https://be.lessurligneurs.eu/pour-le-president-du-mr-la-solution-aux-penuries-est-le-travail-force-assene-paul-magnette/> accessed 23 January 2023.

63 According to an impact survey in January 2023, available at <https://survey.impacttrack.org/6f24fda1-7404-4f0d-9348-3438ad4399f7> accessed 23 January 2023.

be dealt with by using terms such as "in principle" or "notably", but it should not be more than that. To avoid errors, all articles are reviewed by experts in the Editing Committee or outside experts if the topic is not in the area of expertise of the Editing Committee, and always by the Editing Director. If the law is not clear enough, the Editing Director, Jean-Paul Markus, decides to withhold publication, as legal-checking does not have the aim of producing a new legal doctrine on a certain controversy.

Fifth, it may be that some citizens disagree with the law that is being checked and that the legal checking operation sparks a more fundamental debate. To some, the law only represents the established order of the powerful. They reject the rule of law, i.e. the current system of democratic values, and vote for more extremist, antidemocratic political leaders or call for civil disobedience.[64] If the political project were then to change, the law should be adapted too, but it might be contrary to the democratic values. *Les Surligneurs* clearly defends the rule of law (*l'État de droit*), and not simply the current legal framework (*l'état du droit*). This is where the role of *Les Surligneurs* comes close to a "Projective Design" and aims to take part in that broader debate: to change society by reducing disinformation and to ensure better respect for the rule of law.

Lastly, concerning the design aspect of *Les Surligneurs*, it seems to keep up its promises: with its very recognisable features (yellow colour, highlighting, tags...) the website and its content have gained recognition over time, becoming a valued media outlet among other professionals (journalists, lawyers...). *Les Surligneurs (France* and *Belgique*) together with Datagora, an anti-fake news platform focused on the design of statistics, received a grant from the *Organisation internationale de la Francophonie* (OIF) to share knowledge on the fight against disinformation, to build capacity on fact-checking and to draft a white book.[65] They

64 Maxime Charpotier, 'Action de désobéissance civile pour dénoncer l'inaction du gouvernement face à l'urgence climatique et sociale dans les Pyrénées-Orientales' (*La France insoumise*, 27 February 2019) <https://lafranceinsoumise.fr/2019/02/27/cabestany-66-action-de-desobeissance-civile-pour-denoncer-linaction-du-gouvernement-face-a-lurgence-climatique-et-sociale/> accessed 23 January 2023.

65 Les surligneurs, 'Projet DEFI : un partage de connaissances entre initiatives de lutte contre la désinformation et la publication d'un livre blanc' (*Les Surligneurs*, 8 September 2022) <https://www.lessurligneurs.eu/projet-defi-un-partage-de-connaissances-entre-initiatives-de-lutte-contre-la-desinformation/> accessed 23 January 2023.

held workshops in 2022 on Communication Strategy, Information Design and Fact-Checking. It was confirmed that the design strategy of *Les Surligneurs* was on point with a clear and coherent visual identity, with innovative tools (podcasts, quizzes, webinars, legalthons…), with widening partnerships and with a certain presence on social media.

Conclusion

The limitations of the legal design initiatives in France are the result of history and of the approach of those who introduced legal design: cultural shyness, methodological rigidity, notional blur, and little political commitment. The example of *Les Surligneurs* shows how it is possible to go beyond these limitations, because the project was founded and led by a lawyer and a designer. *Les Surligneurs* also shows that legal design should not be made by non-designers who only apply a method. It takes both designers and lawyers to build projects that can go beyond the limitations of legal design.

There are different ways of doing legal design, and there are also various effects of legal design. In the case of *Les Surligneurs*, the effects can be seen on the public debate. But some effects are limited. Those participating in *Les Surligneurs* have reached some of these limitations: the design of public debate – the polarisation of public debate, the growing complexity of the law – makes it difficult to reach out to the public. Also, it remains a challenge to find enough law professors who are willing to participate in the public debate.

Other effects have been unexpected. The most interesting one is that by running *Les Surligneurs*, lawyers have come to a new comprehension of the public debate, as well as a new awareness of society's issues. Also, *Les Surligneurs* questions the role of lawyers in the public debate, and helps to train law students – those who participate in the project – and they have developed a tailor-made service for journalists in legal issues pertaining to the public debate. When combining law and design in the political sphere, many unexpected opportunities emerge.

Bibliography

Adams RS and others, 'Characterizing the Work of Coaching during Design Reviews' (2016) 45 Design Studies 30

Banathy BH, *Designing Social Systems in a Changing World* (Springer US 1996)

Brown T, *Change by Design: How Design Thinking Transforms Organizations and Inspires Innovation* (HarperBusiness 2009)

Chanal V and others, *Former par le design: principes, méthodes et outils pour préparer les étudiants aux enjeux du XXIe siècle* (Éditions EMS, management & société 2022)

Crawford MB, *The World Beyond Your Head: On Becoming an Individual in an Age of Distraction* (Reprint édition, Farrar, Straus and Giroux 2016)

Cross N, *Design Thinking: Understanding How Designers Think and Work* (Berg Publishers 2011)

Dubar C, Tripier P and Boussard V, *Sociologie des professions* (3e éd, A Colin 2011)

Farrell R and Hooker C, 'Values and Norms Between Design and Science' (2014) 30 Design Issues 29

Findeli A, 'Searching for Design~Research Questions: Some Conceptual Clarifications' in Rosan Chow, Jonas Wolfgang and Joost Gesche (eds), *Questions, Hypotheses & Conjectures* (iUniverse 2010)

Findeli A and Bousbaci R, 'L'Eclipse de L'Objet Dans Les Théories Du Projet En Design (The Eclipse of the Object in Design Project Theories)' (2005) 8 The Design Journal 35

Fontaine L, *Qu'est-ce qu'un grand juriste ? Essai sur les juristes et la pensée juridique contemporaine* (LGDJ 2012) <https://www.lgdj.fr/qu-est-ce-qu-un-grand-juriste-9782359710656.html> accessed 12 December 2023

Hagan MD, '1. Legal Design' (*Law By Design*, 26 January 2015) <https://lawbydesign.co/legal-design/> accessed 20 January 2023

Harner M, 'The Value of "Thinking Like a Lawyer"' [2011] Faculty Scholarship <https://digitalcommons.law.umaryland.edu/fac_pubs/1031>

'IFCN Code of Principles' <https://www.ifcncodeofprinciples.poynter.org/profile/les-surligneurs> accessed 20 January 2023

Kantrowitz C, Warzel C and Mac R, 'Facebook Executive In 2016: "Maybe Someone Dies In A Terrorist Attack Coordinated On Our Tools"' (*BuzzFeed News*, 29 March 2018) <https://www.buzzfeednews.com/article/ryanmac/

growth-at-any-cost-top-facebook-executive-defended-data> accessed 12 December 2023

Lawson B, *How Designers Think: The Design Process Demystified* (4th ed, Architectural Press 2005)

Le Gall A, 'Legal Design beyond Design Thinking: Processes and Effects of the Four Spaces of Design Practices for the Legal Field' in Rossana Ducato and Alain Strowel (eds), *Legal Design Perspectives: Theoretical and Practical Insights from the Field* (Ledizioni 2021)

Martin R, 'Design Thinking: Achieving Insights via the "Knowledge Funnel"' (2010) 38 Strategy & Leadership 37

Midal A, *Design - introduction à l'histoire d'une discipline* (POCKET 2009)

'Mireille Delmas-Marty : « Profitons de la pandémie pour faire la paix avec la Terre »' *Le Monde.fr* (17 March 2020) <https://www.lemonde.fr/idees/article/2020/03/17/mireille-delmas-marty-profitons-de-la-pandemie-pour-faire-la-paix-avec-la-terre_6033344_3232.html> accessed 12 December 2023

Mollon M, 'Design pour débattre : comment créer des artefacts dissonants, et leurs situations de communication, afin d'ouvrir des espaces de contestation mutuelle (agonisme) et d'expression des voix marginales (dissensus)' (PhD thesis, Université Paris sciences et lettres 2019) <https://theses.hal.science/tel-03120398> accessed 12 December 2023

Morgan R and Allbon E, 'Is Law Really That Special ?' in Rossana Ducato and Alain Strowel (eds), *Legal Design Perspectives: Theoretical and Practical Insights from the Field* (Ledizioni 2021)

Norman DA and Verganti R, 'Incremental and Radical Innovation: Design Research vs. Technology and Meaning Change' (2014) 30 Design Issues 78

Ost F and van de Kerchove M, *De la pyramide au réseau? pour une théorie dialectique du droit* (Publications Fac St Louis 2002)

'Où sont les Dragons' <https://ousontlesdragons.fr/publications/legal-design-roundtable/> accessed 20 January 2023

Ryan CD and others, 'Monetizing Disinformation in the Attention Economy: The Case of Genetically Modified Organisms (GMOs)' (2020) 38 European Management Journal 7

Schön DA, *The Reflective Practitioner - How Professionals Think In Action* (Basic Books 1983)

Schön DA and DeSanctis V, 'The Reflective Practitioner: How Professionals Think in Action' (1986) 34 The Journal of Continuing Higher Education 29

Seidel VP and Fixson SK, 'Adopting Design Thinking in Novice Multidisciplinary Teams: The Application and Limits of Design Methods and Reflexive Practices' (2013) 30 Journal of Product Innovation Management 19

Tooze A, 'Chartbook #130 Defining Polycrisis - from Crisis Pictures to the Crisis Matrix.' (*Chartbook*, 24 June 2022) <https://adamtooze.substack.com/p/chartbook-130-defining-polycrisis> accessed 12 December 2023

Van Meerbeeck J, 'Penser par cas... Et par principes' (2014) 73 Revue interdisciplinaire d'études juridiques 77

Verganti R, *Design Driven Innovation: Changing the Rules of Competition by Radically Innovating What Things Mean* (Harvard Business Review Press 2009)

Vial S, 'De la spécificité du projet en design : une démonstration' [2014] Communication et organisation. Revue scientifique francophone en Communication organisationnelle 17

Zuboff S, *The Age of Surveillance Capitalism. The Fight for a Human Future at the New Frontier of Power* (PublicAffairs 2019)

12. FROM DARK TO FAIR PATTERNS? HOW CAN DESIGN-DRIVEN INNOVATION AND NEURODESIGN HELP FIGHTING AGAINST DECEPTIVE DESIGN

Marie Potel-Saville

Abstract
Dark patterns are deceptive or manipulative interfaces that modify users' architecture of choice, leading them to act without realising, against their preferences or against their best interests. They are widely spread in the digital environment and there is multi-disciplinary evidence of the individual and structural harms they cause. In this article, we synthesise evidence of the prevalence of dark patterns, evidence of harms and the legal framework. Then, we propose a complementary area of research to contribute to solving the issue: we introduce the concept of fair patterns, as a combination of design-driven innovation and neurodesign, building on the human-centric approach, 'light patterns', 'bright patterns' without paternalism, autonomy preserving protection measures and the newly introduced principle of fairness by design. Beyond the concept, we also propose a grid of criteria to create fair patterns and provide an example of one of our prototypes. We then discuss whether the concept of fair patterns is robust enough to contribute to solving the issue, identify limitations and call for further research, including user testing and a technological solution to scale fair patterns, in addition to training all of the stakeholders.

1. Introduction

Design thinking certainly does not exhaust the role that design plays in innovation,[1] and has attracted criticism among designers themselves,[2]

1 Marcus Jahnke and Ulla Johansson-Sköldberg, 'Introducing Design-Driven Innovation: A Challenging Ride Towards New Possibilities' in Miriam Grace and George Graen (eds), *Millennial Spring: Designing The Future Of Organizations* (Volume IX, Information Age Publishing 2014).

2 Sarah Dawood, 'Pentagram's Natasha Jen: "Design is not a monster you 'unleash' to fix the world"' (Design Week, 8 March 2018) <https://www.designweek.co.uk/issues/5-11-march-2018/pentagrams-natasha-jen-design-monster-un-

namely in regard to 'diluting' design into a corporate, linear and almost 'tick-the-box' (or 'tick-the-post-it-notes') process.

While we still see the value of design thinking in our practice as a starting point, this paper aims at exploring the potential of design-driven innovation,[3] and NeuroDesign[4] in contributing to solving one of the most widespread issues for humans online: dark patterns.[5] In general terms, dark patterns are interfaces that deceive or manipulate users, to act without realising, against their preferences or against their own interests.

Dark patterns are now legally defined in the EU by the Digital Services Act, as interfaces that *'mislead, manipulate, impair or substantially limit the ability of users to make free and informed decisions'*, due to their *'design, organization or the way they are operated'*.[6]

There is also rich scientific literature on the definition and taxonomy of dark patterns. A behavioural study by the European Commission on unfair commercial practices online revealed that 97% of European citizens' preferred e-commerce sites contain at least one dark pattern,[7] while a Princeton/Chicago University study analysed over 11,000 favourite e-commerce sites in the US and found 1,818 dark pattern instances, and even 23 providers offering 'on the shelf' dark patterns.[8]

---

leash-fix-world/> accessed 07 February 2023.

3 Roberto Verganti, 'Design as brokering of languages: Innovation strategies in Italian firms' (2003) 14 Design Management Journal 34.

4 Jan Auernhammer and Bernard Roth, 'The Origin and Evolution of Stanford University's Design Thinking: From Product Design to Design Thinking in Innovation Management' (2021) 38 Journal of Product Innovation Management 623.

5 Some authors such as Harry Brignull and Jennifer King have used the term 'deceptive patterns' to avoid any misunderstanding as to any negative connotation associated with the term 'dark'. We fully adhere to this precaution; however given that recent legislation and regulatory publications have used the term 'dark pattern', we will use it in this article for legal precision purposes.

6 Regulation (EU) 2022/2065 of 19 October 2022 on a Single Market for Digital Services and amending Directive 2000/31/EC [2022] OJ L277/1, (Digital Services Act), art 25.

7 European Commission, Directorate-General for Justice and Consumers and others, 'Behavioural Study On Unfair Commercial Practices In The Digital Environment: Dark Patterns And Manipulative Personalization- Final Report' (Publications Office of the European Union 2022).

8 Arunesh Mathur and others, 'Dark Patterns at Scale: Findings From a Crawl of 11k Shopping Websites'(2019) 3 ACM Human-Computer Interaction 81.

Interestingly, scientific literature has been focusing on debating definitions, taxonomies and the regulation of dark patterns, but little has been published so far on solving the issue, apart from new regulations.[9]

This paper aims at exploring whether design-driven innovation, on its own or combined with NeuroDesign, (which aims at applying the information gained by studying brain functioning to improve and advance design thinking practices[10]) has the potential to counter dark patterns and help create 'fair patterns': interfaces that empower users to make enlightened and free choices.

First, we will present multidisciplinary evidence of the prevalence and harms caused by dark patterns. Second, we will introduce the concept of fair patterns, combining design-driven innovation and NeuroDesign. Finally, we will discuss whether the new concept is robust enough to tackle the issue and what the limitations are, and call for further research. As a conclusion, given the significant gaps between human cognitive abilities and what would be required to truly keep our autonomy online, we call for legislators to take into account neurosciences and cognitive sciences in new legislation regulating the digital economy.

2. Multi-Disciplinary Evidence of the Prevalence of, and Harms Caused by, Dark Patterns

2.1. Rich Literature Defining and Categorising Dark Patterns

There has been rich academic literature on the definitions of dark patterns since the term was coined in 2010 by UX designer and PhD in neurosciences holder, Harry Brignull, referring to 'tricks used in websites and apps that make you do things that you didn't mean to, like buying or

9 Ingvar Tjostheim, 'Dark Pattern: A Serious Game for Learning About the Dangers of Sharing Data' (2022) 16 ECGBL 774; Than H Soe, Cristiana T Santos and Marija Slavkovik, 'Automated Detection Of Dark Patterns in Cookie Banners: How to Do it Poorly and Why it is Hard to do it Any Other Way' (2022) <https://arxiv.org/abs/2204.11836v1> accessed 07 February 2023; Hellen Truong and Axel Dalbard, 'Bright Patterns as an Ethical Approach to Counteract Dark Patterns' (Masters thesis, Jönköping University School of Engineering 2022).

10 Auernhammer and Roth (n 4).

signing up for something'.[11] Most definitions include notions of:
1. deception, manipulation, coercion, or exploitation in the design and wording of user interfaces,
2. playing on humans' cognitive biases,
3. leading users to make decisions unknowingly, against their preferences or against their best interests.[12]

Across the various definitions, Mathur, Kshirsagar and Mayer[13] find that the commonality of dark patterns in the scientific literature is that they "modify the choice architecture presented to users". They do so either by:
- modifying the set of choices available to users: making some choices more burdensome, or less appealing than other choices (usually the most privacy protective or the cheapest for the users), or
- manipulating the information flow to users: making protective information more difficult to find or more difficult to understand or even providing false information.[14]

Either way, dark patterns exploit cognitive biases and in particular seek to trigger Kahneman's 'System 1' thinking: automatic, fast, intuitive

11 'What is Deceptive Design' (Deceptive Design) <https://www.deceptive.design/> accessed 07 February 2023.

12 Gregory Conti and Edward Sobiesk, 'Malicious Interface Design: Exploiting the User' (19th International Conference on World Wide Web, Raleigh NC, April 2010); Christoph Bösch and others, 'Tales from the Dark Side: Privacy Dark Strategies and Privacy Dark Patterns' [2016] Proceedings on Privacy Enhancing Technologies 237; Colin Gray and others, 'The Dark (Patterns) Side of UX design' (CHI 2018, Montréal QC, April 2018); Mathur and others (n 8); Paul Graßl and others, 'Dark and Bright Patterns in Cookie Consent Requests' (2021) 3 Journal of Digital and Social Research 1; Jamie Luguri and Lior Jacob Strahilevitz, 'Shining a light on Dark Patterns' (2021) 3 Journal of Legal Analysis 43; Luiza Jarovsky, 'Dark Patterns in Personal Data Collection: Definition, Taxonomy and Lawfulness' (2022), available at SSRN at <https://ssrn.com/abstract=4048582>; OECD, 'Dark Commercial Patterns' (OECD Digital Economy Papers, No. 336 OECD Publishing 2022).

13 Arunesh Mathur, Jonathan Mayer and Mihir Kshirsagar, 'What Makes A Dark Pattern... Dark? Design Attributes, Normative Considerations, And Measurement Methods' (CHI Conference on Human Factors in Computing Systems (CHI '21), Yokohama, Japan, (2021).

14 OECD (n 12).

decisions with low cognitive effort, rather than 'System 2' thinking: deliberative, conscious and effortful decision-making.[15]

Indeed, neurosciences have established that our brain is a real 'decision machine', from the simplest to the most sophisticated, in particular the prefrontal cortex, at the front of the brain. To make decisions, two main types of mental strategies (i.e., connections and neural networks) have been proposed by psychologist Daniel Kahneman, winner of the Nobel Prize in Economics in 2002:[16]

- System 1: very fast, effective and economical for the brain based on heuristics. It works very well, very often, but not always, and
- System 2: slower, analytical strategies, with cognitive effort. It leads to the correct solution but is costly for the brain.

In addition to these systems, a third system is described nowadays, System 3, inhibition, which is an arbitration system that precisely interrupts – when necessary – the heuristic system (System 1) to activate that of the algorithms (System 2).[17]

Heuristics and cognitive biases are closely linked to System 1, as they provide decision guidance in cases of uncertainty. The concept of cognitive bias was introduced in the 1970s by Daniel Kahneman and Amos Tversky to explain certain irrational decisions in the economic field.[18] It was then extended to many other fields: perception, statistics, logic, causality, social relations, etc.

A cognitive bias can be described as a 'mental shortcut': it is a systematic, irrational pattern impacting judgement and decision making. Cognitive biases can lead to more effective actions or faster decisions in some contexts. They reduce the amount of information to be considered and simplify the processes of judgment and decision-making.

They can be classified into 4 categories according to the problems they help us to address:

---

15 Daniel Kahneman and Amos Tversky, 'The Psychology of Preferences' (1982) 246 Scientific American 160; Bösch and others (n 12); Graßl and others (n 12): Dark patterns push users to make quick heuristic decisions rather than slow and deliberate ones; OECD (n 11).

16 Kahneman and Tversky (n 15).

17 ibid.

18 ibid.

- In cases of information overload: some biases arise from too much information
- In cases of lack of meaning: some biases arise as the brain needs to make sense
- In cases where there is a need to act fast: most biases gain time and resources
- In cases where we are figuring out what needs to be remembered for later: biases relating to memory limits arise.

More than 180 different cognitive biases are described in the literature. The issue with cognitive biases is that they are :
- Based on inputs that are not objectives, decisions then differ from rational choices
- Systematic, replicable and difficult to inhibit
- 'Silent': we can miss factors that influence our decision.

Cognitive biases act like unconscious errors in thinking and may lead to inaccurate judgement and irrational interpretations. Dark patterns rely on several cognitive biases that are implicit to users,[19] mostly:
- Anchoring bias
- Default effect
- Framing effect
- Hyperbolic updating effect
- Optimistic bias
- Overchoice

Given that dark patterns rely on cognitive biases that are implicit, they are often difficult to avoid for users.[20] Therefore, they can be considered as online manipulation as they deprive users of their capacity for independent decision-making.[21]

Several studies have examined the 'efficiency' of dark patterns, namely Utz and others, who demonstrated with a representative sam-

19 Ari Ezra Waldman, 'Cognitive Biases, Dark Patterns, and the 'Privacy Paradox' (2020) 31 Current Issues in Psychology 1; Jarovsky (n 12).

20 Jarovsky (n 12); Waldman (n 19).

21 Daniel Susser, Beate Roessler and Helen Nissenbaum, 'Technology, Autonomy, and Manipulation'(2019) 8 Internal Policy Review 1.

ple of users that dark patterns influence users' consent decisions,[22] Graßl and others, who experimented with dark patterns on cookie banners,[23] and Maier and Harr, who analysed users' awareness and ability to detect them. They reported that most users 'were moderately aware of these deceptive techniques, several of which were perceived as sneaky and dishonest. Respondents further expressed a resigned attitude towards such techniques and primarily blamed businesses for their occurrence'.[24] Bongard-Blanchy and others established that even when users are aware of some dark patterns, for example the blatant 'confirmshaming' (making users feel bad about declining a proposed 'option', usually to buy, subscribe, or share personal data), they cannot resist it.[25]

In addition to being 'silent' and difficult to resist, there is multi-disciplinary evidence of the high prevalence of dark patterns on a global scale.

2.2. World-Wide Evidence of Prevalence, in Spite of Existing Legal Framework

2.2.1. High Prevalence

Significant research efforts have been made to identify the prevalence of dark patterns. Very recently, in 2023, the European Commission and

---

22 Christine Utz and others, '(Un)informed Consent: Studying GDPR Consent Notices in the Field' (ACM SIGSAC Conference on Computer and Communications Security (CCS'19), London, 2019).

23 Graßl and others (n 12). Other studies were conducted either with a non-representative sample (e.g., only students or young university-educated people; Dominique Machuletz, 'Multiple Purposes, Multiple Problems: A User Study of Consent Dialogs after GDPR' (2020) 2 Proceedings on Privacy Enhancing Technologies 481; Rainer Böhme and Stefan Köpsell, 'Trained to Accept? A Field Experiment on Consent Dialogs' (28th International Conference on Human Factors in Computing Systems, Atlanta, April 2010); Midas Nouwens and others, 'Dark Patterns after the GDPR: Scraping Consent Pop-ups and Demonstrating their Influence'(CHI 2020, Honolulu, April 2020) or in a context that cannot be generalised easily (e.g., participants were told to have been automatically signed up for a costly identity-theft protection service; Jamie Luguri and Lior Jacob Strahilevitz, 'Shining a light on Dark Patterns' (2021) 3 Journal of Legal Analysis 43.

24 Maximilian Maier and Rikard Harr, 'Dark Design Patterns: An End-User Perspective' (2020) 16 Human Technology 170.

25 Kerstin Bongard-Blanchy and others, '"I am Definitely Manipulated, Even When I Am Aware of It. It's Ridiculous!" – Dark Patterns from the End-User Perspective' (Designing Interactive Systems Conference, USA, 2021).

national consumer protection authorities of 23 Member States, Norway and Iceland,[26] screened 399 retail sites offering a wide variety of products, and found that nearly 40% contained at least one dark pattern, among only three types of dark patterns that were searched, in relation to consumer protection: fake countdown timers, push & pressure to buy or subscribe, and hidden information.

The OECD Report on dark patterns identifies a large number of studies by researchers, regulatory authorities and consumer protection bodies:

- In 2022, the European Commission study on dark patterns found that 97% of 75 popular e-commerce websites and apps in the EU contained at least one dark pattern;[27]
- Radesky and others[28] found that 80% of popular children's apps contained at least one manipulative design feature;
- Gunawan and others[29] found that all 105 of the most popular online services in the Google Play Store that featured both an app and website format contained at least one dark pattern;
- The Chilean consumer protection authority found that 64% of 103 Chilean e-commerce websites examined featured at least one dark pattern.[30]
- Mathur and others[31] identified that 11.1% of around 11 000 popular e-commerce websites examined featured dark patterns.
- The International Consumer Protection Enforcement Network identified that 24 % of 1754 e-commerce websites/apps investigated featured "dark nudges" (ICPEN, 2019);[32]

26 European Commission, 'Consumer Protection: Manipulative Online Practices Found on 148 Out of 399 Online Shops Screened'(2023) <https://ec.europa.eu/commission/presscorner/detail/en/ip_23_418> accessed 07 February 2023.

27 European Commission (n 7).

28 Jenny Radesky and others, Prevalence and Characteristics of Manipulative Design in Mobile Applications Used by Children (2022) 5 JAMA Network Open 1.

29 Johanna Gunawan and others, 'Towards an Understanding of Dark Patterns Privacy Harms'(2021) ACM <https://doi.org/10.1145/3479521> accessed 07 February 2023.

30 SERNAC, 'Report on the results of the survey of Dark Patterns in Electronic Commerce' (SERNAC, 03 August 2021) <https://www.sernac.cl/portal/619/w3-article-62983.html> accessed 03 January 2023.

31 Mathur and others (n 8).

32 OECD, 'Roundtable on Dark Commercial Patterns Online: Summary of Discussion' (Directorate for Science, Technology and Innovation Committee on Consumer Pol-

- Di Geronimo et al. [33] found that 95% of a sample of 240 popular apps contained at least one dark pattern;
- In 2018, the Norwegian Consumer Protection Council[34] analysed the account creation and management settings of Facebook, Google and Windows 10, and identified dozens of "privacy intrusive" interfaces: leading users to share more personal data than they would have consciously done.

While the precise prevalence varies, mostly depending on the method used to identify them, the breadth and severity of harms caused by dark patterns has led legislators in the US and the EU to expressly prohibit dark patterns, in addition to already applicable legislation.

2.2.2. Numerous Applicable Legal Grounds, and New Emerging Legislation
An analysis of the legislative framework in the EU and the US reveals that even before specific legislation targeting dark patterns, there were numerous legal backgrounds prohibiting them.

At the European level, there is a large body of legislation that is already applicable to dark patterns:
- In consumer law: The Unfair Commercial Practices Directive,[35] Consumer Rights Directive,[36] Unfair Contract Terms Directive[37]

icy 2021).

33 Linda di Geronimo and others, 'UI Dark Patterns and Where to Find Them: A Study on Mobile Applications and User Perception' (CHI 2020, Honolulu HI, 2020).

34 Forbrukkerådet (The Norwegian Consumer Council), *Deceived by design: how tech companies use dark patterns to discourage us from exercising our rights to privacy* (Forbrukkerådet 2018).

35 Directive 2005/29/EC of 11 May 2005 concerning unfair business-to-consumer commercial practices in the internal market and amending Council Directive 84/450/EEC, Directives 97/7/EC, 98/27/EC and 2002/65/EC of the European Parliament and of the Council and Regulation (EC) No 2006/2004 of the European Parliament and of the Council [2022] L149/22 (Unfair Commercial Practices Directive).

36 Directive 2011/83/EU of 25 October 2011 on consumer rights, amending Council Directive 93/13/EEC and Directive 1999/44/EC and repealing Council Directive 85/577/EEC and Directive 97/7/EC [2011] OJ L304/64 (Consumer Rights Directive).

37 Council Directive (EEC) 93/13/EEC of 5 April 1993 on unfair terms in consumer contracts [1993] OJ L95/29 (Unfair Contract Terms Directive).

- In data protection law, the GDPR[38] (namely Articles 4, 4, 12 and 25), the EDPB draft Guidelines on dark patterns on social networks[39] and the e-Privacy Directive,[40] Article 5(3)
- In sector-specific law: The E-commerce Directive[41] (now amended) and the Audiovisual and Media Services Directive,[42] as amended, and
- In competition law, some dark patterns could be qualified as an abuse of dominance[43] (Art. 102 TFEU).

In the US, Section 5 of the FTC Act[44] prohibits "unfair or deceptive conduct or practices affecting commerce". In September 2022, the FTC published a report on dark patterns and announced enforcement measures[45] following a workshop held in 2021.

None of these acts takes account of the fact that the human brain is simply not wired for information overload, which triggers Kahneman's System 1 answer: automatic response. That is why some authors consider for example that online consent is irrelevant, and that privacy regulation should let go of this inefficient mechanism and rather impose fiduciary duties on companies handling our personal data. [46]

38 Regulation (EU) 2016/679 of 27 April 2016 on the protection of natural persons with regard to the processing of personal data and on the free movement of such data, and repealing Directive 95/46/EC [2016] OJ L119/1 (General Data Protection Regulation).

39 Draft Guidelines 3/2022 of 14 March 2022 on Dark Patterns in Social Media Platform Interfaces: How to Recognise and Avoid Them [2022] Version 1.0.

40 Directive 2002/58/EC of 12 July 2002 concerning the processing of personal data and the protection of privacy in the electronic communications sector [2002] OJ L201/37 (Directive on privacy and electronic communications).

41 Directive 2000/31/EC of 8 June 2000 on certain legal aspects of information society services, in particular electronic commerce, in the Internal Market [2000] OJ L178/1 (Directive on electronic commerce).

42 Directive 2010/13/EU of 10 March 2010 on the coordination of certain provisions laid down by law, regulation or administrative action in Member States concerning the provision of audiovisual media services [2010] OJ L95/1 (Audiovisual Media Services Directive).

43 Consolidated Version of the Treaty on the Functioning of the European Union [2008] OJ C202/47.

44 Federal Trade Commission (FTC) Act 1914.

45 Federal Trade Commission (FTC) Bureau of Consumer Protection, 'Bringing Dark Patterns to Light: An FTC Report' (Staff Report 2022).

46 Waldman (n 19).

Given the prevalence of dark patterns, which indicates that the existing legislative framework is not sufficient, new texts have emerged to expressly prohibit them, as 'dark patterns'.

The California Privacy Rights Act, (CPRA), passed in 2020, is considered to be the first piece of legislation to provide a definition of dark patterns: 'a user interface designed or manipulated with the substantial effect of subverting or impairing user autonomy, decision-making, or choice, as further defined by regulation'.[47]

The CPRA provides that 'consent obtained through dark patterns does not constitute consent'. Similar amendments to privacy laws have been introduced in other US states, or are under consideration. Similarly, Canada introduced a bill in 2022, the Digital Charter Implementation Act[48] (Bill C-27), to prohibit and invalidate consent obtained through deception or manipulation. Without expressly mentioning the term, it is considered to cover dark patterns.[49]

In the EU, the Digital Services Act[50] lays down the transparency obligations on online platform providers and defines a dark pattern as a digital interface that 'misleads, manipulates, impairs or substantially limits the ability of users to make free and informed decisions', due to its 'design, organization or the way it is operated'.

In other words, and according to Point 67 of the preamble to the DSA, they are mechanisms that cause users to act involuntarily, or to make undesirable decisions, which may have negative consequences for them. The DSA is due to come into force by February 2024 at the latest.

Most of the major recent texts, which have been adopted or are in the process of being adopted at the time of writing, also prohibit dark patterns in their respective fields. For example, the Digital Markets Act includes an 'anti-circumvention' provision for the main prohibitions imposed on gatekeepers, in practice the GAFAMs, notably through 'in-

47 California Privacy Rights Act 2020.

48 Digital Charter Implementation Act (Bill C-27).

49 Jennifer King and Adriana Stephan, 'Regulating Privacy Dark Patterns in Practice-Drawing Inspiration from California Privacy Rights Act' (2021) 5 Georgetown Law Technology Review 250.

50 Digital Services Act (n 6).

terface design'.[51] The draft Regulation on artificial intelligence[52] also prohibits dark patterns, as artificial intelligence practices contrary to the values of the European Union. The following artificial intelligence practices are prohibited:

1. placing on the market, putting into service or using an AI system that uses subliminal techniques below the threshold of a person's awareness to substantially alter their behaviour in a way that causes or is likely to cause physical or psychological harm to that person or to a third party;
2. the placing on the market, putting into service or use of an AI system that exploits possible vulnerabilities due to the age or physical or mental disability of a given group of persons in order to substantially alter the behaviour of a member of that group in a way that causes or is likely to cause physical or psychological harm to that person or to a third party.

2.3. Multi-Disciplinary Evidence of Individual and Structural Harms

The European Commission's behavioural study on dark patterns[53] recalls that the harmful consequences for consumers have been widely documented in recent years: financial losses, impairment of autonomy and privacy, cognitive burdens, and in some cases mental health impairment (addictions, etc.), in addition to risks of impairment of competition, reduced price transparency and ultimately loss of confidence in markets.

The study also shows that dark patterns particularly affect vulnerable consumers: minors, senior people, and less educated people. For example, one third of Internet users worldwide are minors,[54] who are officially

---

51 Regulation (EU) 2022/1925 of 14 September 2022 on contestable and fair markets in the digital sector and amending Directives (EU) 2019/1937 and (EU) 2020/1828 [2022] OJ L265/1 (Digital Markets Act), Article 4.

52 Proposal COM/2021/206 of 21 April 2021 for a Regulation laying down harmonised rules on artificial intelligence and amending certain union legislative acts COM(2021) 206 final, (Article 5 (a) and 5 (b)).

53 European Commission (n 7).

54 See in particular: Marie Potel-Saville and Elisabeth Talbourdet, 'Empowering Children to Understand and Exercise their Personal Data Rights' in Rossana Ducato and Alain Strowel (eds), *Legal Design Perspectives* (1st edn, Ledizioni 2021).

vulnerable and need greater protection under the GDPR, among other things.

Dark patterns generate two main types of harms, which have been identified in the literature: individual harm and structural harm.

(i) Individual harm

Unsurprisingly, it has been evidenced that dark patterns harm individuals' autonomy:[55] they trick users in deciding against their preferences, deny their choice, or make their choice more difficult. Obviously, dark patterns also harm consumer welfare by generating a financial loss: they make users buy more than intended, or pay more for what they wanted to buy. For example "drip pricing" was evidenced to make users spend 21% more than usual. [56]

In addition, dark patterns create significant privacy harms: they lead users to share more personal data than intended. For example a survey on Australian consumers showed than 1 in 4 consumers shared more personal data owing to dark patterns.[57] They have also been evidenced to create psychological detriment and time loss: they generate frustration and shame and increase our cognitive burden.[58] The European Commission even found that they increase the heart rate, and cause anxiety and alertness.[59]

(ii) Structural harm

Beyond affecting individuals, dark patterns also weaken or alter competition. They do so by preventing consumers from comparing prices, locking consumers into recurring subscriptions and hampering switching. They also affect competition,[60] and can enable firms to increase their sales or the volume of personal data they collect without offering better

55 Mathur and others (n 8) 4.

56 Thomas Blake and others, 'Price Salience and Product Choice' (2021) 40 Marketing Science 619.

57 Consumer Policy Research Centre (CPRC), 'Duped by Design. Manipulative Online Design: Dark Patterns in Australia' (Consumer Policy Research Centre 2022).

58 Mathur and others (n 8) 4.

59 European Commission (n 7).

60 Alexander Rasch, Miriam Thöne and Tobias Wenzel, 'Drip Pricing and its Regulation: Experimental Evidence (2020) 176 Journal of Economic Behaviour and Organization 353.

services or products. In this respect, dark patterns can give them an undue competitive advantage.[61]

Concerns have also been voiced that dominant firms could use dark patterns to neutralise a competitive threat: default settings, nagging or collecting data to offer services in a way that rivals cannot.[62]

To the extent that dark patterns impede consumers' ability to select the best firms on the merits of their product offerings, market use of dark patterns can distort the competitive process as a whole),[63] allowing firms to compete through the "efficiency" of their dark patterns rather than on merit.

Dark patterns also lead to less consumer trust and engagement: much of consumers' behaviour towards online businesses is based on trust, which has been defined as expectations that businesses will behave in a favourable, predictable manner. [64]

Unsurprisingly, many researchers have found that dark patterns alter consumers' trust in sites and apps using them. For example almost 50% of consumers exposed to scarcity and social proof dark patterns on hotel booking sites distrusted these sites as a result.[65] See also Maier and

61 OECD (n 12).

62 ibid; Katharine Kemp, 'Concealed Data Practices and Competition Law: Why Privacy Matters' (2020) 16 European Competition Journal 628; Rebecca Slaughter, 'Opening remarks of acting chairwoman Rebecca Kelly Slaughter at "Bringing dark patterns to light" workshop' (FTC 'Bringing Dark Patterns to Light' Workshop, Virtual, April 2021); Competition and Markets Authority (CMA), 'Online Choice Architecture: How digital design can harm competition and consumers' (Competition and Markets Authority 2022).

63 ibid; Gregory Day and Abbey Stemler, 'Are Dark Patterns Anti-Competitive?' (2020) 72 Alabama Law Review 2.

64 Waldman (n 19).

65 Simon Shaw, 'Consumers Are Becoming Wise to Your Nudge' (Behavioral Scientist, 12 June 2019) <https://behavioralscientist.org/consumers-are-becoming-wise-to-your-nudge/> accessed 08 February 2023.

Harr,[66] Voigt, Schlögl and Groth,[67] Robbert and Roth,[68] and Totzek and Jurgensen.[69]

The harms generated by dark patterns are so serious that it could even put into question whether a market economy is still the system that provides the greatest benefits for consumers.[70] The lack of trust resulting from dark patterns may lead consumers to lose faith in markets and market forces and disengage.[71]

In the US, Maya MacGuineas, chair of the Committee for a Responsible Federal Budget, argued in 2020 that in a well-functioning market, consumers have the freedom to act in their own self-interest and to maximise their well-being, *"but the new powers of the digital age have built their model on strategies that undermine the principles that make capitalism a 'good deal' for most people"*.[72]

3. Introducing the Concept of Fair Patterns, as a Combination of Design-Driven Innovation and Neurodesign

3.1. Building on Design-Driven Innovation, a Human-Centric Approach and 'Light Patterns'

Given that some cognitive biases arise from a lack of meaning, whereas the brain needs to make sense, it is interesting to explore whether design-driven innovation could contribute to solving the issue. Indeed,

66 Maier and Harr (n 24).

67 Christian Voigt, Stephan Schlögl and Aleksander Groth, 'Dark Patterns in Online Shopping: Of Sneaky Tricks, Perceived Annoyance and Respective Brand Trust (HCI International, Washington DC, July 2021).

68 Thomas Robbert and Stephan Roth, 'The Flip Side of Drip Pricing' (2014) 23 Journal of Product & Brand Management 413.

69 Dirk Totzek and Gabriel Jurgensen, 'Many a Little Makes a Mickle: Why do Consumers Negatively React to Sequential Price Disclosure?' (2020) 38 Psychology and Marketing 113.

70 OECD, 'OECD Recommendation of the Council on Consumer Protection in E-Commerce' (OECD Publishing 2016); OECD (n 12).

71 Luguri and Strahilevitz (n 23).

72 Maya MacGuineas, 'Capitalism's Addiction Problem' (The Atlantic, April 2020) <https://www.theatlantic.com/magazine/archive/2020/04/capitalisms-addiction-problem/606769/> accessed 08 February 2023.

design-driven innovation focuses on products' or services' meaning, and the value created by products or services, including utilitarian, emotional, psychological and socio-cultural values.[73] Therefore, 'design-driven innovation broadens the horizon beyond user-centered design and balances knowledge about user needs, technological development and product language'.[74]

Through the lenses of design-driven innovation, we can question the meaning and value for users of cookie banners, online privacy policies and other online contracts – which are often plagued with dark patterns, as demonstrated above. The rocket-high levels of blind signing seem to indicate that their current content and form deprives them of (i) any meaning and consequently (ii) any value for users,[75] who are 'trained to accept'. [76] One of the most blatant examples of the absence of any meaning, let alone value, of most online terms is the result of the Europol experiment conducted in 2015, where users of a public Wi-Fi hotspot agreed to Terms and Conditions that specified that by agreeing, they would give up their firstborn child or a beloved pet to use the hotspot.[77]

Design-driven innovation is based on Krippendorff's interpretation of design as a 'meaning-making activity'.[78] According to Krippendorff,[79] 'design is making sense (of things)', creating products or services that

73 Roberto Verganti, *Design Driven Innovation: Changing the Rules of Competition by Radically Innovating What Things Mean* (Harvard Business Press 2009).

74 Heleen de Goey, Per Hilletofth and Lars Erikson, 'Design-driven innovation: Making meaning for whom?' (2017) 20 The Design Journal 479.

75 OECD, 'Improving online disclosures with behavioral insights' (OECD Publishing 2018).

76 Rainer Böhme and Stefan Köpsell, 'Trained to Accept? A Field Experiment on Consent Dialogs' (28th International Conference on Human Factors in Computing Systems, Atlanta, April 2010); Marie Potel-Saville, 'Shaping the Law to Restore Its Function?' (Master's thesis, École Nationale Supérieure de la Création Industrielle ENSCI-Les Ateliers 2019).

77 Agata Blaszczak-Boxe, 'Give Up Firstborn for Free Wi-Fi? Some Click "I agree' (CBS News, 30 September 2014) <https://www.cbsnews.com/news/give-up-firstborn-for-free-wi-fi-some-click-i-agree/> accessed 22 January 2023.

78 Ulla Johansson-Sköldberg, Jill Woodilla and Meves Çetinya, 'Design Thinking: Past, Present and Possible Futures' (2013) 22 Creativity and Innovation Management 121.

79 Klaus Krippendorff, 'Content Analysis' In Erik Barnouw (eds), *International encyclopedia of communication* (OUP 1989).

are 'understandable and meaningful to someone'. We started exploring how to make sense of privacy policies or compliance programs in 2018,[80] first through a human-centric approach, taking into account the characteristics of the context of use. According to the ISO definition,[81] human-centred design implies a design team with multidisciplinary skills and perspectives, a design based on the context of use (users, tasks and environments), users' involvement throughout design and development, an iterative process, a design addressing the whole user experience and user-centered evaluation to refine solutions.

For example, we applied human-centred design in our project with the CNIL, in which our multi-disciplinary team of designers and lawyers co-created with underage users in creating their ideal privacy information interfaces, which would (i) engage them to read, taking into account their context of use (ii) empower them to understand data privacy concepts or choices easily, and (iii) empower them to better exercise their privacy rights.[82]

King and Stephan,[83] building on Susser [84] and Mathur and others[85] advocate this human-centred approach, placing the *'individual's ability to understand what they are consenting to squarely at the core of what it means to consent',* to create 'light patterns'. King and Stephan define 'light patterns' as the opposite of dark patterns, a non-coercive design.[86] King and Stephan[87] warn against 'false remedies' to dark patterns where users are given more checkboxes or buttons, which are meaningless and fragmented. Instead, they advocate solution mechanisms that are 'more substantive, meaningful, and informative'.

---

80 Potel-Saville (n 76).

81 'Ergonomics of human-system interaction - Part 210: Human-centred design for interactive systems (ISO 9241-210:2019)' (Standards) <https://standards.iteh.ai/catalog/standards/cen/7e97d923-5f48-46d9-b206-7df5819f85aa/en-iso-9241-210-2019#:~:text=CEN%2FTC%20122-,Ergonomics%20of%20human%2Dsystem%20interaction%20%2D%20Part%20210%3A%20Human%2D,of%20computer%2Dbased%20interactive%20systems> accessed 07 February 2023.

82 Potel-Saville and Talbourdet (n 54) 9.

83 King and Stephan (n 49).

84 Susser, Roessler and Nissenbaum (n 8).

85 Mathur, Mayer and Kshirsagar (n 13).

86 King and Stephan (n 49).

87 ibid.

In concrete terms, in relation to data privacy consent, such non-coercive design would translate into:

- existing consent options in the first place: each option to accept should have its equivalent to deny,
- consent options (accept and deny) being placed with equal prominence without favouring one choice over the other,
- no preselected option,
- same colour-contrast and size of the accept and decline buttons, and
- in relation to opting out of data sales,[88] strictly equivalent steps and options to opt-in and opt-out.[89]

Arguably, combined with plain language,[90] these design features would make data privacy information more understandable, which would be an indispensable starting point to become more meaningful, and perhaps have some value to users.

This would be relevant assuming that people make decisions and agree online in a rational way, through conscious weighing of the costs and benefits of each choice option. [91] However, a growing number of researchers question the relevance of this 'rational actor' theory. Indeed, there is compelling, multi-disciplinary evidence that most users online do not make decisions in a rational manner, based on their preferences and values.[92] Rather, they use heuristics, i.e. mental shortcuts, and fall back on cognitive biases.[93]

This leads us to combine design-driven innovation with neurodesign.

---

88 Obviously, such personal data sale is not permissible in the EU under the GDPR.

89 King and Stephan (n 49).

90 ibid.

91 Robert S Laufer and Maxine Wolfe, 'Privacy as a concept and a social issue: A multidimensional developmental theory (1977) 33 Journal of Social Issues 22.

92 Alessandro Acquisti and others, 'Nudges for Privacy and Security: Understanding and Assisting Users' Choices Online' (2017) 50 ACM Computing Surveys 44.

93 Cass R Sunstein, 'Nudges that Fail' (2016) available at SSRN at <https://ssrn.com/abstract=2809658> accessed 08 February 2023.

3.2. Building on Neurodesign and 'Bright Patterns'

Auernhammer and Roth[94] consider that results from neuroscience research are rarely directly applied to design practice, and explore how the emerging field of NeuroDesign might bridge this gap. The point of NeuroDesign is to 'effectively and efficiently apply the information gained by studying brain functioning to the development and teaching of improved design thinking practices'. While Auernhammer studied NeuroDesign to enhance design thinking approaches, this paper aims at exploring how NeuroDesign could go beyond design thinking itself.

In regard to data privacy, Graßl and others[95] identified several factors that make people apply heuristics in cookie banners:

1. Information asymmetry.
2. Ambiguous language (Relying on Simon's concept of bounded rationality,[96] i.e. human rationality is limited to the available cognitive resources and the available time, Acquisti and others consider decision making in condition of uncertainty triggers System 1).[97]
3. Cognitive biases affecting people's privacy decisions: the status-quo bias[98] and the salience bias.[99]

To fight dark patterns, Graßl and others[100] experimented with 'bright patterns', i.e. user interface designs that aim to steer consumers towards consumer-friendly options through nudges.[101] For example, a 'bright

94 Auernhammer and Roth (n 4).

95 Graßl and others (n 12).

96 Herbert A Simon, 'Bounded Rationality' in John Eatwell, Murray Milgate, M Peter Newman (eds), *Utility and Probability* (Palgrave 1990).

97 Acquisti and others (n 92).

98 ibid.

99 ibid.

100 Graßl and others (n 12).

101 Originally, nudging means influencing the decisions of individuals or groups towards good choices (as judged by themselves) through minor changes in the choice environment without compromising freedom of choice. A prominent example is a fly painted on a urinal in a public men's toilet to prevent urine spillage: Richard Thaler and Cass R Sunstein, *Nudge: Improving Decisions about Wealth, Health and Happiness* (rev edn, Penguin Books 2009); Potel-Saville (n 76). If a nudge is used for evil, Thaler considers it is no longer 'nudge', but rather 'sludge' See: Richard Thaler, 'Nudge, not Sludge' (2018) 361 Science 431.

pattern' would make privacy-friendly options easier to select than privacy-intrusive options, e.g. through preselected defaults or aesthetic framing.[102] They also experimented with several types of bright patterns to see whether (i) bright patterns indeed led users to choose the privacy-friendly option and whether (ii) bright patterns deprived users of their perceived control.[103]

The experiment revealed that 10 times more people changed their consent behaviour when nudged towards the privacy-friendly option, using the following nudges: defaults, aesthetic framing and obstructing the privacy-unfriendly option.

Thus, nudging users towards the privacy-friendly option through relatively small changes on the interface is indeed efficient, and does not help users to feel more in control when they make decisions online. In other words, nudges have no effect on the perception of control by the users (who actually have a high perception of control when faced with dark patterns, as shown in Graßl's first experiment).

Nouwens and others[104] conducted experiments on cookie banners with (only) 40 participants with 8 different designs. Although they acknowledge the limitations of the representativity of the sample, their main findings in terms of factors that decrease 'blind consent' are the following:

1. Non-blocking cookie banner (instead of a pop up blocking access)
2. Presence of 'accept all' and 'reject all' on the same page, and equal prominence
3. Displaying more granular consent options on the first page
4. Having a real choice as to consenting or not
5. Understanding the consequences of their choices.

But overall, Nouwens and others consider the consent model not to be efficient, given multi-disciplinary evidence that the rational actor model is flawed, and rather call for legally-binding browser settings, or trusted third parties to manage consent. Waldman considers for the same reason that legislators should shift away from consent as a legal basis (when

102 Graßl and others (n 12).
103 ibid.
104 Nouwens and others (n 23).

applicable) to alternatives such as a fiduciary duty imposed on companies to treat users' data in users' best interests.

3.3. New Concept of Fair Patterns, and Examples of Design

In our opinion, shifting away from consent or nudging users towards privacy or consumer-friendly options implies giving up on humans' capacity to make their own informed choices online, as if the digital economy necessarily contravenes one of our most human attributes: free choice and autonomy.

We do not believe that it is doomed to be this way. Digital per se does not entail any form of exploitation. As explained by Shoshana Zuboff, 'the digital can take many forms depending upon the social and economic logics that brings it to life'.[105] We further argue that dark patterns are not an inevitable expression of the technology they employ, in other words, digital does not imply per se manipulation or deception. On the contrary, given our ever increasingly digital lives, we believe it is precisely indispensable to reinforce and strengthen some of our deepest human attributes, our free choice and capacity to make autonomous decisions online.

As active optimists, we would rather bet on people's intelligence, once 'equipped' with the right knowledge and tools to freely decide for themselves, despite the information asymmetry. In addition, informed consent is to date one of the relevant legal bases under the GDPR, which indeed requires empowering users to understand.

We therefore propose to:

- combine meaning-making activities and NeuroDesign not to nudge, but to trigger System 2, and to
- enhance these approaches with a deeply human attribute, autonomy, and the new principle of 'fairness by design' advocated by the Competition & Markets Authority.[106]

105 Shoshana Zuboff, *The Age of Surveillance Capitalism: The Fight for a Human Future at the New Frontier of Power* (1st edn, Public Affairs 2019).
106 ibid.

Jarovsky introduced the concept of 'Autonomy Preserving Protective Measures' (APPMs), to avoid paternalistic protection, based on her definition of autonomy: *The ability of an individual to:*

independently think (understand, reflect),

decide (critically evaluate) and

choose (act, implement choice) according to his own preferences and values.[107]

Jarovsky[108] identifies three characteristics of APPMs, as non-paternalistic measures:

1. They preserve the individual's capability to make better choices, both on the immediate and next occasions (learning curve);
2. They are transparent in their format and goals;
3. They are not manipulative, can be rationally perceived and can be legally questioned.

In practical terms, Jarovsky identifies several types of APPMs: education, icons, consumer-friendly language, formatting requirements, standardised privacy notices, data collection options.

In its 2022 report on Online Choice Architecture,[109] the Competition & Markets Authority (CMA) proposed the new concept of fairness by design, to take into account users':

- Limited cognitive capacity: limited bandwidth to allocate attention, comprehend information, weight choices and make decisions; thus fairness by design requires information to be made accessible with limited cognitive effort
- Sensitivity to how information is presented: frames and nudges
- Disconnect between intentions and behaviour: guidance, additional information or even protective defaults can be required to have consumers make decisions in their own interests.

The fairness by design duty proposed by the CMA aims at ensuring that 'choices and defaults are presented in a way that facilitates informed consumer choice', 'succinctly, clearly, fairly and in a timely way so that

107 Luiza Jarovsky, 'Improving Consent in Information Privacy through Autonomy-Preserving Protective Measures (APPMs)' (2018) 4 EDPL 447.

108 ibid.

109 CMA (n 62).

consumers can easily make informed choices', and that users are able to 'access the information, assess it and act on it'.

We have been trying to make legal information clear, accessible and actionable under the methodology of 'legal design', combining user-centricity, plain language, some aspects of neurosciences and design to solve problems since 2018, with some measurable results.[110] However, given the depth and multidisciplinary nature of dark patterns, we argue that it is necessary to go beyond, to contribute to fighting dark patterns.

Building on design-driven innovation, NeuroDesign, autonomy preserving protective measures and fairness by design, we introduce the concept of 'fair patterns': interfaces that empower users to make enlightened and free choices.

The term 'fair' seems preferable to 'light' or 'bright' patterns to illustrate that we are not just advocating for the opposite of dark patterns (which would be nudging), but going one step further and empowering users to make their own decisions according to their preferences.:

- Fair as opposed to deceiving and misleading dark patterns, but equipping users with the right knowledge and tools, to preserve their autonomy, which is a central human attribute
- Fair because they empower users to make their own choices, while avoiding paternalism
- Fair because users are informed about the consequences of their choices, and are thus able to make meaningful choices
- Fair because they aim at triggering System 2, or limiting the negative consequences of System 1, to help users pause for a second, reflect and then decide - to do so, we namely rely on the hedonic qualities or interfaces (aesthetic framing) not to nudge, but to engage users to read, reflect and decide
- Fair to foster sustainability of the digital economy, inspired by the fairness by design duty proposed by the CMA.[111]

On this basis, fair patterns include information that is easily:

---

110 Marie Potel-Saville and Mathilde Da Rocha, 'Legal Design beyond the Hype: Measuring the Value' in Marcelo Corrales Compagnucci, Helena Haapio and Mark Fenwick(eds) *Research Handbook on Contract Design* (1st edn, Elgar Online 2022).

111 CMA (n 62).

- Accessible: information and choices are clear and easy to access so that users can easily review and adjust settings
- Balanced: all information and options are presented in a fair and balanced way, using the same colours, fonts, language and other design features across all options.
- Consistent and enabling: periodically remind users of their current choice settings and available controls, e.g. using dashboard.

To be considered 'fair patterns', we propose the criteria below, building on Graßl,[112] Nouwens,[113] Jarovsky[114] and the CMA.[115] In the table below, one criterion can meet several goals:

Goals pursued	Criteria
Triggering System 2 Avoiding consent fatigue namely due to perception of lack of control	enabling action, i.e. explaining consequences of choices short-term boost: explaining legal concepts in plain language, while keeping the technical term for longer term learning curve, quiz and rewards for learning more long-term boost: empowering users to measure their learning progress in not just identifying dark patterns but also resisting them and taking action (e.g. reporting dark patterns to halls of shame, regulators or NGOs to prompt class actions) enhancing perception of control: meaningful control tools by users (not just perception of control) e.g. dashboards

112 Graßl and others (n 12).
113 Nouwens and others (n 23).
114 Jarovsky (n 107).
115 CMA (n 62) 31.

Limiting cognitive effort in System 2	succinct "dosis" of information at the right time of the journey clearly distinguishing between what's mandatory and optional limited mental effort to make choices according to users' preferences, e.g. the call-to-action button on the right-hand-side is the one that corresponds to the action that the user initiated herself/himself formatting: minimum font size for minimum cognitive effort and ease of reading sufficient contrast sufficient spacing icons to support understanding (but not if ends up over-loading the page)
Fighting salience bias (sensi-tivity to frames).	balanced information, i.e. presenting options in a strictly equivalent way (button size, colours etc.)
Fighting status quo bias	neutral defaults (or protective defaults for vulnerable users e.g. minors) periodic reminders to adjust choices, and warnings
Correcting information asym-metry	providing context and guidance plain, succinct and empowering Language: language is so clear that users easily find what they need, understand it upon first reading, and understand the consequence of their choices.
Creating a learning curve	relevant and educative information short- and long term boosts mentioned above transparency in format and goals user tested
Enhancing ability to choose	easily accessible actual choice exists clarity meaningful information: providing context and stakes, including long-term consequences timely information: the right information at the right time of the user journey

Table 1. Fair Patterns Criteria, based on our new actionable and solution-oriented taxonomy of dark and fair patterns[116]

116 Marie Potel-Saville and Mathilde da Rocha, 'From Dark Patterns to Fair Patterns?

At the time of writing, we have created 23 prototypes of fair patterns, which are currently under review by independent experts including neuroscientists, economists, privacy experts, legal scholars and consumer protection experts.

An example of a fair pattern would look like this:

NEUTRAL OR PROTECTIVE DEFAULT

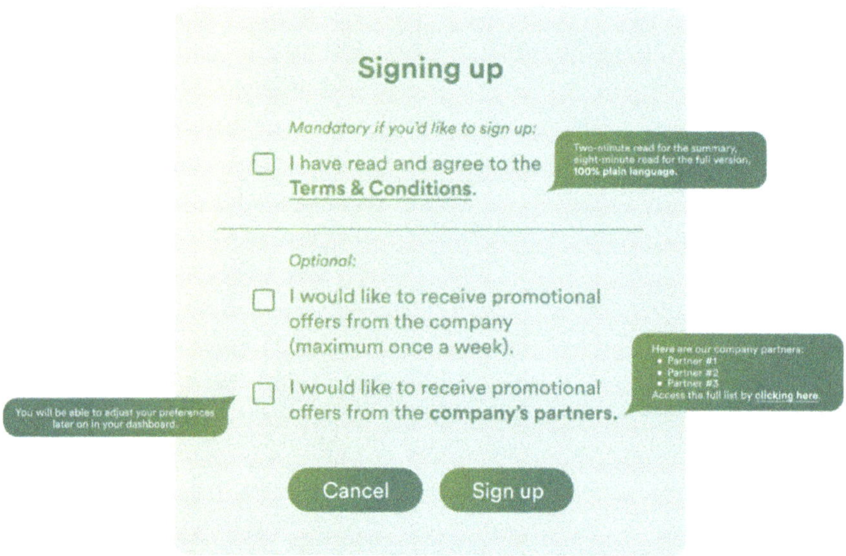

Fig. 1. Prototype of a 'fair pattern' aimed at fighting 'harmful defaults' according to our taxonomy, and creating 'neutral or protective defaults'.[117]

Usable Taxonomy to Contribute Solving the Issue with Countermeasures' Annual Privacy Forum (forthcoming).

117 Amurabi, 'Fair patterns' <https://fairpatterns.com/what-are-dark-patterns/> accessed 12 February 2024.

4. Discussion, Limitations and Next Steps

4.1. Discussion

It is clear that dark patterns are a crucial contemporary issue in the digital economy at a global level, and there is multi-disciplinary evidence for this. The current state of research has demonstrated the individual and structural harms, and regulations are changing around the world.[118]

Among the characteristics that make dark patterns 'efficient', and hence dangerous for users, are the fact that they rely on System 1 and cognitive biases, they are cheap to implement, and easy to scale and 'refine' thanks to frequent A/B testing, potentially combined with algorithmic marketing, and they are particularly efficient towards 'vulnerable' users or users with special needs.[119]

Is the concept of fair patterns and more importantly the criteria grid robust enough to address all these factors? At the time of writing, we have asked ten independent experts in neurosciences, cognitive psychology and UX, privacy, law and technology, design and consumer protection to analyse our work from a conceptual point of view, including our criteria grid, and to review our 23 current prototypes of fair patterns. We have also asked behavioural and competition economists to review our work specifically to identify possible incentives for businesses to switch from dark to fair patterns, or another solution, if better suited.

At this stage, on a conceptual level, given that part of the issue lies in interfaces that trigger System 1, it makes sense to try to activate System 2, namely by increasing the perception of control and fighting against user fatigue.

As regards the fact that dark patterns are cheap and easily scalable, it is important to realise that there is what Mathur and others describe as an 'ecosystem of third-party entities' creating dark patterns and enabling them at scale.[120] In their now famous crawl of about 11,000 shopping websites, they discovered a total of 22 third-party entities, embedded in

118 OECD (n 12) 1.

119 ibid.

120 Mathur and others (n 13).

1,066 of the shopping websites in their dataset, and in 7,769 of the Alexa top million websites. Based on publicly available marketing material on their websites, Mathur and others classified these third-parties into two groups:

- third parties focusing on social proof notifications as a service, and
- third parties providing a wide range of digital marketing services, some of them are dark patterns, mostly scarcity and urgency.

Mathur and others found that many of these third-parties openly advertise manipulative practices, such as '[p]lay upon [customers'] fear of missing out by showing shoppers which products are creating a buzz on your website' (Fresh Relevance), '[c]reate a sense of urgency to boost conversions and speed up sales cycles with Price Alert Web Push' (Insider), '[t]ake advantage of impulse purchases or encourage visitors over shipping thresholds' (Qubit), or even sheer scam such as a Woocommerce notification advertising fake social proof message '[t]he plugin will create fake orders of the selected products'.

This fairly frightening 'ecosystem' led us to create 'off-the shelf' fair patterns which are being developed at the time of writing. The idea is to create very accessible and affordable plug-ins that could be easily integrated into e-commerce sites, for example a fair purchasing funnel, a fair subscription funnel, etc.[121]

As regards the increased efficiency of dark patterns thanks to A/B testing and algorithms, where basically companies can "improve" their dark patterns by testing various versions (A / B) and observe which works the best for their purposes, the OECD[122] notes that currently dark patterns are documented in the literature to operate in the same way for all consumers, regardless of their specificities or behaviours.[123] However, they point out that some researchers consider that dark patterns will be increasingly personalised thanks to algorithmic methods, and thus more able to target users' vulnerabilities at a granular level.[124]

121 We are currently working on the technical aspects, in parallel with the expert audit and further improvement of the concept and of each prototype.

122 OECD (n 12).

123 Arvind Narayanan and others, 'Dark Patterns: Past, Present, and Future: The evolution of tricky user interfaces' (2020) 18 ACM 67.

124 Luguri and Strahilevitz (n 12) 25.

Some researchers argue that 'businesses may be able to target consumers with the dark patterns to which they may be most vulnerable, for instance based on data concerning e.g. where they live (e.g. residents of a retirement village, or people from certain language backgrounds), whether they suffer from a specific health-related vulnerability (e.g. mental illness), or are in a specific emotional or physiological state (e.g. bereavement)'.[125]

These possibilities might trigger a need to rethink the notion of 'vulnerable consumers' itself, to take into account a broader set of circumstances, bearing in mind that some authors consider all users vulnerable online.[126]

At this stage of our work, it might be worth exploring whether fair patterns could be applied in data mining and algorithmic approaches, precisely to prevent this risk. For example, in 2014 Haijan and others introduced the concept of 'fair patterns discovery', aiming at addressing the discrimination risks in data mining, and presented a 'set of pattern sanitization methods'.[127]

4.2. Limitations

It is now clear in the literature that certain subsets of users are particularly vulnerable to dark patterns[128]. The following vulnerable groups have been identified, in a non-extensive way:

- users who are less tech-savvy, such as elderly people with less developed technology skills or less educated people;[129]

---

125 Stigler Committee, 'Stigler Committee on Digital Platforms: Final Report' (Stigler Center for the Economy and the State 2019); Natali Helberger and others, 'Structural asymmetries in digital consumer markets' (EU Consumer Protection 2.0 March 2021) European Commission (n 7) 29.

126 Amelia Fletcher and others, 'Consumer Protection for Online Markets and Large Digital Platforms' (2021) available at https://doi.org/10.2139/ssrn.3923588.

127 Sara Haijan and others, 'Fair patterns discovery' (29th Annual Symposium on Applied Computing, Gyeonju South Korea, March 2014) <https://dl.acm.org/doi/abs/10.1145/2554850.2555043>.

128 Beni Chugh and Pranjal Jain, 'Unpacking Dark Patterns: Understanding Dark Patterns and their Implications for Consumer Protection in the Digital Economy' (2021) 7 Rgnul Student Research Review 1.

129 Stigler Committee (n 125) 49.

- minors, mainly due to the following characteristics: 'having immature executive function; forming imaginative relationships with characters; being susceptible to rewards; being indifferent to or unfamiliar with data privacy; and lacking understanding of virtual currencies',[130] in particular when they use apps[131] or video games;[132]
- less educated consumers, who are more susceptible to 'mild' or subtle dark patterns than better educated consumers, as shown by Bongard-Blanchy and others[133] and the European Commission.[134]

At the time of writing, some of our prototypes take into account minors' vulnerabilities, based on our previous research on privacy,[135] for example by featuring protecting privacy defaults (contrary to neutral default for adults, to avoid paternalism), but we have not yet addressed the wide range of other vulnerabilities, or cultural differences.

It would be worth exploring in particular (i) how fair patterns can be adapted to young adults as well as people with cognitive impairments (on the ASD), mental health disorders (social anxiety or panic disorder, among others) or lower IQ, and (ii) how cultural differences impact users' perception of control, general vulnerability to dark patterns, and triggers to System 2. We plan to advance our work in this aspect as well, and call for further research, building on existing work and experiments, namely by the World Wide Web Foundation.[136]

4.3. Next Steps

In addition to the undergoing expert review, we will be testing our pro-

---

130 Radesky (n 28) 135.

131 Marisa Meyer and others, 'Advertising in Young Children's Apps: A Content Analysis' (2019) 40 Journal of Developmental and Behavioral Pediatrics 32.

132 Forbrukerrådet (n 34) 89.

133 Bongard-Blanchy and others (n 25) 33.

134 European Commission (n 7) 29.

135 Potel and Talbourdet (n 54).

136 Karshalya Gupta and Carlos Iglesias, 'Deceptive Design: Moving Towards Trusted Design Patterns — The Next Challenge for the Tech Policy Design Lab' (World Wide Web Foundation, 21 October 2021) <https://webfoundation.org/2021/10/dark-patterns-moving-towards-trusted-design-the-next-challenge-for-the-tech-policy-design-lab/> accessed 08 February 2023.

totypes of fair patterns with users, ideally in several regions of the world, focusing in particular on measuring the cost of fair patterns on cognitive load compared to other existing patterns (dark or light and bright). This measure seems essential to further improve fair patterns accordingly and reduce potential resistance to change at the individual and corporate level.

We are also developing plug-ins (i) to ease the actionability of fair patterns for businesses, and (ii) for the general public to raise awareness and help trigger System 2.

Raising awareness more generally is essential, and we are producing a dedicated podcast for designers, developers, digital marketers, product owners, lawyers and anyone interested in fighting deceptive practices online. We have also identified two 'halls of shame' where users can name and shame and report dark patterns: one by Harry Brignull[137] and a tipline[138] hosted by the Digital Civil Society Lab at Stanford. However, what seems to be missing is a clear way to report dark patterns to regulators in each jurisdiction – this would be an interesting opportunity for regulators to collaborate across disciplines as data protection authorities have jurisdiction over some dark patterns, while consumer protection regulators have jurisdiction over some others, and competition authorities have jurisdiction if dark patterns are implemented by dominant firms.

In this respect, we note that the Digital Services Act specifies that it is applicable only if other acts are not applicable such as the GDPR or consumer protection legislation. The resulting lack of clarity for users could be a hurdle in reporting dark patterns. Thus, class actions could be necessary, if the conditions are met in the jurisdictions concerned, to more efficiently tackle the issue.

However, it is interesting to note that the European Commission is conducting a "digital fairness fitness check" in the context of the New Consumer Agenda, which is evaluating whether the existing consumer protection legislation (the Unfair Commercial Practices Directive, the Consumer Rights Directive and the Unfair Contract Terms Directive) is

137 'Hall of Shame' <https://www.deceptive.design/hall-of-shame/all> (Deceptive Design) accessed 08 February 2023.

138 'Dark Patterns Tip Line' <https://darkpatternstipline.org/> (Dark Patterns Tip Line) accessed 09 February 2023.

robust enough to protect consumers in the digital environment, namely to protect them from dark patterns and deceptive design. The current trend is therefore to tighten the legislative net around manipulative and deceptive practices online, so that one way or another (consumer law, GDPR, DSA and tomorrow, AI Act), offenders are indeed caught.

5. Conclusion

After decades of policy and regulation relying on the myth of the rational actor, legislators in the US and in the EU are beginning to take into account humans' cognitive biases and the fact that they usually make decisions online in a non-rational way, which is prone to prediction and manipulation. Similarly to King and Stephan, who advocate a fundamental rethinking of online consent mechanisms in the light of dark patterns, as well as a shift towards a human-centred approach, we call for policy design that better takes into account humans as they are, and that enables humans to thrive in the digital economy. The revision of the GDPR could be a timely opportunity to apply human-centric policy (neuro)design.

Furthermore, Margaret Hagan, Director of the Stanford Legal Design Lab, also calls for solutions that would remove the burden from users (of having to read and consent each time) and rather place it on companies: initiatives where users would set up their preferences for given situations once and for all, and companies would have to abide by such expressed preferences.

We are also seeing a growing number of issues emerging with Artificial Intelligence in relation to dark patterns: it is actually quite easy to train generative AI to create deceptive or manipulative practices. In addition, hyper personalisation of interfaces thanks to AI could lead to "hyper manipulation", and all the more in dematerialised interfaces such as connected glasses or VR headsets. We are already seeing examples of anthropomorphism that are meant to deceive users. The draft AI Act already prohibits some forms of dark patterns but it is critical that any future legislation ensures that it captures all forms of AI-enabled manipulative or deceptive experiences.

Bibliography

Acquisti A and others, 'Nudges for Privacy and Security: Understanding and Assisting Users' Choices Online' [2017] ACM Computing Surveys 44

Auernhammer J and Roth B, 'The Origin and Evolution of Stanford University's Design Thinking: From Product Design to Design Thinking in Innovation Management' (2021) Journal of Product Innovation Management 623

Blake T and others, 'Price Salience and Product Choice' (2021) 40 (4) Marketing Science 619

Blaszczak-Boxe A, 'Give Up Firstborn for Free Wi-Fi? Some Click "I agree"' (CBS News) <https://www.cbsnews.com/news/give-up-firstborn-for-free-wi-fi-some-click-i-agree/> accessed 22 January 2022

Bösch C and others, 'Tales from the Dark Side: Privacy Dark Strategies and Privacy Dark Patterns' (2016) Proceedings on Privacy Enhancing Technologies 237

Böhme R and Köpsell S, 'Trained to Accept? A Field Experiment on Consent Dialogs' (28th International Conference on Human Factors in Computing Systems, Atlanta, April 2010)

Bongard-Blanchy K and others, '"I am Definitely Manipulated, Even When I Am Aware of It. It's Ridiculous!" – Dark Patterns from the End-User Perspective' (Designing Interactive Systems Conference, USA, June 2021)

Chugh B and Jain P, 'Unpacking Dark Patterns: Understanding Dark Patterns and their Implications for Consumer Protection in the Digital Economy' (2021) 7 Rgnul Student Research Review 1

Competition and Markets Authority (CMA), 'Online Choice Architecture: How digital design can harm competition and consumers' (Competition and Markets Authority 2022)

Consumer Policy Research Centre (CPRC), 'Duped by Design. Manipulative Online Design: Dark Patterns in Australia' (Consumer Policy Research Centre 2022)

Conti G and Sobiesk E, 'Malicious Interface Design: Exploiting the User' (19th International Conference on World Wide Web, Raleigh NC, April 2010)

'Dark Patterns Tip Line' <https://darkpatternstipline.org/> (Dark Patterns Tip Line) accessed 09 February 2023

Dawood S, 'Pentagram's Natasha Jen: "Design is not a monster you 'unleash' to fix the world"' (Design Week) <https://www.designweek.co.uk/issues/5-11-march-2018/pentagrams-natasha-jen-design-monster-unleash-fix-world/> accessed 07 February 2023

Day G and Stemler A, 'Are Dark Patterns Anti-Competitive?' (2020) 7 Alabama Law Review 2

Deceptive Design, 'What is Deceptive Design' (Deceptive Design) <https://www.deceptive.design/> accessed 07 February 2023

de Goey H, Hilletofth P and Erikson L, 'Design-driven innovation: Making meaning for whom?' (2017) 20 The Design Journal 479

di Geronimo L and others, 'UI Dark Patterns and Where to Find Them: A Study on Mobile Applications and User Perception' (CHI 2020, Honolulu HI, April 2020)

Eatwell, J, Milgate M and Newman P (eds) *Utility and Probability* (Palgrave 1990)

European Commission, Directorate-General for Justice and Consumers and others, 'Behavioural Study On Unfair Commercial Practices In The Digital Environment: Dark Patterns And Manipulative Personalization- Final Report' (Publications Office of the European Union 2022)

—, Consumers, Health, Agriculture and Food Executive Agency, 'Consumer vulnerability across key markets in the European Union' (Publications Office of the European Union 2016) <https://data.europa.eu/doi/10.2818/165625>

—, 'Consumer Protection: Manipulative Online Practices Found on 148 Out of 399 Online Shops Screened' <https://ec.europa.eu/commission/presscorner/detail/en/ip_23_418> accessed 07 February 2023

Federal Trade Commission (FTC) Bureau of Consumer Protection, 'Bringing Dark Patterns to Light: An FTC Report' (Staff Report 2022)

Fletcher A and others, 'Consumer Protection for Online Markets and Large Digital Platforms' (2021) available at <https://doi.org/10.2139/ssrn.3923588 >

Forbrukkerådet (The Norwegian Consumer Council), *Deceived by design: how tech companies use dark patterns to discourage us from exercising our rights to privacy* (Forbrukkerådet 2018)

Graßl P and others, 'Dark and Bright Patterns in Cookie Consent Requests' (2021) 3 Journal of Digital and Social Research 1

Gray C and others, 'The Dark (Patterns) Side of UX design' (CHI 2018, Montréal QC, April 2018)

Gunawan J and others, 'Towards an Understanding of Dark Patterns Privacy Harms'(2021) ACM <https://doi.org/10.1145/3479521> accessed 07 February 2022

Gupta K and Iglesias C, 'Deceptive Design: Moving Towards Trusted Design Patterns — The Next Challenge for the Tech Policy Design Lab' (World Wide

Web Foundation) <https://webfoundation.org/2021/10/dark-patterns-moving-towards-trusted-design-the-next-challenge-for-the-tech-policy-design-lab/> accessed 08 February 2023

'Hall of Shame' <https://www.deceptive.design/hall-of-shame/all> (Deceptive Design) accessed 08 February 2023

Hajian S and others, 'Fair Pattern Discovery' (SAC 2014: Symposium on Applied Computing, Gyeonju Republic of Korea, March 2014) <https://doi.org/10.1145/2554850.2555043>

Helberger H and others, 'Structural asymmetries in digital consumer markets' (EU Consumer Protection 2.0 March 2021)

Jahnke M and Johansson-Sköldberg U, 'Introducing Design-Driven Innovation: A Challenging Ride Towards New Possibilities' in Miriam Grace and George Graen (eds), *Millennial Spring: Designing The Future Of Organizations* (Volume IX, Information Age Publishing 2014)

Jarovsky L, 'Dark Patterns in Personal Data Collection: Definition, Taxonomy and Lawfulness' available at <https://ssrn.com/abstract=4048582>

—, 'Improving Consent in Information Privacy through Autonomy-Preserving Protective Measures (APPMs)' (2018) 4 EDPL 447

Johansson-Sköldberg U, Woodilla J, Çetinya M, 'Design Thinking: Past, Present and Possible Futures' (2013) 22 Creativity and Innovation Management 121

Kahneman D and Tversky A, 'The Psychology of Preferences' (1982) 246 Scientific American 160

Kemp K, 'Concealed Data Practices and Competition Law: Why Privacy Matters' (2020) 16 European Competition Journal 628

King J and Stephan A, 'Regulating Privacy Dark Patterns in Practice- Drawing Inspiration from California Privacy Rights Act' (2021) 5 Georgetown Law Technology Review 250

Krippendorff K, 'Content Analysis' in Erik Barnouw (eds), International encyclopedia of communication (OUP 1989)

Laufer RL and Wolfe M, 'Privacy as a Concept and a Social Issue: A Multidimensional Developmental Theory' (1977) 33 Journal of Social Issues 22

Luguri J and Strahilevitz LJ, 'Shining a light on Dark Patterns' (2021) 3 Journal of Legal Analysis 43

MacGuineas M, 'Capitalism's Addiction Problem' (The Atlantic) <https://www.theatlantic.com/magazine/archive/2020/04/capitalisms-addiction-problem/606769/> accessed 08 February 2023

Machuletz D, 'Multiple Purposes, Multiple Problems: A User Study of Consent Dialogs after GDPR' (2020) 2 Proceedings on Privacy Enhancing Technologies 481

Maier M and Harr R, 'Dark Design Patterns: An End-User Perspective' (2020) 16 Human Technology 170

Mathur A and others, 'Dark Patterns at Scale: Findings From a Crawl of 11k Shopping Websites'(2019) 3 ACM Human-Computer Interaction 81

Mathur A, Mayer J and Kshirsagar M, 'What Makes A Dark Pattern... Dark? Design Attributes, Normative Considerations, And Measurement Methods' (CHI Conference on Human Factors in Computing Systems (CHI '21, Yokohama, Japan, 2021)

Meyer M and others, 'Advertising in Young Children's Apps: A Content Analysis' (2019) 40 Journal of Developmental and Behavioral Pediatrics 32

Narayanan A and others, 'Dark Patterns: Past, Present, and Future: The Evolution of Tricky User Interfaces' (2020) 18 ACM 67

Nouwens M and others, 'Dark Patterns after the GDPR: Scraping Consent Pop-ups and Demonstrating their Influence'(CHI 2020, Honolulu, April 2020)

OECD, 'OECD Recommendation of the Council on Consumer Protection in E-Commerce' (OECD Publishing 2016)

—, 'Improving online disclosures with behavioral insights' (OECD Publishing 2018)

—, 'Roundtable on Dark Commercial Patterns Online: Summary of Discussion' (Directorate for Science, Technology and Innovation Committee on Consumer Policy 2021)

—, 'Dark Commercial Patterns' (OECD Digital Economy Papers, No. 336 OECD Publishing 2022)

Potel-Saville M, 'Shaping the Law to Restore Its Function?' (Master's thesis, École Nationale Supérieure de la Création Industrielle ENSCI-Les Ateliers 2019)

Potel-Saville M and da Rocha M, 'From Dark Patterns to Fair Patterns? Usable Taxonomy to Contribute Solving the Issue with Countermeasures' Annual Privacy Forum (forthcoming)

—, 'Legal Design beyond the Hype: Measuring the Value' in Marcelo Corrales Compagnucci, Helena Haapio and Mark Fenwick (eds) *Research Handbook on Contract Design* (1st edn, Elgar Online 2022)

Potel-Saville M and Talbourdet E, 'Empowering Children to Understand and Exercise their Personal Data Rights' in Rossana Ducato and Alain Strowel (eds), *Legal Design Perspectives* (1st edn, Ledizioni 2021)

Radesky J and others, 'Prevalence and Characteristics of Manipulative Design in Mobile Applications Used by Children' (2022) 5 JAMA Network Open 1

Rasch A, Thöne M and Wenzel T, 'Drip Pricing and its Regulation: Experimental Evidence' (2020) 176 Journal of Economic Behaviour and Organization 353

Robbert T and Roth S, 'The Flip Side of Drip Pricing' (2014) 23 Journal of Product & Brand Management 413

SERNAC, 'Report on the results of the survey of Dark Patterns in electronic commerce' (SERNAC) <https://www.sernac.cl/portal/619/w3-article-62983.html> accessed 03 January 2023

Shaw S, 'Consumers Are Becoming Wise to Your Nudge' (Behavioral Scientist) <https://behavioralscientist.org/consumers-are-becoming-wise-to-your-nudge/> accessed 08 February 2023

Simon HA, 'Bounded Rationality' in Eatwell J, Milgate M, Newman P (eds) *Utility and Probability* (Palgrave 1990)

Slaughter R, 'Opening remarks of acting chairwoman Rebecca Kelly Slaughter at "Bringing dark patterns to light" workshop' (FTC 'Bringing Dark Patterns to Light' Workshop, Virtual, April 2021)

Sobolev M and Lesic V, 'Online Choice Architecture: The Good, The Bad, and The Complicated' (2022) available at <http://dx.doi.org/10.2139/ssrn.4241296> accessed 08 February 2023

Soe TH and Santos CT and Slavkovik M, 'Automated Detection Of Dark Patterns in Cookie Banners: How to Do it Poorly and Why it is Hard to do it Any Other Way' (2022) available at <https://arxiv.org/abs/2204.11836v1> accessed 07 February 2023

Susser D and Roessler B and Nissenbaum H, 'Technology, Autonomy, and Manipulation'(2019) 8 Internal Policy Review 1

Sunstein CR, 'Nudges that Fail' (2016) available at <https://dx.doi.org/10.2139/ssrn.2809658> accessed 08 February 2023

Stigler Committee, 'Stigler Committee on Digital Platforms: Final Report' (Stigler Center for the Economy and the State 2019)

Utz and others, '(Un)informed Consent: Studying GDPR Consent Notices in the Field' Degeling, Fahl, Schaub, and Holz (ACM SIGSAC Conference on Computer and Communications Security (CCS'19), London, 2019)

Thaler R, ‘Nudge, not Sludge’ (2018) 361 Science 431

Thaler R and Sunstein CR, *Nudge: Improving Decisions about Wealth, Health and Happiness* (rev edn, Penguin Books 2009)

Truong H and Dalbard A, ‘Bright Patterns as an Ethical Approach to Counteract Dark Patterns’ (Masters thesis, Jönköping University School of Engineering 2022)

Verganti R, ‘Design as brokering of languages: Innovation strategies in Italian firms’ (2003) 14 Design Management Journal 34

—, *Design Driven Innovation: Changing the Rules of Competition by Radically Innovating What Things Mean* (Harvard Business Press 2009)

Voigt C, Schlögl S and Groth A, ‘Dark Patterns in Online Shopping: Of Sneaky Tricks, Perceived Annoyance and Respective Brand Trust (HCI International, Washington DC, July 2021)

Waldman AE, ‘Cognitive Biases, Dark Patterns, and the ‘Privacy Paradox’ (2020) 31 Current Issues in Psychology 1

Tjostheim I, ‘Dark Pattern: A Serious Game for Learning About the Dangers of Sharing Data’ (2022) 16 ECGBL 774

Totzek D and Jurgensen G, ‘Many a Little Makes a Mickle: Why do Consumers Negatively React to Sequential Price Disclosure?’ (2020) 38 Psychology and Marketing 113

Zuboff S, *The Age of Surveillance Capitalism: The Fight for a Human Future at the New Frontier of Power* (Public Affairs 2019)

www.ingramcontent.com/pod-product-compliance
Ingram Content Group UK Ltd.
Pitfield, Milton Keynes, MK11 3LW, UK
UKHW062008041026
15591UKWH00017B/1237

9 791256 000845